Self-Help Housing, the Poor, and the State in the Caribbean

Self-Help Housing, the Poor, and the State in the Caribbean

Edited by Robert B. Potter and Dennis Conway

The University of Tennessee Press / Knoxville
and
The Press University of the West Indies
Jamaica • Barbados • Trinidad and Tobago

Published by The University of Tennessee Press / Knoxville.
Published simultaneously in the Caribbean by The Press University of the West Indies.
Copyright © 1997 by The University of Tennessee Press / Knoxville.
All Rights Reserved. Manufactured in the United States of America.
First Edition.

ISBN 0-87049-963-7 The University of Tennessee Press

ISBN 976-640-024-5 The Press University of the West Indies

The paper in this book meets the minimum requirements of the
American National Standard for Permanence of Paper for Printed
Library Materials. ∞ The binding materials have been chosen
for strength and durability.

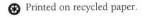 Printed on recycled paper.

Library of Congress Cataloging-in-Publication Data

Self-help housing, the poor, and the state in
the Caribbean/edited by Robert B. Potter
and Dennis Conway. —1st ed.
p. cm.
Includes bibliographical references and index.
ISBN 0-87049-963-7 (pbk. : alk. paper)
1. Poor—Housing—Caribbean Area.
2. Self-help housing—Caribbean Area.
3. Housing policy—Caribbean Area.
I. Potter, Robert B. II. Conway, Dennis.
HD7287.96.C27S44 1997
363.5'83—dc20   96-25220
                                  CIP

Self-help housing, the poor, and the state in
the Caribbean/edited by Robert B. Potter
and Dennis Conway. —1st ed.
p. cm.
Includes bibliographical references and index.
ISBN 976-640-024-5
1. Housing—West Indies—Finance.
2. Housing policy—West Indies. 3. Self-help
housing—West Indies. 4. Poor—Housing—
West Indies. 5. Housing, Cooperative—West
Indies. I. Potter, Robert B. II. Conway,
Dennis.
HD7314.A4S44   1997
363.582—dc20

For Virginia and Katherine,
Rebecca and Michael
and
In loving memory of
Gladys Ruth Potter,
March 1916–August 1996

Contents

Illustrations

Figures

Maps

Tables

Preface

The idea of this book took shape in 1990, following discussions between the joint editors at the Caribbean Studies Association Annual Conference held in Port-of-Spain, Trinidad, in May of that year. The editors bemoaned the fact that, despite the distinctive nature of housing in the region, the evident housing stress which afflicts so many areas, and the diversity of state policies, so little has, in fact, been written on the topic by academics. We resolved, therefore, to commission a series of specially written chapters by experts working in various parts of the region. We were convinced that the focus should be placed on the interfaces between self-help housing, the poor, and the state, but rather than inviting the contributors to address this nexus under various country or island chapter headings, we invited them to stress thematic issues of particular salience and topicality. In order to help, the contributors were asked to give particular thought to four principal themes, covering the history of housing, extant housing conditions, housing policy, and likely future issues. Efforts were made to encourage responses on all parts of the Caribbean region. However, in the end, we did not manage to secure contributions on either Hispaniola or the Netherlands Antilles. Similarly, a contribution on international aid agencies and Caribbean housing did not materialize for inclusion.

Rob Potter would like to thank the Economic & Social Research Council and the Nuffield Foundation for the grants they provided which allowed him to undertake firsthand research on housing conditions and housing policies in the eastern Caribbean, and which thereby led to the publication of this volume. Dennis Conway would like to acknowledge the support of the Office of International Programs, the Indiana Center on Global Change and World Peace, at Indiana University, Bloomington, and the John D. and Catherine MacArthur Foundation for support of travel and fieldwork in the Caribbean which contributed to this volume.

Particular thanks are owed to Kathy Roberts and Caroline Stafford of the Department of Geography, Royal Holloway, University of London, for all the hard work they jointly put into revising and reformatting the original contributions received from the authors.

Chapter 1

Caribbean Housing, the State, and Self-Help: An Overview

Dennis Conway and
Robert B. Potter

In common with most, if not all, developing countries, those of the Caribbean exhibit a plethora of housing problems for their burgeoning poor. Recent history has witnessed the struggle for adequate shelter in this urbanizing region. This is in a highly inequitable social context where, as early as 1964, Charles Abrams reported on the desperate plight of the poor in Trenchtown, Jamaica, the Kingston "shanty-town" which was later to be immortalized by Bob Marley.

Housing problems in the region include dilapidated and overcrowded inner-city tenements, sprawling and largely uncontrolled spontaneous settlements (each island variant acquiring its own pejorative label), limited rental accommodation, and highly distorted real estate markets. In the largest cities, overcrowding is perhaps the most obvious problem, along with inadequate housing facilities and services. However, the problems of insufficient and unsatisfactory accommodation afflict rural and peripheral areas as much if not more than urban zones, a salient feature highlighted in several contributions to this volume.

Legacies of colonial domination and a region-wide experience of accumulated unmet housing needs were rendered even worse by the constant state of economic stagnation and crisis during the first three decades of the twentieth century. Colonial administrations could be accused of neglect—indeed the record shows it—but it is largely the post-colonial experiences of the Caribbean that interest us here. How did the newly independent governments go about the business of delivering shelter to their newly enfranchised polity? Was the state *really* determined to play a major role in improving housing conditions for the poor? What have been the effects of changes in political regimes? This volume addresses the role of the state, as well as concentrating on the ways the poor have sought shelter and accommodation via self-help initiatives.

Adequate shelter provision has ostensibly been an important objective of the state in many of these peripherally capitalist, decolonizing Caribbean nations. Unfortunately, practice has rarely reflected policy, rhetoric, or legislation. This is in large part to be expected because the newly independent *state apparatuses* were scarcely fully functional at Independence, whilst the others did not attain full functionality because of continued "dependent" relations, either with colonial "mother-countries" or neo-colonial masters. The overburdened, limited resource bases of these developing nations have more often than not contributed to either an evasive or a benign neglect of the housing sector by public institutions, state enterprises, and government ministries alike. But other functional dimensions were equally nascent or underdeveloped. Dear and Clark (1978) and Clark and Dear (1981) outline the state's four main functional roles as follows: 1) as "supplier" of public or social goods and services; 2) as "regulator and facilitator" of the operation of the market place; 3) as "social engineer" in the sense of intervening in the marketplace to achieve its own social objectives; and 4) as "arbiter" between competing groups or classes (Clark and Dear 1981: 49). Throughout the Caribbean, the state struggled to define its agendas, and housing more often than not remained low on the priority list, rarely warranting the attention it deserved. Regime changes did not help either, nor did radical shifts in policies, though there were some signs of maturity in state-mandated programs in a few cases.

More recently, the externally imposed, restructuring imperatives of today's neoliberal global agenda have reinforced the state's avoidance of the responsibility to provide affordable accommodation for the poor and homeless. This theme emerges strongly in a number of the contributions to the present comparative volume. But again, there are some exceptions to this generalization regarding externally directed mandates. As Hewitt's chapter reveals, in Trinidad an externally directed initiative of the IADB actually maintained a progressive squatter-regularization program, despite a regime change that might have otherwise signaled a more regressive change in policy. Other contributions, however, confirm the generality of this observation on Caribbean states' interdependent condition.

Where low-income housing has been provided by government agencies, in all-too-many Caribbean countries this has led to the construction of a very limited number of over-specified units, frequently at a cost well beyond the means of the poor majority which makes up the population. There are, of course, exceptions to this generalization in the region. Indeed, our pan-regional comparison of the differing responses of the state to housing problems is illuminating in respect of what the future might hold, or the ways in which the future might better be structured and charted.

Ironically, the persistence of a mismatch between supply and demand for affordable housing in so many Caribbean countries has occurred in a regional context where folk and vernacular architectural forms of habitation have always demonstrated the capability for modular, expandable, upgradable, self-built, and self-improved homes. The poor, largely excluded from entering the legal (and fragmented) housing and land markets, have responded to their plight with self-help strategies: they have accessed the limited but growing rental market and adapted vernacular forms of shelter to their new transitional realities, whether urban or rural.

The present comparative volume pays special attention to folk and vernacular house forms since they have evolved as highly appropriate systems, yet they appear to remain both stigmatized and undervalued. However, debating whether such systems should be reified is not our objective. But the question as to whether they should be incorporated into a revived state-provided or state-assisted set of housing policies is a highly pertinent and pressing one. The evidence provided in the chapters which make up this book, especially those by Hudson, Watson and Potter, Potter, and Duany, is unequivocal in suggesting that folk and vernacular housing styles address the environmental challenges of this tropical region, in ways that the introduced, invariably "modern," temperate latitude designs do not. Resonances of this argument are also to be found in the chapters presented by Eyre and Klak on the contemporary housing situation in Jamaica.

The international aid fraternity has scarcely made a contribution to alleviate the region's housing woes. Even Robert McNamara's International Bank for Reconstruction and Development (IBRD) with its "site and services" emphasis did not go far enough to help meet the urban housing deficits in these developing and struggling Caribbean countries. With international and local attention towards housing provision for the poor being overtaken by more immediate problems of economic-sectoral development, the unfulfilled demand for accommodation continues to plague overburdened state institutions, while the poor have to resort to their own initiatives to gain access to shelter. The current involvement of the World Bank through IBRD and the International Monetary Fund (IMF) in imposing restructuring "conditionalities," with an emphasis on cost recovery, affordability, and private-sector involvement (facilitated, but scarcely organized by state oversight and services), also seems to be leading to the implementation of housing schemes which provide homes for the wealthier few, rather than much needed habitable accommodation for the poor majority. The recognition of adequate housing for the poor as a *basic need* remains long overdue in the region.

The latest era of restructuring has seen Caribbean countries embarking upon housing plans and policies, many of which involve private sector cooperation and dominance. This is clearly highlighted in the accounts provided on housing in

Barbados, Jamaica, and Trinidad in this volume. In a few exceptional cases, Cuba, Puerto Rico, and the French West Indies, for example, the state has undertaken comprehensive and drastic housing provision measures to address the problems of adequate shelter provision for the poorer segments of society, for rural as well as urban residents. Indeed, Mathéy's contribution to this volume challenges us to evaluate this "alternative" Caribbean experience as a potential model to follow. Condon and Ogden also add the francophone example provided by the French West Indies. However, the past record of state performance in housing and residential services provision in the wider region scarcely engenders confidence that this new era of restructuring and reorganization will see the region's housing problems being brought under control. The experiences of Jamaica, Puerto Rico, Guyana, and Trinidad, as evidenced in the respective contributions of Eyre, Klak, Duany, Peake, and Hewitt, are extremely disappointing, if not downright disenchanting, in this regard.

In a book published in 1989 under the title *Urbanization, Planning and Development in the Caribbean,* one of the present editors marshaled an impressive set of commentaries on the contemporary record of urbanization and planning in the region (Potter 1989). This earlier Caribbean-wide anthology documented the historical role of the state, the common experiences of inadequate planning, and the emergence of autonomous actions by the urban poor in providing their own shelter solutions, including self-help housing. The present follow-up volume essentially takes up where that regional compendium left the argument. The issues and deliberations were introduced and documented in the previous volume as an island-by-island account, while in this collection, a comparative, thematic, critical evaluation is provided.

The constraints facing the state in its attempts to alleviate housing shortages and to improve the quality of shelter, residential infrastructure, and services, and to generally achieve a level of accommodation accessibility which is socially just and provident in the Caribbean are many and varied. And, in all fairness, we need to recognize the tremendous institutional obstacles these newly independent state apparatuses faced when attempting to meet their multidimensional responsibilities: as housing supplier, social engineer, and intermediary, as "regulator and facilitator," or as class arbiter (see Clark and Dear 1981). Where would "shelter for the poor" fit, how would it play in the political arena? With inheriting colonial regimes, practices, and biases, the institutional shortcomings of post-colonial governments might be expected to diminish through time. But the Caribbean experience scarcely demonstrates such a "learning" curve in the states' approaches to housing provision and other related welfare provisions for the poor.

Competing for scarce resources and for housing and land are the middle and upper classes of these transitional, peripheral capitalist societies. One clear expression of this conflict situation is the widespread occurrence of uncontrolled or mismanaged land subdivisions and low-density residential developments. These are frequently associated with middle-class housing schemes, both private- and public-sponsored, or with land market distortions which encourage property speculation and overseas investment. The state's role is again challenged, and all-too-often found wanting. In addition, the openness of Caribbean economies, along with unmanaged tourism entrepreneurialism, remittance investments, and externally controlled flows of capital, are all believed to contribute to this anarchic state of housing and land markets in the Caribbean region. It is not so much a case of state mismanagement; rather, it is that institution's powerlessness or functional limitations or both. Housing the poor, whether they are rural-based or on the urban periphery, is an obligation the state would prefer not to deliberate upon, but knows it must.

In the Caribbean, and common to other regions of the "South," the struggle between the relatively powerless under classes and the socially and economically more powerful middle and upper classes is an unequal one. The body-politic has inevitably acceded to the more powerful, in the name of "modernization" and "development" if nothing else. Be this as it may, the political-economic responsibility of the nation state should not be so retrogressive and the acknowledged energy of autonomous, community-based efforts by the Caribbean poor to find their own means of access to shelter suggest that the situation is far from entirely hopeless. Self-help strategies have frequently been employed by the urban and rural lower classes in the region. The burgeoning shantytown, a reliance on urban squatting as an alternative to legal residential processes, reliance on informal networks to finance accommodation alternatives, dependence upon informal activities in the construction sector, and varied land access strategies developed in response to different forms of land tenure all characterize the Caribbean. There is community empowerment, but it is of a particular and somewhat limited kind. The accounts presented in this volume demonstrate this all too clearly.

These circumstances mean that the Caribbean region is an ideal context for a volume seeking to examine critically self-help and state strategies with regard to low-income housing provision in the less-developed world. Small island states bring scale issues to the fore, and the sociohistorical legacies and cultural diversity that characterize the region provide our comparative framework with the richness of geographical variety, while enabling commonalities to be identified among the various housing experiences.

The Pedigree of Self-Help Housing

There is, of course, a well-developed academic discourse on the issue of self-help housing. Starting with Charles Abrams (1964), if not before (see George 1935), and initiated by such advocates as John F. C. Turner, the degree of autonomy that self-help housing solutions has provided the impoverished population of rapidly growing urban centers throughout the developing world has been the subject of a vigorous, if sometimes unnecessarily acerbic, debate (Burgess 1977, 1982; Conway 1981, 1982; Harms 1976, 1992; Turner 1967, 1968a, 1968b, 1976, 1982; Turner and Fichter 1972; Ward 1982).

First there was the Turner-Burgess debate (Turner 1976, Burgess 1977; Conway 1982, 1985). Somewhat of a milestone in the unfolding discourse was Peter Ward's (1982) collection, *Self Help Housing: A Critique,* which refined and developed the arguments, both pro and con. Others weighed in with their collections, either dealing with specific continental realms: Dwyer (1975) on Asia, Gilbert (1990) on Latin America, for example; or undertaking international comparisons: Skinner and Rodell (1983); Patton (1988); and Payne (1984) among others. Most recently, one of our contributors, Kosta Mathéy (1992), has broadened the scope to include comparisons from socialist and advanced capitalist countries, and his collection, under the title *Beyond Self-Help Housing,* has provided the debate with both hindsight and a firmer sense of currency and topicality. The availability of adequate supplies of land for low-income housing, whether state-provided or spontaneously settled, has also emerged as a long-standing and constantly debated issue surrounding the viability of the self-built urban-environmental option to adequately house the poor (Conway 1985). There is an ongoing and vigorous empirical and theoretical thrust-and-parry of ideas concerning how the differing land-tenure systems, when "articulated" in peripheral capitalist regimes, would behave and constrain whatever policy formulations might be designed (Angel et al. 1983; Cullen and Woolery 1982; Darin-Drabkin 1977; Doebele 1983a, 1983b; Gilbert 1990; Gilbert and Healey 1985; Jones 1991; Ward 1989).

Gilbert (1990, 1993) also weighed in with his arguments on the importance of rental accommodation for the urban poor and with his reflections on the growing importance of "shared housing." Gilbert also noted the changing patterns of occupancy in Latin American sites, which demonstrate increasing residential densities. These observations add to the general comparative framework that the contributions in this volume draw upon.

The "self-help housing," "rental versus owner-built," and "land for housing the poor" debates, therefore, rage eloquently and furiously. Of course, ideological concepts underpinned much of the discourse too. Whether such debates have ever been of that much applied significance and value for Caribbean housing policymakers and urban planners is open to debate. The inevitable parochiality of such European and North American scholarship, not to mention the pressing imperatives to address the immediate needs facing those Caribbean institutions responsible for devising and implementing housing programs, leads to an uneasy mismatch between academic, theoretical understanding, and critical appraisal on the one hand, and local and regional understanding of housing and urban problems on the other. However, some of the central issues involved in the Turner-Burgess and liberal-radical debates are returned to by our contributors, particularly Mathéy and Potter, in considering Cuba and the eastern Caribbean territories respectively.

If we achieve nothing else, the contributions to this critical, comparative volume have every intention of bringing such debates to the notice of the region's decision makers and their international advisory communities. This, then, is one of our main purposes in presenting this collection of firsthand accounts.

Themes of the Volume

The comparative investigation of the contemporary housing situations in several islands and island groups of the Caribbean is likely not only to highlight the alarming situation these nations face in providing adequate and appropriate shelter for their under classes, but also to implicate governments in past failures and poor performances. The lessons to be learned from the investigation of specific Caribbean planning initiatives, whether they are with or without international cooperation and resources, provide invaluable insights for those endeavoring to implement new workable and realistic strategies to build communities and provide shelter.

The expert analyses provided in this collection afford pointers and insights into the formulation of progressive policies and plans for the provision of housing and shelter in the future. They also draw on theoretical debates, concerning, for example, the articulation of modes of production under pre-capitalist, capitalist, and state socialist formulations, and, indeed, the very role of self-help housing itself. Issues relating to sustainable development, the empowerment of the poor, and the influence of structural adjustment programs also receive prominence in the various chapters which make up the volume. The Caribbean is an ideal context for political and economic comparisons to be drawn across nations which show great similarities in many other respects.

The volume comprises a series of specially commissioned chapters, each dealing with a specific island or group of islands, written from a particular thematic point of view. The chapters have been written by internationally known authors from the Caribbean, United States, Canada, Britain, Germany, France, and Australia. All of the authors are Caribbeanists and social scientists with current knowledge of housing provision and policymaking in the respective islands or subcontinental regions with which they deal. In order to enhance the comparative utility of the volume and provide it with coherence and focus, the contributors were initially invited to consider the salience of four principal issues:

1. *The history of housing since colonization,* with comments where appropriate concerning the evolution of the vernacular form, especially in so far as this has a bearing on the potential for spontaneous and aided self-help;

2. *The assessment of current housing conditions,* focusing both on particular problems (overcrowding, squatting, rent yards, illegal subdivision) and problem
   areas in both rural and urban environments;
3. *Housing policy in the twentieth century,* charting the degree of involvement of
   the state and the effect of public policies, set against private-sector developments and self-help, both aided and spontaneous, including an assessment
   of the housing and land markets and the various managerialist forces which
   serve to shape them;
4. *State and private-sector involvement in the contemporary era of structural read-
   justment,* addressing the future interplay of the state, private capital, local
   community needs, and the scope for autonomous self-help solutions in
   building sustainable residential environments for Caribbean societies as a
   whole.

The contributors address these four themes by drawing upon their own empirical evidence and insights; some stress state policies, others vernacular traditions,
and others concentrate upon differences in housing quality. This empirically derived autonomy has proved worthwhile, in that the sum of the parts turns out to
be greater than the individual contributions. The collection is accordingly ar-
ranged to bring out the complementary nature of the island-specific contributions.

This introductory chapter overviews the themes and objectives of the volume
and sets out the collection's agenda. The chapters which follow are organized in
three broadly defined, mutually reinforcing sections. Each section is a comparative collection in and of itself. The concluding "synthesis" chapter, however, attempts to chart the way forward, not only drawing upon the insights provided by
the contributors' findings, but by means of building a case for shelter provision
out of the recent discourses on sustainable development and people empowerment.

Chapters 2, 3, and 4 deal specifically with vernacular housing. The second
chapter, Brian Hudson's "Houses in the Caribbean: Homes and Heritage," stresses
the rich heritage of vernacular housing traditions throughout the region. Change
there is for certain, and the introduced and absorbed transformations of architectural technologies has markedly reduced the vernacular housing stock, and all
but replaced it in many Caribbean urban areas. Nevertheless, the distinctive styles
remain, and they are coming to be recognized as an integral part of the local
landscape, although at present probably more as part of the distinctive "heritage-
tourism" ensembles that characterize the Caribbean, rather than in the realm of
housing policy per se (Dann and Potter 1994; Potter and Dann 1994).

There then follow two chapters by Rob Potter. Chapter 3, co-authored with
Mark Watson, addresses the specific character of Barbados's chattel housing and
tenantries; chapter 4 presents his own treatment of housing provision in the small
eastern Caribbean islands of St. Vincent and the Grenadines, Grenada, St. Lucia,

and Dominica. In Barbados, the state is directly and heavily involved in physical planning, low-income housing policymaking, and housing provision, albeit with mixed results and a wide gap between policy mandates and actual practices. Not that low-income housing and tenantry development have not been accomplished in Barbados; they have. However, the record is far from exemplary, and middle- and upper-income housing developments have been far more extensive—and have become major contributors to the transformation of the urban and peri-urban/rural landscapes of Barbados—than have housing for the island's poor. The situation in the eastern Caribbean is very different, however. The state has, by and large, avoided any responsibility for the provision of low-income housing, and self-help, autonomous, and community-sponsored housing initiatives are the common means adopted by the poor in these rapidly transforming small islands states.

The next set of chapters focus attention on the failed or failing state-directed housing policies of the largest three Commonwealth Caribbean countries: Jamaica, Guyana, and Trinidad and Tobago. There are four chapters in this part; two assess Jamaica's low-income housing practices; the other two detail the all-too-obvious and deleterious links between the waxing and waning of national economic fortunes and the poor's housing opportunities in Guyana and Trinidad, respectively. Eyre, for instance, in a very personal and immediate account, stresses the long tradition of self-help housing in Jamaica and the fact that this tradition has generally been supported by politicians and the police. But, alarmingly, 1994 saw a turnaround with the state evicting squatters. Eyre argues that global capitalism and the free market seem to be leading to those who felt they would eventually receive title to land being evicted, with the IMF, World Bank, and the government of Jamaica now branding squatters as immoral and antisocial. Klak picks up the theme of the rich tradition of people incrementally improving their homes, but suggests that current market forces and inequalities are hampering this long-standing process. In the theoretical part of Klak's contribution, regime effects, dependency conditions, and other structural constraints the state face are treated thoroughly and convincingly. Most recently, and with neo-liberal politics dominant, the state has avoided helping the popular sector, concentrating instead on providing mortgages via the private sector. What has changed is that land is now wanted for profit, in the manner exemplified by Potter in the eastern Caribbean, while USAID maintains that it is unwilling to fund "slums." Peake also charts the effects of changes in regime in Guyana and, not surprisingly, indicts the Burnham regime for its mismanagement. She ends more optimistically, however, showing how housing is back on the agenda in Guyana, but once again the emphasis is on middle-income groups. Without special support for the poorest, plus a focus on low-income women and community participation, the already poor housing conditions will become even more unequal. Hewitt's account also serves to stress how the poor have generally been left to fend for themselves, throughout the some thirty years of political independence. In Trinidad, as in Jamaica and Guyana, whilst political rhetoric espoused state concern for housing the poor, state action scarcely ever followed through. The twists and turns of state positions on their multiple roles, vis-à-vis the private sector, contributed to the disappointing record. Sometimes acting as social engineer, and at other times as arbiter, facilitator, intervenor, but more often than not "experimenter," the Trinidad government generally failed to deliver on its promises. Now, under the guidance of World Bank/IMF conditionalities, the Trinidad State is perhaps at its latest crossroads. Hewitt's account presents a picture of the severity of the resulting crisis.

A final grouping of contributions deal with state housing policies and practices and the accompanying autonomous self-help responses of the urban poor in other Caribbean countries: Cuba, the French West Indies, and Puerto Rico. Here the comparative framework is extended much wider to examine markedly different cultural milieus, different societal models, and different resultant low-income housing scenarios. Mathéy proposes the Cuban experience as an alternative vision that other Caribbean state policies might well learn from or, at the very least, might compare to their own. Mathéy argues effectively that the review of self-help largely conducted under capitalism is not complete without considering the case of Cuba. The effectiveness of *microbrigades* is highlighted in this discussion of the socialist alternative. Further, the state's actions during the current hardships Cuba is facing during its Special Period of adjustment are examined, and this all-too-clearly stresses the low priority housing provision stands on Caribbean national agendas. Suffice it to record that housing needs are considered secondary to other national sectoral needs. Ogden and Condon portray the French West Indian State's direct involvement in mass-housing provision as partially successful, although this has inflicted a heavy price on metropolitan revenues, and provision for the rural areas has remained poor. Duany's depiction of Puerto Rico's wholesale societal transformation, and accompanying uncontrolled urbanization experience, suggests more immediate parallels with other Caribbean countries' experiences, rather than with the Cuban or French West Indian cases. In particular, Duany shows how the public-housing projects embarked upon have been far from successful. Duany maintains that the "social cancer" originally attributed to squatter settlements has now been transferred to public-housing projects, while the state has overlooked vernacular, self-help housing.

A common thread emerging among these accounts of large-scale, mass-public housing provision is the cross-cultural acceptance of "concrete" as a status symbol, and as a "modern" building material which is socially preferable to local, folk, or "old-fashioned" housing styles. Interestingly, but not surprisingly, the power of middle-class values is as dominant as that class's political power in its persuasion that modern, concrete-block housing conveys status, regardless of Caribbean cultural milieu: whether French, English, American, Spanish, or Dutch. How does this play against our positions for better acceptance of local, vernacular styles? Clearly, it poses a major obstacle and suggests that radical changes in cultural awareness need to be accomplished. The need is to re-evaluate the region's indigenous heritages, which are both distinctive to each people's homeland and pan-regional. There have been well-articulated calls for such revaluations by such luminaries as Nobel laureate Derek Walcott and Rex Nettleford (1989, 1990).

The concluding editorial chapter provides a synthesis, and it points to a future where the provision of environmentally sustainable living spaces for all members of Caribbean societies, the poor and not-so-poor equally, should be the objective of state-facilitated and state-assisted projects. Local democratic decision making, people's involvement, and empowerment, by helping to build their living spaces, and the appropriate technical and infrastructural assistance provided by the state, NGO's, and other advisory agencies are all identified as pieces to the future puzzle.

No one model of housing provision should be considered applicable to all contexts. Each Caribbean people's experiences, whether self-help or state-involved, has to be set against the common pattern of current legacies of accumulated deficits. For some groups there are additional legacies of decades of uncontrolled settlement; for others, neglect of rural housing stocks and a failure to promote their renewal. Regionwide, there appears to be a societal reluctance to consider the substitution of vernacular styles for their more expensive "modern" equivalents, and, unless there is a marked change in the class values of Caribbean societies, there is the chance that our advocacy of such a policy may fall on deaf ears. As we move toward the twenty-first century, the challenges presented by Caribbean shelter remain as fundamental and as pressing as this.

References

Abrams, C. (1964) *Man's Struggle for Shelter in an Urbanizing World.* Cambridge, Mass: MIT Press.

Angel, S., et al., eds. (1983) *Land for Housing the Poor.* Singapore: Select Books.

Besson, J., and J. Momsen, eds. (1987) *Land and Development in the Caribbean.* London: Macmillan.

Burgess, R. (1977) "Self-Help Housing: A New Imperialist Strategy? A Critique of the Turner School." *Antipode* 9: 50–59.

———. (1982) "Self-Help Housing Advocacy: A Curious Form of Radicalism: A Critique of the work of John F. C. Turner." In P. M. Ward, ed., *Self-Help Housing: A Critique,* 56–97. Oxford: Alexandrine Press.

Clark, G., and M. Dear. (1981) "The State in Capitalism and the Capitalist State." In M. Dear and A. J. Scott, eds., *Urbanization and Urban Planning in Capitalist Society,* 45–62. London and New York: Methuen.

Conway, D. (1981) "Fact or Opinion on Uncontrolled Peripheral Settlement in Trinidad: Or How Different Conclusions Arise from the Same Data." *Ekistics* 286 (Jan./Feb.): 37–43.

———. (1982) "Self-Help Housing, the Commodity Nature of Housing and Amelioration of the Housing Deficit: Continuing the Turner-Burgess Debate." *Antipode* 14: 40–46.

———. (1985) "Changing Perspectives on Squatter Settlements, Intraurban Mobility, and Constraints on Housing Choice of the Third World Urban Poor." *Urban Geography* 6 (2): 170–92.

Cullen, M., and S. Woolery. (1982) *World Congress on Land Policy, 1980.* Lexington, Mass: D. C. Heath and Co., Lexington Books.

Dann, G. M. S., and R. B. Potter. (1994) "Tourism and Postmodernity in a Caribbean Setting." *Cahiers du Tourisme.* Series C, no. 185.

Darin-Drabkin, H. (1977) *Land Policy and Urban Growth.* New York: Pergamon.

Dear, M., and G. Clark. (1978) "The State and Geographic Process: A Critical Review." *Environment and Planning A* 10: 173–83.

Doebele, W. A. (1983a) "Concepts of Urban Land Tenure." In H. B. Dunkerley, ed., *Urban Land Policy: Issues and Opportunities,* 63–107. Washington, D.C.: IBRD.

———. (1983b) "The Provision of Land for the Urban Poor: Concepts, Instruments and Prospects." In S. Angel et al., eds., *Land for Housing the Poor,* 348–74. Singapore: Select Books.

Dwyer, D. J. (1975) *People and Housing in Third World Cities: Perspectives on the Problems of Spontaneous Settlements.* New York: Longman.

George, H. (1935) *The Land Question, Property in Land, the Condition of Labor.* New York: Robert Schalkenbach Foundation.

Gilbert, A. (1990) "Urbanization at the Periphery: Reflections on the Changing Dynamics of Housing and Employment in Latin American Cities." In D. Drakakis-Smith, ed., *Economic Growth and Urbanization in Developing Areas,* 73–124. London and New York: Routledge.

———. (1993) *In Search of a Home: Rental and Shared Housing in Latin America.* Tuscon, Arizona: University of Arizona Press.

Gilbert, A., and P. Healey. (1985) *The Political Economy of Land: Urban Development in an Oil Economy.* Aldershot, Hampshire: Gower.

Hardoy, J. E., and D. Satterthwaite. (1989) *Squatter Citizen.* London: Earthscan Publications.

Harms, H. (1976) "Limitations of Self-Help." *Architectural Design* 46: 230–31.

———. (1992) "Self-Help Housing in Developed and Third World Countries." In K. Mathéy, ed., *Beyond Self-Help Housing,* 33–52. London and New York: Mansell.

Harvey, D. (1973) *Social Justice and the City.* London: Edward Arnold.

Jones, G. (1991) "The Commercialisation of the Land Market?" *Third World Planning Review* 13 (2): 129–53.

Mathéy, K. (1992) *Beyond Self-Help Housing.* London and New York: Mansell.

Nettleford, R. (1989) "Caribbean Crisis and Challenges to Year 2000." *Caribbean Quarterly* 35 (1/ 2): 6–16.

———. (1990) "Threats to National and Cultural Identity." In A. T. Bryan, J. E. Green, and T. M. Shaw, eds., *Peace, Development and Security in the Caribbean: Perspectives to the Year 2000,* 241–54. New York: St. Martin's Press.

Patton, C. V. (1988) *Spontaneous Shelter: International Perspectives and Prospects.* Philadelphia: Temple University Press.

Payne, G., ed. (1984) *Low Income Housing in the Developing World.* New York: John Wiley and Sons.

Potter, R. B., ed. (1989) *Urbanization, Planning and Development in the Caribbean.* London and New York: Mansell Press.

Potter, R. B., and G. M. S. Dann. (1994) "Some Observations concerning Postmodernity and Development in the Caribbean." *Caribbean Geography* 5: 91–101.

Skinner, R. J., and M. J. Rodell. (1983) *People, Poverty and Shelter: Problems of Self-Help Housing in the Third World.* New York: Methuen.

Turner, J. F. C. (1967) "Barriers and Channels for Housing Development in Modernizing Countries." *Journal of the American Institute of Planners* 33: 167–81.

————. (1968a) "Housing Priorities, Settlement Patterns and Urban Development in Modernizing Countries." *Journal of the American Institute of Planners* 34: 254–63.

————. (1968b) "The Squatter Settlement: Architecture that Works." *Architectural Design* 38: 355–60.

————. (1976) *Housing by People: Towards Autonomy in Building Environments.* London: Marion Boyars.

————. (1982) "Issues in Self-Help and Self-Managed Housing." In P. M. Ward, ed., *Self-Help Housing: A Critique,* 99–113. Oxford: Alexandrine Press.

Turner, J. F. C., and R. Fichter. (1972) *Freedom to Build: Dweller Control of the Housing Process.* New York: Macmillan.

————. (1992). "Foreword." In K. Mathéy, ed. *Beyond Self-Help Housing,* xi–xiv. London and New York: Mansell.

UNCHS. (1983) *Land for Human Settlements: Recommendations for National and International Action.* Helsinki: United Nations Commission on Human Settlements; HS/C/6/3/Add.1.

Ward, P. M. (1982) *Self-Help Housing: A Critique.* Oxford: Alexandrine Press.

————. (1989) "Land Values and Valorization Processes in Latin American Cities: A Research Agenda." *Bulletin of Latin American Research* 8 (1): 47–66.

Chapter 2

Houses in the Caribbean: Homes and Heritage

Brian J. Hudson

In December 1980 a small archaeological team from the University of the West Indies conducted a dig at the site of a slave village on the Montpelier Estate near Montego Bay, Jamaica. Our excavation work was limited to one of the former slave dwellings of which practically nothing of the structure remained except for a few stones that formed part of the base of the modest building. Indeed, the whole site of the settlement was nothing more than some low hummocks among the grass on either side of the long, shallow depression which marked the position of the former village street. Once home to generations of poor Jamaicans of African descent, the old village was now just part of a cattle pasture. In contrast, the large eighteenth-century great house, built about 1775 of local cut limestone, still stood in view of the abandoned village site and continued to be inhabited. Nearby, substantial remains of the old sugar estate buildings survived to remind us of the days when Montpelier was one of hundreds of West Indian estates and plantations which created enormous wealth that even today is expressed in many magnificent eighteenth- and nineteenth-century buildings on both sides of the Atlantic.

Despite this rich architectural heritage, in Europe, as in the Caribbean, very little remains of the former homes of the poor majority of the population. Splendid and substantially built mansions, palaces, churches, fortresses, and the like often stand for centuries, but the unprepossessing and insubstantial dwellings of the poor are usually constructed of much less durable materials and are destroyed with indifference when those in power decide to clear them away for other purposes, a theme which is of considerable relevance to the contemporary Caribbean housing situation. Even many of the smaller old houses which contribute to the picturesque charm of the historic towns and villages of Europe were originally the homes of better-off residents, the contemporary inferior dwellings of the poorer classes having been swept away by the ravages of time or in later improvement schemes.

Today, the dwellings of the poor, when considered at all, are generally regarded as substandard structures which need to be replaced by modern buildings designed in accordance with officially approved standards of health and amenity and provided as economically as possible. To this end, governments often seek solutions in the employment of modern technology, commonly hoping to obtain economic advantage in standardized mass-production methods. In the Caribbean, as in many parts of the Third World, the technology, design standards, and often the building materials themselves have been largely imported from abroad, thus increasing dependence on foreign countries and organizations.

The widespread failure of this approach has encouraged many governments and international aid organizations to turn increasingly to self-help housing of various types, such as "core houses" and "site and services projects," which attempt to revive and capitalize on the age-old tradition of building one's own home. All too commonly, however, official attempts to harness the energies and the individual and community self-help traditions of the poor in the field of housing retain considerable reliance on imported modern technology-based solutions. The theme of this chapter is that they generally ignore the heritage of vernacular buildings which the people themselves developed over many generations in response to their problems, often creating housing forms which are remarkably well adapted to their physical, cultural, and economic environments, as well as being aesthetically pleasing. As Edwards (1980) has observed: "The folk architectural traditions of the Caribbean remain, perhaps, the least studied major institution of the culture of these islands" (291), and Potter (1993), too, has commented on the surprising neglect of the Caribbean vernacular house: "This is exemplified by the general lack of scholarly attention that has been paid to such housing. It is also reflected in the fact that in the realm of state housing policy and provision, the efforts of low-income groups to house themselves have been almost totally neglected as a socio-cultural resource of major importance" (46).

"Folk" and "vernacular" are terms which are often employed with many different meanings, and it may be helpful to adopt the distinction made by Edwards (1980: 297). "Folk architecture" refers to buildings which are designed and constructed primarily by the people who live in them, whereas a "vernacular tradition" is one in which houses are built under the direction of a master builder or carpenter who normally receives payment for his services. Edwards applies the term "polite" architecture to buildings involving three levels of differentiation: the consumer, the builder, now usually literate, and the architect.

Since the present volume about self-help housing in the Caribbean region as a whole draws specific attention to, and makes frequent mention of, traditional houses and construction methods, the purpose of this chapter is to provide the reader with a concise account of Caribbean folk and vernacular houses and their origins, tracing their history and evolution from the pre-Columbian period to the present. Thus informed, the reader may be better able to evaluate the heritage of Caribbean domestic architecture and to judge whether there are useful lessons to be drawn from the West Indian peoples' tradition of house building.

The Caribbean Popular House: Diversity and Unity

Caribbean architecture reflects the diverse physical and cultural character of the region itself. The diversity of geology, vegetation, and cultural influences derived from different parts of Europe, Africa, and Asia tends to give variety to buildings in terms of construction materials and architectural styles. Traditional building materials include timber, wattle and daub, stone of different kinds and brick, some locally made, some imported as ship's ballast, with roofing of thatch, wooden shingles, tiles, slate, and, more recently, the ubiquitous corrugated galvanized iron. Homes of the wealthier classes, including many of the more modest dwellings of those at a lower socioeconomic level, normally reflected the architectural fashions of the European nations which took possession of the islands between the late fifteenth and nineteenth centuries.

Some islands, such as Cuba and Puerto Rico, were dominated by Spanish influence; others, including Martinique and Guadeloupe, were dominated by the French; Barbados and Antigua by the English; Curaçao and Aruba by the Dutch; the U.S. Virgin Islands by the Danish. Still others, such as Trinidad, St. Lucia, and Dominica, inherited a very mixed European cultural influence, reflecting the changing fortunes of the colonial powers in their long struggles for possession of the islands. This diversity of European cultural influence is particularly evident in the languages spoken on the different islands, but, in the case of Caribbean architecture, there is a degree of unity which has its origins in the European Renaissance and the classical architectural style which the colonizers brought to the West Indies. Adaptations to local conditions, particularly the climate, gave rise to a creolized form of classical architecture distinguished from the European models by features such as louvers, jalousies, verandahs, and the extensive use of fretwork, creating a distinctively West Indian style, sometimes referred to in the English-speaking islands as "Caribbean Georgian."

Writers such as Acworth (1949), Radcliffe (1976), Buisseret (1980), and Gosner (1982) have created considerable awareness of this remarkable Caribbean architectural heritage, but relatively little attention has been given to the Caribbean popular house or cabin. There are signs of change, however, with an increasing number of scholarly studies of West Indian folk and vernacular architecture (Doran 1962; Edwards 1980; Potter 1991; Potter 1992; Potter 1993; Watson and Potter 1993), and the recent publication of more popular works which celebrate the humbler dwellings of the Caribbean (Berthelot and Gaumé 1982; Fraser and Hughes 1982; Slesin et al. 1985; Binney et al. 1991).

As with the "high" or "polite" architecture of the Caribbean, the folk and vernacular architectural traditions of the region reflect strong overseas influences, largely European and African, best displayed in the popular house or cabin, typically a rectangular, two-roomed structure, twice as long as it is wide, with the door placed on the long side and a gabled or hipped roof. These features appear to derive from a fusion of African and northwest European—perhaps mainly southern English—folk architectural traditions which were brought together in the Caribbean in the seventeenth century, creating a distinctive dwelling type which later diffused to many parts of the region except Cuba and Puerto Rico (Doran 1962; Edwards 1980). While circular buildings were (and remain) common in much of Africa, as indeed they once were in Europe, the houses were mainly rectangular in those parts of the continent from which came most of the Africans brought as slaves to the West Indies. In its general proportions, its division into two spaces, and the placement of the entrance, the African house closely resembled that of its southern English counterpart, differing mainly in the larger size of the latter. English and Welsh houses of the fourteenth to seventeenth centuries normally measured at least five meters in width, but few African houses of this period were more than four meters wide (Edwards 1980).

It would be misleading to consider the cabin in its original or expanded form without reference to the adjacent area which is used by the occupants as an integral part of the residential space. As Berthelot and Gaumé (1982) rightly emphasize, "We should speak less of 'the hut with its annexed spaces' than of an inhabited space of which the hut is only one part: one that could be qualified as 'highly structured'" (13–14). Typically, the inhabited area is a carefully maintained space which includes the following: the hut or cabin itself; the kitchen, a separate structure for the preparation of meals, normally situated downwind; the hearth space, defined by large rocks, and sometimes by a sheet-metal screen that gives protection from the wind; the latrine; farmyard spaces for livestock such as chickens and pigs; the kitchen garden area for the cultivation of food and medicinal plants; a decorative space in front of the house, with ornamental flowers, shrubs, seashells and the like; space reserved for waste; the washing and laundry space;

and transitional spaces and passageways. While this chapter focuses on the house, on the building itself, it is necessary to remember the importance of the related outdoor spaces, particularly in rural areas where the kitchen garden plays an essential role in the social and economic life of the people (Brierley 1991).

Pre-Columbian Dwellings

The earliest written records we have of houses in the Caribbean are found in the log books and other accounts of the Europeans who explored the region in the late fifteenth and early sixteenth centuries. In his log book entry of 17 October 1492, Columbus, having reached Long Island in the Bahamas, made the following reference to the homes of the Arawak people who lived there: "The men who had gone for water told me that they had entered their houses and that they were very clean and well swept and that their beds and blankets are like cotton nets. The houses are like large tents. They are high and have good chimneys. But of all the villages I saw, none consisted of more than a dozen or fifteen houses" (Cohen 1969: 66). In Cuba, too, Columbus and his men saw villages of tentlike circular dwellings, including one "of fifty houses, all very large and built of wood with thatched roofs. These houses were round and tent-shaped like all the others they had seen. There must have been some thousands of inhabitants, since in each house lived all the members of a family" (Cohen 1969: 75). It was in Cuba that they learned that the suspended net beds noted earlier by Columbus were called hammocks. In Hispaniola, Columbus saw "many Indian villages with round houses thatched with straw . . . doors . . . so low that you have to bend to get in" (Cohen 1969: 161). In a Carib village on Guadeloupe, however, "The houses were square, not round as on other islands" (Cohen 1969: 196).

The Amerindian peoples of the Caribbean islands were soon almost entirely annihilated in consequence of their contact with the Europeans, and very little trace of their villages remains. Modern reconstructions of their dwellings show the Arawak houses as circular with steep, conical roofs, while those of the Caribs are rectangular with ridge roofs (Honychurch n.d.). An interesting feature of the Arawak dwelling was the flat stone placed over the smoke hole at the intersection of the roof poles, no doubt the "good chimney" which Columbus noted in his log book. Today very little remains of the culture of the Amerindians who occupied the islands before the arrival of the Europeans, and the architecture of the region, including the traditional cottages, probably owes little or nothing to the original inhabitants. True, the pioneer European settlers erected hurriedly built huts which resembled inferior versions of the native dwelling which they no doubt copied, using forked sticks as supports, wattled or palmetto-thatched walls, and thatched roofs, but when the newcomers began to erect more permanent buildings they were on the European model (Edwards 1980; Gosner 1982).

The Transplanted European Cottage

Well into the eighteenth century European settlers were building cottages which were essentially similar to the one- and two-roomed medieval dwellings of their homelands. Timber-framed buildings on brick or stone foundations with wattle and daub, masonry, and other infilling were common, although for the very poor the pole hut often served as their primitive shelter. Now seen only in the very poorest areas, especially in Haiti, these dwellings are basically simple rectangles of poles set vertically in the ground with woven twigs between, plastered with a mixture of mud and chopped grass or leaves, and roofed with palm thatch on a pole framework (Gosner 1982). Huts of this kind were common in Carib, African, and medieval European societies from which they may be said to have been derived, but this form of building occurs almost inevitably at a primitive stage in society wherever the appropriate construction materials are found. Perhaps because of their drier climate and scrubby vegetation and possibly influenced by Latin American construction methods, in Aruba, Bonaire, and Curaçao the traditional cottage is built with a greater proportion of mud to pole, essentially an adobe house. The thick walls are generally built wider at the bottom and are commonly buttressed and brightly painted, and the paint serves a functional as well as an aesthetic role, as it helps to weatherproof the building (fig. 2.1).

Fig. 2.1. A cottage on the island of Curaçao, where the use of a greater proportion of mud to pole creates something resembling an adobe structure. Typical features include thick walls, wider at the bottom, corner buttresses, and a brightly painted exterior. The corrugated metal roof probably replaced an original one of thatch.

Not only in the Dutch Antilles did local conditions influence the way in which houses were built. As the forests were cleared for agriculture and for timber, suitable accessible wood for construction became increasingly scarce, necessitating greater use of other materials. There was usually good building stone, commonly limestone or soft volcanic rock suitable for ashlar masonry, to be had, and bricks were imported and, in some places, locally made; but these materials were generally costly and thus not normally available to the poor. Throughout the Caribbean, however, there was plenty of limestone, coral rock, or seashell that could be burned to make lime for mortar, and which made possible the widespread use of small stones and rubble in the construction of humble cottages as well as more substantial houses.

Today lime mortar has been almost replaced by cement. Not only has this manufactured product become increasingly available, but wood required for lime burning has become harder to obtain with the cutting down of trees for lumber, firewood, and charcoal. Concrete nog, as it is called in Jamaica, is a type of wall construction which is widely used in house building in the Caribbean. The origins of this practice predate the introduction of cement; the old term "nogging" comes from England, where it applies to a brickwork panel set in a timber frame (Brunskill 1987). As Ann Hodges (1987: 4) explains, "In Jamaica nog is a generic term for masonry in a timber frame; so we have stone nog, brick nog and, nowadays, concrete nog" (fig. 2.2). Stone nog, variously known as "Spanish walling" or "tabby" is perhaps the most typical traditional wall construction in the region, the precise method and materials used varying from island to island, and even between different parts of individual islands (Gosner 1982). Hodges (1987) has described Jamaican nog construction in great detail, and the following is part of her account of Spanish walling:

> To build a Spanish wall house, a frame is first constructed of four-inch (c. 10 cm) round or square timbers, with a sill and wallplate, and uprights about three feet (c.1 metre) apart, driven into the ground, with diagonal bracing at the corners. Horizontal planks are notched into the posts to support the windows. Pest resistant wood such as braziletto or guango is used. Usually, the roof is put on and covered with thatch or shingle before the walls are infilled between the posts.

> Once lime is burned and ready for use the mortar can be mixed, using red dirt. The resulting mortar is like a dry putty.

> Boards are then fixed to the outside of the house, and the mason breaks stones and packs them in mortar against the board between the posts from the inside. First a layer of mortar, then a layer of stones, then mortar then another row of stones "bruck joint" to the row below. The boards are left in

place for a day or two and then removed and replaced higher up, until the whole wall is filled in. The stone pieces are about four inches (c.10 cm) at the bottom of the wall, reducing to three inches (c.7.6 cm) at the top.

The wall is rendered using the same three to one earth/lime mortar mixed to a soft consistency, thrown on, levelled with a board and then trowelled with a mason's trowel to get a smooth finish.

And so in a Spanish wall house, wood, earth and stone, found right there on the site are combined to provide a durable, smooth masonry wall. The grout used in the smoothing is made by mixing additional lime and water with some of the same mortar. (Hodges 1987)

Fig. 2.2. This cottage in St. Elizabeth, Jamaica, is a good example of Spanish walling, the "nog" construction covered by a traditional rendering of earth and lime mortar. Thatched roofs such as this are becoming rare as they are replaced by corrugated galvanized iron or "zinc" sheets.

Concrete nog construction is similar except that a mixture of stone, sand, and cement is used. As the concrete is more liquid than lime mortar, it has to be shuttered with board on both sides and often barbed wire is stretched between the posts in the plane of the wall to give added reinforcement. The concrete is poured about 0.6 meter at a time and stones are added (Hodges 1987).

Increasing the proportion of stone, Spanish walling merges into rubble masonry for which wooden forms are unnecessary and less timber is required in construction. In many places, however, timber remains a very important building material, both in well-forested islands such as Dominica, and in islands which have been almost totally deforested, such as Barbados, where houses have long been constructed of imported wood.

Prefabrication and Modular Construction

Not only building materials and construction methods have been imported into the Caribbean but buildings themselves were shipped from overseas in prefabricated sections. Frequent destruction of buildings by natural and other disasters to which the islands are prone, notably hurricanes, earthquakes, and fires, probably encouraged the importation of prefabricated houses. As early as 1652, Barbados sent to Boston for ready-made house frames, and records reveal that the wooden dwellings imported from New England were of clapboard construction, roofed with cedar shingles (Edwards 1980). The standard module was a rectangular structure, its length twice its width, measuring three by six meters, at most, the door with a window on each side of it at the front. This form lends itself to modular expansion typified in the Barbadian chattel house. Normally, this is extended by the addition of more units behind the original dwelling, itself usually partitioned into a bedroom and a larger living/dining/kitchen space (Berthelot and Gaumé 1982; Potter 1989).

A different module is found in some of the non–English-speaking islands, such as Puerto Rico, Guadeloupe and Aruba, a form possibly originating in the former French colony of Louisiana. Comprising one square room of about three by three meters, this module always has an opening in the middle of each side, usually doors in Guadeloupe, more often windows in Puerto Rico. Several modules make up the dwelling, a type of construction lending itself to the provision of a corner verandah as when three units are put together in an **L** shape, as the space enclosed by the two wings is easily adapted to this purpose (Berthelot and Gaumé 1982).

Dwellings of prefabricated units and modular construction were highly appropriate in the industrialized, slave-labor-based plantation economies which developed in the Caribbean islands from the late seventeenth century. Having no security of tenure, slaves could be ordered off the land they occupied and had to remove their dwellings when the requirements of agriculture or the whim of the planter required them to shift. Even after the end of slavery, when the people did not have title to the land on which they lived, insecurity of tenure encouraged the retention of simple cottages that could be transported easily from one site to another, a theme taken up by Watson and Potter in the next chapter. This practice remains common today; in some places the hut is removed bodily, in others the building is first dismantled into flat sections of panels to facilitate transportation (Potter 1992; Watson and Potter 1993).

The African Influence

Like the forms of the houses in which they lived, the majority of the people of the Caribbean were either imported, mainly from Africa, or descended from those thus brought to the islands. On arrival in the West Indies, many of the African slaves had to build their own shelter, commonly constructing their traditional two-roomed huts similar to those of their homelands and not unlike those of the European settlers. There were differences which contemporary observers noticed, however. Apart from being smaller than the European cottages, the African dwellings were generally darker inside and less well ventilated (Edwards 1980; Berthelot and Gaumé 1982). While these features may be seen as a reflection of the extremely poor conditions under which the slaves had to live, some of these architectural characteristics may have been part of a building tradition which the Africans brought with them to the Caribbean. From my own observations of rural and small urban settlements in West Africa, windows or similar openings are not usually provided in most traditional dwellings, and the entrances are often very small, sometimes so low as to make it necessary to bend down in order to pass through. This may be at least partly explained by the largely outdoor domestic life of the people, much of which takes place under shade trees near the dwellings. In contrast, the climate of northwest Europe encourages a more indoor way of life centered on the house and hearth. Smoke from indoor fires used for cooking and heating would further encourage improved ventilation such as the provision of window openings to supplement the chimney.

As slaves in the Caribbean, the Africans usually retained little control over the way they lived. Their housing came under strong European influence and, indeed, was often subject to strict control. Slave villages were sometimes laid out in highly regimented patterns of straight lines as at the Roehampton Estate in Jamaica, where the hillside terraces on which the rows of dwellings formerly stood could still be seen when I visited it in 1980. Some planters provided barrack accommodation for their slaves, sometimes erecting rows of attached dwellings built of stone, but these were unpopular with the Africans, many of whom refused to live in them. Others adapted the accommodation provided for them by making additions such as external kitchens and outbuildings, thus "spoiling" the regularity of the original layout (Higman 1974).

The Caribbean House

In the Caribbean environment, both the European and African building traditions evolved and merged by a process of syncretism (Edwards 1980). Among the most significant changes to the original models were the abandonment of the climatically inappropriate European cottage fireplace and chimney and the adoption of windows for improved lighting and ventilation in the African homes. The widespread Caribbean practice of raising the house above the ground on supports of loose rocks or timber posts derives in part from the wish to exclude as far as possible vermin and other pests, to improve ventilation, and in some places as a precaution against flooding, but it is also commonly related to the requirement for mobility where many residents do not have secure tenure to the land they occupy (fig. 2.3). These circumstances discourage the construction of permanent foundations where the dwelling is firmly attached to the ground.

With improved living standards, internal developments included the replacement of earth floors by wooden boards, and often the inside surfaces of walls were covered with plain boards or, more rarely, with plaster. The roofs, however, generally remained unceiled for better ventilation. For similar reasons internal partitions between rooms normally did not extend above the eaves, although the space between the top of the walls and the roof might be filled with some form of wooden latticework.

Today one of the most typical features of the Caribbean house, large or small, is the verandah, a semi-enclosed area transitional between the outdoors and the interior of the house proper. The origins of the verandah are much disputed by scholars, but its diffusion throughout much of the world, in temperate as well as tropical zones, is strongly related to the influence of European imperialism (Hudson 1993). Possibly influenced by early Portuguese contacts with India and perhaps at least partly derived from the arcaded or colonnaded courtyards and plazas of Mediterranean Europe, the verandah may confidently be said to have been introduced into the Caribbean by the Europeans, first by the Spanish. Verandah-like structures were common features of some Caribbean house types before the arrival of the Europeans, however, notably the partly enclosed front portion of the Carib hut. Indeed, similar features are common in many parts of the world, their widespread popularity possibly being due as much to deeply engrained human aesthetic responses to landscape as to their undoubted practical value (Hudson 1993).

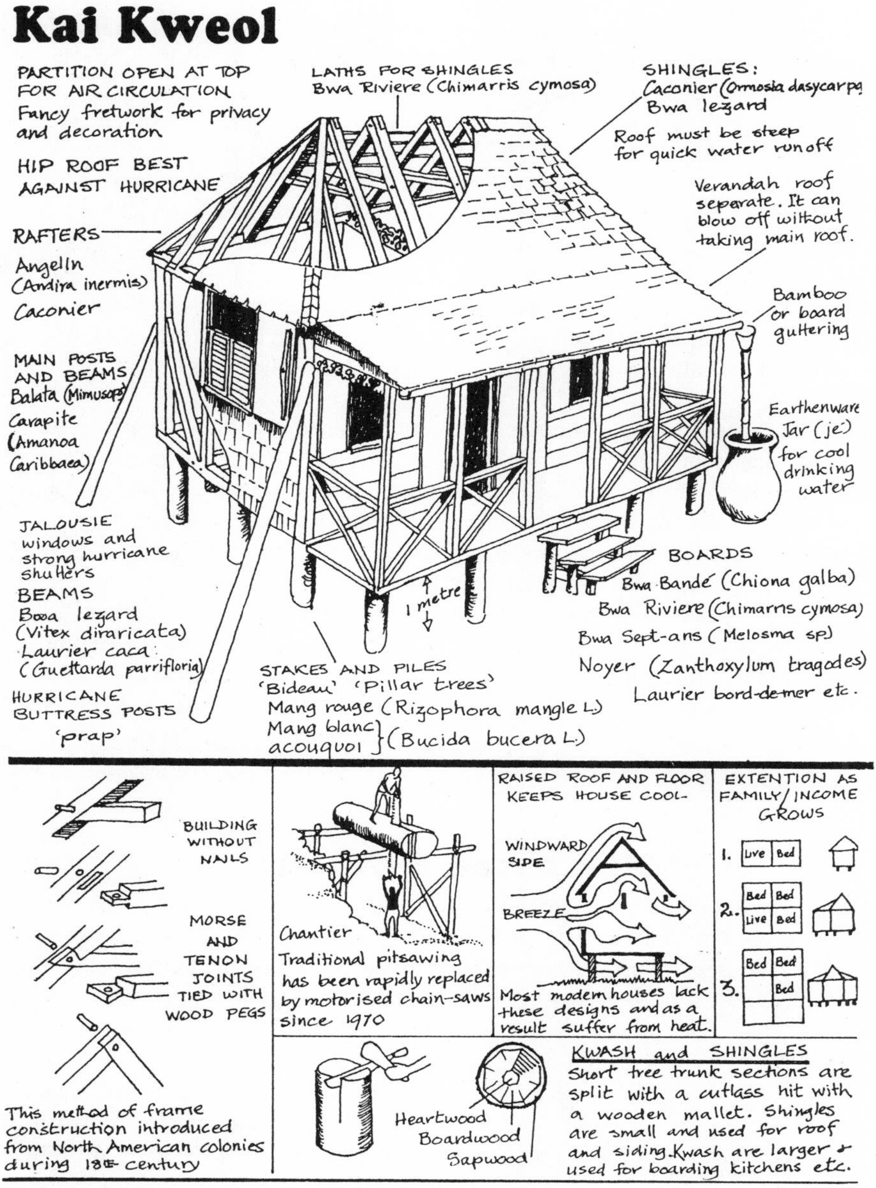

Kai Kweol

PARTITION OPEN AT TOP FOR AIR CIRCULATION. Fancy fretwork for privacy and decoration

HIP ROOF BEST AGAINST HURRICANE

RAFTERS

Angelin (Andira inermis)
Caconier

MAIN POSTS AND BEAMS
Balata (Mimusops)
Carapite (Amanoa Caribbaea)

JALOUSIE windows and strong hurricane shutters

BEAMS
Bwa lezard (Vitex divaricata)
Laurier caca (Guettarda parriflorra)

HURRICANE BUTTRESS POSTS
'prap'

LATHS FOR SHINGLES
Bwa Riviere (Chimarris cymosa)

SHINGLES:
Caconier (Ormosia dasycarpa)
Bwa lezard

Roof must be steep for quick water runoff

Verandah roof separate. It can blow off without taking main roof.

Bamboo or board guttering

Earthenware Jar (je) for cool drinking water

1 metre

STAKES AND PILES
'Bideau' 'Pillar trees'
Mang rouge (Rizophora mangle L.)
Mang blanc } (Bucida bucera L.)
acouquoi }

BOARDS
Bwa Bandé (Chiona galba)
Bwa Riviere (Chimarns cymosa)
Bwa Sept-ans (Melosma sp.)
Noyer (Zanthoxylum tragodes)
Laurier bord-de-mer etc.

BUILDING WITHOUT NAILS

MORSE AND TENON JOINTS TIED WITH WOOD PEGS

This method of frame construction introduced from North American colonies during 18th century

Chantier
Traditional pitsawing has been rapidly replaced by motorised chain-saws since 1970

RAISED ROOF AND FLOOR KEEPS HOUSE COOL

WINDWARD SIDE

BREEZE

Most modern houses lack these designs and as a result suffer from heat.

EXTENTION AS FAMILY/INCOME GROWS

1. | Live | Bed |

2. | Bed | Bed |
   | Live | Bed |

3. | Bed | Bed |
   | | Bed |

Heartwood
Boardwood
Sapwood

KWASH and SHINGLES
Short tree trunk sections are split with a cutlass hit with a wooden mallet. Shingles are small and used for roof and siding. Kwash are larger & used for boarding kitchens etc.

Fig. 2.3. Details of the Caribbean Popular House. Courtesy of L. Honychurch.

An effective protection against the heat and glare of the sun and against the rain, the verandah commonly performs additional functions, such as providing access to rooms and providing space for work, play, and storage. It is a popular place to relax and watch the world go by and to meet callers without admitting them into the privacy of one's home. While not an essential part of the basic Caribbean hut or cabin, a verandah is commonly added as soon as means allow, its separate roof being capable of being blown off in a high wind without taking with it the main roof of the house, thus reducing potential storm damage (fig. 2.3). Verandahs are usually built on the front of the dwelling, but back and side verandahs are also common. Some are highly decorated, often with ornate woodwork. Edwards (1980) attributes designs frequently occurring in the former British West Indies to the influence of British naval architecture of the period from 1670 to 1760.

The eighteenth and early nineteenth centuries, when the prosperity of the West Indian plantation economy was at its height, was also the period when the classical influence was strong in European architecture, notably in the British Georgian style. Most strongly evident in the official buildings and great houses of the Caribbean, the classical influence can also be discerned in more modest dwellings, often in the symmetry and simple elegant proportions of the building and in some architectural details. With adaptions to climate, such as louvered windows and jalousies or coolers, and extensive use of verandahs, together with cultural features such as the common use of brightly colored paint and decorative woodwork, this has created a distinctive Caribbean architectural style, the small cottages as well as the great houses displaying considerable elegance and charm.

The Asian Influence

Among the important migrant groups not so far mentioned are those who came from India and China as indentured laborers in the nineteenth and early twentieth centuries. Although the architectural influence of these minority immigrant peoples is sometimes strikingly evident in their religious and other community buildings, and the ornamentation of the homes of the better-off families often reflects the Asian origins of the owners, the Indian and Chinese folk and vernacular traditions appear to have made little or no impact on the Caribbean traditional dwelling. Trinidad is exceptional in having a relatively large Indian population, which is roughly equal to the number of people of African descent. In his study of a small, rural Indian community in Trinidad, Klass (1961) distinguishes three house types: the "ajoupa," the "creole," and the "modern." "Ajoupa" is a word of Carib origin, taken by East Indians from French-Creole patois. The ajoupa, or "trash house," is considered in Trinidad to be the typical dwelling of the poor rural East Indian. It has mud walls constructed round a simple wooden frame, a mud floor, and a thatched ("trash") roof and may be constructed by one person and family, perhaps with the aid of a single paid carpenter. Improved ajoupas have slab-board floors or galvanized iron roofs or both. The "creole" house is associated with higher socioeconomic status and is built of wood with a wooden floor resting on the ground on concrete pillars about one and one-half meters tall. The roofs are of shingles or galvanized iron. Built by skilled local carpenters, these houses have little in their appearance that is distinctively Indian. Even more competent carpenters, masons, and other specialists are employed in the construction of the "modern" house, for which materials such as bricks, cement blocks, and poured concrete, as well as wood, plaster, and galvanized iron are commonly used. Typically raised above the ground on concrete pillars at least two meters tall, these dwellings often remain long in a state of partial completion due to financial constraints. Among the distinctly East Indian characteristics associated with such houses are the "puja" room for prayers and household religious ceremonies in the wealthier homes, and sometimes the retention of the family's old ajoupa serving as a kitchen and dining room for the old people who feel more at home in these familiar surroundings (Klass 1961).

In his description of East Indian dwelling types in Trinidad, Klass (1961) makes no mention of the verandah, which some scholars suggest has its origins in India. But there is clear evidence that verandah-like structures were prominent features of some of the wattle-walled, thatch-roofed dwellings in which East Indians in Jamaica lived. A West Indies Reference Library photograph of a post-indentureship Indian settlement in Jamaica reproduced in a paper by Mansingh and Mansingh (1976) shows several such houses with thatched roofs extending beyond the walls supported on wooden posts. Further research may indicate whether this particular architectural feature was introduced from India or was merely a copy of the West Indian verandah which was already common throughout the Caribbean region when the Indians first arrived.

A Disappearing Heritage Rediscovered?

Of course, it is not only among the Indian population that modern building materials and forms are replacing the traditional Caribbean popular house. In terms of durability and hygiene, modern dwellings commonly built of concrete blocks, often with steel reinforcement, and having concrete or galvanized iron roofs may represent a considerable improvement on the folk and vernacular dwellings described in this chapter. Nevertheless, the abandonment of traditional methods and forms of building has not been all gain, particularly in terms of comfort, economy, and aesthetic quality. For many years architects in the Caribbean have been discussing the relevance of local vernacular architecture to contemporary buildings in the region (Richards 1971), but this discussion appears to have been largely ignored, especially in the field of government-funded or government-assisted low-cost housing. More recently Potter (1991, 1992; see also Watson and Potter 1993) has been among those who have been urging Caribbean governments to encourage the greater use of traditional building methods, materials, and forms in the provision of low-cost housing, while others have argued for the conservation of the heritage of West Indian folk and vernacular architecture on the grounds of both its intrinsic cultural importance and its economic value as a resource for cultural tourism (see also Binney et al. 1991; Fraser 1982; Mayes n.d.). One of the main arguments of the present volume is that vernacular housing is cost effective, energy efficient, and draws on both local building materials and human capital. Thus, such housing provides an important alternative between homelessness and flimsy shanty housing on the one hand and high-technology, imported solutions on the other.

In the words of Pamela Gosner (1982): "More than any other type of building, these small houses are in danger of disappearing; they should be saved, both for their contribution to the general ambience of the islands, and for the lessons they have to teach about adaption to the climate" (76). No less important is the potential value that the folk and vernacular traditions of self-help housing may have in efforts to find economic solutions to one of the Caribbean's most pressing contemporary problems, that of housing the poor.

References

Acworth, A. W. (1949) *Treasure in the Caribbean: A First Study of Georgian Buildings in the British West Indies*. London: Pleiades Book.

Berthelot, J., and M. Gaumé. (1982) *Kay Antiye jan moun ka rété (Caribbean Popular Dwelling)*. Point-à-Pitre, Guadeloupe: Editions Perspectives Creoles.

Binney, M., J. Harris, K. Martin, and M. Curtin. (1991) *Jamaica's Heritage, an Untapped Resource*. Kingston, Jamaica: The Mill Press.

Brierley, J. S. (1991) "Kitchen Gardens in the Caribbean, Past and Present: Their Role in Small Farm Development." *Caribbean Geography* 3: 15–28.

Brunskill, R. W. (1987) *Illustrated Handbook of Vernacular Architecture*, 3d ed. London and Boston: Faber and Faber.

Buisseret, D. (1980) *Historic Architecture of the Caribbean*. London, Kingston, and Port of Spain: Heinemann.

Cohen, J. M., ed. and trans. (1969) *The Four Voyages of Christopher Columbus*. Harmondsworth: Penguin Books.

Doran, E. (1962) "The West Indian Hip-Roofed Cottage." *Californian Geographer* 3: 97–104.

Edwards, J. D. (1980) "The Evolution of Vernacular Architecture in the Western Caribbean." In S. J. Wilkinson, ed., *Cultural Traditions and Caribbean Identity: The Question of Patrimony*, 291–339. Gainesville, Fla.: Center for Latin American Studies, University of Florida.

Fraser, H. S. (1982) "Our architectural heritage—an SOS." *The Bajan* (Jan. 1982): 21–22.

Fraser, H. S., and R. Hughes. (1982) *Historic Houses of Barbados: A Collection of Drawings with Historical and Architectural Notes*. St. Michael, Barbados: Barbados National Trust.

Gosner, P. (1982) *Caribbean Georgian. The Great and Small Houses of the West Indies*. Washington, D.C.: Three Continents Press.

Higman, B. (1974) "A Report on Excavations at Montpelier and Roehampton." *Jamaica Journal* 8: 40–45.

Hodges, A. (1987) "Jamaican Traditional Building Materials and Techniques . . . 2, Lime and Earth." *Jamaica Journal* 20: 2–9.

Honychurch, L. (n.d.) Our Island Culture. Roseau, Dominica: Dominica Cultural Council.

Hudson, B. J. (1981) "Tourism Development and the Jamaican Landscape." *The Masterbuilder* (Jamaica) 19: 31–34.

———. (1993) "The View from the Verandah: Prospect, Refuge and Leisure." *Australian Geographical Studies* 31: 70–78.

Klass, M. (1961) *East Indians in Trinidad. A Study of Cultural Persistence*. New York and London: Columbia University Press.

Mansingh, L., and A. Mansingh. (1976) "Indian Heritage in Jamaica." *Jamaica Journal* 10: 10–19.

Mayes, P. (1974) "Conserving Prehistoric and Historic Jamaica." In B. Hudson, ed., *Conservation in Jamaica,* 29–43. Kingston, Jamaica: Jamaican Geographical Society.

Potter, R. B. (1989) "Urban Housing in Barbados, West Indies." *Geographical Journal* 155: 81–93.

———. (1991) "Caribbean Popular Housing: Cinderella of Research and Policy." *Caribbean Studies Newsletter* 18: 19–21.

———. (1992) *Housing Conditions in Barbados: A Geographical Analysis*. Mona, Jamaica: Institute of Social and Economic Research, University of the West Indies.

———. (1993) "The Neglect of Caribbean Vernacular Architecture." *Bahamas Journal of Science* 1: 46–51.

Radcliffe, V. (1976) *The Caribbean Heritage*. New York: Walker and Company.

Richards, N. O. (1971) "Vernacular Housing, a Stylistic Base?" *Jamaica Architect* 8: 30–37.

Slesin, S., S. Cliff, J. Berthelot, M. Gaumé, and D. Rozensetroch. (1985) *Caribbean Style*. London: Thames and Hudson.

Watson, M., and R. B. Potter. (1993) "Housing and Housing Policy in Barbados: The Relevance of the Chattel House." *Third World Planning Review* 15: 373–95.

Chapter 3

Housing Conditions, Vernacular Architecture, and State Policy in Barbados

Mark R. Watson
and Robert B. Potter

With good reason, Barbados is known as "the singular island," being located some one hundred miles to the east of the Caribbean archipelago. Such singularity is undoubtedly reflected in the island's folk architectural tradition, which has given rise to a housing situation that Charles Abrams once described as being "virtually without counterpart anywhere in the world" (Abrams 1963: 4). Although Barbados does share many of the characteristics of its Caribbean neighbors in terms of its shelter mechanism, such as a strong colonial legacy, evident vernacular heritage, and a perpetuation of the self-help tradition, the small island state can be considered unique in several respects. Most saliently, whilst throughout the region illegal land subdivisions, shantytowns, and squatters are commonplace, this is not the case in Barbados, in which officially less than 1 percent of the population are squatters according to the 1990 census.

The present chapter documents the origins of the traditional movable chattel house in the plantation economy, specifically in relation to the evolution of the plantation tenantries. Subsequently, the spontaneous self-help and incremental upgrading experience of Barbados is examined in the context of current housing conditions. The sections of the chapter dealing with these topics draw on earlier expositions by Potter (1989, 1992) and Watson and Potter (1993). Past and present developments in state housing policy are then reviewed, with reference to key shelter projects, the managerialist role of the state and the private sector, and the importance of financing lower-income households.

It is stressed that the timber chattel house as part of site and service and core housing programs would give full recognition of the appropriate, progressive self-help character of the indigenous Barbadian housing system. Finally, the chapter examines the problems and prospects facing the island's planners and policy-makers in attempting to facilitate the provision of adequate shelter in the aftermath of recent economic vicissitudes.

The Origins of the Barbadian Vernacular Landscape

Despite an increasing awareness among both architects and academics of what we may refer to as vernacular architecture, the folk architectural heritage of the West Indies in general, and Barbados in particular, has until recently received relatively little attention from these groups, as stressed by Hudson in the previous chapter. However, recent offerings by Berthelot and Gaumé (1982), Slesin and Rozensetroch (1986), Potter (1989, 1992, 1995), and Watson and Potter (1993) represent the awakening of a nascent interest in such aspects of housing and design practice in the West Indies.

Such a neglect is surprising, for as reviewed by Potter (1989, 1992) and Watson and Potter (1993), as early as 1980, Edwards proposed an interesting five-stage model for the evolution of the Caribbean popular dwelling (table 3.1). In Edwards's terminology, Stage 0 covers the period of the earliest English settlement, between 1627 and 1675, of islands such as Barbados and Nevis, where the planter-pioneers built crude huts constructed with supports of forked sticks and comprising palmetto-thatched or wattled walls.

Table 3.1

Five-Stage Sequence in the Development of Vernacular Architecture in the Caribbean

Stage	Description	Time Period
0	Antecedents	ca. 1627–75
I	Preadaptation and the grounding of separate folk/vernacular traditions	1628–ca. 1660
II	Simplification: reduction of Old World variability	1642–ca.1800
III	Initial amalgamation and reinterpretation	ca. 1650–1700
IV	Elaboration: innovation and borrowing	ca. 1670–present

SOURCE: Edwards (1980).

Edwards recognized Stage I (1628–1660) as the *preadaptation and grounding of separate folk/vernacular traditions*. This period was marked by the construction of small English-style cottages by the planters, as sawn timber became available. Significantly, these rectangular cottages followed the floor plan of the ubiquitous southern England clapboard cottage of the period. Edwards (1980) suggests that "until after the middle of the seventeenth century, many West Indian buildings were simply copies of English cottages" (301). Furthermore, the transportation of slave labor from West Africa contributed to the existence of rectangular, gabled-roof dwellings. Essentially, in both English and African homes of this period, the structure was that of a two-roomed module, with the door placed asymmetrically on the long wall of the house, the roof usually taking the form of a thatched gable.

Little elaboration or synthesis of such distinct forms occurred until Stage II—the *simplification and reduction of Old World variability*. Covering the period between 1642 and 1800, this was a time during which basic commonalities were united to produce a new regional form. In Barbados, the mass periodic destruction of the majority of the housing stock by hurricanes and fires meant that improved and more substantial structures replaced earlier forms. Moreover, standardization was enhanced with the necessary importation of fitted house frames from Boston, Massachusetts.

Thus Stage III—referred to as a period of *initial amalgamation and reinterpretation*—ensued between 1650 and 1700. The basic rectangular cottage common to both English and African cultures now became the norm for houses within the region, with their two-by-one dimensions and standardized geometry. Distinct styles arose as a response to prevailing environmental and climatic conditions, such as the raising of structures off the ground to prevent infestation and destruction by ants, termites, vermin, and groundwater penetration. The architect Richard Ligon can be credited with initiating the first serious attempt to accommodate English vernacular architecture to the West Indian climate. According to Bridenbaugh and Bridenbaugh (1972: 174), Ligon suggested that buildings be raised off the ground, that they be oriented to the direction of the prevailing trade winds, and that they incorporate large shuttered windows into their design.

Edwards identifies a fifth stage in this evolutionary model, Stage IV—*innovation and borrowing*—covering the period 1670 to the present day, specifically in relation to the islands of the western Caribbean. However, as observed by Potter (1989: 84), in Barbados, a strong Georgian influence can be recognized, as exemplified by the inclusion of verandahs and terraces and a strong tendency toward symmetry of the front façade.

The evolution and development of Barbadian vernacular architecture remains highly evident on the island today, as manifest in the ubiquity of small timber chattel houses (fig. 3.1). Saliently, such dwellings represent the espousal of self-help principles. By definition, they are both unpretentious and strenuously individualistic in character, although they adhere closely to the dictates of the

Fig. 3.1 Example of Barbadian chattel house.

vernacular form. However, the evolution of this distinctive form of shelter cannot be explained by reference to architectural history alone. In fact, its development is inextricably linked to the history of the island's social, economic, and cultural conditions.

Historical Perspectives on Housing in Barbados

Europe's transition to the capitalist mode of production allowed it to pursue a pattern of capital accumulation which led to the rapid expansion of the capitalist system and the subsequent integration of the underdeveloped regions of the world into the global economy. In the Caribbean, the imposition of the capitalist mode of production effectively prevented indigenous development, stifled local production and self-sufficiency, and thereby established in their place highly unequal and hierarchical patterns of interaction with developed capitalist centers. Payne-Drakes (1985) argues that such an unequal relationship also found its expression in the plantation system so common to the Caribbean: "Barbados offered little resistance to plantation domination. The plantation thus evolved as a total institution, dominating the polity, economy and society . . . the masses were therefore deprived of access to wealth and assets such as land. This deprivation then reflected itself in poverty and generally poor housing and living conditions" (Payne-Drakes 1985:10).

In the post-emancipation period, some colonies, such as Jamaica, Trinidad, and the Windward Islands, experienced rapid growth in the numbers of peasants in the years after 1838. Barbados, however, with its high ratio of population to available land did not fall into this category. Nearly all the productive land was utilized for sugar-cane production and was concentrated in the hands of the plantation owners. The landless proletariat thus had no alternative but to sell its labor back to the former masters.

Under the *Master and Servants Act* of 1840, workers were able to occupy a house built by themselves in return for their exclusive labor at stipulated wages. As described by Abrams (1963: 4), the worker was assigned a "spot" on which to erect a chattel house. The spot would generally be designated by the planter on the plantation itself. The house spots would usually be located on infertile, inaccessible tracts of land at the margins of the plantation, on what was commonly referred to as "rab" land (Potter 1989). Furthermore, insecurity of tenure meant that the workers occupied the land at the pleasure of their landlords and, if dismissed, eviction necessitated the wholesale removal of the house from the land to another spot at a different locality. The act permitted eviction as a penalty for breach of duty. The *Landlord and Tenant Act* of 1897 was little better: it made it lawful for either party to terminate occupancy by giving only one month's notice to quit.

Thus, the house was generally a movable timber two-room cabin, approximately eighteen by nine feet in dimension and built on a loose rockpile foundation. Such was the evolution of the *plantation tenantries* in Barbados. They grew as a mere adjunct to the all-embracing plantation system and thus reflected the inequalities expressed in the wider sphere of the capitalist system. Such tenantry areas are located throughout the country and today still account for approximately one-third of the national housing stock. A survey undertaken by the Ministry of Housing and Lands in Barbados during the early 1980s identified some 603 potential tenantry areas, approximately two-thirds of which were rural-based plantation tenantries. The distribution of these is depicted in Map 3.1. The remaining one-third were considered to be *private* or nonplantation tenantries, which were generally located within the principal urban concentration.

Spontaneous Self-Help and the Upgrading Experience in Barbados

As described in the previous section, the long-enduring system of land tenure in Barbados has had a profound effect on the nature of the island's housing mechanism. Payne-Drakes (1985) and Potter (1987) both identify such insecurity of tenure as having major implications for the present-day quality of housing in Barbados. Indeed, it has been observed that "the inability to affix the dwelling unit to

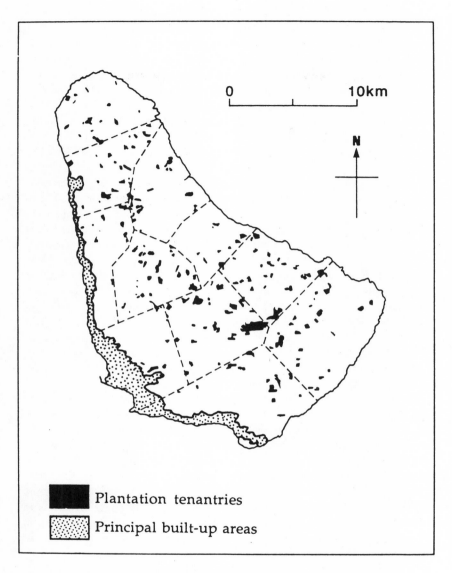

0   10km

N

Plantation tenantries

Principal built-up areas

Map 3.1. The plantation tenantries of Barbados.

the earth gives rise to the perpetuation of chattel houses in tenantries . . . furthermore, there is the perpetuation of disorderly and inefficient layouts which are
poorly served by physical infrastructure" (Payne-Drakes 1985: 22).

Moreover, as noted by Jones (1987), under the tenantry system, whilst it was possible for households to improve their dwellings either by expanding or maintaining them, they were unable to upgrade the loose rock foundation on which they were placed. In addition, the system also served to preserve the pit latrine as the principal means of sewage disposal, since the landlord's permission for conversion to a water-borne system had to be sought and was rarely, if ever, granted. Thus, in 1990, over 42 percent of all Barbadian homes still utilized the pit latrine system.

Despite such restrictions on improvement, upgrading has occurred in Barbados, and many of the occupants of chattel houses appear to epitomize the most fundamental principles of self-help. Jones (1987) notes that the upgrading experience has been one of piecemeal improvement undertaken by individual households, who often paid for the installation of basic services themselves as financial circumstances permitted. Thus, the traditional upgrading model comprises three distinct stages. From the basic timber unit (a single-gable structure divided internally into two rooms), stage two in the upgrading process would normally involve the addition of a second gable to form a "bipartite chattel" (fig. 3.2) and, in time, another to produce a "tripartite chattel" (Potter 1989, 1992). The conversion of the unit is indicative of a degree of security of tenure, and, over time, the remainder of the unit may be converted into a concrete-block or masonry structure, signifying the final stage in the upgrading process. Essentially, Barbados has a strong tradition of incremental house construction, with one of the most recent manifestations being the addition of a wall structure to the rear of the house for an indoor bathroom and kitchen (Dubinsky 1984: 1).

As argued by Potter (1989), the housing situation can best be described as *quasi self-help* in the sense that insecurity of tenure has placed firm restrictions on what individual households have been able to achieve in terms of upgrading. Although the time and cost associated with upgrading can be considerable, the slow process of improvement has meant that households have not generally found it necessary to resort to obtaining loans. Rather, as Jones (1987) points out, they have paid for such improvements in cash or have purchased materials on credit from builder's merchants. In this regard it can be argued that the chattel system is an excellent example of an appropriate system of self-help housing, albeit one in which a clear upper limit has been placed on the types of improvement that can be undertaken (see Potter 1989: 5).

An Overview of Housing Conditions in Barbados

As previously discussed, the evolution of the Barbadian housing system as a consequence of colonial domination has culminated in a highly distinctive form of shelter. The wooden chattel house seen by tourists may be perceived merely as

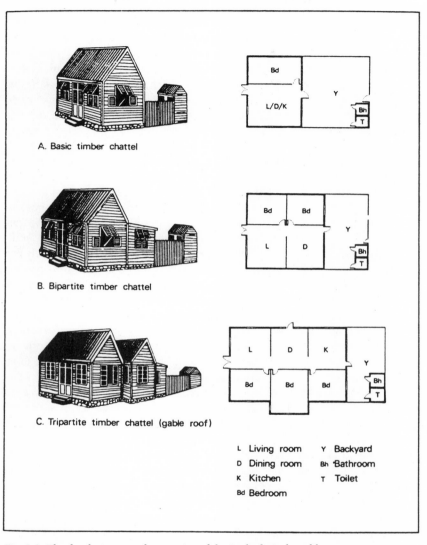

A. Basic timber chattel

B. Bipartite timber chattel

C. Tripartite timber chattel (gable roof)

L Living room   Y Backyard
D Dining room   Bh 'Bathroom
K Kitchen   T Toilet
Bd Bedroom

Fig. 3.2. The development and expansion of the Barbadian chattel house.

quaint, but each house has its own extended history. As an example of the vernacular style, the chattel house is perhaps one of the most distinctive forms of this type of architectural expression. Indigenous Barbadian housing is highly flexible and dwellings are designed in harmony with prevailing climatic conditions. Moreover, the spirit of self-help is built to the system, since upgrading can be carried out in accordance with the household's economic circumstances. Such dwellings are the antithesis of "unplanned," conforming as they do to a clearly codified folk/vernacular blueprint.

However, as identified by Potter (1989, 1992), there are certain underlying housing trends that still persist and which give genuine cause for concern. The well-known paradox is that whilst Barbados exhibits a very high level of outright homeownership at some 76.12 percent in 1990, this directly reflects the outcome of the plantation-related located labor system. In this way, houses were owned but the land upon which they were sited was not, thus perpetuating the problem of insecurity of tenure. It is of paramount importance that in examining the contemporary housing situation, one is intimately aware of the historical legacy that underlies the current housing problem.

An examination of census data provides a useful insight into housing conditions in Barbados. The geographical analysis of the 1980 census provided by Potter (1992) represents the most comprehensive guide to national housing conditions. Most saliently, the 1980 data demonstrate how one may refer to Barbados as a "divided nation" in terms of housing quality. For example, the total proportion of timber dwellings, 57.31 percent, conceals marked spatial variations. Indeed, in one enumeration district located within metropolitan Bridgetown, 91.2 percent of the housing stock found therein was built entirely of wood. Moreover, the high incidence of pit latrine toilets in some areas was indicative of variations in housing quality and diagnostic of the problems associated with insecurity of tenure. Potter (1989, 1992) calculated the incidence of pit latrines in 1980 to be 52.22 percent for Barbados as a whole, although over half the enumeration districts exceeded this figure. Indeed, a quarter of them reached levels in excess of 70.8 percent. The city of Bridgetown exhibited a high incidence of structures twenty-one years old or more—a figure of 54.63 percent compared with a mean national average of 46.78 percent (Potter 1989, 1992).

At the end of the analysis, eight key housing variables were finally factor-analyzed for the 210 enumeration districts which make up non-metropolitan Barbados. The results, summarized in table 3.2, show that the first major component of residential variability is a measure of overall housing disamenity.

The scores of the original enumeration districts on this component are outlined in map 3.2. This shows that poor housing is associated with the entire rural-urban zone, especially St. Lucy, eastern St. Peter, St. Thomas, St. Andrew, St. Joseph, eastern St. George, through to western St. John.

Comparative analysis of the 1990 census data in relation to 1980 (table 3.3) shows two major features. First, housing conditions have continued to improve at the national scale. Thus, the use of standpipes has decreased from 9.96 percent to 1.84 percent, whilst ownership has increased from 70.19 to 76.12 percent. The percentage of houses constructed entirely of wood stood at 39.89 per cent in 1990, having increased from 57.31 percent in 1980. Similarly, pit latrine usage

Table 3.2

Results of the Factor Analysis of the Housing Variables for Barbados

Factor 1: Housing Disamenity, 53.3%		Factor 2: Owned Separate Houses, 13.0%		Factor 3: Age of Housing,	12.3%
Pit latrine toilet	0.91	Separate houses	0.57	Built before 1960	0.91
Constructed of wood	0.89	Owned	0.47	Owned	-0.34
Gas for cooking	-0.79	Electric lighting	0.44		
Electric light	-0.75				
Public standpipe	0.75				

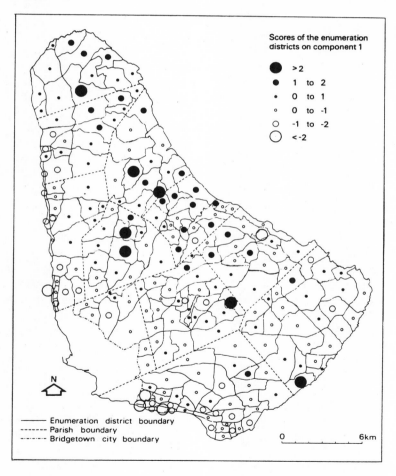

Map 3.2. Scores of the enumeration districts of Barbados on principal component 1: a measure of housing disamenity.

fell from 52.22 percent to 32.09 percent. However, the proportion of houses built over twenty years ago decreased only marginally, from 46.78 to 44.91 percent. Second, it becomes clear that the rural-urban disparity in housing conditions and housing quality still persists. Although it was the index which changed most during the period 1980–90, those who obtained water from a public standpipe remained above 4 percent of all households for rural St. Andrew and St. Joseph (map 3.3).

Table 3.3

Key Indices of Housing Quality in Barbados, 1980 and 1990

	Percentage of Households Possessing the Attribute:	
Index	1980	1990
Owner occupied	70.19	76.12
Water from a standpipe	9.96	1.84
Pit latrine toilet	52.22	32.09
Constructed entirely of wood	57.31	39.89
Built over 20 years ago	46.78	44.91
Electrical lighting	83.02	92.58
Gas used for cooking	66.44	73.50

Likewise, pit latrine usage is still above 45 percent for the same two parishes, and above 40 percent in St. John, St. Thomas, and St. Lucy. The rural north and east is strongly highlighted by the proportion of houses built entirely of wood, standing at above 45 percent. All-wood houses are most prevalent in St. Andrew, at over 50 percent. As expected, electrical lighting shows a reverse pattern, with the coastal strip of St. James, St. Michael, and Christ Church uniformly showing levels over 89 percent. The parishes of St. Joseph and St. Lucy show levels below 89 percent.

Clearly, rural local-scale housing problems remain characteristic of the emerging structure of Barbados. Housing clearly is continuing to improve in overall terms, but a strong geographical division still pertains. This begs the question as to why this should be the case.

Government Housing Policy in Barbados since 1937: State Intervention versus Self-Help

In a report to the government of Barbados in 1976, recommending the introduction of what he termed "rural-scale housing," Louis Redman provided a history of

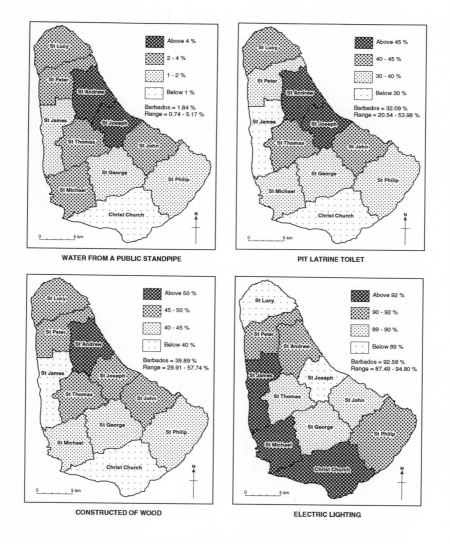

WATER FROM A PUBLIC STANDPIPE

Above 4 %
2 - 4 %
1 - 2 %
Below 1 %

Barbados = 1.84 %
Range = 0.74 - 5.17 %

PIT LATRINE TOILET

Above 45 %
40 - 45 %
30 - 40 %
Below 30 %

Barbados = 32.09 %
Range = 20.54 - 53.98 %

CONSTRUCTED OF WOOD

Above 50 %
45 - 50 %
40 - 45 %
Below 40 %

Barbados = 39.89 %
Range = 29.91 - 57.74 %

ELECTRIC LIGHTING

Above 92 %
90 - 92 %
89 - 90 %
Below 89 %

Barbados = 92.58 %
Range = 87.49 - 94.80 %

Map 3.3. Selected housing conditions in 1990 by parish, Barbados.

state intervention in housing the people of Barbados. Redman acknowledged the year 1937 as the start of the government's interest in housing, as it marked the appointment of the West Indian Royal Commission, charged with examining the causes which lay behind the civil disturbances of that year. Redman (1976) argues that "the first formal housing programme in Barbados was one of the results of the recommendations of the Royal Commission" (6). In 1939, a Housing Board was appointed to formulate a policy program for housing those with low incomes, and, in 1944, the board initiated a program to compulsory purchase and subsequently started to redevelop several of the slum areas of metropolitan Bridgetown (De Syllas 1944). This culminated in the development of the Pine Estate in Bridgetown during that decade (Potter and Wilson 1989).

Redman suggests that the board functioned in a limited way until the destruction caused by Hurricane Janet in 1955 forced the government to restructure and enlarge the existing body, thereby creating the Barbadian National Housing Authority (NHA). After alleviating the immediate short-term effects of the hurricane damage through the provision of some low-income housing units, the National Housing Authority made plans to address the long-term goal of improving the quality of the existing housing stock by replacing obsolete units and adding new developments as population expansion necessitated growth (Redman 1976). Redman argues that, from its inception, the National Housing Authority found it impossible to satisfy the annual housing requirement, which was in the order of some two thousand units. Saliently, Redman views the problems which hindered the work of this body from the outset as those that still plague successive government attempts to formulate and execute a viable housing program. These can broadly be categorized as problems of finance, land availability, development costs, and management skills. Redman argues that finance badly needed for housing was redirected and channeled into the development and promotion of tourism by the Barbadian government, and that the state perceived housing as an economically nonproductive entity—an attitude encountered throughout the Caribbean, as well as in the developing world in general. Such a situation, he suggests, has seriously curtailed activity in the production of houses by the private and state sectors alike. By the mid-1970s, the Barbadian National Housing Authority had provided a total of 4,282 housing units. Of these, 3,316 were rental units, accounting in 1980 for just 4.94 percent of the national housing stock.

One of the landmarks in the history of Barbadian State housing policy was the year 1963, when Charles Abrams, at the request of the government, drafted a consultancy report on housing finance and provision. This highly critical appraisal of the situation identified several key issues which underpinned the housing problem existing at that time, including the question of loan and rent repayments by tenants, the inadequacies of personnel and administrative structures, the need to re-examine the relationship between central and local government, the problems associated with land in both urban and rural areas, and the need to promote mortgage finance. Abrams thus proposed that the government apply for a team of planners from the United Nations to produce a radical physical development plan for the island. Significantly, he advocated the establishment of a mortgage finance system and the use of core housing schemes in order to allow Barbadians to capitalize on their long-established house-construction skills. Abrams (1963) preferred core housing to self-help programs, since the main advantage of the former is in providing a place in which the owner can live upon completion, and such units are relatively cheap (Abrams 1963: 45). However, the government of Barbados rejected Abrams's advice wholesale. Throughout the 1970s, state housing took the form of units for sale aimed at the lower-middle and middle classes, rather than units for rental and ownership by low-income families. As noted by Potter (1992): "Abrams' advice to the Barbadian government . . . was ignored for the best part of twenty-five years" (66).

Despite being overlooked by officialdom, Charles Abrams identified the central problem of the threat of eviction associated with insecurity of tenure among many tenantry residents, who felt unable to upgrade their properties as fully as they would like unless they owned the land upon which their houses stood. From 1965, most tenants were granted some semblance of security of tenure through the new Tenantries (Control and Development) Act, although they did not have the right to purchase. The act, argues Payne-Drakes (1985), was an advancement on the 1955 Security of Tenure and Smallholdings Act, which failed to ameliorate the threat of eviction.

It was not until the 1980 Tenantries Freehold Purchase Act, however, that the notion of security of tenure became a reality for the residents of the tenantries (Potter 1986). The new act created the right for individuals who had resided on tenantries for five years or more to purchase the freehold of their lots (Barrow 1985). On plantation tenantries, the purchase price was set at one Barbadian dollar for every square meter, the minimum total statutory price being Bds$300. As noted by Potter (1986: 257), there were, of course, exclusion clauses. The right to buy could not be exercised if the chief town planner certified that the lot was unsuitable for purchase due to its location or for any other valid reason. However, in these instances, the tenant was allowed to remain as such on the existing spot or have the landlord relocate him or her to another which was deemed suitable for purchase. The right to purchase was also waived if the land were required for public purposes by the Crown or any other statutory board. Hailed by some as nothing less than a social revolution, the implementation of the act has been somewhat problematic, notably by virtue of the reluctance of those landlords who owned urban tenantries to sell their lots at what was effectively one-thirtieth of the open-market price of land for development in other areas.

The Tenantries Development Act of 1980 was an attempt to provide for the parallel physical infrastructural development of these areas, within the government's overall program of house upgrading (Barrow 1985; Potter 1986). However, despite the good intentions of the act, the criticism must be faced that, whilst a substantial number of tenantries have been designated as in need of upgrading, formal improvement schemes have been few and far between (Potter 1992). Indeed, the only recognizable signs of infrastructural improvement on the majority of tenantries has been the provision of slippered roads by the Ministry of Transport. Moreover, the time lag between the passing of the 1965 Tenantry Act and the current legislation should not go unnoticed. Such a time interval highlights the common gradualist approach which characterizes many reform measures in the Caribbean region.

To assist tenants in the purchase of their lots, a loan scheme was established in 1982 to be administered by the Barbados National Bank at a fixed interest rate, the loans to be repaid in ten years. Another government scheme set up in the early 1980s was the Housing Credit Fund. Established in 1983, the program provided finance for housing to low-income earners. Loans were restricted to persons whose family income did not exceed Bds$16,000 per annum and the funds had to be used for home improvements, house purchases, or construction. A fundamental actor in the Barbadian housing system is the Barbados Mortgage Finance Company (BMFC), which is a wholly-owned subsidiary of the Barbados National Bank. However, due to a general paucity of funds available for on-lending, the BMFC currently grants loans only for the acquisition of new houses. The number of lots conveyed under the Tenantries Programme annually between 1983 and 1991 has ranged between 223 and 379. The largest number of sales occurred in the rural and suburban parishes of St. John, St. Philip, St. George, St. Thomas, and Christ Church.

Progress within the Tenantries

A recent survey carried out by Watson (1996) indicates that housing conditions within the island's plantation tenantry areas do indeed appear to be in a process of transition and improvement. In the survey, 150 plantation tenantries were sampled at random, representing some 58.8 percent of all such settlements identified by the government of Barbados in 1993. The survey revealed that, although vernacular architecture still predominates, as reflected in the high incidence of stand-alone timber dwellings, significant levels of upgrading and modernization have occurred in tenantries throughout the island since the 1980s as a direct consequence of state housing policy.

Indeed, although 55.59 percent of the 3,598 tenantry homes sampled were constructed entirely of wood, indicating that the chattel house can hardly be dismissed as a thing of the past, some 17.39 percent of housing units had undergone a process of wood to wall conversion in the last twelve years. Although commentators such as Dubinsky (1984: 1) and Jones (1987: 54) perceive such conversions as almost inevitable, given both the nature of the Barbadian housing system and the impact of the 1980s Tenantries Programme, the phenomenon is perhaps not as widespread as anticipated, at least within plantation tenantries. More significant is the incidence of houses constructed entirely of permanent walling materials, such as concrete blocks and masonry. The field survey revealed that, overall, 27.37 percent of the houses within the sample utilized such materials (map 3.4). Furthermore, at the microscale, a number of tenantries showed significant signs of improvement and a move towards permanent construction materials. For example, at Sedgepond tenantry in the northeastern parish of St. Andrew, 25.95 percent of the units are built entirely of concrete blocks or masonry. It is therefore posited that through the granting of security of tenure and the right to purchase among tenantry households, post-1980 legislation has facilitated both the upgrading and development of specific tenantry housing areas and individual dwellings themselves, in a manner that has capitalized upon the very nature of the indigenous Barbadian housing mechanism.

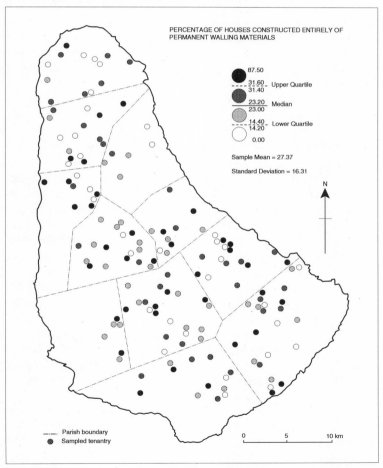

Map 3.4. Houses constructed entirely of permanent walling materials (concrete blocks and masonry), Barbados.

However, an examination of thirty-three key variables considered to be diagnostic of tenantry housing conditions revealed that there are significant disparities in the overall quality of individual tenantry dwellings and of tenantry areas themselves. Saliently, several of the variables showed strong spatial-geographical patterns, which effectively divide the nation. This serves to corroborate Potter's (1992) finding that Barbados is a highly divided nation in terms of overall housing quality. Specifically, the survey data reveal such variations when examining the percentage of houses with pit latrines, level of wood to wall conversions, incidence of permanent wall units, utilization of water closets, incidence of both loose rock and masonry foundations, and levels of infrastructural development within plantation tenantries. Clearly, the government of Barbados can pride itself on the overall level of upgrading that has taken place within plantation tenantries during the last twelve years. However, despite such change, the argument that an approach which capitalizes on the long-standing vernacular housing system should form the core for policies in other areas is a strong one, but has still to gain credibility among the island's housing planning fraternity.

Housing Policy and the Future

One of the most important changes to note with regard to Barbados's housing situation since 1980 is the government's strong advocacy of the potential of private-sector involvement in the housing market. Indeed, both the *White Paper on Housing* (Housing Planning Unit, 1984) and the *National Housing Plan* (Ministry of Housing and Lands, 1986) recommended private-sector intervention in the construction of expandable "starter homes" and wet core units. As described by Ishmael (1985: 66), masonry core units ranging in size from 30–40 square meters were proposed on lots of approximately 280 square meters. The units consisted of a kitchen, toilet/bath, living area, and bedroom (fig. 3.3, phase 2), and can be expanded to incorporate three bedrooms, lounge, and dining room (fig. 3.3, phase 4). Such measures were central to the proposals for a National Urban Low Income Housing Project, suitable for funding under the terms of a World Bank loan (Ishmael 1985: 66), although ultimately external funding for such a scheme was not secured. Most conspicuously, phase 1 (fig. 3.3), involving the linking of a traditional chattel house adjacent to the most elementary core unit, has not been realized as a viable policy option.

As described by Potter (1992: 69), two types of starter home have been envisaged, these being referred to as the *Twin Core Starter House* and the *National Housing Corporation (NHC) Starter House*. During the 1980s, several experimental NHC starter house units were constructed in the northwestern section of the Bridgetown urban zone. Curiously, as noted above, early designs envisaged the incorporation of a chattel house into the design of the twin core option (fig. 3.3, phase 1),

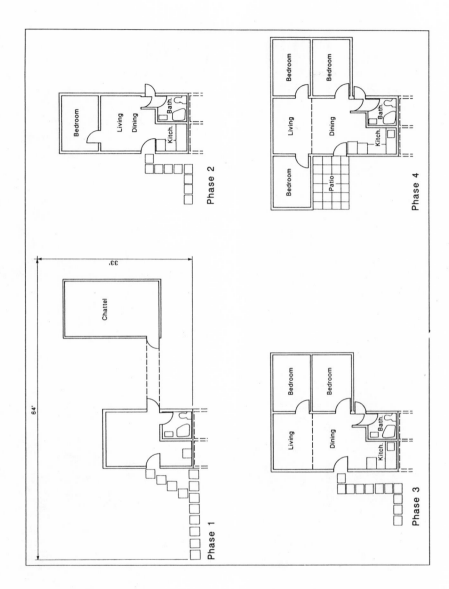

Fig. 3.3. *Proposed expansion of starter homes incorporating the traditional chattel house at Stage 1.*

thereby exemplifying the notions of Charles Abrams and, to some extent, those of Louis Redman, who in 1976 proposed the possibility of constructing a timber "core" house for the island's rural parishes. This option has never been taken up, and concrete starter houses only have been produced over the past eight to ten years (fig. 3.4).

Evidently, it appears that the construction of the basic NHC starter home witnesses the continuation of a somewhat disturbing trend, one that rejects the beauty and simplicity of the indigenous housing system which has characterized the island since emancipation; that is, a trend towards the incorporation of precast concrete as the principal construction material for new low-income homes facilitated by the state. If nothing else, this type of development is inappropriate for low-income earners, since the cost of building a concrete starter house would be prohibitive to this critical section of Barbados's population. Indeed, government estimates put the cost of the twin core option at Bds$35,800 and the NHC starter home as high as Bds$42,000. Even the lower of the two figures would be well beyond the means of the lowest third of Barbadian income earners (Potter 1992).

In terms of contemporary housing supply in Barbados, the capability of the state to act as a viable provider has been strongly challenged both by the growth of private-sector construction firms catering to low- and lower-middle-income families and by the relative inefficiency of the state in providing adequate shelter

Fig. 3.4. The NHC concrete starter house.

for the masses. Indeed, it is strongly believed in certain Barbadian political circles that there are no longer valid reasons for direct government participation in residential construction and that house building should be solely the domain of the private sector. Certainly, one only has to examine the position of the government of Barbados's housing executive, the National Housing Corporation (NHC), for evidence to support such a contention. The corporation continues to exhibit major problems, such as cost overruns, poor house designs, and, most disturbingly, huge rental arrears. Given such conditions, coupled with the added burden of an ever-decreasing annual budget from the central government, NHC finds it increasingly difficult to effectively execute the policies of the Ministry of Housing and Lands and to maintain its existing housing stock. However, although agencies such as the United States Agency for International Development (USAID) are firmly committed to the belief that the state should be removed from the production of residential units for lower- and middle-income earners and to utilize private sector assistance, the present Barbadian administration perceives that it still has a substantial role to play in the production of such housing. Such a belief is highly evident in the government's continued thrust towards joint ventures, in which the state assumes a highly intimate position with the private sector contractor as an active participant and not the role of a bona fide client.

Furthermore, although the argument that government should be removed from housing production is a convincing one for the reasons stated above, we feel that there remain valid arguments for continued state involvement in housing aimed at low-income families in Barbados. Indeed, if the right conditions must be created in order to induce the private sector to produce low-income housing, there may be a strong case for government intervention. However, there no longer appears to be a valid reason for state participation in middle-income housing projects, which should become the remit of the private sector. In fact, as far back as 1984, one senior USAID official argued that the government of Barbados should "do those things that individuals cannot do for themselves" (Dubinsky 1984: 51) and that the main thrust of state intervention should be to "facilitate the provision of land and basic services at an affordable price with minimum subsidization" (51). Saliently, Dubinsky (1984) suggests that future state housing programs should be "built on the longstanding tradition of self-help over time" (51).

Essentially, Barbados's private-sector construction industry can be divided into three distinct groups. The first group comprises large-scale developers with the resources to provide over fifty dwellings per annum. The second group, referred to as moderate-size contractors, produce between ten and fifty units in a given year. At the other end of the spectrum are the small-scale individual builders, who, with the assistance of two or three fellow craftsmen or laborers, produce only a handful of dwellings each year. The first two groups are perhaps the most significant since they interact with the state's housing machinery and, as such, exert a strong managerialist influence in serving to shape the nature of the island's housing market. Indeed, the government of Barbados has strongly favored the participation of both large-scale and moderate-size firms drawn from the private sector to produce a significant proportion of its existing housing stock through a series of joint-venture schemes since the mid-1980s; a policy that it continues to advocate at present, with the recent completion of the Church Village project in the southeastern parish of St. Philip in 1992. However, due to the state's desire to remain an intimate partner in all such joint ventures, private contractors have tended to reduce their level of involvement in government housing programs aimed at lower-income earners, favoring instead those projects with a high foreign-exchange content. Simply put, projects which are ostensibly aimed at middle- and upper-income groups are now perceived as those from which substantial profits can be realized, since the inherent high cost of finished houses built by private-sector contractors effectively precludes majority low-income families. For these groups, the alternatives are to seek state assistance or to rely on more traditional means of housing production.

In general terms, the private-sector construction industry has performed well in Barbados, despite the problems of building within a small island economy. It is therefore suggested that the private sector is in the best position to build most houses; it has both the technical expertise and the human and financial resources. However, we would maintain strongly that this is true only for the middle and upper classes. With regard to the future, the state remains the most fundamental actor within the Barbadian housing system, especially for those in receipt of low incomes.

References

Abrams, C. (1963) *Report to the Barbados Government and Barbados Housing Authority on Land Tenure, Housing Policy and Home Finance.* New York.

Barrow, P. Y. (1985) *A Description of Government Housing Programmes.* Barbados: Housing Planning Unit, Ministry of Housing and Lands.

Berthelot, J., and M. Gaumé (1982): *Kaz Antiye jan moun ka rété (Caribbean Popular Dwelling).* Pointe-a-Pitre, Guadeloupe: Editions Perspectives Créoles.

Bridenbaugh, C., and R. Bridenbaugh. (1972) *No Peace Beyond the Line: The English in the Caribbean 1624–1690.* New York: Oxford University Press.

De Syllas, L. M. (1944) *Report on Preliminary Housing of Two Blocks of Chapman's Lane Tenantry, Bridgetown, Barbados.* Unpublished report.

Dubinsky, R. (1984) *Housing Costs in Barbados. Office of Housing and Urban Programs.* Washington, D.C.: United States Agency for International Development.

Edwards, J. D. (1980) "The Evolution of Vernacular Architecture in the Western Caribbean." In S. J. K. Wilkersenn, ed., *Cultural Traditions and Caribbean Identity: the Question of Patrimony.* Gainesville, Fla.: Center of Latin American Studies, University of Florida. 291–339.

Government of Barbados. (1993) *Report on Plantation Tenantries.* Bridgetown, Barbados: Housing Planning Unit, Ministry of Housing and Lands.

Housing Planning Unit. (1984) *White Paper on Housing.* Bridgetown, Barbados: Ministry of Housing and Lands.

Ishmael, L. A. (1985) *A Description of How the Private Sector Is Involved in Housing and How Its Efficiency and Capacity Could Be Improved.* Bridgetown, Barbados: Ministry of Housing and Lands.

Jones, A. (1987) "The Housing Experience of Barbados." *Cities* 4: 52–57.

Ministry of Housing and Lands. (1986) *National Housing Plan.* Bridgetown, Barbados.

Payne-Drakes, H. (1985) "An Assessment of the Socio-Economic Impact of the Tenantries Freehold Purchase Act 1980." B.A. diss., Cave Hill, Barbados, University of the West Indies.

Potter, R. B. (1986) "Housing Upgrading in Barbados: The Tenantries Programme." *Geography* 71: 255–57.

———. (1987) "Housing in Barbados: Good, Bad or Beautiful?" *The New Bajan* 1: 26–32.

———. (1989) "Urban Housing in Barbados, West Indies." *Geographical Journal* 155: 81–93.

———. (1992) *Housing Conditions in Barbados: A Geographical Analysis.* Mona, Jamaica: Institute of Social and Economic Research, University of the West Indies.

———. (1995) *Low-Income Housing and State Policy in the Eastern Caribbean.* Kingston, Jamaica: University of the West Indies Press.

Potter, R. B., and M. Wilson. (1989) "Barbados." Chapter 5 in R. B. Potter, ed., *Urbanization, Planning and Development in the Caribbean.* London and New York: Mansell. 114–39.

Redman, L. (1976) "Proposals for Rural-Scale Housing in Barbados." Paper presented at the Twenty-Seventh International Conference on Housing, Planning and Building, Rotterdam.

Slesin, S., and D. Rozensetroch. (1986) *Caribbean Style.* London: Thames and Hudson.

Watson, M. R., and R. B. Potter. (1993) "Housing and Housing Policy in Barbados: The Relevance of the Chattel House." *Third World Planning Review* 15: 373–95.

Chapter 4

Housing and the State in the Eastern Caribbean

Robert B. Potter

The small island nations of the eastern Caribbean—Dominica, Grenada, St. Lucia, and St. Vincent and the Grenadines, in common with others in the Caribbean region, possess indigenous self-help housing systems that are based on expandable and moveable wooden units (Potter 1995). The central theme of the present chapter is that such houses, built by the people for the people, represent a surprisingly neglected architectural, cultural, and planning resource, a theme that was explored in the more highly developed context of Barbados in the previous chapter. Here, attention is placed on discussing housing conditions and housing quality at the outset, by recourse to available census data. Following this, attention turns to state housing policies in the region. The theme is the lack of clear pro-active policies in the case of such states. With very few exceptions, the state has only been seen to intervene directly when the demand for land for commercial purposes has suggested the efficacy of clearing squatters and low-income groups from particular residential areas. Another instance when the state has become involved is where dwellings have been threatened by the likelihood of environmental disasters such as flooding and storm damage. Examples illustrating both of these types of state intervention are provided in the present chapter.

However, in almost all other circumstances, it is suggested that the state has basically left low-income groups to provide for themselves. As such, housing policies have at best amounted to a form of benign neglect. State policy, it is argued, has largely failed to incorporate the positive aspects of the vernacular house form into viable housing programs and policies. In conclusion, the chapter turns to articulation theory in order to provide a theoretical rationale for these empirical observations.

An Overview of Housing Conditions in the Eastern Caribbean

The Windward Islands are poor, ruggedly mountainous, and economically dependent territories. Currently, their Gross Domestic Products per capita stand at around the US$2,300 level, whilst each of their populations amount to somewhat around 100,000. Although the tourist and construction sectors of the economy have grown quite rapidly over the last few years, agriculture—in particular bananas—remains the most important economic activity throughout the region. Industry, on the other hand, is generally in its infancy, accounting for less than 10 percent of GDP among the islands. Tourism grew during the 1970s and 1980s, employing almost one-quarter of the labor force of the Windwards and currently provides between 50 and 70 percent of the area's foreign exchange (Fraser 1985; Potter 1993a, 1993b).

A useful insight into housing conditions in these islands is afforded by the data provided by the census. Unfortunately, data from the 1990–91 census were not fully available at the time of writing, and so reliance had to be placed upon the 1980–81 population census. Using this data source, the basic characteristics of housing are summarized in table 4.1 for the three islands which formed the focus of a project carried out by the author, which was funded by the British Economic and Social Research Council between 1990 and 1992. This work concentrated on St. Lucia, St. Vincent and the Grenadines, and Grenada. Although Dominica was visited during the project, it was not possible to put together the same data set as that collected for the other territories.

The typical household in the Commonwealth Caribbean lives in a separate dwelling unit, and flats and apartments are a comparative rarity, although this is somewhat less so in the main urban-tourist zones. This is shown to be true of all three of the eastern Caribbean countries under consideration, with the proportion living in separate dwelling units ranging from a low of 83.18 percent in the case of St. Lucia to a high of 90.78 percent for Grenada. As elsewhere in the Caribbean, most houses are owned by the occupants. It is vital to stress, however, that in the 1980–81 census, this question referred to the legal tenure of the dwelling unit and not the land. This explains the very low number of squatters recorded in the census.

Houses in the region which conform to the traditional vernacular form have

Table 4.1

Key Indices of Housing Quality for Grenada, St. Lucia, and St. Vincent and the Grenadines in 1980/81

Country/Area	Percentage of total households possessing the attribute:							
	Built before 1960	Constructed entirely of wood	Pit latrine toilet	Public standpipe	Separate houses	Owner occupied	Electrical lighting	Gas for cooking
Grenada	48.26	60.74	61.82	34.21	90.78	74.10	39.08	28.11
St. Lucia	38.82	73.62	51.40	40.74	83.18	64.74	40.77	24.52
St. Vincent	37.42	45.29	68.66	45.33	89.22	72.06	52.03	27.96
All three	40.65	60.82	60.01	40.07	87.46	69.97	43.69	26.72
Barbados	46.78	57.31	52.22	9.96	90.70	70.19	83.02	66.44

generally been constructed entirely of wood, as shown in fig. 4.1, although minor stylistic variations in the template can be seen from island to island. Unlike Barbadian houses, the door is usually positioned asymmetrically on the long wall of the dwelling. This pattern is undergoing a rapid transformation in most countries, with a marked swing toward building in permanent materials. But, as shown by table 4.1, even in 1980, the proportion of dwellings constructed entirely of wood remained extremely high in St. Lucia, standing at nearly three-quarters of the housing stock. It is notably lower, at just less than half, in St. Vincent. For Grenada the proportion is just over 60 percent, close to the average for the three nations taken as a whole.

In situations where half to three-quarters of all homes are built of wood, the age of construction of dwellings necessitates a great deal of repainting and upgrading of timbers (see fig. 4.2). One way of examining the repairing of timbers is the percentage of houses that were over twenty years old at the time of the census. According to table 4.1, housing in both St. Vincent (where 37.42 percent of the dwellings are over twenty years old) and St. Lucia (where 38.82 percent are over twenty years old) is noticeably less aged than in the case of Grenada (where 48.26 percent are over twenty years old). Despite progress being made in the region with regard to the supply of water, the communal public standpipe as opposed to water piped into the yard or into the dwelling itself remains the predominant form of water supply for a very large proportion of households. This form of water supply accounts for nearly half of all connections in St. Vincent (45.33 percent). The equivalent statistics for the other two islands remain over one-third. The public standpipe is still very much part of the daily scene in the eastern Caribbean.

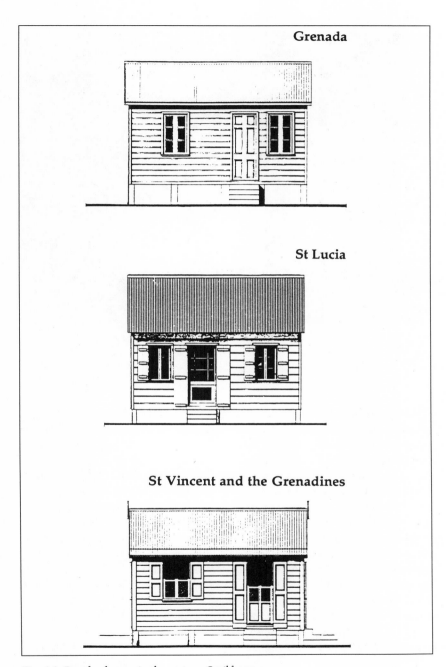

Fig. 4.1. Popular houses in the eastern Caribbean.

Fig. 4.2. *Unconsolidated and consolidated houses on the outskirts of Kingstown, St. Vincent.*

A water closet type of toilet is relatively uncommon in the Commonwealth Caribbean (Singh 1988), and pit latrine toilets are still the most frequent type of facility. The overall level of use is almost exactly 60 percent, varying from 68.66 percent for St. Vincent to 51.40 percent for St. Lucia. An index of relative modernity such as the presence of electrical lighting shows that St. Vincent fairs relatively well once again, whilst the use of gas for cooking stands at only one-quarter of households in each of the territories under consideration.

A straightforward index of housing disamenity may be constructed from the rows of table 4.1. High percentage values on variables 1 to 4 can be regarded as signifying housing disamenity and can be summed together. Variables 5 and 6—separate houses and owner occupied—measure traits that appear to vary little across the countries and can thus be excluded from the index. The variables in the last two columns—the provision of electrical lighting and the employment of gas for cooking purposes—are effective measures of amenity. They can be subtracted from the sum of the first set of variables to give a crude general index of housing disamenity. Thus, the higher the score, the greater the implied level of disamenity. The results suggest that St. Lucia shows the poorest relative conditions, with an index score of 23.22, followed closely by Grenada, with 22.97. The lowest total, and therefore the lowest disamenity score applies to St. Vincent at 19.45. To put the analysis in context, on the same calculation, Barbados records a value as low as 2.80, some ten times less than those characterizing the Windward Islands. In comparison, the difference between GDP per capita for Barbados and the Windwards is approximately four to five times.

Geographically, of course, the important point is that the condition of housing disamenity is expressed geographically. The analysis of the full data set has been presented in Potter (1991, 1994). One example, that of St. Vincent and the Grenadines, will suffice here (map 4.1). The incidence of public standpipe use shows a very strong north-south pattern. Levels are conspicuously high in the case of Barrouallie, Chateaubelair, Sandy Bay, and Georgetown, and lower in the southern part of the island and the Grenadines. The lowest levels of public standpipe use apply to central Kingstown and the North and South Grenadines. The eastern suburban areas of Marriaqua and Calliaqua show levels of usage between 25 and 50 percent. Turning to an index of amenity, the availability of gas for cooking purposes reaches a peak in the city center and in Calliaqua and then declines progressively with movement from these urban-suburban areas. Once again, the northern Grenadines show relatively high levels of housing amenity.

The eight housing variables employed in the analysis were finally factor-analyzed in an effort to search for general patterns in the case of each of the three countries. The overall results of the analysis are listed in table 4.2. In all three islands a highly general first factor was derived, which accounted for a large proportion of the variance contained in the original data set. This accounted for 69.3 percent variance in the case of Grenada, 58.3 percent in St. Vincent and 57.6 percent with regard to St. Lucia.

In each instance the first factor is a general measure of disamenity, as was so in the case of Barbados in Chapter 3. In the case of Grenada, variables such as wood, owned houses, separate dwellings, and pit latrines load positively on the first component, while the use of gas and electricity are negatively associated with it. The same sort of pattern applies to St. Vincent where public standpipe, wood, separate houses, owned, and pit latrine load positively, and electricity plus gas load negatively. In respect to St. Lucia, the variables ownership and constructed of wood load positively once more, and the use of gas and electricity negatively.

The pattern of census area scores of the first factors for the three countries were as follows. In the case of Grenada, housing conditions were on average best in central St. George's, followed by the parishes of St. George's South and St. George's North in that order. St. Andrew's North on the northeast coast recorded by far the highest disamenity score. Middle to high disamenity scores applied to St. David's, St. Andrew's South, St. Patrick's, and St. John's, plus the island of Carriacou. A much lower score characterized St. Mark's on the northwest leeward coast.

Turning to St. Lucia, the same urban-rural patterning was discernible in the

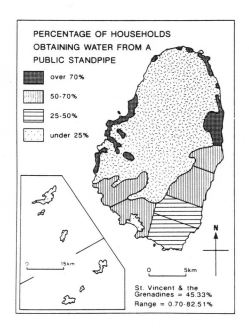

PERCENTAGE OF HOUSEHOLDS
OBTAINING WATER FROM A
PUBLIC STANDPIPE

- over 70%
- 50-70%
- 25-50%
- under 25%

0   15km

0   5km

St. Vincent & the
Grenadines = 45.33%
Range = 0.70-82.51%

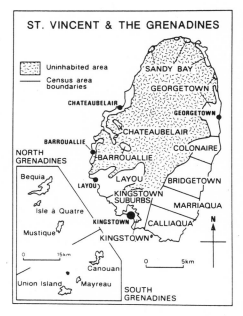

ST. VINCENT & THE GRENADINES

- Uninhabited area
- Census area boundaries

SANDY BAY

GEORGETOWN

CHATEAUBELAIR

GEORGETOWN

CHATEAUBELAIR

NORTH
GRENADINES

BARROUALLIE

BARROUALLIE

COLONAIRE

Bequia

LAYOU

LAYOU

BRIDGETOWN

Isle à Quatre

KINGSTOWN
SUBURBS

MARRIAQUA

Mustique

KINGSTOWN

KINGSTOWN

CALLIAQUA

0   15km

0   5km

Canouan

Union Island   Mayreau

SOUTH
GRENADINES

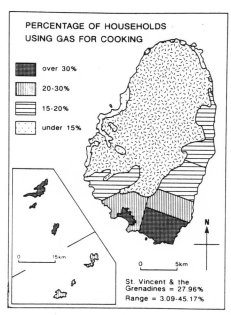

PERCENTAGE OF HOUSEHOLDS
USING GAS FOR COOKING

- over 30%
- 20-30%
- 15-20%
- under 15%

0   15km

0   5km

St. Vincent & the
Grenadines = 27.96%
Range = 3.09-45.17%

Map 4.1. Some aspects of housing quality in St. Vincent and the Grenadines.

Table 4.2

Results of the Factor Analysis of the Housing Variables for Grenada, St. Lucia, and St. Vincent for 1980/81

Grenada

Factor 1: 69.3% variance		Factor 2: 16.4% variance	
Wood	+0.97	Built before 1960	-0.95
Owned	+0.94	Public standpipe	+0.58
Gas	-0.94		
Electricity	-0.93		
Separate houses	+0.92		
Pit latrine	+0.88		

St. Lucia

Factor 1: 57.6% variance		Factor 2: 20.9% variance	
Separate houses	-0.91	Pit latrine	+0.78
Owned	+0.87	Built before 1960	-0.55
Wood	+0.86		
Electricity	-0.84		
Gas	-0.83		

St. Vincent

Factor 1: 58.3% variance		Factor 2: 17.1 % variance	
Electricity	-0.90	Built before 1960	-0.94
Public standpipe	+0.89		
Gas	-0.88		
Wood	+0.79		
Separate houses	+0.76		
Owned	+0.75		
Pit latrine	+0.74		

scores. Progressively larger negative scores were achieved on the disamenity factor as one progressed from the rural areas of Castries quarter to the suburbs and to the city itself. The highest disamenity scores pertained to the two southern rural areas of Choiseul and Laborie, followed some way behind by Anse-la-Raye and Canaries.

For St. Vincent and the Grenadines, the largest negative score on the housing disamenity factor was returned by central Kingstown, and the next highest applied to the North and South Grenadines rather than the immediate environs of the capital. This reflects the tourist and expatriate orientations of these islands. The next lowest amenity scores pertained to the Calliaqua area to the east of the capital city and to the suburbs of Kingstown. Housing disamenity scores reached their peak in the northern peripheral census zone of Sandy Bay. On the west coast, Barrouallie exhibited a high score, as did Bridgetown, Colonaire, and Georgetown on the eastern Atlantic coast. Layou and Chateaubelair showed relatively low scores on the housing amenity factor.

This analysis stresses the fact that there are marked and consistent bases to the geographical variations which characterize housing conditions in the three Windward Islands under study. In particular, they serve to highlight that, in overall terms, the poorest housing is to be found in the rural areas and not the principal urban zones, a point which is all too frequently either ignored or obfuscated in the realm of housing policy. Such geographical inequalities in housing circumstances reflect not only the colonial past, but also the persistence of urban bias in development since independence.

The State Apparatus for Housing

The first point to stress is that despite the existence of such obvious housing stress few Commonwealth eastern Caribbean territories have an explicit national housing plan, nor a formal housing planning machinery. This is true of all three of the Windward Islands under examination here. Even Barbados, as a larger more developed country, only moved to this position in 1984 (Ministry of Housing and Lands 1984; Potter 1992).

In a seemingly paradoxical manner, in most states in the region, the Ministry of Housing has had little or nothing to do in a direct sense with the production of houses. Such a state of affairs is partly reflected in the fact that the ministerial function of housing is frequently combined together with a series of other portfolios. For example, in 1991, the Ministry of Housing in St. Vincent and the Grenadines was linked with Local Government and Community Services and, in discussions, the permanent secretary stressed that there was no officer who specifically dealt with housing issues. In a similar vein, in St. Lucia, the Ministry of Housing forms part of a wider Ministry of Health, Housing and Labour and has undertaken no housing projects whatsoever. Phillip (1988) comments that the "Ministry is therefore the least effective and active in the field of housing" (59).

The same situation is reflected in the minuscule proportion of the housing stocks of these three territories which is provided by the state. The government-rented housing stock is largest in St. Lucia at 1.50 percent of total households. However, the proportions are as low as 0.18 and 0.36 percent in the case of Grenada and St. Vincent and the Grenadines respectively. This may be compared with a figure of 4.50 percent in Barbados. In the case of St. Lucia, for instance, the state's involvement in housing dates from the fire which destroyed Central Castries in 1948. Between 1949 and 1959, the state built 357 apartment blocks in Central Castries. The units vary from one to four bedrooms and, in 1990, fetched rents from EC$70 to EC$200 per month. In the final analysis, these units were deemed totally inappropriate, whereupon the state has almost entirely withdrawn from the housing market.

In all three nations under examination, the function of providing and overseeing housing is vested in a technically oriented national housing agency. In St. Vincent and the Grenadines this is referred to as the *Housing and Land Development Corporation*. In the case of St. Lucia it is the *Housing and Urban Development Corporation,* while in Grenada it is styled the *National Housing Authority.* These units are expected to be self-financing, working on the basis of cost recovery and replicability, by means of purchasing land for the next scheme from money recouped from the previous one. It is not expected that they will receive funding from the state, nor that they will provide lower-income groups with subsidized housing.

The overall result is that very few houses have been built in the public sector, and a minimal number of improvement programs have been carried out. Further, the few houses that have been constructed by these respective corporations have turned out to be well beyond the means of those who are most in need. For example, in St. Lucia, the Housing and Urban Development Corporation was originally established in 1971, but was totally dormant from the early 1980s to 1989, when it was reconstituted. During its 'active' period, however, it was involved in only one scheme which was specifically geared toward the lower end of the housing market. This was the construction of 110 timber houses at Independence City in the Entrepot area of Castries. The units, which were built in 1975, measured about 39 square meters. Although they were ostensibly designed for low-income earners, the fact that they were sold at EC$11,000 meant that a significant proportion of the houses were eventually purchased by middle-income earners. In another, somewhat earlier scheme, undertaken at Sans Souci in 1971, masonry units of some 93 square meters were constructed. These were priced between EC$12,000 and EC$14,000 and, as a direct result, were also purchased by middle-income earners.

In contrast to this manifestly poor performance, 1980 saw the establishment of the *Housing Rehabilitation Project* (HRP) in St. Lucia, following the destruction caused by Hurricane Allen in August of that year. The scheme was, in fact, physically located within the Housing and Urban Development Corporation, despite the long-standing quiescence of the latter. The aim of the HRP was to provide direct assistance to the 1,940 families whose homes were devastated by the storm. As Louis (1986) has effectively demonstrated, the salient point of the project was that many of the housing units provided were factory prefabricated and were transported to the site of construction. Thus, he argues that, with proper management, stringent financial control and an effective loan recovery operation, the prefabrication of houses for low-income earners could well be a feasible venture in the region. When informal interviews were being conducted by the present author in late 1990, the general manager of the Housing and Urban Development Corporation said that they were looking at the possibility of introducing a two-room, one-bedroom starter house, designed for expansion by the occupant over time. It was envisaged at that time that such units would sell at EC$30,000 or thereabouts.

In a remarkably similar manner, it has been argued that the public sector *Housing and Land Development Corporation* (HLDC) in St. Vincent has failed to provide effective low-income shelter. The corporation was established in June 1976 by an act of parliament. In a report made to the United Nations Center for Human Settlements (UNCHS) Ishmael (1989) puts the failure down to a mixture of internal mismanagement and the lack of clearly designed housing policies in the first place. Although charged with remaining economically viable from its inception, the corporation always provided some subsidies. This was true in the case of the sale of building materials by HLDC. The criteria for eligibility for subsidized building materials were a maximum income of EC$15,000 per annum, total assets of EC$40,000, whilst an upper limit of EC$60,000 was placed on the house price. However, it was well known that relatively wealthy people were purchasing building materials from HLDC at discounted rates. By the financial year 1989–90, the corporation had run up a EC$1.9 million overdraft, and the public image of the corporation had become severely tarnished. Indeed, Ishmael (1989) recommended that HLDC be dissolved legislatively and a new Housing Finance Institution be established in its place, together with its own integral Technical Service Agency.

Over the past few years, however, there have been signs of a changing awareness of the housing problem in the case of St. Vincent and the Grenadines. In September 1988, the then minister of housing outlined the St. Vincent and the Grenadines government's intended approach to housing. The enlightened point here was that it was announced that future policy was to focus mainly on the provision of site and services schemes and the upgrading of existing low-income housing areas. Since then, HLDC has been endeavoring to upgrade two areas per year, with each of these consisting of twenty-five to thirty houses. This is a very small total, but a step in the right direction. In areas such as Upper New Montrose and the Malla Valley, footpaths have been improved and two standpipes provided. It is envisaged that other upgrading efforts will focus on areas such as Camden Park, Routcher Bay, Coconut Range, Gibson Corner, Fair Hall, and Largo Heights.

In discussions with the author in 1989, the then general manager of the National Housing Authority (NHA) of Grenada confirmed that there was no national housing plan. Further, given that the government to that point had thought exclusively in terms of producing entire houses, there was seen to be no need to apply to external agencies such as the World Bank or USAID for housing funds. It was further reported that only at that stage were the government and NHA thinking of establishing a small site-and-service scheme at Corinth. In fact, between 1975 and 1989, official statistics show that national housing schemes saw only 327 houses built (Grenada Planning Office, n.d.), and most of these were affordable only to middle-income families (Wirt 1987).

The essential aim of the present section of this chapter has been to establish that the eastern Caribbean countries under study do not currently possess overt national housing plans in any shape or form. Their respective ministries of housing have been dormant, and the responsibility for improving the housing lot of those on low incomes has been placed at the feet of technically oriented national housing corporations. These have been expected to run on the basis of cost recovery, with minimal subsidies being transferred to the poor. As a result, most of the houses constructed by these divisions have been way beyond the means of those on low incomes. In the case of St. Vincent and the Grenadines, there has been a recent step towards a more pro-active policy, with the espousal of the need for squatter upgrading programs on the steep hillsides around the capital, Kingstown. This has followed a period during which the national housing agency was far from successful. However, in both St. Lucia and Grenada, there are no upgrading or rehabilitation schemes for the existing housing stocks.

The Question of Housing Finance

In general terms, the housing finance opportunities available in these Caribbean territories, like those in many Third World nations, mean that the poor are largely, if not entirely, excluded from the opportunity of obtaining a mortgage given the price of housing and land in the formal sector.

For example, in the mid-1980s, the cheapest unit constructed in the formal sector in St. Lucia cost EC$33,000 (Phillip 1988). At a mortgage interest rate of 12 percent per annum over a repayment period of fifteen years—the general terms prevailing at the time—such a house was not affordable to the lowest 60 percent of income earners. At about the same juncture, Central Planning Unit data showed that approximately 300 units were being produced per year by the formal building sector. The reported average cost of these units was EC$86,191, which could only be afforded by the top 10 percent of income earners. Hence, although funds for lending are available through the St. Lucia Development Bank, the St. Lucia Mortgage Finance Corporation, the National Insurance Scheme, and the St. Lucia Co-Operative League (comprised of a group of credit unions), these are all effectively out of the reach of low-income house searchers (see Louis 1986: 64–68 for further details).

In St. Vincent and the Grenadines, there are approximately twenty institutions, mainly banks and credit unions, that are involved in dispensing mortgages. Since 1988, the main source of mortgage finance has been the government-owned National Commercial Bank (NCB). The funds derive from a loan of EC$4.05 million from the Caribbean Development Bank, together with a matched pool of funds from the National Insurance Scheme, making EC$10.7 million available in all. NCB loans can be used to cover 90 percent of the market value of land and new construction. However, with a 10 percent interest rate over twenty years, the bulk of funds have served the needs of only the top 25 percent of Vincentian income earners. Ishmael (1989) notes that approximately 75 percent of the population earn under EC$10,000 per annum, whilst the bottom 20 percent earn less than EC$3,000 per year. Even if such groups could afford a mortgage, the maximum purchase they could manage would be in the EC$18,000–20,000 range. The cheapest unit available in the formal housing market in 1989 cost EC$35,000, close to the average cost in the case of St. Lucia.

Thus, low-income groups in these societies are unable to service their shelter needs within the formal housing, finance, and credit sectors. At the same time, the government is not involved in providing housing or, indeed, in providing housing subsidies. Hence, the bottom 60 to 75 percent of income earners have no option but to provide their own housing by whatever means they can. In short, as is replicated in so many contexts, those groups who are most in need of housing are not reached by the formal sector, nor by the state.

Squatter Settlements, Rent Yards, and Shantytowns

The account thus far has detailed how poor groups within the societies under study are marginalized and excluded from the formal housing sector. Those with low incomes have no option but to provide their own homes by informal means (for example, see fig. 4.3). As a result, squatting has become more and more common around the capitals of these territories, especially on the steep hills which surround Kingstown, Castries, and St. George's. Some authorities talk in terms of 30 percent of the households in such areas being squatters. Squatting has become particularly prevalent on land which is marginal for other purposes—for example, on steep slopes and poorly drained land, as well as on Crown or public lands. A recent analysis of the preliminary results of the 1991 census for St. Vincent and the Grenadines shows the rapid growth of population in the Kingstown suburbs and Calliaqua, with growth rates well over 16 percent between 1980 and 1991 (Potter 1993c). In contrast, Kingstown proper actually lost population during this period.

There are two major areas where people have been squatting for some time in Castries, St. Lucia. These are both shown in map 4.2. The first is the Conway area located just to the north of the Central Business District (CBD), adjacent to the harbor. The second is the Four à Chaud area, which is also located adjacent to the harbor, this time directly to the west of the CBD. The Four à Chaud area was originally settled in 1972, and today houses approximately 428 dwellings with a population in excess of 2,000. The area was originally swampy, and residents stress that they were encouraged to settle by members of the then government, albeit on a temporary basis. In a study of the area Phillip (1988) stresses that many

Fig. 4.3. An informal house and "psychic zone" in central Castries, St. Lucia.

of the inhabitants feel that they own the plots on which they reside, as a direct result of the fact that they have filled in the lots themselves by paying truck drivers to deliver soil to their plots in an effort to make them suitable for building. However, the origins of the area are shown by the fact that it is still very prone to waterlogging and periodic flooding during the wet season. Drainage in the area is very poor, consisting of a few open drains. There is only one public facility comprising a shower and toilets and a single public standpipe, which is reported as serving the 153 households that do not have water piped into the house or yard. As high a proportion as 70 percent of the population use the public facility as the means of sewage disposal, 22 percent use the pit latrines, and 8 percent use "other" methods (Phillip 1988). The land is ultimately zoned for warehousing activity as a part of the Port Zone, and Phillip (1988) reports widespread concern among the residents about the possibility of relocation.

The other main squatter area of Castries, known as Conway (map 4.2), is built on land which was originally owned privately by a single family and which was being developed as a rent yard. The area grew rapidly during the 1940s and 1950s as a result of the flourishing trade which occurred in Castries harbor during the period. Stevedores, in particular, needed to be near the harbor and so were prepared to pay the low rents charged and build their own homes on an informal

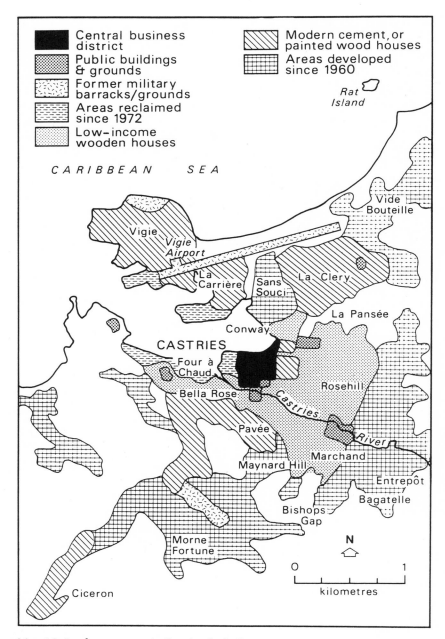

Map 4.2. Land use patterns in Castries, St. Lucia.

and largely ad hoc basis (Phillip 1988). Eventually, the owners of the land felt that they could not keep abreast of the rent yard type of development, which made rent collection difficult. They therefore sold the land to the government in the early 1960s, whereupon the area effectively became a squatter settlement, as the state did not bother to collect rents for the spots. By this stage the area consisted of well over three hundred houses.

But the Conway area affords an interesting lesson concerning the role of the state in housing matters in the region. Generally, as elsewhere, the state has not intervened and squatters have been left to get on with the job of building for themselves. But the state has recently become involved in the Conway area. As long ago as the 1970s, the area was scheduled for commercial redevelopment. The plan envisaged a central Piazza, with commercial offices being built along the water-front, facing the John Compton Highway. Nothing happened, however, for approximately twenty years. Then, in the middle of the 1980s, a new duty-free tourist facility was developed across the harbor at Pointe Seraphine. In 1986, after the opening of the duty-free facility, the government announced its plans to clear part of the Conway area—the first intervention of its kind in St. Lucia—and build commercial and governmental offices. The western part of the squatter zone was cleared with considerable haste between April and July 1986, with a total of 162 houses being relocated in three phases. These former residents of Conway were moved to Ciceron, some three kilometers to the southwest of the CBD. The Housing and Urban Development Corporation had land here, and the inhabitants of Conway were given the incentive of EC$1,000, either as a direct deduction from the cost of the land or in the form of materials for renovating the unit. The government provided free transport for the dismantled houses to be carried to their new sites. Two meetings were held with members of the area, but both took place after the relocation process itself had begun.

It seems clear that the process of state involvement in housing after a period of extended quiescence reflects the interests of capital. The moves were made on economic grounds in order to release prime, valuable land in the city center. It is hard not to ponder whether it also witnessed the desire to remove what might be considered an eyesore in the vicinity of a large, new tourist-oriented development.

A noticeable recent development in Castries has, however, been the creation of two new squatter settlements close to the urban core, and it is hard to envisage that these two sets of circumstances are not linked. The first has occurred where squatters have started to build houses in and around the small cemetery which is located just to the east of the Four à Chaud area. The second area is one farther along the harbor from Four à Chaud, at Bananes Point, which is in the process of being developed as a self-help fishing community (fig. 4.4).

Fig. 4.4. The informal fishing village developing at Bananes Point, Castries.

Essentially similar examples could be presented in respect of both St. Vincent and Grenada. Suffice it to say here that squatting has become all too frequent an occurrence in and around Kingstown, St. Vincent. Ishmael (1988) reports that most squatting occurs on Crown Lands and is strongly based on the apparent lack of past reaction on the part of the authorities. Some local experts argue that this explains why the housing stock of St. Vincent is found to be better than those in other states. Central Kingston, in particular, is surrounded on the east by rapidly growing squatter communities which are extending up the mountain slopes. This is, of course, exacerbating problems of deforestation, soil erosion, and increasing agricultural resource tensions. There are well-established squatter settlements in Upper New Montrose and Malla Valley, where densities are high due to infilling.

A recent development in St. Vincent appears to parallel the one elaborated above in relation to Conway, St. Lucia. There are a number of squatter areas on the slopes which overlook the southwest running valley which slopes down to a very scenic beach at Ottley Hall to the northwest of the capital, Kingstown. For some time it has been intended to develop this area as a marina and resort, and there has been talk of clearing the squatters from the area as a part of this development. Planning permission has been granted and a $135 million marina and luxury cruise ship port will be developed over the next few years.

Evidence from the region confirms that housing is a strongly political issue, with squatting being actively encouraged and supported by politicians in the periods immediately prior to elections. At the same time, existing shanty and squatter areas are likely to see the provision of basic services during such periods. In a survey carried out by Ishmael (1988), 78 percent of those interviewed in two areas claimed to have been authorized to squat either by politicians or HLDC officials. After elections, the settlements continue to be neglected. In this way, self-help housing may be used as a political tool in return for electoral support. At the same time squatters have, with the few exceptions outlined above, rarely been disturbed by the authorities. Thus, in St. Vincent, in particular, walled houses are quite common, and in 1981, for instance, such houses formed a larger proportion of the total housing stock in this impoverished country (65 percent) than they did in Barbados (45 percent). It is worth quoting a regional writer in this regard, Louis (1986), who stated that "one would hate to believe that squatter settlements are a deliberate method of satisfying housing needs without the massive investments that would have been expected, had it been a controlled development" (275).

Another instance where the state may become involved in housing is where environmental factors threaten the safety of settlements. An instance of this was provided earlier in relation to the rehabilitation of housing after the passage of Hurricane Allen in St. Lucia. A second example serves to exemplify the marked lack of emphasis which is accorded low-income housing in general in the region. On mainland St. Vincent, a large number of self-help houses are to be found located on the upper parts of the beach on the windward side of the island. Examples of these dwellings are shown in figs. 4.5 and 4.6. A large constellation of such houses is to be found in the Mangrove, Gorse, and Byera areas. Similar communities are to be found just to the south of Georgetown.

The precise location of such dwellings along the Mangrove, Gorse, and Byera section of the east coast is shown in map 4.3, which has been adapted from Robertson (1987). It is estimated that the beach in this area is home to about 116 households. The history of these dwellings can be traced to Hadley Brothers Enterprise Limited, a plantation growing coconuts and bananas. In the early 1960s, all households on the estate were ordered to relocate onto the coastal beach flats. At first, such "lands" were occupied free of charge, although HLDC files show that subsequently the occupants were asked to pay "peppercorn" rents amounting to twelve dollars annually. In 1973, in a further development, the occupants were asked to purchase the spots at ten cents per square foot, in the case of laborers, and twenty cents per square foot for nonlaborers.

However, with the passage of Hurricane Allen on 4 August 1980, extensive flooding caused damage to housing, possessions, and livestock along the Gorse-Mangrove-Byera area. Following these events, the coastal beach was regarded as a danger zone for housing. Accordingly, a proposal for a scheme to relocate the beach dwellers was put before the British Development Division (BDD) on 8

Fig. 4.5. Example of a beach house at Byera, St. Vincent.

Fig. 4.6. A row of houses located on the beach at Byera.

December 1980. The total funding required was estimated at EC$448,271, with approximately three-quarters coming from BDD. The land for a resettlement village was made available by the Mt. William Estate. The precise location of the new inland village is shown in map 4.3.

Progress with the scheme was very slow at first, but by 1985–86, some 60 percent of the original households residing on the beach had been relocated to the new village. However, as might be anticipated in the situation of a housing shortage, there remain to this day a substantial number of beach dwellers. Clearly, the children of some of those residing in older housing units remained in the beach houses when their parents moved, whilst in other instances new residents moved into the zone. Thus, some thirteen or so years after the original incident occurred, the threat of severe flooding and storm loss remains, testifying once again to the "afterthought" nature of housing in the eastern Caribbean.

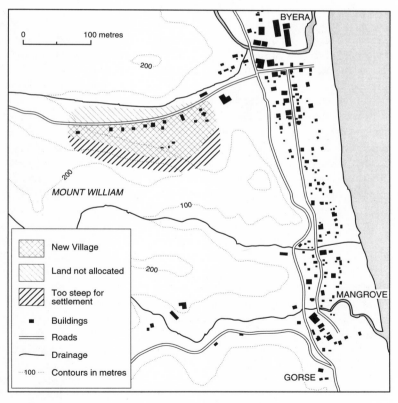

Map 4.3. The Mangrove-Gorse-Byera area and resettlement village.

Housing and the State:
Past, Present, and Future

It is argued here that facts add up to a form of nonpolicy with regard to low-income housing. The onus of producing housing has remained firmly and squarely with the poor themselves. Most strangely of all, the governments of Caribbean territories have rarely seen fit to place the local vernacular cottage at the center of systems of state-aided self-help. In this sense, they have not planned *with the local people* and their distinctive sociocultural innovations. As noted in chapter 1, this argument may be situated in the debate between liberals, such as John Turner, who argue that the state should confine its attention to helping the poor to help themselves (see Turner 1967, 1968, 1976, 1982), and Burgess (1982, 1990, 1992), who, from the radical stance, argues that taken to extreme, self-help principles allow the state to abdicate its responsibility within the housing arena (see also Conway 1982).

Some would argue that this is because there are just too few votes to be had from providing appropriate aided self-help housing in the region. More votes are to be obtained from legitimizing or otherwise spontaneous self-help houses. In addition, the argument runs that symbolic schemes, which involve providing a few houses at a high technical specification have far more visual and political impact. This also helps to explain why housing conditions are found to be so much poorer in the rural areas of these territories, a feature pinpointed earlier in this chapter. Further, leaving the poor to fend for themselves helps to maintain a pool of labor, affords the context for powerful patron-client relationships and formidable patronage systems, as well as serving to maintain relatively low wage levels.

The implications of these observations for the development of a theoretical framework for the consideration of eastern Caribbean housing can be summarized. The failure to produce explicit housing policy statements can be seen as an implicit state policy of allowing the poor to fend for themselves. Thus, no policy must be seen as a clear policy. This can be interpreted in the light of ideas emanating from *articulation theory* concerning modes of production under capitalist development (see also McGee 1979; Wolpe 1980; Burgess 1990). In simple terms the argument goes that capitalism *conserves* traditional precapitalist forms that work in its favor, but specifically seeks to *dissolve* those which do not.

Thus, the stance of governments may be interpreted as one of primarily seeking to conserve the "precapitalist" or "informal" housing system in its most basic form. The process involves the fostering of strict self-help, involving minimalist systems of state assistance. It is associated with poverty, hard work, and exploitation at both work and at home. The brief flirtation with complete state housing systems, consisting of too high a specification, can be seen to be leading to the ultimate *conservation* of the folk/vernacular architectural form at its most *basic* level, although at first this seems to be leading to dissolution. Such a situation involves modernization, symbolic schemes, and tokenism. However, the intermediate position of improving such housing by means of appropriately financed state-aided self-help housing has largely been ignored.

Such a policy stance would involve the future provision of small, low-interest loans and technical assistance on site. It would almost certainly entail producing core units associated with wooden houses built along traditional lines. It would witness the enhancement of the local vernacular architectural system, not its maintenance at a most basic and exploitative level. The Caribbean vernacular house—built by the people for the people—is a surprisingly neglected cultural artifact in the Caribbean region. This is exemplified by the general lack of scholarly attention that has been paid to such housing. It is also reflected in the fact that, in the realm of state housing policy and provision, the efforts of low-income groups to house themselves have been almost totally neglected as a sociocultural resource of major importance (Potter 1989, 1992).

For far too long, the policy potential of the Caribbean popular dwelling has remained unrecognized by politicians and development planners alike. The work carried out as part of the present project suggests that only when the appropriate, basic needs, and self-help characteristics of such people-built houses are fully recognized will genuine progress be made in improving low-income housing in the region. Just as the grand Georgian house may be interpreted as the outcome of imposed colonial power, so the vernacular architectural form can be construed as a form of sociocultural resistance to the inequities of that earlier colonial domination.

References

Burgess, R. (1982) "Self-Help Housing Advocacy: A Curious Form of Radicalism: A Critique of the Work of J. F. C. Turner." In P. M. Ward, ed., *Self-Help Housing: A Critique*. Mansell: London. 55–97.

———. (1990) "The State and Self-Help Building in Pereira, Colombia." Ph.D. thesis, University of London.

———. (1992) "Helping Some to Help Themselves: Third World Housing Policies and Development Strategies." In K. Mathéy, ed., *Beyond Self-Help Housing*, 75–91. Mansell: London.

Conway, D. (1982) "Self-Help Housing, the Commodity Nature of Housing and Amelioration of the Housing Deficit: Continuing the Turner-Burgess Debate." *Antipode* 14: 40–46.

Fraser, P. (1985) *Caribbean Economic Handbook*. Euromonitor: London.

Grenada Planning Office (n.d.) *Sectoral Issue Papers—Draft Grenada National Physical Development Plan*. St. George's, Grenada.

Ishmael, L. (1988) "Informal Sector Factor Mobilization: The Process by which Poor People Shelter Themselves and Implications for Policy Focus on the Caribbean: St. Vincent and Dominica." Ph.D. diss., University of Pennsylvania.

———. (1989) *Housing Sector Overview*. Government of St. Vincent and the Grenadines and United Nations Center for Human Settlements and United Nations Development Programme.

Louis, E. L. (1986) "A Critical Analysis of Low-Income Housing in St. Lucia." M.Sc. diss., St. Augustine Campus of the University of the West Indies.

McGee, T. (1979) "Conservation and Dissolution in the Third World City: The 'Shanty Town' as an Element of Conservation." *Development and Change* 10: 1–22.

Ministry of Housing and Lands (1984) *White Paper on Housing.* Barbados Government Printing Office.

Phillip, M. P. (1988) "Urban Low Income Housing in St. Lucia: An Analysis of the Formal and Informal Sectors." M.Phil. thesis, University of London.

Potter, R. B. (1989) "Urban Housing in Barbados, West Indies." *Geographical Journal* 155: 81–93.

———. (1991) "An Analysis of Housing in Grenada, St. Lucia and St. Vincent and the Grenadines." *Caribbean Geography* 3: 106–25.

———. (1992) *Housing Conditions in Barbados: A Geographical Analysis.* Kingston, Jamaica: University of the West Indies, Institute of Social and Economic Research (ISER).

———. (1993a) "Basic Needs and Development in the Small Island States of the Eastern Caribbean." In D. Lockhart, D. Drakakis-Smith, and J. Schembri, eds., 92–116. *The Development Process in Small Island States.* London and New York: Routledge.

———. (1993b) "Urbanization in the Caribbean and Trends of Global Convergence-Divergence." *Geographical Journal* 159: 1–21.

———. (1993c) "Demographic Change in a Small Island State: St. Vincent and the Grenadines, 1980–1991." *Geography* 77: 374–76.

———. (1994) *Low-Income Housing and the State in the Eastern Caribbean.* Barbados, Jamaica, Trinidad, and Tobago: University of the West Indies Press.

Robertson, R. E. A. (1987) "Disaster Management in St. Vincent and the Grenadines." B.Sc. diss., University of the West Indies.

Singh, S. (1988) *Housing in the English-Speaking Caribbean: Recent Conditions and Trends.* Trinidad and Tobago: Central Statistical Printing Office.

Turner, J. F. C. (1967) "Barriers and Channels for Housing Development in Modernizing Countries." *Journal of the American Institute of Planners* 33: 167–81.

———. (1968) "Housing Priorities, Settlement Patterns and Urban Development in Modernizing Countries." *Journal of the American Institute of Planners* 34: 354–63.

———. (1976) *Housing by People: Towards Autonomy in Building Environments.* London: Marion Boyars.

———. (1982) "Issues in Self-Help and Self-Managed Housing." In P. M. Ward, ed., *Self-Help Housing: A Critique.* London: Mansell. 99–113.

Wirt, D. S. (1987) *An Assessment of Socio-Economic Conditions of Human Settlements.* Grenada: Department of Regional Development, Organization of American States.

Wolpe, H., ed. (1980) *The Articulation of Modes of Production.* London: Routledge and Kegan Paul.

Chapter 5

Self-Help Housing in Jamaica

L. Alan Eyre

God hath not promised
Sun without rain
Joy without sorrow
Peace without pain.

But God hath promised
Strength for the day
Rest for the labourer
Light on the way
Grace for the trials
Help from above
Unfailing sympathy
Undying love.

There hath not failed one word of all His good promise.
I Kings 8:56

During the research for this chapter in Jamaica's Riverton City, the poorest and most desperate shantytown in the Caribbean, this was observed on a wall of the building used by one of the gentlest and bravest crusaders for the basic humanity of all shantytown dwellers worldwide, Father Ron Peters of Guyana. In 1993, he was betrayed and gunned down by ruthless dons who bitterly resented the love and devotion shown to him by the thousands whom he sought to uplift. This chapter is dedicated to his memory.

The significance and seriousness of the issues addressed in this volume are vividly highlighted by the fact that while this chapter was being prepared, on 18 April 1994, in a politician's home in the town of Lucea, Jamaica, *police were attempting to control a riot at the gate. Crowds of angry squatters and other shantytown dwellers were waving banners and placards demanding water and roads and, ironically, police protection.* The politician, with the police inspector's protective arm around his shoulder, was pleading for calm, but was helpless to offer anything but the usual promises, which the mob well knows are worthless. The crowds are sufficiently astute politically to know that only if, and when, they rise up and visibly and audibly disrupt the normal life of this town will their voices be heard (fig. 5.1). And their anger is in large measure due to their frustration at the increasing hopelessness of their plight. For several years now, they have seen society's sympathy for squatters evaporate and indeed turn against them as "law and order" rightist politics have become more deeply entrenched, and the wheel of political fortune spins once again, in Lucea and the whole world, towards free market capitalism and the "rights" of the wealthy, the big landowners, and the multinational financial institutions.

Fig. 5.1. Protest demonstration by shantytown residents demanding water, better access, and police protection, April 1994.

They do not know, these crowds, that a few months before a similar number of people from among the managers of the world's resources and wealth had gathered at the American University in Washington, D.C., to consider "actions to reduce poverty" and to "offer the poor the means to become more productive and hence control their own lives" (*Environmental Bulletin* 1993–94). They care little for the roster of world luminaries who addressed the distinguished gathering, including former President Jimmy Carter, World Bank Vice-President Ismail Serageldin, and U.N. General Secretary Boutros Boutros-Ghali. Since the 1950s, these shantytown dwellers, and their parents, had been told by the politicians that the way to "control their own lives" was to invade abandoned or unused land, land that no one seemed to care about, land that, whoever had a paper title to it, really belonged to the masses, and thereupon they should erect their own self-help housing. Now in 1994 the same politicians from the same parties that led squatter marches are telling them that this is immoral, unlawful, antisocial, indeed criminal. And, as that morning I looked out of the window at the shouting crowds squaring off against the police, I beheld bitterness, betrayal, and despair.

A Long Tradition

Jamaica has a very long tradition of self-help housing. A majority of rural Jamaicans and a large proportion of urban residents live in dwellings to which they have contributed all or most of the construction input by self-help methods. No exact figures are available, but more than two-thirds of the population of the city of Montego Bay (67,000 out of 97,000) are in this category (Eyre 1979a). Half of Spanish Town's population, at least 49,000 out of 99,000, inhabit the 36 present or former shantytowns within the urban perimeter and occupy homes which were first built by self-help on either capture or rent land (Eyre 1984c). The proportion in metropolitan Kingston and St. Andrew is lower, but absolute numbers make the Jamaican capital the premier example of genuinely informal self-help housing in the Commonwealth Caribbean, rivaled only in the entire region by the vast shantytowns of Port-au-Prince, Haiti, and Santo Domingo in the Dominican Republic.

This tradition of self-help shelter in Jamaica began with the slave plantation. Higman (1988) documents self-help housing built by plantation slaves. After Emancipation in 1838 the tradition intensified and virtually all free villages which were established in the nineteenth century consisted entirely of self-help housing. This rural tradition persists. I have lived more than half my working life in such a village, established originally by freed slaves from a half-dozen neighboring coffee plantations. All dwellings, without exception and including my own residence in that village, may be categorized as informal housing and were sited and built, often over many years, by some form of self-help.

For many decades earlier this century, *provision* of housing by the state or the private sector was largely confined to the towns of the sugar belt (Eyre 1965a) and to rehabilitation of the urban population after disasters. "Hurricane housing" such as at Maverly and August Town was in the 1950s almost the only shelter built directly by government (Eyre 1984a). Private funding provided the mazes of "tenement rent yards" in all Jamaica's towns, but this kind of provision was (and still is) entirely uncoordinated. Mass provision of housing in Jamaica had to await the state- and aid-funded low-income schemes like Tivoli Gardens, Trench Town, and Zimbabwe in the 1960s and 1970s and (for a higher-income bracket) those of the West Indies Home Construction Company, a Matalon family firm that uses prefabrication methods to reduce costs and increase its share of the market.

Low Incomes Make Self-Help Housing a Necessity for Many

Jamaica is unusual, though not of course unique, in having a high capital value of housing stock relative to incomes. The author's surveys over many years indicate that a majority of Jamaicans live in dwellings that they could never have financed from income derived solely from the local economy. Remittances from abroad, foreign aid, exceptional thrift from casual and "informal" activities, and, in some cases, income from export of prohibited substances have all contributed to this situation. A superficial overview of the quality of the housing stock throughout the country gives a false picture if it is used to measure the levels and strength of the Jamaican economy or average locally generated income. In general, housing quality is superior to what might be expected in a country with a per capita income of US$1,350 per annum (according to 1994 statistics).

It is a stark fact that 41 percent of all employees in Jamaica earn less than US$3 per working day (US$930 per year) and cannot qualify for housing provision of any kind, public or private. In addition, there is the one-fifth of all adults who are officially unemployed and unable to afford anything at all. In these conditions, self-help housing is not an option, it is a necessity. The problem needing to be discussed is not *whether* but only *how* it is to be facilitated.

Low incomes are not the only adverse factor. Jamaica is in a major zone of natural hazards, so that hurricanes (e.g., 1951, 1963, 1980, 1988), earthquakes (e.g., 1907, 1957) and floods (e.g., 1979, 1986, 1990) have on occasion dramatically, though temporarily, reduced the overall inhabitable housing inventory by between 5 and 25 percent. The "tribal war" of 1976–81 resulted in the total destruction, by arson and other violent acts, of an estimated 3,500 dwellings within five years throughout the nation, 2,000 of these in just two adjacent political constituencies (Eyre 1984b, 1986a, 1986b).

No comprehensive inventory of self-help housing throughout Jamaica has ever been made, or is ever likely to be made, given present financial constraints. The most detailed studies have been of the shantytowns of Montego Bay (Eyre 1972, 1979a). Hanson (1975) studied informal settlements in metropolitan Kingston and St. Andrew at all stages between initial *capture* or squatting to full absorption into the urban fabric. Clarke (1983) examined self-help housing in the context of a study of the historical development of Kingston as a primate colonial and post-colonial capital city. Eyre (1984c) included Spanish Town in a national sample. Some publications are widely available; the more comprehensive ones, for reasons of publication cost, have had a very limited distribution, and are relatively difficult for scholars to utilize.

Forms and Stages of Shantytowns

Geographers, like all scientists, are classifiers, and aim to generalize and reduce to order. Consequently, the great complexity which characterizes the physical and social forms of informal settlements have been subjected to some fairly rigorous categorization procedures. These are still tentative, and, like all classifications in the social sciences, bristle with exceptions. However, self-help housing manifests (at least) the following four classic forms:

1. Shantytowns on captured land which pass through several stages of improvement until they are absorbed into the formal urban fabric.
2. Shantytowns on captured land which are aborted and eventually removed by the state or by private owners.
3. Shantytowns on rent land where there are severe limitations on physical improvement, since notice can be given at any time or the land may be sold to another owner. These settlements tend to remain in stasis more or less permanently, though the structures themselves have value and may be bought and sold (Clarke and Ward, 1980). Some dwellings may be quite substantial but capable of being transported elsewhere. In many of these settlements, activists may pressure government to acquire the land and give the occupiers security of tenure.
4. Shantytowns on captured land or rent land, where tenure is controversial, restricting improvement and leaving the population in a kind of tense limbo of perpetual uncertainty. The degree of controversy and uncertainty affects the initiative for improvement, and may restrict it altogether. Activists in these settlements often adopt a confrontational and adversarial attitude towards the wider society, including government.

1994: "The Year of the Squatter"?

From 1965, when the resilient shantytown dwellers of Lionel Town first welcomed me to their embattled community and to their hearts, until 1993, attempts to put the issue of self-help housing firmly and prominently on the national and regional agenda in the Caribbean have largely failed (Angel et al. 1983; Conway 1982; Eyre 1965b, 1979b; Potter 1985, 1989, 1992). Political directorates, local councils, national parliaments, financial institutions, and most decision makers in the society side-stepped or otherwise ignored the growing crisis. During those years a few intellectuals and low-level functionaries from government and the private sector met from time to time to discuss the problem. At conferences, academics and professional consultants analyzed trends and presented models (Kingsley 1990), but all the while a social volcano was rumbling. As recently as 1989, a prominent Jamaican politician led hundreds of capturers on to the multi-million-dollar estate of a "big man" in Montego Bay and urged them to build their own homes there—as substantial as they liked.

So far, 1994 has been very different. By its end it may well have become the "year of the squatter" in the Caribbean. Consider some of the events of 1994:

1. Guyanese President Cheddi Jagan said his government is committed to regularizing four thousand squatting areas annually in its drive to ease the country's worsening housing shortage.
2. A record number of Haitians died at sea, or in camps, or on waterless cays in the Bahamas, fleeing the intolerable conditions in the shantytowns of Port-au-Prince and other cities in that country, especially during the period when President Bertrand Aristide, the hope and champion of the poor squatters of Haiti, had been abandoned by the wealthy and powerful nations of the hemisphere. The politically and culturally vibrant shantytown dwellers, especially the heroic women who struggle to feed and raise their families there, may now see at least some hope in the fragile democracy that has been restored with the return of President Aristide.
3. Cuba, after contending for decades that its unique version of self-help housing had completely solved the need for adequate shelter, officially acknowledged that it had not prevented the development of shantytowns and that these constituted a problem that must be addressed even in a centrally controlled society.
4. During the first four months of 1994, Jamaican squatters and residents of self-help settlements rioted violently in Montego Bay, Portland, Holland Bamboo, and Negril, and demonstrated peacefully in several other areas.
5. Rioting also broke out at the National Stadium in Jamaica during a routine allocation of private housing units to queuing applicants.
6. In April, the National Housing Trust (NHT) in Jamaica, a semi-autonomous statutory body with enormous powers, bulldozed substantial houses nearing completion on lands at Rosemount, St. James, and "vowed to continue the drive by removing forthwith any new squatters." However, completed

homes have not been demolished. The owners have been given an opportunity to buy lots (*Gleaner,* 11 April 1994). Incidentally, no private landowner could possibly have done what the NHT did without lengthy litigation.

7. On 3 April, the minister of the Public Service and the Environment in Jamaica announced that government "will soon be removing squatters from the Fern Gully, Seville, Roaring River, White River and Ocho Rios areas of St. Ann" (*Sunday Herald,* 3 April 1994).

In order to examine in detail processes in Jamaican self-help settlements, a series of five case studies from metropolitan, urban, and rural Jamaica is presented. All were surveyed by the author in 1994. These include geographical analyses of Riverton City, a very low-income marginal shantytown in metropolitan St. Andrew; Hangman Burial Ground, a long established *capture* settlement in Spanish Town; Whitehall, a new semi-legal self-help suburb of Negril, Jamaica's fastest growing tourist resort; Flankers, a dynamic settlement with all ranges of income in the long-established tourist city of Montego Bay; and Holland Bamboo, a rural community in the sugar belt. The location of these settlements is indicated on map 5.1. The causes of recent violent disturbances in the last three of these settlements are examined in detail. These studies confirm that, in regard to self-help housing, Jamaica is at a major crisis point.

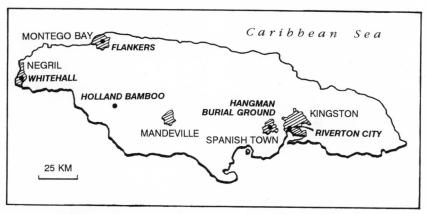

Map 5.1 Map of Jamaica showing locations of case studies.

Riverton City

In the ambitious plans for the post-Independence development of Kingston in the 1960s, Riverton City was envisaged as a major industrial zone, in particular for highly capitalized manufacturing plants of the corporate type employing large numbers of blue-collar workers. At that time these were the model in Europe and North America, and thus coveted by a post-colonial nation with aspirations for development based upon rapid industrialization. Loans were used to build a costly physical infrastructure, comparable to advanced world standards. The anticipated industrial expansion failed to materialize. With rising social tensions in the 1970s, financial institutions considered the location to be dangerous, and interest in its development on the part of both public and private sectors steadily waned. Riverton City was a refugee area for embittered and disillusioned People's National Party supporters after the 1980 parliamentary elections, and over the next decade acquired an unenviable reputation as the nation's poorest and most ungovernable shantytown (map 5.2). Jones (1990) has summarized the present situation:

> The Riverton City area of Kingston is . . . an example of captured use in that the area was zoned for industrial use, but is today occupied by a large squatter settlement and a major urban refuse dump. This dump has expanded in tandem with the need for solid waste disposal for the Kingston Metropolitan Area, and this site poses health and safety hazards as it is not managed. The river passing through this area picks up garbage and other deleterious substances which are transported to the Kingston Harbour to aggravate the high levels of pollution and ecological destruction in that body of water. (60)

It should be clearly understood that the settlement and the dump are not *adjacent,* but co-spatial. The houses are *on* the dump (fig. 5.2). Jones's three laconic sentences in fact describe a self-help housing area of fascinating complexity, fierce independence, deep squalor, social degradation, and individual courage. A volunteer social worker recently described living conditions in this notorious settlement as "absolutely desperate," a depiction with which, from a rather different perspective, I wholly concur.

Approximately five thousand people are commonly reported (by the police, church authorities, and the media) to live in Riverton City. From my own recent surveys, I believe this is a figure grossly inflated by ignorance about the community and fear. There are approximately four hundred very small residential structures. Unless household size is incredibly larger than the average for shantytowns in Jamaica, this implies a population of about two thousand. Individual residential structures average 11 square meters in floor area, with a standard deviation of 3.3 square meters. This is the lowest average and smallest standard deviation of any shantytown I have ever researched, and it is an indicator of the depth of poverty levels, with an absolute minimum of upgrading. The sense of insecurity is very high, the constant fear of eviction being unconducive to self-help improvement (fig. 5.3).

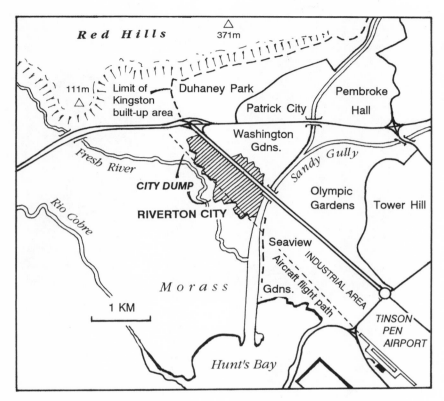

Map 5.2. Riverton City, St. Andrew.

Fig. 5.2. The perpetual pall of smoke and noxious fumes over Riverton City is a serious health hazard for all residents.

Fig. 5.3. Self-help housing at its most basic level: zinc sheets, sent as aid after hurricane Gilbert in 1988, surround compounds in Rivertown City.

Most of the dwelling units are occupied by a single household, but the composition of households is extremely varied, with many members having only brief residence before moving elsewhere. Although there is no way to quantify the fact, it is evident that the community harbors many fugitives from justice (as the larger society and the police view them) or folk hero figures (as they consider themselves and are viewed within Riverton City). Younger females within the community vie competitively for the sexual attentions of these *macho* alpha males, who, in turn, respond by "giving them a belly" as well as assisting them with minor improvements to their premises. Social workers are of the opinion that the more stable households are interested in reducing family size, and I concur: this trend is obvious to anyone working in the community. The cohort of those from five to nine years old is much larger than the one which follows it, newborns to four-year-olds.

There is a widespread perception that Riverton City houses many Rastafarian families (Eyre 1985). This is not true. Religious Rastafarians make up barely 2 percent of the population. *Dreads*—males adopting some visible characteristics of Rastafarianism, but without religious convictions, form about 18 percent of males under forty. However, though a minority, these *dreads* view themselves, and are often considered by outsiders, to be typical of the community.

The police rarely make searches within the area—even, or perhaps especially, in cases of homicides and gun crimes. Arrests of citizens, if made at all, are carried out while they are elsewhere. In fact, occasions when governmental involvement of any kind occurs in Riverton City are very rare indeed. Officially, the settlement and its two thousand residents simply do not exist. Significantly, even the map of the political constituency published by the Statistical Institute of Jamaica gives no inkling of its whereabouts. In stark contrast, its location within the parish of the dynamic priest Monseigneur Richard Albert has meant that the Roman Catholic Church has been instrumental in providing a Basic School, a Health Clinic, and water to a central standpipe. In addition, some assistance has been given towards educating children who show scholastic promise and to assist with the cultivation of *kalalu,* a major constituent of *irie* (that is, natural Rastafarian) cuisine.

Early in 1994, a number of spontaneous fires on the dump coalesced and were completely out of control for almost a week, threatening the homes of residents. Total evacuation was a possibility at one stage, but though this was averted, all residents suffered respiratory disorders or at least serious discomfort for several weeks.

The wider society, including government, has little appreciation of the strength and intensity of cohesion and sense of community within Riverton City. It is a cohesion fostered by the syndrome of ostracism, cynicism, and neglect. When I first researched the area in the late 1970s, the predominant sources of income were casual labor with government contractors (males), combing the dump for recyclable items (males and females), and low-paid domestic work and vending (mostly females). With the shrinkage of the public sector, by 1990 the first of these had almost disappeared, while recycling items from the dump and vending had increased in importance. In a much more sinister trend, income based upon relatively petty *anansi*-ism, or confidence trickery, that has always been endemic has now been augmented by that from violent crime carried out with sophisticated weaponry. Frustration at the unfulfilled promises of political figures, fueled by the prevailing culture of the media, the movies, videos, and the dance hall, has contributed significantly to the present volatility. Criminality is now rife and overt and glorified by many, so that—a far cry from a decade ago—violence has become a way of life. The violent deeds and deaths of community "heroes" Sandokan and Natty Morgan are legendary. Both departed leaving behind many teenage girls with unborn children in Riverton City. Not all residents, of course, approve of the trend towards institutionalized violence: some have left the area. A few seek to pacify the community by providing a more religious or socially acceptable lifestyle, but the peace is *viewed as within* the community rather than between the community and the wider society.

The immediate physical environment in Riverton City is the most unsatisfactory for any sizable population in Jamaica. The dump is a permanent health hazard, sending noxious and toxic chemicals upwards in a huge smoke plume covering Riverton City, downwards into the soil and ground water, and *in situ* in the form of uncompacted piles of untreated solid waste. No research has been done on these effects from the vast dump, or *dungle* (dunghill) as it is termed locally, but the acrid choking fumes that constantly envelop all the residents day and night must have respiratory effects and can only be a form of not-so-slow poisoning, despite the great tolerance of the human body.

Riverton City represents the hard core of the self-help housing problem: land-utilization conflicts, pollution, no likelihood of secure tenure, no infrastructure provision, little improvement in physical fabric over time, increasing social and political tension, drug trafficking, and growing hostility between the settlement and the society at large.

Hangman Burial Ground, Spanish Town

The unconsecrated portion of the Number Five Cemetery in Spanish Town, where those executed on the gallows of the St. Catherine District Prison were interred, provides a number of innovative capturers with free land for self-help housing. The settlement is squeezed between railway, road, canal, and middle-income subdivisions and is the closest to the historic center among the thirty-six shantytowns identified on a map of the Ministry of Construction (Housing) published in 1977. Of these thirty-six, sixteen are larger than five hectares and twenty are smaller. My recent survey, conducted seventeen years after this map, indicates that Hangman Burial Ground houses a vibrant and progressive community of approximately one thousand people. Individual residential structures average a floor area of forty-nine square meters, with a standard deviation of forty square meters. This is fairly high for what was originally a squatter settlement, but many rooms within individual family homes are rented out to single-person households.

Although some aspects of Rastafarian culture are looked upon as acceptable and even normative, with folk art on walls, music, and other manifestations reflecting this, the number of cult Rastafarians is even smaller here than in Riverton City, whereas the proportion of *dreads* is about the same—15 percent of males under forty years of age.

Hangman Burial Ground is very highly politicized. It is recognized as a "garrison constituency" of the Jamaica Labour Party and, on a personal basis, of its chairman, Bruce Golding, who is a member of Parliament. There is certainly an intense loyalty to him in the community, and the fact that the party is at the time of writing in the opposition leads to a certain tension and a coolness towards outsiders.

Hangman Burial Ground has been transformed into a stable, largely owner-occupier community. In 1987, the *capturers* or their successors were told that they are now the owners of their property. Roads were paved and utilities provided. Electricity and water are metered and in general paid for on time. Obtaining actual legal titles to the land has been a very slow process. Nevertheless, a sense of well-being pervades the community. Most citizens complain at the behavior of a minority of "out-of-order" (undisciplined) youth, and the central location within the city makes it rather vulnerable to criminal activity from outside. The informal leaders of the community claim that the residents are law abiding, and whenever the police enter seeking criminals, the latter are outsiders being sheltered by relatives.

Regardless of squatter origin and the present informal site plan, it can be said that Hangman Burial Ground has now reached the stage of full absorption into the urban fabric (fig. 5.4). It can be considered a success story for those who see self-help housing as a viable route to homeownership and adequate shelter for the poor.

Whitehall, Negril

The laid-back, informal, and casually homely atmosphere with which Negril is synonymous in the international leisure industry was rudely disrupted at the start

Fig. 5.4. Squeezed between railway, highway, canal, low-income high-rise housing and middle-income subdivisions, Hangman Burial Ground originally provided reasonable shelter for capturers at minimal cost. Now, it is a vibrant self-help community.

of the 1993–94 tourist season, when rioting erupted. The shantytown dwellers of Whitehall, close to the town center, demonstrated violently, blocking roads, threatening hoteliers and visitors, and seriously damaging one hotel. The reason: eviction notices had been served, ostensibly by the Urban Development Corporation (a statutory body), but in actuality by the People's National Party government of P. J. Patterson.

Worried at the effect on the vital tourist industry, immediate efforts were made to downplay the disturbance and defuse tensions. A few weeks later, a photograph of a benign and smiling prime minister accompanied a press announcement that 370 Whitehall "settlers" would be relocated on lands at Non Pareil, about three kilometers from Negril (map 5.3). With rather unseemly haste, forest

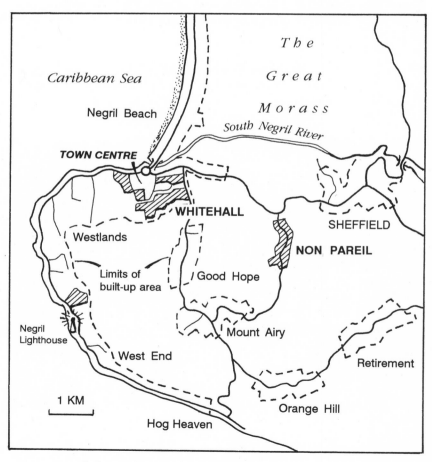

Map 5.3. Negril, showing location of Whitehall and Non Pareil.

is being cleared and lots surveyed. In place of the squatter settlement, there will rise luxury housing, a new town center, a sports complex, and a sewage treatment plant.

This sudden and uncharacteristic concern for the shantytown dweller has arisen directly, although in a complex manner, from the fact that land which migrant job seekers to Negril were encouraged to capture has become, with the triumph of global capitalism, immensely valuable—a situation obtaining in all tourist areas and which was predicted forcefully by government geographer-planner Vincent George in the 1980s (according to unpublished government memoranda). The Ministry of Finance and the Bank of Jamaica have advised that government can make a much-needed financial windfall by selling its Whitehall lands— prospective purchasers are already in the wings—and moreover a subsequent annual bonanza in property taxes will ensue. Government is so strapped for cash, such a prospect is impossible to forgo. The Ministry of Finance has been tight-lipped about land values, but it is widely known that the price of land at Whitehall has risen to rival that in some parts of New York City.

The story of the Whitehall holdings of the Ministry of Construction (Housing) is a prime example of the effects of the changing political attitudes towards self-help housing, land, wealth, and people outlined earlier in this chapter. A succession of "people-oriented" politicians encouraged squatting. During the 1980s, other alternative sites were available, but none were offered. In 1985, the Negril Chamber of Commerce sounded the alarm when there were twenty shacks. In the following eight years an average of ten shacks a month were erected by illegal squatters. Half of these have managed to acquire legal title by various means and are paying at least some of the costs of land acquisition. Most have built substantial homes. The other half are unreformed *capturers,* unable or unwilling to buy or rent shelter in Negril, who have been urged by political activists to resist all efforts to move them or pay anything for the land they occupy. Many of these, having been encouraged to build at Whitehall, feel angry and betrayed.

From 1985 to 1994 the attitude of government, both JLP and PNP, was one of total disinterest and unconcern. The chamber of commerce made representation at Gordon House (Parliament), pointing out the potentially explosive nature of the development, but these pleas were ignored. Tourists began to avoid the area, and later many Jamaicans did the same. Political elements external to Negril began to exploit the situation. When some lots and plots were allocated, partisan politics became an abrasive issue.

While the pressure on government to sell the land was intensifying, in late 1993, *everybody* was given seven days' notice to quit Whitehall, whatever the size or material of their home, and whether or not they had been allocated surveyed building plots. This was received with outrage: the demonstrations followed.

The proximate causes of the Whitehall impasse are not difficult to perceive. Tourist development has created thousands of low-paying jobs, but no low-income housing and very little commuter transport as an alternative have been provided by either the public or private sectors. Each sector claims the other should provide them. In point of fact, some hotels have developed a network of commuter buses for permanent staff, which is of great assistance. But it is not feasible for the tourist sector to finance housing for several thousand casual workers, especially given the current land prices in and around Negril. An area of hills south of the town which was looked upon as a possible inexpensive site has been preempted for high-income development by the Hogg family interests.

Relatively recent arrivals to Whitehall, with small self-help homes, will definitely be evicted: they have no hope whatever of tenure. However, no *terminus a quo* has yet been decided upon, so an air of uncertainty still prevails. Government is ambivalent towards the hundreds of former capturers who have been allocated or promised lots, many of whom have built very substantial homes (US$40,000 and up). So, some uncertainty remains amongst them also (fig. 5.5). Exactly who will be moved to Non Pareil and at whose expense are decisions yet to be made.

The Negril Chamber of Commerce has consistently warned that, in the new regime of free market forces, there are few options but to regret the inertia of the past, grasp the nettle, and clear as much of Whitehall as possible to attract investors. Its every prediction has been verified, but the chamber now finds itself the

Fig. 5.5. Residents of this section of Whitehall have been promised secure tenure on several occasions, but they were recently given eviction notices by the Urban Development Corporation. Their future is very uncertain.

victim and scapegoat for the problems rather than a facilitator of solutions, which would obviously be more congenial.

Whitehall epitomizes all the worst features of, and the worst mistakes that may be made in regard to, self-help housing as a shelter option. Consider what was done and not done:

1. Rapid and maximum development of a key sector in the economy, with high casual and informal employment-generating capacity, was encouraged without any provision for affordable shelter in the locality.
2. The capturing of premium land of high salable and taxable value was permitted and even encouraged.
3. Short-term political expediency overruled any sound economic management of an extremely valuable resource asset.
4. Government inertia, failure to monitor events or heed warnings, and bureaucratic bungling led to an explosive situation.
5. Even now, the quick-fix mentality is the official response. Seeking scapegoats, defusing tensions, and deflecting anger remain more important than the long-term welfare of the people, despite the professed administration policy of "putting people first."
6. Fear of losing electoral support is hampering efforts to be politically equitable in the distribution of scarce resources. Epithets and charges of criminality, exploitation and victimization are being made on a partisan basis, and are hindering cooperation.
7. The deliberate encouragement of migration to Negril by individuals from as far away as Portland (250 kilometers) has exacerbated the situation. It is said that most of these persons are political activists.

Flankers, Montego Bay

When in 1992 I chose Flankers as one of the five case studies for this chapter, I did not know that subsequent events there would become an international sensation. I had worked in Flankers on and off for more than a quarter of a century and shared with its patient residents a growth from a few tin and cardboard shacks to a community of more than six thousand with a total residential value—almost all by self-help—of US$300 million or more than J$9.5 billion Jamaican dollars (Eyre 1972). In 1992, Flankers might have been chosen to illustrate just how tremendously successful self-help housing can be in the geographical context of the Caribbean region.

But on 11 March 1994, police and residents battled along streets littered with rocks, tree trunks, and old car bodies, fires raged out of control, and the worst riot in Montego Bay since before Emancipation in 1838 marred the international image of the tourist city. What had gone so wrong?

Once again, a historical perspective is required. The first residents of Flankers captured land which was supposed to be kept clear of buildings as part of the safety zone around Sir Donald Sangster International Airport (map 5.4). Because an area of thirty-seven hectares was on the opposite side of the perimeter main road around the airport, it was not fenced or guarded. Therefore, under intense pressure from their constituents, certain leftist politicians encouraged self-help construction of housing on—so they emphasized at the time—a "mere eight per cent" of the entire airport reserve (Eyre 1979a). Surely, it was argued, "the people" who were served by the airport ought to have a right to occupy a portion of the reserve, since no other lands in the area were then available. The fact that at any time international air-traffic standards might be applied has been consistently ignored in the interest of housing the masses. Indeed such standards could still be enforced now and in the future, despite the present size and value of the settlement.

In the mid-1970s, Joe Whitter, a Jamaican who had amassed considerable wealth in Britain, bought several square kilometers of land adjoining the airport reserve on the east as an investment. At the time, land prices were low because of political uncertainty and unrest in Jamaica. The tourist industry, nationalized by the government, was depressed. Whitter had faith in the future of Montego Bay as a tourist resort, and he proceeded slowly with the development of his property, known collectively as Ironshore Estates. By the late 1980s, however, the Flankers land had reached capacity, and self-help housing construction was spilling over

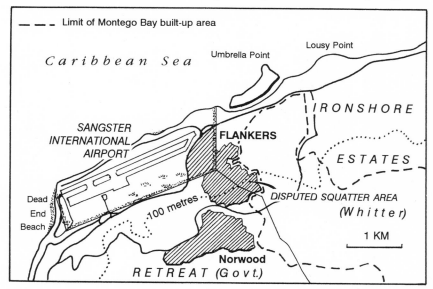

Map 5.4. Flankers, Montego Bay, and environs.

onto a part of Whitter's land which was "undeveloped." Certain politicians encouraged—even personally led—capturers to invade the Whitter property and build large concrete block homes quickly, so that, it was confidently asserted, they could not be evicted. It is alleged that many capturers did not even know at the time who owned the land they were occupying.

Whitter asserts that he gave eviction notices several times between 1987 and 1994 and began lengthy legal proceedings to evict the capturers. But by the end of 1993, several hundred homes had been erected on twenty-seven hectares of his land, many of them described in the media as "palatial mansions." By the time the Supreme Court finally got around to making a judgment in the suit, at least US$10 million worth of self-help housing was in place, and the squatters were so confident of their tenure that they were freely selling "lots" and houses on Whitter's land. The land on which the capturers had built was, in 1993, worth on the open market at least US$13,850,000, and Whitter was negotiating with potential purchasers, both local and overseas.

The Supreme Court judgment, given the present social and political realities, was a foregone conclusion. Joe Whitter was given the legal right to use the force of the state to evict anyone he chose from his lands. And he did so only, so he claims, after years of long suffering. The experience of an acquaintance of mine

Fig. 5.6. Development at Flankers has expanded rapidly from west (left) to east (right). The boundary between the airport and the Whitter lands runs from the lower left corner diagonally to about one-third from the top left.

may introduce the next series of events. Under a personal "good faith" arrangement with the previous landowner from whom Whitter had purchased the property, she had built a large, popular restaurant opposite the famed Holiday Inn, Jamaica's largest resort hotel. One day she arrived to find the restaurant bulldozed to the ground and a for sale notice in its place.

In the small hours of the morning of 11 March 1994, a detachment of police under Inspector Roach entered Flankers and began carrying out the court order, demolishing homes on the Whitter lands. The ensuing resistance developed into full-scale riots which required the Jamaica Defence Force to enter the area in support of the police. An angry mob ransacked and burned down the offices of Whitter's land development company in downtown Montego Bay, destroying nearly all the files, titles, records of sales, and other financial instruments belonging to a wide international clientele (fig. 5.7).

The government prevaricated, at first summarily dismissing Roach and all his men, asserting that the evictions were immoral and unjust and an insult to the masses. A few days later, when the new realities began to dawn upon the prime minister's cabinet, they were all fully reinstated and exonerated of all wrongdoing. Now, squatting was publicly stated, by no less than a senior government minister, to be "immoral and antisocial." The dilemma of government over self-help housing so clearly described by Angel et al (1983) in the quotation at the end of this chapter was never more vividly revealed as on the afternoon of 11 March 1994 in Montego Bay, Jamaica.

At the time of this writing, there was an uneasy truce between Joe Whitter and the squatters, with government in the role of an uncomfortable and unhappy referee. Whitter has been urged to allow those capturers who have already built "very substantial" houses to remain, provided they pay for the land they occupy. No decision on price has yet been made. Cries that Whitter has enough land to make him the richest man in the Caribbean and that he should just leave the squatters alone are irrelevant, since the real problem is neither Whitter nor the self-help builders, but the steep rise in the value of the land to a level which makes its use for self-help housing absolutely impracticable. The desperate poor building shacks on hilltop sites with spectacular million-dollar panoramic views over the Caribbean Sea and its golden beaches is an anomaly that, in 1994, not even a populist government dared ignore (fig. 5.8). 11 March 1994 may prove to be a critical turning point in the whole issue of self-help housing in Jamaica, the Caribbean, and perhaps the world.

Holland Bamboo, St. Elizabeth

The Holland Bamboo case highlights several of the complex historical factors which underlie the current crisis in housing provision in the Caribbean. The disturbance in January 1994 during which the famous and picturesque Bamboo

Fig. 5.7. A new shack being erected by a squatter at Flankers, March 1994. The land is estimated by its owner (a local heavy equipment contractor) to be worth at least US$3 million (J$100 million) a hectare.

Fig. 5.8. The burned-out offices of Ironshore Estates Development company in downtown Montego Bay, March 1994.

Avenue—a major tourist attraction—was set ablaze can be seen as the culmination of a long process of confrontation between various local and Caribbean sectoral interest groups over a period of nearly two hundred years.

Self-help housing was an issue when Holland Estate was a typical sugar plantation, as Laborie (1798) indicates: "A few planters suffer their negroes to make their own huts themselves, and in what form they please; but these will always be very incorrect, and perhaps insufficient. Besides, it seems that this building of houses, is one of the obligations of the master" (95–96). Although Laborie's immediate context was the coffee economy of Saint Domingue (Haiti), it was doubtless equally applicable to a sugar estate such as Holland. Beckford (1790) confirms the desire of slave owners to have some control over Negro housing: "It is the custom now to have them [the Negro houses] built in straight lines, constructed with some degree of uniformity and strength, but totally divested of trees and shrubs" (20). Higman (1988), interpreting many plantation maps of the period, comments on the direct provision or control of slave housing: "The peak period of geometric layouts [around 1810] suggests a relationship with the interventionist policies adopted by planters in many areas of slave life after 1790, sometimes referred to as an 'amelioration' of conditions. It was related also to the ideas of 'improvement' common in British agriculture at the time and to the social engineering associated with industrialization." On the other hand, he notes that self-help housing was evident even in a major, famous sugar estate such as Hope in

St. Andrew, where "houses were generally built by the slaves without the planter's close supervision and in layouts ordered by the slaves themselves" (244).

After Emancipation in 1838, Holland continued to be the property of various sugar planters, of whom the most notable was John Gladstone, father of the famous British prime minister, and it has remained a sugar estate until the present time, although the hectareage in cane has varied greatly. Essentially, the geography of Holland depicted on the detailed map commissioned by John Gladstone in 1835 remained unaltered until the drastic changes of February 1994 (map 5.5).

As in slavery time, Holland Bamboo Village consists of very basic housing provided originally for sugar workers on plantation land, which in most cases has been enlarged by self-help under certain guidelines. The greater part of the present value of the individual homes in Holland Bamboo is due to their owners' own efforts. Although many residents have paid by installments for their own lots and surveys have been made, no proper registered titles have been issued for the small house lots. These lots and homes were never intended to be farms, but simply to house permanent workers on the estate, tying them economically and socially to the plantation system.

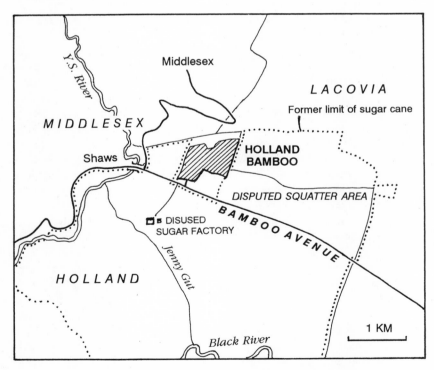

Map 5.5. Holland Estate, St. Elizabeth, showing location of Holland Bamboo village.

A change took place, however, when the Henriques interests disposed of Holland Estate in the early 1980s and made an arrangement with the Jamaica Labour Party member of Parliament for the area, Neville Lewis. Under this arrangement approximately five hundred resident "owners" of the Holland Bamboo housing scheme, who had almost all been made redundant, were each "given" about half a hectare of land north of the Holland Bamboo grove. The exact terms of the contract, and indeed whether it was a contract at all, are matters of deep controversy at the present time. The fact that there is great uncertainty over what actually took place between a wealthy sugar baron and a populist politician illustrates the very crux of the issue of self-help housing in the Caribbean: all important decisions were made for not by those requiring the housing. For thirteen years, from 1981 until 1994, the people of Holland Bamboo built self-help homes and worked their little plots in the belief that ultimately all the land would be theirs.

It is widely asserted that Mel Brown, the People's National Party candidate, promised the people of Holland Bamboo that if he was elected in 1989, he would soon get everyone titles to their land. He was successful, and displaced Neville Lewis in Parliament. Suspicions were aroused, however, when a list of thirteen persons appeared in the *Gleaner* newspaper, headed by the new member of Parliament and including a prominent local judge, stating that they were now owners of the land north of the Bamboo grove. Shortly afterwards, fencing of the land began in order to exclude the people of Holland Bamboo from the land on which they had their crops and livestock. Rioting broke out and a portion of the Bamboo grove was burned. Neville Lewis, the JLP caretaker for the constituency, demanded a meeting with the deputy prime minister and Minister of Agriculture Seymour Mullings. It transpired that the new "owners" had in fact obtained proper registered titles to the land, and so cannot legally be removed. The people of Holland Bamboo were told that they will not lose their house spots, but the remainder of the land from which they derive their livelihood is now in the hands of professional farmers who will ensure that it is used in a highly efficient manner and, unlike the four hundred people of Holland Bamboo, will be able to pay substantial property taxes on the rich and productive alluvial land. Pressing financial considerations, and the need to modernize and to compete internationally, far outweigh any obligations to the rural poor.

Once again, indecision and unconcern, and also failure to understand and apply some basic principles of political equity in the provision of shelter, have resulted in bitterness and a sense of betrayal. The people of Holland Bamboo village have learned with shock that in this new era of global capitalism and the free market, vague, plantation-style notions of paternalism have no place, even if the government claims to be of a democratic socialist persuasion and "puts people first." The present reality for the four hundred families is that their attractive self-help homes are now trapped on small plots in a remote rural housing scheme served by a deteriorating infrastructure and surrounded by large mechanized farms on prime land carved out of a famous but now moribund sugar estate owned by members of a distant urban elite.

The Jamaican government, supported or directed by the International Monetary Fund, the World Bank, and all the bilateral aid agencies, is saying that this is the only way forward. To one who has worked for the past thirty-five years to promote and encourage self-help as a way of providing shelter for the poor in Jamaica and other post-colonial societies, Holland Bamboo is a heavy blow.

Self-Help Housing in Jamaica: Conclusions

The whole issue of self-help housing in Jamaica is at a crossroads. Formerly encouraged as a solution to the problem of shelter for the poor and even championed by socialist politicians, it is now officially stigmatized as "immoral and antisocial." After a hiatus of several decades, confrontation with shantytown dwellers is the order of the day, and the bulldozing of homes has now definitely been put on the national agenda. As a result, the Jamaican government has a severe case of hypertension and is treading very delicately on the issue. Easton Douglas, minister of the Public Service and the Environment, at a press conference on 30 March 1994, parried criticisms that the government had no policy and cautioned that "while there are many requests to settle squatter issues, a lasting and comprehensive solution can only come over time" (*Sunday Herald,* 3 April 1994).

I leave the final word to Angel et al. (1983):

> Since governments see themselves in the role of keeping the peace as well as ensuring the rule of law, they face a serious dilemma. Mass evictions are certainly a threat to peace, while refraining from assisting landlords who legally own plots of land and want to benefit from them cannot be justified. Governments have found it difficult, therefore, to adopt a consistent position on this issue and have often either wavered in taking appropriate action or avoided the issue altogether. This has not, unfortunately, eased the pressure on government to mediate and resolve land conflicts. Radical solutions, such as mass evictions on the one hand or the refusal to protect ownership rights on the other, appear to hold little promise in the majority of cases. There does appear, however, to be room for compromise based on sharing the land between the people who need it for housing and the landowners who want it for commercial exploitation. (25)

Except that the signs of the compromise are extremely tentative so far, that is *exactly* where the issue of self-help housing in Jamaica stands in mid-1994.

Fig. 5.9. Father Ron Peters. In 1993, Peters was betrayed and gunned down by ruthless dons who bitterly resented the love and devotion shown to him by the thousands whom he sought to uplift. This chapter is dedicated to his memory.

Acknowledgments

The author wishes to express sincere appreciation to Monseigneur Richard Albert and the dedicated staff of the parish of St. Patrick's in western St. Andrew, especially those who labor so sacrificially in Riverton City; to Mr. Ray Arthurs, chairman of the Negril Chamber of Commerce; and to Dr. Omar Davies, minister of finance, for the time they all unstintingly gave from their busy schedules to discuss in detail the issues and events raised in this chapter. An even more fervent debt of thanks is due to all the community leaders in the five shantytowns discussed, who, at their own request, will not be named. Their perception of the issues, though biased, is unmatched by any official, however well educated. The entire problem, in all its ramifications, was vigorously debated over a period of several weeks in the Jamaican media, and serious scholars should peruse the columns of the *Gleaner,* the *Jamaica Herald,* and the *Observer* during March and April, and the *Weekend Star* of 18 March 1994.

References

Angel, S., R. W. Archer, S. Tanphiphat, and E. A. Wegelin. (1983) *Land for Housing the Poor.* Singapore: Select Books.

Beckford, W. (1790) *A Descriptive Account of the Island of Jamaica.* London: Egerton.

Clarke, G. C. (1983) "Dependency and Marginality in Kingston, Jamaica." *Journal of Geography* 82 (5): 227–35.

Clarke, G. C., and P. M. Ward. (1980) "Stasis in Makeshift Housing: Perspectives from Mexico and the Caribbean." *Comparative Urban Research* 8: 117–27.

Conway, D. (1982) "Self-Help Housing, the Commodity Nature of Housing and Amelioration of the Housing Deficit: Continuing the Turner-Burgess Debate." *Antipode* 14: 40–46.

Environmental Bulletin (1993–94) "Actions to Reduce Poverty Pledged by International Leaders." 6 (1): 1–3.

Eyre, L. A. (1965a) *Land and Population in the Sugar Belt of Jamaica*. Occasional Paper 1. Dept. of Geography, University of the West Indies, Mona, Jamaica.

———. (1965b) *Shantytowns, A Reappraisal*. Research Notes 3. Dept. of Geography, University of the West Indies, Mona, Jamaica.

———. (1972) "The Shanty Towns of Montego Bay." *Geographical Review* 62 (3): 394–413.

———. (1979a) *Growth in Squatter and Informal Areas in Montego Bay 1958–1978*. Kingston: Ministry of Housing, Sites and Services Division.

———. (1979b) "Quasi-Urban Melange Settlements." *Caribbean Review* 8 (2): 32–35.

———. (1984a) *Field Guide to August Town and Maverly 1951 Hurricane Housing Reconstruction*. Ocho Rios, Jamaica: International Conference on Disaster Mitigation.

———. (1984b) "Political Violence and Urban Geography in Kingston, Jamaica." *Geographical Review* 74 (1): 24–37.

———. (1984c) "The Internal Dynamics of Shanty Towns in Jamaica." *Caribbean Geography* 1 (4): 256–70.

———. (1985) "Biblical Symbolism and the Role of Fantasy Geography among the Rastafarians of Jamaica." *Journal of Geography* 84 (4): 144–48.

———. (1986a) "Party Political Violence and the Struggle for Residential Space in Jamaica." *Nederlands Geografische Studies* 25: 125–39.

———. (1986b) "The Effects of Political Terrorism on the Residential Location of the Poor in Kingston Urban Region, Jamaica, West Indies." *Urban Geography* 7 (3): 227–42.

Hanson, G. T. (1975) "Shantytown Stage Development: the Case of Kingston, Jamaica." Ph.D. diss., Louisiana State University.

Higman, B. W. (1988) *Jamaica Surveyed*. Kingston: Institute of Jamaica Publications.

Jones, E. (1990) "Urban Land Management: A Case for Environmental Cost Benefit Analysis." In *Proceedings of Conference on Urban Management*, 59–73, Bridgetown, Barbados, Sept. 5–7, 1990.

Kingsley, G. T. (1990) "The Urban-Economic Nexus in Caribbean Development." In *Proceedings of Conference on Urban Management*, 17–37. Bridgetown, Barbados, Sept. 5–7, 1990.

Laborie, P. J. (1798) *The Coffee Planter of Saint Domingo*. London: Cadell and Davies.

Potter, R. B. (1985) *Urbanization and Planning in the Third World*. New York: St. Martin's Press.

———. (1992) *Urbanisation in the Third World*. Oxford: Oxford University Press.

———, ed. (1989) *Urbanization, Planning and Development in the Caribbean*. London and New York: Mansell Press.

Chapter 6

Obstacles to Low-Income Housing Assistance in the Capitalist Periphery: The Case of Jamaica

Thomas Klak

The previous chapter by Alan Eyre in this volume underscores the rich tradition and continuing prominence of self-help housing among Jamaica's popular sectors. In essence, Eyre describes an island where perhaps a majority of homes have been built by the occupants themselves, but, at the same time, where the need for secure access to land and decent housing is increasingly acute. His account naturally raises the question as to what the Jamaican state has been doing to assist citizens to secure better shelter. This becomes a more curious question considering the importance of political clientelism in Jamaican society (Stone 1980; Edie 1991), leading one to expect both large demands from constituencies for housing aid and large payoffs to politicians providing it. It becomes a burning question when one considers that, over the past three decades, the Jamaican State has accumulated vast resources from forced payroll deductions and international loans with the express purpose of providing "a roof over the heads of as many families as possible," and to distribute the aid according to "need" (*Gleaner* 1976a, 1976b; NHT n.d.; Ford 1976: 10C; Jackson 1988a). By uniting these points, several incongruities underlying the Jamaican housing crisis are revealed. The country has an especially rich tradition of people incrementally improving and expanding their own accommodations over time, but state resources have gone almost entirely towards facilitating the private housing market or, in other words, towards financing long-term mortgages for a relatively few and expensive multibedroom completed units.

This chapter aims to reveal more precisely the Jamaican State's role in housing and how it has managed largely to avoid helping the popular sectors. Four state agencies comprise the main players. Recent decades have witnessed the Jamaican State's heavy involvement in capital accumulation for housing finance via several agencies which differ in funding, philosophy, and markets served. The vast majority of state housing finance in Jamaica takes the form of home mortgages held by two parastatal or semiautonomous state agencies: The National Housing Trust (NHT) and Caribbean Housing Finance Corporation (CHFC). NHT is by far the largest housing agency, as it is endowed by a massive and steady inflow of funds from compulsory payroll deductions. CHFC is the country's second largest housing agency in terms of asset base and is funded primarily from loans from the United States Agency for International Development (USAID). Jamaica's Ministry of Construction (Housing), or MOC(H), is a third major player. Although it received sizable USAID and World Bank loans in the 1970s and early 1980s, it is underfunded compared to NHT and CHFC. The Ministry of Construction (Housing) has the greatest focus on building low-income shelter. Since the late 1980s the MOC(H) has incrementally turned over its mortgage portfolio to the responsibility of CHFC (TFH and PIJ 1992; PIJ 1992). Besides lending funds for home mortgages, USAID is also influential in funding broader housing policy reform studies (Jones et al. 1987; Peterson and Klak 1990), and it uses its aid packages as leverage to affect housing policy.

Beginning with a description of the creation of NHT in the mid-1970s, this chapter provides a broad multidecade review of state housing activity. The aim is to identify the major trends, while avoiding placing undo emphasis on short-term aberrations or highly publicized but unrepresentative housing activity. In light of this aim, more emphasis is given to the completed records of the administrations of Michael Manley in the 1970s and Edward Seaga in the 1980s than to the Manley-Patterson government of the 1990s, whose housing priorities have yet to be fully disclosed. By similar reasoning, greatest attention is given to the National Housing Trust, the largest and most powerful player in Jamaica's housing system. Because CHFC also controls large pools of housing financial resources, it provides a secondary focus. The roles of USAID and MOC(H) are also considered but are given less emphasis.

Forces Shaping State Housing Programs: Regime, Dependency, and Structural Adjustment

To understand what happens to housing programs from the conceptual stage to full implementation, it is useful to consider three forces that shape them. In reality the forces are not independent of one another, but they have distinct enough historical trajectories to be considered separately. First there is *regime ideology,* referring to the development philosophy and priorities of the administration in power. The National Housing Trust, for example, was born in the democratic socialist movement of Michael Manley's People National Party (PNP) government of the 1970s. This origin has shaped the agency's aims and organization and has generated stalwart defenders among PNP party faithfuls as well as archenemies among free market advocates such as some USAID workers. To a significant extent, such support or opposition is ideologically based, regardless of NHT's actual record. Regime influence on policy has decreased over time in Jamaica, just as it has across Latin America and the rest of the Caribbean, and is at present the weakest of the three forces. Governments of various political persuasions are now lining up to endorse and echo a neoliberal approach to development (Klak 1995). Political debate has largely narrowed to questions of whether neoliberal reform should continue unabated, or if it will be more successful when accompanied by state spending on welfare and services for the many it impoverishes (Lowenthal 1993). Today, there is no mistaking that the goals of the dominant economic model take precedence over those of working people.

A second force derives from the *structure of a country's political economy* or, in other words, from conditions of *dependency.* These refer to the economic base, the level of development, the distribution of wealth, and the traditional role of government, all of which tend to shape housing programs into their own image. Put another way, housing programs tend to reinforce the *status quo,* rather than radically redistributing resources. No matter how ambitious a low-income housing program may be at the conceptual stage, it will encounter many practical obstacles if attempted in a context characterized by massive inequality, poverty, underemployment, and economic dependence, as the Jamaican case illustrates. In sum, conditions of underdevelopment and external dependency provide a long-term and ongoing constraint on progressive housing policy (Klak 1993).

Third, *influences from international development agencies* (the IMF, the World Bank, USAID) have shaped housing policy in Latin America and the Caribbean since its formative years of the 1960s (Klak 1990; Klak 1993). The collapse of traditional exports, the debt crisis, and numerous ensuing *structural adjustment* agreements have, beginning in the late 1970s for Jamaica, considerably strengthened this international influence (Girvan and Bernal 1982; Klak 1995). The agencies themselves have, over time, shifted priorities regarding what they see as the proper role of government in the provision of housing. Whereas housing agencies such as the National Housing Trust and Caribbean Housing were earlier deemed worthy of financial support, by the late 1980s they were being denounced as obstructions to the private market, hopelessly bureaucratic, and wasteful (USAID 1988; Smith 1989). Of course, the housing agencies themselves have evolved over the decades, as documented below. However, the emphasis in the current neo-liberal development model on exports and foreign-exchange generation, nontraditional industries, and privatization leaves little room for active interventionist government housing agencies.

The confluence of these three sets of forces determines such crucial issues as an agency's level of output of housing assistance compared to its intake of financial resources, the number of housing beneficiaries, and the type of assistance that is emphasized. These are revealed in this Jamaican case study.

The Form of Housing Policy in Jamaica

This chapter now traces public housing finances from institutional sources to household beneficiaries so that the social impacts of this state activity can be ascertained. This section sets the stage for that analysis of financial flows by reviewing the funding sources and objectives of NHT and Caribbean Housing.

The National Housing Trust

If size is measured in terms of asset base, then the National Housing Trust has for a considerable number of years been the third largest of all financial institutions in Jamaica, smaller only than two international banks. By 1987 NHT's mortgage portfolio was worth considerably more than that of any *collection* of private financial institutions, such as credit unions or building societies (which are similar to savings and loan institutions in the United States). At that time the Housing Trust held 28 percent of all mortgages by value and a much larger share by number, considering that, on average, private institutions provide larger loans. NHT collects about 80 percent of the outstanding government mortgage funds, which have been distributed to over twenty-five thousand of Jamaica's more than four hundred thousand households (Peterson and Klak 1990).

The National Housing Trust was created as a central component of Michael Manley's broad package of democratic socialist reforms (Girvan, Bernal, and Hughes 1980: 117–18). One enthusiastic columnist at that time called NHT "the most far reaching and fundamental policy of social change attempted by the Manley government" (Hope 1976: 10A). To combat the inequalities produced by the private housing market, early pledges by the Manley government were to allocate housing assistance in socially progressive ways. One such idea was to divide housing assistance equally among income groups. That is, the allocation criteria were designed so that all income groups contributing to the NHT would have more or less the same proportion of mortgages. This would disregard market-related rules of allocation such as purchasing power and the size of the loan relative to the contribution (Smallman 1977). The thinking within the Manley regime was that capitalism allocates resources unfairly and therefore yields little affordable working-class housing. NHT should correct for this by extracting "social surplus" from the middle class and above and should redistribute it to the poor (Gilfillian 1978). Such an analysis of capitalistic defects and state interventions to correct for them were typical of the Manley regime of the 1970s. Below we will assess how well NHT has followed through on this socially progressive pledge.

NHT has historically obtained most of its funds from a 2 percent compulsory savings withdrawal from the payroll of employees and a corresponding 3 percent tax on employers on the same payroll. The combination of employee and employer contributions amounts to a capturing of two and one-half weeks of wages per formal sector employee per year. This produces a great volume of resources that, in the face of currency devaluations and deteriorating terms of trade, is relatively secure and consistent over time. Employees are entitled to a refund of their contributions, plus 3 percent annual interest on the sum, seven years after it was deducted from the paycheck (*Gleaner* 1975). However, inflation has averaged over 18 percent per year since the 1970s, making these refunds small compared to their original value (PIJ 1988; PIJ 1992). The refunds are therefore offered as political tokens, and many contributors never even bother to collect theirs. However, the value of those same funds while they are under NHT's control becomes proportionally greater. Which ever social groups and uses have been the principal recipients of NHT's funds, they have benefited from a vast pool of cheap money, subsidized by the entire formal sector work force.

The Caribbean Housing Finance Corporation

Whereas the Housing Trust is high profile and politicized, CHFC is the opposite. Many Jamaicans have never heard of it, and the 1991 and 1993 editions of the *Economic and Social Survey* of Jamaica prepared by the Planning Institute failed even to mention it (PIJ 1992; PIJ 1994). Staying out of the limelight is an intentional strategy of CHFC in order to avoid the public oversight and criticism that have plagued NHT (Smallman 1977; Cargill 1987; Klak 1992b). That cause is aided by the fact that CHFC's funds are primarily from foreign loans. Despite the public obligation to use them to improve housing conditions and to repay them, foreign loans do not carry the perception of public liability that accompanies NHT's payroll deductions. In reality, Caribbean Housing has played a long, prominent, and growing role in Jamaica's financial system. Since its creation under British colonial rule in 1960, CHFC has been dedicated to providing "social needs" housing (Jackson 1988a). By 1987 the value of its portfolio equaled more than 6 percent of outstanding mortgages held among the many public and private lenders in the country. Because private institutions generally finance much higher-priced housing than CHFC, its role, like that of NHT, is significantly larger in terms of the number of mortgages, of which it had over sixteen thousand by the late 1980s. Since then CHFC has continued to expand by taking over mortgage servicing responsibilities from other public agencies, particularly the Ministry of Construction (Housing), through USAID-inspired housing policy reforms. As of 1990 it was acting as a wholesaler of US$55 million in housing funds provided by USAID (Peterson and Klak 1990). USAID attaches a 1 percent servicing fee on the monies it on-lends for private U.S. financial institutions.

The U.S. Congress stipulates that the beneficiaries of USAID's housing loans in a peripheral capitalist country earn less than the *median income* of that country. When this rule is applied in a poor, dependent, and highly unequal country such as Jamaica, however, it creates a financial bottleneck. Caribbean Housing has held huge sums of money from USAID in Jamaican bank accounts. It is difficult to finance a completed two- or three-bedroom house that is affordable to a household earning less than the median income. CHFC and NHT have not been comfortable with offering housing solutions that the poor can afford. These would include serviced lots or core housing, a structurally complete and serviced housing unit that the occupants complete internal work on. Sentiments of USAID leadership are similar, to keep its funds from financing "slums" (i.e., less-than-completed units occupied by the poor). Additional constraints to providing low-income mortgages from foreign loans derive from uncertainty about future currency devaluations and the perceived risks of lending to the poor. All the while, the poor are being forced to crowd more people into existing units or to build makeshift shelter, often on land of disputed ownership and without security of title.

Access to Housing Assistance for Key Social Groups

Let me now move on to a more detailed examination of the social interests served and excluded by state housing activity. Various social groups possess substantially different capacities to influence the state. Groups interested in state housing provisions include the middle class, unionized workers such as teachers, the police, and government employees, poor people with insecure informal employment, and women, especially those heading households. This section describes and compares these interest groups' records of access to the housing finance programs of NHT and CHFC. Much of the discussion summarizes original analysis of the internal computerized data files of NHT and CHFC conducted over the last six years. Readers desiring a more detailed account of the methodology and findings should consult the original analysis (Klak 1989; Peterson and Klak 1990; Klak 1991; Klak 1992a, 1992b; Klak and Hey 1992; Klak 1993).

Patterns of Housing Finance with Respect to Income

A few basic statistics indicating Jamaica's exorbitant housing costs and low-income levels will illustrate why there is a national housing crisis. According to a private Jamaican developer, "more than 50 percent of the selling price of a housing unit is accountable in interest to banks" (*Gleaner* 1985: 18). As Eyre notes in the previous chapter on Jamaican self-help housing, 41 percent of employees in Jamaica are paid under US$3 per day (US$930 per year). When income levels and private housing costs are compared, less than 10 percent of Jamaican households appear able to afford the least expensive private-sector housing (Jones et al. 1987; *Gleaner* 1991). The price-wage gap is not much better for public sector housing. One reason for this is the well-known practice by the oligopolistic developers who build most housing on government contract to mark up the selling price of the housing 100 percent over costs.

These statistics for income and housing prices also help to account for the considerable gaps between the wage levels of working people in general, of NHT contributors, and of NHT beneficiaries (table 6.1). Perhaps one-half of the work force comprises employees of micro- or informal enterprises, whose meager earnings leave no surplus to contribute to the NHT. Thus, despite its intent to distribute housing according to need, NHT's requirement that beneficiaries make regular payroll-based contributions excludes at the outset the vast majority of those most poorly housed. Even within the contributor population, beneficiaries are chosen from the high-income end (table 6.1). The median income for the beneficiary population is 80 percent higher than that of the rest of the contributors. A similarly large difference separates the mean incomes of contributors and beneficiaries (Klak 1989; Peterson and Klak 1990).

Beyond these general features of loan allocation by NHT suggesting its higher-income orientation, others require a more detailed examination. When set in the context of Jamaica's high housing costs and skewed income distribution, NHT's attempt to operationalize its pledge to provide housing assistance to all income levels independent of their contributions to the NHT produces some contradictory results. On the one hand, as suggested by the high average income levels of beneficiaries, contributors in the upper half of the income distribution have had the greatest probability of obtaining an NHT loan. On the other hand, when comparing contributions to the Trust to loan amounts for each income level, an element of socially progressive allocation within the contributor population emerges. That is, the largest reallocation of housing funds has gone to the bottom third of wage earners. Lower-income groups have paid into the housing fund relatively little compared to the value of mortgages they have been granted. The problem for low-income people, however, is that they have been granted only a relatively few loans, loans which vastly offset the tiny payroll deductions of the low-income

Table 6.1

A Comparison of Income Levels of Jamaican Workforce, NHT Contributors, and NHT Mortgagers, 1980

Weekly Wage in 1980 J$[a]	Employed Work Force[b] %	Contributors[c] %	Mortgagers[c] %
No Income	6.1	0	0
>0–10	5.4	13.7	1.0
>10–20	10.8	0.8	0.2
>20–30	11.6	1.0	0.3
>30–40	12.7	3.1	0.8
>40–50	10.5	0.8	0.3
>50–100	24.8	15.3	15.5
>100	18.1	65.4	81.8

NOTES:[a]When access to NHT computer records was obtained in 1988, income data for 1980 were the most recent available. In 1980, J$1.78 = US$1. Mortgagers include all those receiving a housing loan between 1976 and Sept. 1988.
[b]According to Golding (1982: 14) as of Oct. 1981.
[c]NHT (1988).

group. A contributor in the bottom third of the income distribution is highly unlikely to receive a loan. In other words, among those whose need for housing assistance is greatest, NHT has provided only a few, exceptional loans (Klak 1989). This reflects the fundamental contradiction in NHT's method of gathering funds and allocating housing assistance. Low-income people are unable to contribute to the housing fund in sufficient quantities to finance their own housing, and they do not have adequate incomes to afford the monthly mortgage for the completed housing units that are NHT's priority type of shelter assistance.

Let me turn now to the Caribbean Housing Finance Corporation to see what adjustments it makes to contend with the problem of mortgages that are unaffordable for the majority of Jamaicans. Given the tendencies for housing programs to drift toward a higher-income clientele and the fact that USAID loans provide the major funding source, CHFC's principal beneficiaries are predictable. To meet U.S. congressional restrictions, income levels of CHFC's mortgagors can be expected to be at or near the median wage for the population as a whole. This pattern is borne out in analysis of its internal records (Peterson and Klak 1990). This median-income constraint has forced CHFC to serve a significantly lower-income clientele than the National Housing Trust (Klak 1992a). Non-USAID funds allocated by CHFC are not restricted in that way and therefore tend to serve groups above the median income: union-organized public servants, for example.

In recent years there has been political pressure to dispense with the median-income restriction. In the late 1980s, Jamaican state and USAID representatives discussed raising the "official" median income from J$18,000 to J$22,000 or more, an increase of over 20 percent during a period of little economic growth (Boyd 1988). The campaign to raise the median wage was largely detached from its empirical meaning and whether or not it actually increased by more than 20 percent. The quantitative evidence presented to support the argument that the median income should be raised was based on the assumption that the mean and median are about equal. Such an assumption is scarcely valid when the national income distribution is so highly skewed as in Jamaica. The pressure to raise the official median wage was based on the desire to make USAID funds available to income groups with significantly more purchasing power. The general manager of CHFC argued that raising the median income to J$25,000 would allow young college-educated professionals to obtain USAID-funded housing, and therefore "those in need are the ones who [would benefit]" (Jackson 1988b: 3). She also expressed fear that if CHFC's housing provision is not adjusted upward in terms of income and housing quality, young professionals will simply take their skills abroad (Jackson 1988b).

This discussion of the median-income issue illustrates how housing "need" gets redefined over time by the leadership of state agencies. It also shows how higher-income groups can indirectly put pressure on the state so that it shifts more public resources in their direction. In the process, those with the greatest housing problems get increasingly marginalized (Klak 1992a).

Key Social Groups' Access to Housing Finance

The State Sector

The concentration of NHT mortgages among government employees is heavy. Although government employees make up less than 10 percent of the official work force, they have obtained a remarkable 58 percent of all NHT loans. Men take advantage of access via the state more than women. While state-employed men constitute a relatively small portion of the official work force (4 percent), they have captured the largest share of NHT loans (33 percent) of any employment type, male or female (Klak and Hey 1992).

This amassing of home loans in the hands of state employees results from at least two processes. First there is an insider's network. NHT employees understand all the details of the complicated system of loan allocation and can adjust their applications accordingly (Gleaner 1982, 1989). Some employees of the Trust have been able to obtain as many as six NHT homes, even though the rules limit them to one per customer (THA 1988). Insider information can also be obtained by the many public employees with regular contact with NHT, such as those in planning, land titling, and tax records. Second, public employee unions, such as those of teachers, police, and nurses, are well-organized, vocal, and effective lob-byists for housing assistance. They have been able to arrange for the construction and finance of many multiunit housing schemes through both NHT and CHFC.

Another important way that state employees directly benefit from public-housing resources is through NHT's huge payroll and overhead costs. NHT's internal consumption of funds is captured in the notion of "point spread," defined as the difference between the agency's cost of funds interest rate and the interest rate it charges mortgagors. CHFC's point spread is only 1 to 2 percent. Largely because its financial sources are relatively high-interest foreign loans, the Caribbean Housing Finance Corporation is pressured to be a low-overhead and cost-efficient agency. In contrast, NHT, the larger agency with lower-cost funds, maintains a point spread in excess of 7 percent. This is higher than government housing agencies in other Latin American countries (Klak 1993) and higher than private lending agencies such as the credit unions and the building societies. Unlike most financial institutions, NHT is under few constraints to keep its costs down, and so it can consume a large share of the housing resources itself (Cargill 1987).

Informal Workers

Those working in the informal sector face several obstacles in their quest for public-housing assistance, as illustrated by Jamaica's higglers. Higglers are vendors of consumer nondurables, primarily female, and high-profile members of the informal work force (LeFranc 1988). Some of Jamaica's more than eighty thousand higglers have amassed reasonable wealth, particularly those who travel to Miami or Colón, Panama, to purchase items cheaply for resale on the streets of Jamaica. Higgler success stories are widely used to ostracize them for being unjustly rich, exploitative, and unlawful.

The National Housing Trust has tried to bring informal workers into its contributor population, classifying them as "self-employed" and requesting voluntary contributions (*Gleaner* 1975: 15). Despite the fact that they have the greatest need for improved housing conditions, in actuality, few informal sector workers participate in NHT, presumably because of the low probability that a low-income person will receive a loan (McLeod 1987). Informal workers are unattractive customers to state housing agencies for other reasons. These include the tendency for their earnings to fluctuate and a lack of official documentation such as pay stubs and credit history. When a high-ranking CHFC employee was asked if it would be possible to match mortgage payments to the seasonality of higgler income (for example, Christmas, Easter), I was told that this was not necessary because the higglers could make monthly payments ahead of time. Clearly, to pay in advance, an informal worker would need a much larger income than a formal worker with regular wages.

Women

Female-headed households make up half the total in many cities of Latin America and the Caribbean, and they live in some of the worst housing (Moser 1987: 14). Women headed 41 percent of all Jamaican households in the mid-1980s, and 47 percent in the capital city, Kingston (Statin 1987a, 1987b). Like the patterns of public-housing finance with respect to low-income groups, those for women contain a contradiction. On the one hand, the greatest obstacle facing many women seeking housing assistance from NHT is that they are excluded from the contributor population because they disproportionately work in the informal sector and in micro-enterprises. That 64 percent of NHT contributors are men suggests a significant denigration of women's work. Further, nearly 60 percent of all mortgagers are men. On the other hand, if NHT practice is assessed according to its own criteria that housing loan recipients must also be contributors to the Trust, we identify aspects of accessibility that favor women within this relatively privileged group. First, female contributors have a slightly higher probability of obtaining a loan than male contributors. Second, women are able to obtain comparable-sized loans with incomes that average only 75 percent of that of men. Women have achieved this access to state housing through their greater persistence in pursuit of state housing assistance, greater responsibility in loan repayment, and, most significantly, because of state employment. However, NHT's favoring of select female contributors does not overcome the effects of the overall biases that prevent women, particularly poor women, from entering the contributor population. In other words, the loan award procedure should not be separated from the multistage process of selection and screening of which it is only a part. Prior to the selection of loan applicants, NHT's attachment to the more secure portion of the formal sector has excluded most poor women (Klak and Hey 1992).

Regime Effects

The previous section reveals that, despite the objectives of Jamaica's housing programs to allocate assistance according to "need," in practice they have not prioritized low-income people. The question then arises as to the extent to which this higher-income reorientation occurred under Seaga during the 1980s as opposed to under the creator of NHT, Michael Manley, in the 1970s. Like the social group analysis above, this regime effect can be measured from NHT's internal records, in this case using a three-step calculation. First, the proportion of contributors at each income level receiving housing loans can be compared. A second comparison can be made between each income level's contribution to the housing fund and the value of its housing loans. Third, the two measures of reallocation can be combined to produce a synthesis measure that takes account of both loan likelihood and the financial flow in and out of each income level (for more detail, see Klak 1989).

During the Manley administration of the 1970s, the income groups receiving the best combination of return on contributions to NHT and loan likelihood were the sixth and seventh income deciles. This is the 20 percent of employees just above the median-income level. The eighth income decile had the next best combination of monetary returns and loan probability. In other words, employees in approximately the third income quartile were favored. The top decile fared relatively poorly. Besides the favored status of the third quartile and the relative exclusion of the top decile from benefits, housing opportunities were widely disbursed across the income groups contributing to NHT.

Some shift in emphasis occurred under the Seaga administration of the 1980s. The income group with the best combination of returns on contributions and loan likelihood was the eighth income decile, followed by the seventh and ninth income deciles. Notably low were the combinations of return on contributions and loan likelihood for employees below the median wage. The highest income decile fell in between these extremes. Thus, under Seaga, NHT's lending continued to favor the upper half of the income distribution, but with most favored access given to the eighth decile, and with preferential status declining in both directions from this group.

To summarize, both administrations favored the upper half of formal sector wage earners. This suggests that forces that redirect socially progressive policy toward more market-like behavior transcend the regime in power. The critical difference between these regimes is that under Seaga there was a movement of benefits up the income distribution, and a concentration of it within the highest preference group. Both regimes favored higher-income contributors, but Seaga's did so to a greater extent, both in terms of income level and concentration of housing benefits. These findings are corroborated in other research on Jamaican housing policy (Jones, Webber, and Turner 1987: 62).

Following nearly a decade of dwindling numbers of low-cost housing units financed under the Seaga administration, there is now some evidence of a progressive shift in the state's social priorities under Manley and Patterson. A ten-thousand-unit development in Portmore, a working-class suburb of Kingston, and several other large moderate-income projects are underway (PIJ 1992). Even more relevant to the poor is the renewed vigor with which the MOC(H) has been constructing core housing units, and NHT's new initiative in which it provides loans for construction materials while low-income mortgagers invest labor to keep costs down (PIJ 1992; *Gleaner* 1993). While such low-income housing activity is at a significantly higher level than under Seaga, it is important to note that this level of activity is scarcely making a dent in the accumulated and still growing housing deficit of the poor. Even more problematic for the poor is the recent wave of destruction of self-help housing, as chapter 5 by Eyre documents. The Jamaican government has in recent years felt increased pressure from land developers, domestic and foreign, to remove squatters from profitable land. The government has bulldozed several illegal communities recently, even when politicians had earlier encouraged the invasion in the spirit of Jamaican political clientelism (Stone 1980; Edie 1991). Taken together, these trends suggest that socially progressive regime imperatives to meet low-income housing needs are dwindling and that there is a corresponding increase in influence of forces furthering dependency because Jamaica is preoccupied with neoliberal structural adjustment imperatives. In other words, there is growing power in the hands of those, both domestic and foreign, who advocate the application of private market rules to land and housing.

Other Impacts of Crisis and Structural Adjustment on Housing Policy

The growing presence of international development agencies in the Third World affects housing programs in other, broader ways. In small, resource-weak, dependent, and underdeveloped economies such as Jamaica's, state housing programs consume scarce foreign exchange. This is because the share of the value of materials for formal sector construction that must be imported is around 60 percent and rising (Goldson 1983–84; *Gleaner* 1988; PIJ 1994). The presiding sentiment in international development agencies is that there are better uses for foreign exchange than to meet housing needs, especially low-income needs. Government housing programs therefore become a major target for cutbacks during debt renegotiations.

A related structural adjustment-based constraint on government housing provision is the reserve requirement. As a component of monetary reforms, international agencies often want governments to hold larger sums of capital in reserve to pay the debt, to lend to the private sector, and generally increase financial stability. In the negotiations over structural adjustment, housing funds such as those of NHT are often argued to be better put to "productive" uses such as industry, agriculture, or tourism. The large pools of capital in the hands of state housing agencies are easy targets, and restrictions have been placed on their use (fig. 6.1) (see *Gleaner* 1985). This has major redistributional consequences. The working class pays into the housing fund but contributions may fund business expansion. Or they may simply fund an oversized bureaucracy and seep overseas as ongoing debt payments.

State housing programs are also clearly at odds with the currently popular "privatization" ideology. This doctrine holds that basic service delivery systems should be handed over to the private sector (Ohnesorgen 1990). International development agencies have specifically raised concerns about the "overall appropriateness" of an institution such as NHT that uses compulsory contributions to

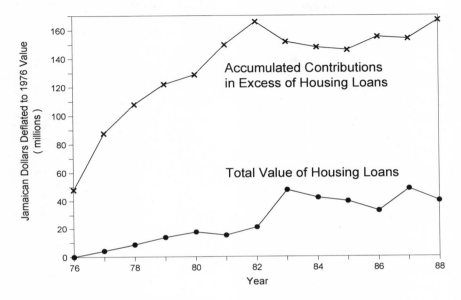

Fig. 6.1. Value of National Housing Trust contributions versus loans.

finance housing at below market interest rates (USAID 1988: 40). Despite the prominence worldwide of such pro-market, anti-state arguments, it must be recalled that government housing programs were created because of the short-comings of the formal private sector, which, compared to the state's offerings, are characterized by even higher prices, greater exclusiveness, and very small quan-tity (*Gleaner* 1986; PIJ 1992; Knopp and Kujawa 1993). No matter what the state does, the private formal sector in peripheral capitalism does not provide the basic requirements for working-class reproduction.

The neoliberal climate of the 1990s is restricting state housing assistance even further. The current hegemonic thinking about Third World development is that it must be private sector–based and externally oriented in terms of investment, comparative advantage, trade, exports, and market niches. In this model, domes-tic housing subsidies are seen as an inefficient and unproductive use of scarce resources. Within the last few years, the international agencies have made a slight shift in discourse to advocate *social development* (Grimond 1993; World Bank 1993). Neoliberalism is still dominant, but there is now recognition at the highest institutional levels that there are limits to the negative impacts lower-income people will absorb without threatening the system. This provides some political room for low-income housing assistance, as illustrated by the recent increase in provision of core units and sites and services by the Ministry of Construction

(Housing). However, in the present development model for Latin America and the Caribbean, the "social" plays the role of damage control and not that of a twin pillar to "development."

Conclusion

This overview of public housing resource flows in Jamaica during recent decades has helped expose the state's priorities and its allegiances to particular social groups. It has also revealed that there are severe obstacles to large-scale provision of low-income housing in a capitalist peripheral region like the Caribbean. Many of the trends in state housing can be explained by considering the roles of three forces: regime ideology, dependency, and structural adjustment. A regime effect is clearly present in Jamaica. The country's largest housing institution, NHT, was a child of democratic socialism and an attempt to bring better shelter to all citizens regardless of purchasing power. To some extent, words were followed by actions. Manley's party delivered more low-income housing assistance in the 1970s and 1990s than did Seaga's party, with its free market ideology, in the 1980s.

That said, the regime effect has been minor compared to the effects of the other two forces: those of dependency and of neoliberal, structural adjustment policies. By dependency I refer to forces rooted in Jamaica's political economy, such as grave inequalities, a lack of economic vibrancy and adequate employment, and a large state bureaucracy (Klak 1992a, 1995). Set in this context, NHT has been able to accumulate vast resources from formal sector payroll deductions, but has pitched its housing aid above the median income of the contributor population. CHFC serves a somewhat lower-wage group (around the median income for the country as a whole), but this occurs mainly because of USAID's constraints on its earmarked loans. Both major sources of public housing resources have, by and large, excluded those with the greatest housing needs. It would take the full exploitation of the massive financial resources of these two institutions to make a significant dent in the low-income housing problem.

Jamaica has been under structural adjustment policies since the late 1970s. In recent years, Jamaica has followed the regional pattern whereby the priorities of international development agencies are influencing a greater number of economic, governmental, and social activities. This influence takes many forms, from wholesale policy shifts towards nontraditional, export-oriented development and social spending restrictions to reserve requirements that hold vast housing resources in bank accounts. Resources are reallocated to pay the foreign debt, and domestic and international forces continue to pressure the state to downsize and privatize its activities. The overall mood at present is that the state has been an obstacle to growth and development and so its activities must be severely reigned in or curtailed entirely.

Given that most public housing resources accumulated in Jamaica over several decades have not gone to improve the shelter conditions of those most in need, one could argue that structural adjustment restrictions on state housing activity are irrelevant to the cause of decent shelter for those of low income. I think this is a mistaken view. The poor can hardly be worse off than if resource distributions are relegated completely to the anarchy of the market in a peripheral capitalist context. Recent demolitions of self-help housing in order to free space for more profitable uses underscores this point. The existence of public housing agencies and funds holds open the possibility that resources could be allocated in socially progressive ways. Those resources could complement the rich traditions of self-help and of vernacular home building are entrenched and dynamic. Low-income people themselves hold the potential of using whatever mechanisms that are available through Jamaica's electoral system and through popular organizing to pressure the state to turn such resources in their direction.

References

Boyd, D. (1988) *Economic Management, Income Distribution, and Poverty in Jamaica.* New York: Praeger.

Cargill, M. (1987) "The NHT Ripoff." *Gleaner,* 12 Feb.

Edie, C. (1991) *Democracy by Default: Dependency and Clientelism in Jamaica.* Boulder: Lynn Rienner.

Ford, F. (1976) "National Housing Trust: Role in the Building Industry." *Gleaner,* 16 May, 9–10C. Text of paper presented to Building Seminar of Joint Consultative Committee of the Building Industry.

Gilfillian, K. (1978) "The Role of Government and NHT in housing." In *Housing for Jamaica—Workshops on Science & Technology, Jamaica,* 80–83. Sponsored by OAS, Published by Kingston Scientific Research Council/NPA.

Girvan, N., and R. Bernal. (1982) "The IMF and the Foreclosure of Development Options: The Case of Jamaica." *Monthly Review* 33.

Girvan, N., R. Bernal, and W. Hughes. (1980) "The IMF and the Third World: The Case of Jamaica, 1974–80." *Development Dialogue* 2: 113–55.

Gleaner. (1975) "Text of Prime Minister's Statement." 9 Oct., 1A.

———. (1976a) "Proposed National Housing Trust Operations Outlined." 17 Feb., 5.

———. (1976b) "House Approves National Housing Trust." 18 Mar., 12–16.

———. (1982) "NHT: Now It's Points System." 29 Dec.

———. (1985) "Agency Has Money but Few NHT Units this Year for Contributors." 23 Feb.

———. (1986) "Jamaica Said Producing Fifth of Housing Required." 8 Mar.

———. (1988) "Cost of Housing." Weekly Edition, 11 July, 6.

———. (1989) "Hole in the Housing Trust's Bucket." Weekly Edition, 16 Oct., 16.

———. (1991) "What Is Middle-Income Housing: for Whom? 75% Earn Less than $25,000 per Annum." 16 Mar.

———. (1993) "NHT Assigns $2.5 M to Low-Income Projects." 22 May, 12.

Golding, B. (1982) *A National Housing Policy for Jamaica.* Kingston: Ministry of Construction (Housing).

———. (1983–84) "Trends in Housing Costs II." *Housing and Finance* (Winter): 16–18.

Grimond, J. (1993) "Yes, We Have No Mañanas." *The Economist,* 13 Nov.

Hope, P. (1976) "Uncensored." *Gleaner,* 22 May, 10A.

Jackson, S. (general manager of CHFC). (1988a) "Caribbean Housing Finance Corporation Limited: A Case Analysis." Master's paper, Nova University.

———. (1988b) Letter to USAID. Regional Housing and Urban Development Office, 9 June.

Jones, E., M. Webber, and M. A. Turner. (1987) *Jamaica Shelter Sector Strategy, Phase 1.* Final Report. USAID Sponsored "U.I. Project 3666–02." Feb.

Klak, T. (1989) "From Socially Progressive Policy to Socially Regressive Program: The Case of Jamaica's National Housing Trust." Paper presented at the Association of American Geographers annual meeting, Baltimore (available from author).

———. (1990) "Spatially and Socially Progressive State Policy and Programs: The Case of Brazil's National Housing Bank." *Annals of the Association of American Geographers* 50: 571–89.

———. (1991) "Analysis of Government Mortgage Records: Insights for State Theory and Housing Policy with Reference to Jamaica." In A. G. Tipple and K. Willis, eds., 96–112, *Housing the Poor in the Developing World: Methods of Analysis, Case Studies and Policy.* London and New York: Routledge.

———. (1992a) "Excluding the Poor from Low-Income Housing Programs: The Roles of State Agencies and USAID in Jamaica." *Antipode* 24: 87–112.

———. (1992b) "What Causes Arrears in Government Housing Programs? Perceptions and the Empirical Evidence from Jamaica." *Journal of the American Planning Association (JAPA)* 58 (3): 336–45.

———. (1993) "Contextualizing State Housing Programs in Latin America: Evidence from Leading Housing Agencies in Brazil, Ecuador and Jamaica." *Environment and Planning, A* 25 (5): 653–76.

———. (1995) "A Framework for Studying Caribbean Industrial Policy." *Economic Geography* 71 (3): 297–316.

Klak, T., and J. Hey. (1992) "Gender and State Bias in Jamaican Housing Programs." *World Development* 20: 213–27.

Knopp, L., and R. Kujawa. (1993) "Ideology and Urban Landscapes: Conceptions of the Market in Portland, Maine." *Antipode* 25: 114–39.

LeFranc, E. (1988) "Higglering in Kingston." *Caribbean Review* 1 (Spring): 15–17, 35.

Lowenthal, A. F. (1993) "Latin America: Ready for Partnership?" *Foreign Affairs* 72: 74–92.

McLeod, R. (1987) *Low-Income Shelter Strategies in Kingston: Solutions of the Informal Sector.* Report for RHUDO (Regional Housing and Urban Development Office). Kingston: USAID.

Moser, C. (1987) "Women, Human Settlements, and Housing: A Conceptual Framework for Analysis and Policy-Making." In C. Moser and L. Peake, eds., 12–32. *Women, Human Settlements, and Housing.* London: Tavistock.

NHT (National Housing Trust). (1988) Contributor and Mortgage master files, computer data files containing records for NHT contributors and beneficiaries, Kingston.

———. (n.d.) "Objectives of the NHT." Internal document, Kingston.

Ohnesorgen, F. (1990) "Special Committee on Solid Waste and Waste Water Disposal of the City of Guayaquil, Ecuador." Appraisal report on committee's proposal to privatize solid waste services. (Report obtained from USAID, Quito).

Peterson, G., and T. Klak. (1990) "Shelter Sector Mortgage Credit and Subsidy Policy: The National Housing Trust and Caribbean Housing Finance Corporation. Executive Report." Kingston: USAID and the Jamaican Ministries of Construction (Housing) and Development, Planning and Production, Contract no. PDC 0000-I-00-6168-00.

PIJ (Planning Institute of Jamaica). (1988) *Economic and Social Survey, Jamaica, 1987.* Kingston: PIJ.

———. (1992) *Economic and Social Survey, Jamaica, 1991.* Kingston: PIJ.

————. (1994) *Economic and Social Survey, Jamaica, 1993*. Kingston: PIJ.

Smallman, P. (1977) "The Housing Trust: A History of Non-performance." *Gleaner,* 3 Dec., 23.

Smith, L. (then director of RHUDO, Regional Housing and Urban Development Office, U.S. Agency for International Development, Kingston). (1989) Personal Communication, 31 July. Kingston.

Statin (Statistical Institute of Jamaica). (1987a) *Statistical Abstract 1986*. Kingston: Statin.

————. (1987b) *Household Expenditure Survey 1984,* vol. 2. Kingston: Statin.

Stone, C. (1980) *Democracy and Clientelism in Jamaica*. New Brunswick, N.J.: Transaction Books.

TFH (Task Force on Housing) and PIJ (Planning Institute of Jamaica). (1992). *Jamaica Five Year Development Plan 1990–1995 Housing*. Kingston: PIJ.

THA (Trevor Hamilton and Associates). (1988) *Alternative Approaches to Improving Mortgage Affordability: Final Report*. Report submitted to NHT (Oct.). Kingston.

USAID (United States Agency for International Development). (1988) Jamaica Project Paper: Jamaica Shelter and Urban Services Policy. Washington, D.C.: USAID.

World Bank (1993). *World Development Report 1993: Investing in Health*. New York: Oxford University Press.

From Cooperative Socialism to a Social Housing Policy? Declines and Revivals in Housing Policy in Guyana

Linda Peake

Overcrowding, insecure shelter, and increasing levels of homelessness are the primary characteristics of the housing situation in Guyana in the early 1990s. Moreover, these conditions characterize not only the poor but salaried employees in both state and private-sector enterprises and skilled wage earners in traditionally middle-class occupations in the education and health care sectors. Two decades after the declaration of the People's National Congress (PNC) that it intended to house the nation, state-managed housing is in near collapse, and in the cooperative and private sectors, building has been at a virtual standstill. The significance of the state's withdrawal from housing provision lies in the fact that, since before Independence, it has played a major role in the provision of housing for all social groups. Thus, the crisis in housing affects all but the wealthiest sectors of society.

This chapter analyzes the factors that have shaped the development of housing policy in Guyana. It commences with a brief historical overview of the pattern of urbanization to establish the geographical and historical contexts within which housing policy has developed. Attention then turns to periods in which the PNC, through the use of specific policy instruments, has shaped the nature and particular forms of housing; an evaluation of these periods concludes that there has not been a recognizable housing policy in Guyana since Independence in 1966. The chapter ends with an assessment of the current crisis in housing facing the recently elected People's Progressive Party (PPP) and the forces most likely to shape housing provision in the future.

Urbanization

Guyana faces a crisis in housing even though its population has been in decline; the estimated total population of 739,553, of which 32 percent is urbanized, is less than 60 percent of that projected from the 1970 census (Bureau of Statistics 1992; UNICEF 1993). Most of the urban population lives in the capital, Georgetown, which houses approximately two hundred thousand persons. Other principal urban centers are Linden, an interior bauxite-mining town, and New Amsterdam, a small port and service center for the region of Berbice. Density is low at an average of nine persons per square mile, but this figure hides a spatially skewed distribution with approximately 90 percent of the population living along the coastal strip, much of which is below sea level and dissected by three rivers, the Essequibo, the Demerara, and the Berbice.

The pattern of urbanization cannot fully be understood without addressing the factors that have led to the geographical bases of support for the two largest political parties, the PNC and the PPP. Support for the PNC has traditionally come from the Afro-Guyanese population, which throughout the twentieth century has become more urbanized. The PPP receives its support from the Indo-Guyanese population, which has always had a rural base, although it is currently also moving into the urban areas. These bases have their origins in the racial composition of the labor force and the settlement pattern, both of which arose from the colonial systems of slavery and indentured labor. Both African slaves (from approximately the 1650s to 1834) and East Indian indentured laborers (from 1838 to 1917) were used to establish sugar plantations on the fertile alluvial coastland (Daly 1976). Following emancipation ex-slaves set up rural villages next to the sugar estates. They were joined by East Indians at the end of the period of indenture, although substantial numbers remained on the estates, continuing to live in logies and range houses. The villages were multiracial until the race riots of the early 1960s; since then they have largely become differentiated between Indo- and Afro-Guyanese.

During this period, Georgetown continued to thrive, being a major transportation hub, the legislative center, and increasingly the location of the Afro-Guyanese middle classes (Potter 1987). Outside the coastal area, the only urban settlement of any note is Linden, which developed more recently—during the Second World War—as a foreign-enclave bauxite-mining center.[1] By 1970, it had developed from being a company town to the second largest urban center with a population of thirty-one thousand in 1990. The pattern of settlement outside Georgetown and the sugar estates is relatively sparse. North of the Essequibo there is only the small township of Anna Regina and dispersed small villages and farms. The coastal belt to the east and west of the Demerara is the most densely populated area with large villages lining the coastal road on either side of Georgetown. Land south of the Berbice River is serviced by the small port of New Amsterdam and the townships of Corriverton and Rose Hall. There are also a number of Amerindian peoples living in small, scattered communities along the major rivers in the interior.[2]

The low figure for the rate of urbanization, which in 1980 stood at only 1 percent, masks the real growth that has taken place in the Greater Georgetown area (Central Housing and Planning Authority n.d.). Hemmed in by surrounding sugar estate lands and the Atlantic Ocean, its increasing population was forced to locate on the east bank (of the Demerara River) and the East Coast (the Atlantic seaboard). In the 1980s, however, substantial squatting has taken place on these sugar lands. Potter (1987) claims that the entire area within about thirty kilometers of the capital is now periurban, given the growth of industrial production and the decline in agricultural production that has taken place within these villages. Moreover, the demographic structure of the population in Georgetown is shifting due to the differential rates between Afro- and Indo-Guyanese, fertility, and out-migration. The absolute decline in the population is attributable to a decline in the fertility rate and the exceptionally high level of out-migration. Higher levels of fertility of the Indo-Guyanese population have led to their becoming the largest group in the population (approximately 50 percent). They also have begun to move into urban areas. In 1980 Indo-Guyanese made up 27.4 percent of the population of Georgetown, but by 1990 this figure had risen to approximately 43 percent. The impact these demographic changes will have on future housing policy is unclear. As the following section reveals, the PNC adopted a policy of political patronage in relation to housing. Consequently, its projects focused largely on member of the Afro-Guyanese population, who were based in the urban areas. If the recently elected PPP adopts a similar strategy it would have to address the housing needs of Indo-Guyanese in both urban and rural areas.

Stages in the Development of Housing Policy in Guyana

The Colonial Era, 1831–1966

British Guiana was formed in 1831 with the amalgamation of Demerara, Essequibo, and Berbice and remained a British colony until 1966. During the nineteenth century and until the Second World War, the provision of housing was mostly by private individuals and sugar estates. Workers on the estates could obtain finance for housing from the Sugar Industry Labour Welfare Fund (SILWF).

This fund was originally financed by a levy for each ton of sugar exported, with workers being granted interest-free loans on a ten-year repayment plan.

The building of logies, however, continued on the estates until the 1930s and improvements in accommodation were slow; in 1952, 948 ranges were still occupied (Cummings 1954). Cummings (1954) reported that "Housing in the Colony prior to 1939 was unsatisfactory. It is certain that overcrowding existed in low income dwellings throughout the Colony; but accommodation for middle and upper income groups appeared to be adequate" (1). Housing for these latter groups was financed by the only other formal financing institution besides the SILWF, the British Guiana Building Society Limited (later the New Building Society).

Conditions in Georgetown began to deteriorate in the early 1940s with the rise in population following the eradication of malaria and migration from the rural areas. A survey of 7,994 houses in Georgetown in 1945 indicated that 2,309 were unfit for habitation and 5,303 were in need of repair (Dick 1984). In order to deal with the deteriorating housing situation, the Central Housing and Planning Authority (CHPA) was formed in 1946, primarily for providing houses for the working class (Dick 1984). This was the first national-level housing body to be formed, and it focused its attention on slum clearance and redevelopment of Wortmanville and Albouystown, identified as the worst slum areas in Georgetown. The CHPA adopted a multifaceted approach, housing the lowest income groups in government rental housing and preparing land for lower middle-income groups on which to build their own homes, as well as providing loans for higher-income groups through credit corporations. Self-help housing was formally introduced in 1953–54 when the government, together with the Caribbean Development Corporation, sponsored ten projects, each providing fifteen homes, along the coastal strip. With the introduction of the ministerial system in 1953, the Ministry of Labour, Health and Housing was established to take over the responsibilities of the CHPA (see table 7.1).

In 1957, with the first noncolonial administration in place, the PPP inherited a larger housing program that had been initiated by the interim government. The following year, however, the PPP cut the housing budget by nearly 50 percent (Dick 1984), and between 1960 and 1964 fewer than 400 dwellings were built by the government. Since this time, expenditure on housing has continued to show a progressive decline. For example, whereas between 1954 an 1964 the government built 3,900 units, the SILWF built 10,785.

The Era of Nationalism and Cooperativism, 1966–1980

Four years after the granting of Independence and the election of the PNC, it was announced that the country was adopting socialism and had become a Coopera-

Table 7.1

Chronology of the Development of Housing Administration

Date established	Name	Comment
1948	Central Housing and Planning Authority	A statutory body responsible for enforcing all planning schemes
1954	Ministry of Labour, Health and Housing	
1966	Ministry of Housing and Reconstruction	
1970	Ministry of Health, Housing and Labour	
1972	Ministry of Works, Transport and Housing	
1983	Ministry of Health and Public Welfare (Housing)	
1986	Ministry of Manpower and Housing	
1990	Ministry of Housing abolished	
1993	Human Services, Social Services and Housing	

tive Socialist Republic; housing was to become a priority item on the national agenda. Cooperatives were to be the instruments through which the social and economic reorganization of Guyanese society was to be achieved, and their application to housing provision and construction was an obvious step. Thus, in common with other Third World governments in the early 1970s, Guyana emphasized "bottom-up" self-help projects. Housing was viewed not only in terms of having a roof over one's head but also in terms of community membership. The slogan of the 1972–76 Second Development Plan, "Feed, house and clothe the nation," reiterated this philosophy. The government's aim was to increase the level of self-sufficiency among the population, and it assumed that cooperative maintenance of property would provide the basis for collective participation in other activities. It is also possible, however, to view the PNC's housing policy merely as a continuation of that of the interim government. The British colonial authorities first introduced cooperatives in 1948, and the PNC adopted the same policy instruments of self-help, rental housing, plot preparation, and hire purchase, albeit with different emphases.[3]

Self-Help Housing

Although self-help housing was introduced in Guyana as early as 1953, it was not until the cooperative movement of the PNC government was established that self-help was actively promoted. As early as 1968, self-help projects were brought within the remit of the then Ministry of Housing and Reconstruction, but by 1982 it was estimated that only four thousand families had been housed by them (Hanson 1981). There were two varieties of self-help projects in Guyana: 1) Aided Self-help (ASH) Housing Societies and 2) Co-operative Self-help Housing Groups

(Ministry of Public Welfare [Housing] 1981).[4] In the former, members paid for house lots at the cost of development and repaid the ministry for loans covering the cost of materials used in construction. With escalating costs of building materials and land development, many ASH housing society members were unable to repay their mortgage loans and were encouraged to join cooperative self-help groups. Members of these paid a fixed percentage of their income towards the cost of their homes, with payments spread over varying periods according to the ability to pay of the members. These housing cooperatives comprised two types: those concerned only with acquiring land and houses and those wanting to further utilize the principles of cooperativism to develop a sense of sharing and self-reliance within a Community Cooperative Village (Ministry of Health and Public Welfare [Housing] 1981).[5]

The most important period for self-help housing was in the mid-1970s, when government subsidies included salary costs and reduced interest payments on mortgage loans. From 1974 to 1976, and in 1978, public-sector employees were released from their workplaces on full pay (although the level of production at their workplace had to be maintained at the same level). From 1973, self-help groups were also granted mortgages by the Guyana Co-operative Mortgage Finance Bank (GCMFB) at interest rates of 6 percent per annum (commercial rates in 1981 were 12–14 percent), and approximately 80 percent of the bank's funds were allocated to low-income borrowers. In addition, the CHPA gave subsidies to self-help groups, amounting to 40 percent of the total cost, for materials, infrastructure works, technical supervision, and instruction from skilled construction workers and transportation of materials and equipment to sites (Ministry of Health and Public Welfare [Housing] 1981).

By 1977, with a deterioration in trade and faced with economic recession, the PNC government was unable to continue providing financial support for cooperative housing.[6] Whereas the 1972–76 plan allocated 18.1 percent of expenditure to housing, health, and roads, the 1978–81 plan allocated only 6.8 percent. In the early 1980s, the removal of government support resulted in self-help groups working in their own free time without the benefit of professional instruction, and applicants were no longer screened to decide whether they could afford their mortgage payments.

Perhaps more significant than these financial criteria was the fact that the PNC government did little to foster a conducive environment in a country with little history of cooperativism. When building activity finished, the cooperative society would cease to function. The majority of cooperatives existed in name only and made no substantial contribution to economic activity nor to increasing the power of low-income groups to control the distribution of resources in society. In practice, the public and private sectors, via commercial builders and landlords, dominated the economy with little space for cooperatives. The 1970 census revealed that 66 percent of households owned or were paying for their dwelling, while a further 31 percent were renting, although these figures varied between the urban and rural areas. In the predominantly Indo-Guyanese rural areas, homeownership was three times as common as in urban areas where renting, primarily through private landlords, was the norm.

Rental Housing

Although the government in the 1970s was to focus on ASH, it was not the only instrument of housing policy. The 1970 Housing Development Act provided for the operation of a Revolving Fund (in the then Ministry of Health, Housing and Labour), which enabled the ministry to purchase, develop, and sell land and to finance the construction of homes for sale and for rent. The Housing Fund provided "front-end finance": after houses were allocated, the GCMFB would reimburse to the fund its expenditure and would then formally register individual occupants as mortgagees. With the Housing Fund the GCMFB could ostensibly restructure the pattern of the mortgage market by channeling funds towards those officially designated as lower-income groups. The broad guidelines adopted were that families with incomes below G$250 per month qualified for government rental apartments. People were encouraged to join cooperative housing groups and build by self-help if they had an income of G$250 per month or higher; they could purchase leveled plots with infrastructure on which to build their own homes individually or in cooperative groups. However, Hanson (1981) estimated that if a household were to receive a mortgage loan of G$30,000–35,000 (the official "low-income" housing range) it would need an annual income of over G$7,000. The 1977 Labour Force Survey revealed that 50 percent of households had annual incomes of less than G$2,800. Hanson estimated that over 77 percent of the urban population and 96 percent of the rural population could not afford to buy houses in this price range. Thus, government rental housing was the only formal option open to a large segment of the population.

A major focus, then, during the 1970s was the building of government housing to rent. Initially, these new dwellings were supposed to rehouse residents of slum clearance programs. But these programs were not executed, thus the dwellings were used to rehouse families from overcrowded areas in Georgetown. They were allocated, as was ASH housing, more on financial criteria than need, and increasingly they became allocated to the Afro-Guyanese sector of the population, on the perceived (and real) basis of political support for the PNC. My study in the mid-1980s (Peake 1987) of a random sample of applicants for government rental housing found that over 95 percent were Afro-Guyanese women. Not only did they face long delays, they also had only a small chance of being allocated a dwelling. Many low-income women were forced into the option of individual self-build housing. This was particularly disadvantageous to women who headed households, had less time available to participate in construction, and had low and often irregular income that did not enable them to contract skilled labor.

Although there was a massive shortage of rental properties, government building having practically stopped in the late 1970s, rents were minimal and commonly were often not collected. The rents ranged (at 1985 prices) from G$5 to G$60 per month, and had not been raised since 1961 (Peake 1986). Officials in the Ministry of Housing, in 1985, did not know how many properties they operated and could only put figures between 2,000 and 7,000. Similarly, for the decade 1970–80, official statistics on the number of new dwellings constructed by the government differ widely, ranging from 2,206 to 3,088 (Hinckson n.d.). These numbers fell far short of estimates which suggested that anywhere between 2,000 and 6,000 new dwelling units per annum were needed in Guyana between 1970 and 1980.[7] One estimate of new constructions for both the public and private sectors was 30,180 (Ministry of Health, Public Welfare and Housing 1981). Undoubtedly, the vast bulk of these new dwellings was constructed by the private sector for middle- and upper-income groups.

The Era of Restructuring, 1980–1990

Throughout the 1980s the PNC continued to increase its hold over the economy and civil society, as witnessed by an increase in political oppression and increasing attempts to restructure the economy towards socialist objectives in the face of the World Bank and the IMF establishing a program of structural adjustment. Overall the decade witnessed increasing poverty and, by its end, the virtual abandonment of socialist rhetoric (Potter 1987).

Although a few self-help schemes were still operating in the 1980s, the norm was still for private households to build their own homes. By 1982 it was estimated that private households were building approximately 70 percent of the new housing stock per annum, with the remainder being accounted for by private developers (Dick 1984; Hanson 1981). Although hampered by a lack of finances (every year since 1981 debt servicing has taken increasingly large portions of government revenue), the government's commitment to house low-income groups, as well as others, was nonexistent by the early 1980s. The government's low level of political commitment to the spirit of cooperativism was exemplified in its virtual reversal in policy: housing was downgraded from an integral element of development to a mere item of welfare. This was evidenced in 1983 when the portfolio for housing was removed from the Ministry of Works and Housing to the low-status and overburdened Ministry of Health and Public Welfare. By early 1985, the government had also ceased funding cooperative housing and had decided to sell its rental housing, thereby denying tenants the right to future maintenance and repairs.

Although a national housing plan was drafted in November 1986, it was neither adopted nor implemented, resulting in the absence of a national housing policy.[8] In 1990, the Ministry of Housing was abolished, and the CHPA took over its role as the statutory body for housing, but with a reduction in staff from 200–250 to 60. Suffering from a shortage of skilled personnel it has continued to function on an ad hoc basis. In July 1990, for example, the Welfare and Estate Management section of the Housing Department was virtually abolished in a further restructuring exercise. In the first 6 months of 1990, over 700 visits had been made to government housing estates to deal with welfare management matters and repairs were made to over 50 dwellings. Since July 1990, there have been no such visits or repairs. The other major activity of the CHPA, the selling of government properties to tenants, although ostensibly an ongoing process since 1985, has been held up because of a lack of basic documentation on their locations and total number, and because the necessary legal framework was not in place until 1989, when the Condominium (Regulation and Miscellaneous Provisions) Act was passed allowing the Certificate of Title to be transferred to the tenant.[9] Since 1989, however, only one area, Campbellville, has received individual titles.

Private Sector

Very little is known about housing provision in the 1980s outside the sphere of state provision. This is especially true of the private rental sector in both the urban and rural areas. To the best of my knowledge there is no documentation on private-sector housing. It is generally agreed that conditions in urban areas have been characterized by overcrowding, insecurity of tenure, and dilapidated buildings with inadequate sanitary facilities. Rental accommodation has been provided both by major landlords and people letting rooms in their own homes, often to relatives. Apart from a few individuals who have been unscrupulous in renting out substandard dwellings, most landlords appear to be poor themselves, supplementing their limited incomes from rent but not being able to live from this income alone. Renting does not, therefore, appear to have been particularly exploitative. However, the extent to which private rental housing has been used to buy political support and defuse demands for radical change is unknown. Neither is it known whether petty landlordism will develop into large-scale capitalist activity. The shortage of rental housing has also resulted in a low level of mobility, added to by the fact that most renters are too poor to own and have been renting for long periods.

The urban power base of the PNC resulted in a failure to address the housing needs of the rural-based Indo-Guyanese, for whom private renting is common in both established villages and squatter settlements. A survey I conducted in 1993 in the village of Meten Meer Zorg, West Coast Demerara, found that renting was common among divorced and widowed women and among young married couples. Landlords were owners who invariably lived locally, or were the relatives of homeowners who were absent, usually overseas.

Squatting

Since the mid-1980s, with the cessation of government provision of housing, those unable to afford to build or buy their own homes were restricted to finding their own solutions to their housing needs; squatting became a significant activity among low-income groups. Squatting in Guyana has not traditionally been the result of rapid population growth, but rather a result of racial conflicts, which started the first wave of squatting in the 1960s. These conflicts culminated in the movement of approximately fifteen thousand people out of racially integrated communities into racially segregated ones. Large numbers had no option but to squat on government-owned land. The 1980s increase in the number of households turning to squatter settlements is a result of squalid urban housing conditions and overcrowded premises in which households are no longer willing to live. The greatest concentration of squatter settlements is to be found on the periphery of Greater Georgetown, the Green Belt area. Since it is unregulated, this land has no sanitary facilities or infrastructure of any kind, and now it is estimated to house a population of over twelve thousand (UNICEF 1993). Squatter settlements are also present in rural areas, particularly in the sugar belt where vacant land is available.

Squatting has tended to take place in an orderly fashion, with individual households or whole communities applying for land titles and making representations for communal services and infrastructure to their Regional Democratic Council.[10] Residents are often very willing to participate in consolidation of their settlement—by digging drains, laying water pipes, and building access roads—if they feel they will be granted title to their land. Because of financial constraints, the Town and Country Planning Department has recommended a lowering of standards for squatter upgrading. These include building claybrick roads instead of bitumen roads; earth drains instead of concrete ones; communal standpipes instead of individual water pipes to each house; and no provision of electricity, which would instead be supplied by individual households.

A typical long-established squatting area, such as that of Meten Meer Zorg on the East Coast Demerara, has houses built from a variety of materials, usually with wooden or zinc walls, wooden or occasionally glass windows, and roofs of zinc, wood, or trooley leaves. They usually comprise two bedrooms, a small living room, and kitchen. Pit latrines and a small wooden structure for bathing are to be found on most house lots. Since early 1994, there has been electricity, but there is still no running water, with only two standpipes at the front of the settlement. Household appliances are limited to a flat iron and an oven, with the latter usually built out of clay, with maybe a box oven for baking. The desire to upgrade is strong, especially among women, who, when they have an opportunity to save money, usually spend it on improving their home. Figures 7.1 and 7.2 show the home of a small nuclear family in Meten Meer Zorg, which was upgraded in August 1993, with savings acquired by the woman of the household and gives a clear indication of what can be achieved.

Fig. 7.1. A house in Meten Meer Zorg before consolidation.

Fig. 7.2. The same house after consolidation in 1993.

The Context of the Housing Crisis in the 1990s

In October 1992, Guyana emerged from twenty-eight years of rule by the PNC, a period characterized by a sublimation of the democratic rights of the people to the aggrandizement of the party, a process enshrined in 1974 in the Declaration of Sophia, which established the paramountcy of the party over the state. The rigging of elections during this period served not only to disenfranchise the electorate but also to generate a political crisis that spilled over into civil society, resulting in its demobilization.

Moreover, the mismanagement of the economy, characterized by high levels of corruption, has been exacerbated by the Economic Recovery Programme (ERP), implemented since 1988 under the auspices of the World Bank/International Monetary Fund's Structural Adjustment Programme (SAP). Although there has been some growth in the economy, the devaluation of the Guyanese dollar and the corresponding rise in prices, accompanied by the removal of subsidies and a reduction in government spending on services such as health care, education, and housing, has led to the growth of an impoverished middle class, causing the process of pauperization to envelop the vast majority of the Guyanese population (Roopnarine 1992).[11] It is estimated that between 67 and 86 percent of the population now live below the poverty line (Thomas 1993). It is within this context that the magnitude of the current crisis in housing can be ascertained.

A broad range of problems is faced in both urban and rural environments. Since the mid-1980s electricity blackouts have been a common, everyday occurrence, and the piped water supply is also erratic and of such variable quality that it is commonly boiled before using it for drinking. Only the wealthiest residents can afford their own generators, so most of the country comes to a standstill during the blackouts. Indeed, there has been a marked decline in the functioning of all physical infrastructure both at the level of hardware and services. The public education and health care sectors have virtually collapsed, and there has also been an increase in levels of malnutrition (UNICEF 1993). Supplies of essential items such as flour, cooking oil, and even rice and sugar have vied between being sporadic and nonexistent. In order to survive, many households have depended on the parallel market. The severity of this situation is evidenced in increasing levels of crime, with all residential areas, regardless of status, being subject to increasing numbers of break-ins, which have been particularly violent in rural areas.

Perhaps the unhealthiest aspect of the housing situation in Guyana is the critical shortage in housing in the urban areas, particularly in Georgetown. Although there has been a nationwide shortfall in accommodation, it is in Georgetown that the shortages have been most acute. This has resulted in increasing numbers of homeless families, in squatting, and in multiple occupancy with exorbitant levels of overcrowding which not only have detrimental effects on sanitation and hygiene, but also have led to an intolerable stress on family units witnessed by high levels of domestic violence against both women and children.[12]

The results of a survey conducted in 1992, which covered 8 percent of the population of Georgetown (GOG/IDB 1993b), reveal that over 60 percent of households shared their homes with at least one other person and over 47 percent expressed the need for owner-constructed housing units (with 93 percent of these declaring a willingness to be involved in self-help housing projects). In terms of tenure, 46 percent were owner occupiers, 33 percent rented, and 13 percent lived rent free.[13] Rents were highly skewed; 29 percent had rents of less than G$500 per month; 63 percent paid rents of G$500–4,000; and only 7 percent paid above G$4,000. When the distribution of household income is taken into account, it is clear that households spend a very small proportion of income on rent. While 7 percent of households earned less than G$1,700 per month, 25 percent earned between G$1,800 and G$5,300, 36 percent between G$5,400 and G$8,000, and 33 percent over G$8,000. It should be noted that only 47 percent of the respondents answered questions on income, but among these respondents expenditure across all households showed that over four times the amount of money spent on rent was spent on food.

The housing shortage is a result of several factors: 1) the diversion of quality housing into a high-cost rental housing market serving Guyanese nationals and expatriates working temporarily in the country; 2) the advanced state of decay and dilapidation of a large proportion of the housing stock; 3) the decision of the PNC government in the mid-1980s to cease building and subsidizing public-sector housing; 4) the almost total cessation of the building of new houses by private-sector businesses and trade unions (construction costs are approximately G$1,000–1,500 per square foot); 5) the irregular supply of building materials; 6) a fragmented pattern of landownership; and 7) the decline in real wages, preventing workers from saving and, hence, from having sufficient capital to finance new building. In the 1990s starter homes with two bedrooms cost at least G$500,000, with prices rising to G$950,000 (Anon. 1993b). These prices are far outside the reach of even the middle-class sector of the population. At current rates of interest (ranging from 17 to 25 percent) over 80 percent of the population cannot afford to buy a home, and even at a 5 percent rate of interest, 50 percent of the population would still be excluded. Moreover, the building that has taken place has been characterized by an ostentatiousness not witnessed before in Guyana: there has been the development of a new architectural style that symbolizes housing as an item of conspicuous consumption.[14]

Future Policy

The future focus of housing policy would appear to reflect a common shift already witnessed in several Third World countries; that is, a move from an emphasis on self-help to the upgrading of slums and unauthorized areas. In 1993, the PPP government reinstated housing as a ministerial responsibility, within the Ministry of Labour and Human Services, suggesting that housing may again become a national priority. This was verified when early in 1994 the government claimed it intended to ensure the regularization of squatter settlements as well as the building of thirty-one thousand houses by the year 2000 (Barclay 1994). The emphasis throughout the 1990s, however, at the macro level, will continue to be determined by structural adjustment policies, focusing primarily upon the efficiency of the market. Government will take more of an enabling role as opposed to that of a provider; corresponding with this reduced role of government is that of an enhanced role for the private sector, which will continue as the main force of development.

This is not to argue that the PPP is repeating history and merely adopting the policy instruments of its predecessors. There are significant differences between past and current housing policy that arise not so much from party politics, but from the international economic climate. The World Bank has assumed that a restructuring of national economic policies requires a corresponding process of urban adjustment: "In the field of housing, this means that urban (low-income) housing will no longer be 'projectised'. Instead, the Bank will try to bring about structural policy changes through a 'policy dialogue' on the performance of urban land and housing markets, the role of the government and the like" (Baken and Van der Linden 1993: 3). It is anticipated that enhancing the efficiency of land and housing markets will trigger an urban adjustment process by reducing constraints on urban productivity and alleviating urban poverty. The former involves upgrading infrastructure, making the regulatory framework more amenable to private-sector involvement, and improving financial services and the capacity of municipal institutions. Instruments for the latter include enhancing the productivity of urban households, improving access to basic needs, and providing safety-net assistance to the most marginal groups.

Some of these policy instruments are already established in Guyana. And, although there has been a recent recognition that housing is a basic need, the housing needs of the poor are still considered to be most likely met from the trickling down of macroeconomic improvements. The provision of housing is being promoted as a channel for the alleviation of urban poverty, but the latter will be achieved primarily by reducing the constraints on urban productivity; that is, housing is viewed as a commodity as opposed to a social service. The mechanisms for controlling change in urban land and housing markets are, however, poorly developed. For example, in March 1994 the government passed a Landlords Registration Act with the intention of reducing tax evasion by private-sector landlords who failed to declare rental income. Although it is unclear how this will affect tenants, a likely scenario is that tax increases will be passed on to tenants as increased rents. The underlying objective of such legislation is clearly fiscal in nature, but it also aims to make the regulatory framework more amenable to private-sector involvement. Although rent-restriction legislation exists, preventing land-lords from making excessive increases, it is rarely applied. High levels of inflation in the last decade have already led to huge increases in rent, although many domestic buildings remain empty because landlords are reluctant to rent given the difficulty of evicting tenants and the uncertainty surrounding the use of the Rent Restriction Act. In order to address the needs of tenants, however, there needs to be a focus on improving the application of rent-restriction legislation as well as informing tenants of their rights.

The priorities of the current minister for housing appear to be to institutional-ize a process of cost recovery and to remove hidden subsidies. These are evident in his current activities (Jeffreys 1993), which have included continuing the pro-cess of selling government dwellings, accessing loans from the IBD and the neigh-boring country of Venezuela to help reduce mortgage rates, and investigating the use of new technologies to provide low-cost building materials.[15] Moreover, these priorities also determine the nature of activities directly addressing the alleviation of urban poverty, such as the regularization of squatter settlements and the allo-cation of land both to low-income groups and private developers.

With its emphasis on cost recovery, the allocation of land has been a source of tension. The government has started to distribute 2,000 plots of state land (mea-suring 40 by 80 feet) on which people can build their own homes. It plans to distribute 4,000 plots per annum to low-income groups.[16] The plots are priced at approximately G$8,000 to cover the cost of surveying, clearing, and drainage; this price is still beyond that which many households can pay.

A recent assertion of the PPP government is that it will not tolerate an un-abated process of squatting, although it will not evict people from established squatting areas—that is, those that were settled by 1 March 1993 (Anon. 1993b). The upgrading of existing squatter settlements is usually a two-stage process of legalization and improvement. The first stage provides security of tenure by en-abling residents to become legal owners or lessees of the land on which they dwell. Improvement usually refers to provision, by the government, of the infrastructure that the residents often cannot supply themselves, such as electricity, water, sew-erage, and the like. The regularization of squatter areas has been an ongoing ac-tivity. Many squatter households or the illegal "landlords" to whom they pay rent, have been attempting to acquire transports for the land, which has often greatly increased in value since being originally settled. The government plans to regular-ize 4,000 units per year up to the year 2000 (Persaud 1994). The objective is not to give title of the land to the squatters, but rather to produce a plan for a recom-mended layout and arrangement of house lots to satisfy the requirements of the Central Board of Health (CBH) and the CHPA. The CBH can then give approval to individual residents for the First and Second Certificates. These certificates are required before the building of infrastructure and upgrading of properties can commence, and they are the prerequisites for passing of title to the land by the Land Registry (Peake 1987). While in theory these certificates could both be acquired within a one-year period, in practice it takes much longer.[17]

In addition, two major slum upgrading projects have been administered by the offices of the CHPA by international agencies in the 1990s: the Urban Rehabilitation Project, sponsored by the Inter-American Development Bank, and the Albouystown Upgrading Pilot Project, sponsored by the United Nations Development Programme. The latter, based in one of the poorest neighborhoods of Georgetown, commenced in January 1990 and is focusing on improving housing through the use of low-cost building materials, infrastructure, and social services. It has faced problems within Albouystown because of entrenched political loyalties, which have resulted in certain groups attempting to usurp the project. The approach of the IDB Urban Rehabilitation Programme is that of improving the physical infrastructure in five urban areas (Georgetown, New Amsterdam, Corriverton, Rose Hall, and Linden), including roads, canals, drains, water supply, sewerage, and street lighting. While socioeconomic surveys were conducted to identify the components of a rehabilitation program, their aim was also to assess the ability of households to pay for infrastructure and services.

In addition there have been no attempts to control the increasing bifurcation of the rental sector into a dual housing market. Renovations of houses, mostly by expatriate Guyanese, for short- and long-term rentals, have resulted in rents being set at approximately US$50 per day. The need by private-sector investors to immediately recoup capital investment costs make it unlikely that this sector will provide housing for low-income groups. The government has stated, however, that it will provide land for private-sector construction of housing to purchase and to rent for all income groups. This would involve an estimated US$31 million per annum, or 7.4 percent of the GDP. The government is also committed to providing G$4 billion for mortgage financing. Of the 4,434 houses to be built each year, over 90 percent will be for low-income units, those costing less than G$1,000,000. But G$1,000,000 is still far too high for low-income groups who, despite the government's assertion of its intention to house low-income groups, still have no alternative to squatting.

Conclusion

After a period of forty years, housing is once again on the national agenda in Guyana. But unlike the 1970s when housing was, at least in rhetoric, recognized as a basic need and human right, the 1990s have heralded in a weak version of a social housing policy. The focus is not on creating redistribution mechanisms to ensure that all are adequately housed, but rather on questions of who will have access to what type of housing and at what standard (see Schlyter 1990). Although low-income groups are considered in current policy, primarily through squatter upgrading and the provision of plots of land, the emphasis is on housing for middle-income groups. Without coherent planning policies which explicitly focus on the needs of low-income groups, and the policy instruments through which they can be met, little can be done to alleviate the dismal conditions under which the vast majority of the population live. Without special efforts to support the poorest, housing conditions will become even more unequal (as exemplified in the lowering of standards for the poorest, rather than an emphasis on bringing high-standard units within their financial reach, which could be achieved, for example, by a repromotion of aided self-help housing). Moreover, the underlying emphasis of current housing policy appears to be the promotion of economic development. For a socially oriented housing policy there also needs to be a consideration of its role in, for example, promoting regional balance and family stability. Any policy initiatives aimed at low-income groups must consider the need for initial low costs and incremental building and servicing. It is these very features that make squatter settlements such an attractive option for the poor and, at the same time, exclude them from formal sector operations.

Until the current government addresses the poverty and loss of hope that characterizes Guyanese life little can change. Although there has been an opening up of political space with the election of the PPP into office, it remains to be seen to what extent it will abandon the authoritarian political culture of its predecessor, the PNC.[18] Yet, the disengagement of the state from commanding all aspects of political, economic, and social affairs is imperative if the Guyanese people are to exercise their democratic rights. Trade unions, NGOs, community groups, and international agencies can all play a role in the provision of housing. For their participation to be meaningful, the support of the government and guidance and coordination by the Ministry of Labour is needed. This would allow both internal and external agencies to concentrate on the mobilization and reconstruction of existing communities. And it is through addressing the needs of low-income women in these communities that the most propitious use will be made of scarce resources. These women have shown themselves to be engaged in the provision and maintenance of housing for themselves and their children at a level that far exceeds that of men (Moser and Peake 1987; Peake 1986, 1987). The current minister for housing recognizes that "the social dynamics of the community centre around women" (Jeffreys 1993). Women's needs for housing are great, given their responsibilities for employment and family survival and their overrepresentation among low-income groups. With a policy focus that puts the empowerment of low-income groups at its core, defined by the needs of low-income women, community participation in squatter upgrading and neighborhood renewal may be the strategy that has most potential in uniting the government and the people and restoring hope to Guyana.

Notes

I would like to thank Rawle Edinboro, Denise de Souza, and Karen de Souza for their comments on an earlier draft. The author alone remains responsible for the views expressed in this chapter.

1. There is also an interior settlement at Bartica which acts as a service center for gold and diamond miners. It had a population of only 6,200 in 1980. The settlement of Anna Regina, on the West Coast Demerara, was officially declared a township in 1990, but its population is approximately only 2,500.

2. An almost complete absence of data prevents the author from including information on Amerindian housing.

3. This is evidenced in the report by Hinckson (n.d.). The section headed "Housing Development in Guyana from 1969–79" outlines a policy that is identical to the one outlined by the interim government in Cummings (1954).

4. The first Aided Self-Help housing scheme was Meadow Brook Gardens Housing Scheme in Greater Georgetown, with 132 two-bedroomed houses (Dick 1984).

5. One example of the latter is Melanie Damishana, situated on the coast, fifteen miles east of Georgetown. Established in 1974, it was built with over four hundred homes, a shopping complex, and a garment factory run by the women's wing of the PNC, the Women's Revolutionary Socialist Movement (WRSM). In the early 1980s collective farming of ten acres of rice was started. Although the village was successful in its establishment (all houses have potable water and electricity) it is now in a state of disrepair. The shopping complex, the WRSM factory and the collective farming venture have all been abandoned. As early as 1965, members established a building cooperative but the decision to own and manage the homes cooperatively was not their own. After the first houses were constructed government officials decided to establish it as a cooperative village. This was not formally communicated to the self-helpers until after a formal announcement by the Prime Minister (Anon. n.d.b). The residents, therefore, were not to receive individual titles until the mortgage for the whole village had been paid in full, but in the mid-1980s they were given individual titles because of confusion caused by communal ownership. The cooperative financial institutions holding the mortgage were ostensibly run on commercial principles (Thomas 1983), hence they wanted individual transports so that they knew to whom they were lending money. Moreover, until they received individual transports, residents defaulted on payments not knowing exactly what they were paying for. The settlement has faced a number of other problems preventing it from operating on the basis of self-reliance. Most of the original occupants worked in Georgetown, preventing the community from developing its own economic base, although there is a range of small industrial establishments within a few miles of the village. Furthermore, its residents were housed not on the basis of need but on the basis of political patronage. The village is well known for housing PNC supporters from the police and the army, and for allegations that members repaid the housing cooperative according to their income rather than the value of the property (Potter 1987).

6. The third development plan (1977–81) was largely undermined by the collapse of world markets for Guyana's staple products (bauxite, sugar, and rice) and by widespread levels of administrative and managerial incompetence.

7. A UNDP report in 1981 took 3,600 units as its starting point. All these figures are substantially below the standard equation of 10 dwelling units per 1,000 population per annum to meet housing need. A population of approximately 740,000 would give a figure of 7,400 new units per annum. The difference in these figures could be attributed to the low level of new household formation, which, in part, is due to the shortage of housing.

8. Since 1990 the CHPA has not produced any annual reports. The CHPA now has three de-

partments: Housing, Town and Country Planning, and Support Services. Town and Country Planning has always been well developed and staffed but the Housing Department only came into being in 1982. Before this housing was considered only in the light of a construction activity.

9. By 1993 it was known that the government had 2,025 rental dwellings on 17 estates, many of which rented for as low as G$18 per month and are in a deplorable condition. Of these 1,767 are to be sold under the Condominium Act of 1990 (this figures include both rental purchase apartments as well as straight rentals).

10. Regional Democratic Councils are the administrative units of local government, spread over ten regions. The system was formalized in 1980 with the Local Democratic Organs Act (plus Acts 28/01 and 28/02). Up to 1973, the precolonial system of local government was in place. Between 1973 and 1980 the system existed without a legal framework, comprising six regions and the three urban areas of Georgetown, New Amsterdam, and Linden. Each of the ten Regional Democratic Councils has attached to them a Regional Planning Unit, ostensibly to allow each region to become the major agent in promoting its own economic development. In practice local government suffers from maladministration and patronage. As opposed to increasing local autonomy the local government system only served to increase the hold the PNC had on aspects of daily life (Strachan 1989). This may change with the democratization of the political system.

11. Various social and economic indicators serve to express the importance of the crises faced by the Guyanese people: the 1990 World Bank Report rated Guyana as the poorest country in the Western hemisphere, placing it, along with Haiti, in the category of the "least developed"; the external debt of US$2.1 billion gives Guyana the highest per capita debt in the world; and in 1991 the minimum wage was the equivalent of US$0.96 per hour (UNICEF 1993).

12. Raw sewage is common in drains because of cracked yard pipes. It is estimated that 90 percent of these pipes are cracked (GOG/IDB 1993a). In most of the low-income, densely populated areas in Georgetown, water supply problems are increasing because of low water pressure. Because the residents do not have storage tanks, it is common practice to break into the water mains to obtain water and the "problem of solid waste management in Georgetown is critical nearing the state of a crisis" (GOG/IDB 1993a: 15).

13. In the smaller urban areas of Linden and New Amsterdam, the percentage of owner occupiers was higher at 48 percent and 64 percent respectively, with a corresponding reduction in the size of the rental sector, at 28 percent and 25 percent respectively.

14. In Toronto, Canada, similar housing styles are called "monster" homes. It is commonly believed that a large proportion of this new building is financed by money from illegal activities such as gold and drug smuggling.

15. Currently under investigation is the use of seashell as an alternative to cement, as well as the use of unfired clay bricks.

16. The government has recently acquired ten thousand acres from the Sugar Corporation for distribution to individuals and private-sector companies.

17. My 1987 study of a women's ASH cooperative housing group, the Virginia Women's Homestead, set up in the 1970s when the housing drive was at its peak, revealed that it took them over four years to acquire their certificates.

18. Also it remains to be seen to what extent the election of the PPP will serve to stem the flow of Indo-Guyanese out of the country. If Indo-Guyanese now perceive that there is a role for them to play in the economy and the rate of out-migration falls, then the shortage of housing will become an even greater problem.

References

Anon. (n.d.a) "The Role of Women in Housing." Unpublished paper. Ministry of Housing, Georgetown.

————. (n.d.b) "Melanie Damishana. Development as a Co-operative Community." Unpublished paper, Ministry of Housing, Georgetown.

————. (1993a) "Labour Ministry Now Responsible for Housing." *Sunday Mirror,* 7 Feb., 1.

————. (1993b) "Homes for Sale!" *Stabroek News,* 14 Apr., 20.

Baken, R., and J. van der Linden. (1993) "Getting the Incentives Right; Banking on the Formal Private Sector. A Critique of World Bank Thinking on Low-Income Housing Delivery in World Cities." *Third World Planning Review* 15 (1): 1–23.

Barclay, G. (1994) "Jeffrey Announces Plans for 31,035 houses by 2000." *Guyana Chronicle,* 16 Mar.

Bureau of Statistics. (1992) *Guyana Statistical Bulletin, 1992.* Georgetown: Bureau of Statistics.

Central Housing and Planning Authority. (n.d.) *Draft National Housing Policy.* Georgetown: Central Planning and Housing Authority.

Central Housing and Planning Authority. (1990) *Annual Report.* Georgetown: Central Housing and Planning Authority.

Cummings, P. (1954) "Housing Policy." Unpublished paper. Ministry of Labour, Health and Housing, Georgetown.

Daly, V. T. (1976) *A Short History of the Guyanese People.* London: Macmillan Education.

Dick, C. (1984) "A Review of Official Policies and Achievements Regarding Housing in Guyana under the People's National Congress Government." Unpublished paper. Ministry of Housing, Georgetown.

GOG\IDB (Government of Guyana/Inter American Development Bank). (1993a) *Urban Rehabilitation Program. Draft Report on Condition of Physical Components.* Georgetown: Government of Guyana.

————. (1993b) *Urban Rehabilitation Program. Report on Socio-Economic Surveys, 1992.* Georgetown: Government of Guyana.

Hanson, D. (1981) "Low Income Housing." Discussion paper. World Bank/ CHPA, Georgetown.

Hinckson, J. (n.d.) "A Decade of Housing in Guyana." Unpublished paper. CHPA, Georgetown.

Jeffreys, H. (1993) Personal interview, Aug. Conducted at Central Planning and Housing Authority, Georgetown.

Moser, C., and L. Peake, eds. (1987) *Women, Human Settlements and Housing.* London: Tavistock.

Ministry of Public Welfare (Housing). (1981) *Guyana's Housing Drive.* Georgetown: Ministry of Public Welfare (Housing).

Peake, L. (1986) "Low-Income Women's Participation in the Housing Process: A Case Study from Guyana." *Development and Planning Unit Gender and Planning Working Paper* 10. University College, London.

————. (1987) "Government Housing Policy and Its Implications for Women in Guyana." In C. Moser and L. Peake, eds., *Women, Human Settlements and Housing,* 113–38. London: Tavistock.

Persaud, G. (1994) "'I Am Not the Minister of Squatting'—Jeffrey." *Stabroek News,* 16 Mar.

Potter, L. (1987) "Guyana: Co-operative Socialism, Planning and Reality." In D. Forbes and N. Thrift, eds., *The Socialist Third World: Urban Development and Territorial Planning,* 214–49. London: Blackwell.

Roopnaraine, R. (1992) "Presentation and Panel Discussion II." In D. Watson and C. Craig, eds., *Guyana at the Crossroads,* 25–32. North-South Centre, University of Miami.

Schlyter, A. (1990) "Zimbabwe." In K. Mathéy, ed., *Housing Policies in the Socialist Third World,* 197–226. London: Mansell.

Strachan, A. (1989) "Guyana." in R. B. Potter, ed., *Urbanization, Planning and Development in the Caribbean,* 140–60. London: Mansell.

Thomas, C. (1983) "State Capitalism in Guyana: An Assessment of Burnham's Co-operative Socialist Republic." In F. Ambursley and R. Cohen, eds. *Crisis in the Caribbean,* 27–48. London: Heinemann.

———. (1993) "Poverty in Guyana." Revised draft report prepared for the Economic Commission for Latin America and the Caribbean.

UNICEF. (1993) *Analysis of the Situation of Women and Children in Guyana.* Georgetown: UNICEF, UNDP.

Chapter 8

A Critical Review of State Involvement in Housing in Trinidad and Tobago

Linda Hewitt

Contemporary housing problems in Trinidad and Tobago are no different from the fundamental issues debated globally and regionally about the role of the state, the policy measures it should adopt, and whether it should become directly involved in construction activity to deliver homes to people in need. As the chapters in this volume show, in every Caribbean country, a significant proportion of the population is poor and has insufficient means to provide affordable homes, thereby becoming dependent upon the state. The latter, recognizing its responsibility of maintaining a population that is adequately housed, must determine what the bounds of this responsibility should be, given other competing demands. The inevitable question is: can the state ensure that people have their basic need for shelter adequately met?

A further difficulty facing the Trinidadian housing sector today is that unmet needs are being felt by wealthier income groups, during the prolonged recessionary trend which has been experienced by Caribbean countries, among others, in the hemisphere. The state has found itself more unable than ever to adequately provide for the increasing number of people, the poor and not-so-poor, whose disadvantaged situations have become much more pronounced in the wake of structural adjustment policies and programs. Many have seen their means diminished, either on account of income loss or unemployment. The poor are thereby doubly disadvantaged in the competition for scarce housing.

To a great extent, the history of low-income housing in Trinidad and Tobago has been closely tied to phases of development of the plantation economy which characterize colonial dependencies in the Caribbean. As Trinidad and Tobago passed through successive phases—of enslaved labor which ended with emancipation, indentureship, and then to varying dimensions of the private- and state-controlled plantocracy—different housing styles have evolved, many of which are still on view today.

The population censuses, taken every ten years, evidence the gradual disappearance of earlier housing forms, with "modern construction forms" displacing vernacular styles in all but the most rural and remote regions of the country. Particularly during the last century, progressive changes in the economic order enabled some among the population to ascend to occupations providing reliable incomes. This enabled them to acquire housing for their families, independent of the state. During the last three decades, there has been some sharing of responsibility for the provision of low-income shelter, with the state, a few private companies involved in agricultural and petroleum production, and the people themselves contributing. Today, while a large proportion of the more than three hundred thousand households have been able to avail themselves of some form of reasonable housing, a significant proportion remain in need. The state now faces a major challenge to relieve conditions which have accumulated as a consequence of the prolonged housing deficiency situation. These include extensive squatting on state and private lands, increasing homelessness and vagrancy, urban-accommodation overcrowding and severely limited rental markets, and the situation of many rural households still living in substandard housing (see Potter and O'Flaherty 1995).

This chapter about state involvement in housing in Trinidad and Tobago critically reviews the evolution of the housing problem and how the state has responded over the years to meeting citizens' housing needs. Over the years, the response of the state to housing needs can be cast within definite time periods associated with regime shifts and transitions: namely, before 1956, the periods 1956–62, 1963–72, 1973–85, 1986–90, and 1991 to the present. All of these phases represent periods of economic and social significance in the economic history of the country and in the twists and turns of state policy and practices towards housing the poor and the not-so-poor. Such regime effects (also discussed by Klak and Peake in chapters 6 and 7), are seen to be strongly influenced by external agency directives, especially during the transitions of governments. However, these external influences appear to have contributed to continuities in housing policy directions, rather than a usurpation of state mandates, as neoliberal theorizing would dictate.

A Brief Profile of Trinidad and Tobago

Trinidad and Tobago is a small island state of 1.2 million people distributed over a relatively small land area which is further constrained by topographic extremes limiting human settlement. A little over half of this land area (57 percent), measuring 1,236,750 acres, consists of natural and secondary forest and swamplands, while 34 percent is either under agricultural cultivation or reserved for it. Of the remaining area, 9 percent consists of built-up areas and the rest accommodates scattered settlements and other miscellaneous usages. The limited land area is shared among twelve major administrative regions, as shown in table 8.1. Housing demand and supply must therefore be understood within the context of these limiting circumstances of scarce physical infrastructural endowments.

Politically, the country was "discovered" in 1498, the result of Spanish conquest, but was subsequently fought over several times, becoming the object of virtual tug-o-wars involving the British, Spanish, French, and Dutch colonial powers. It thus came to bear the mark of each of these sovereignties, even in legacies of housing and architecture. The occupations of the latter two powers were largely short-lived, but Spanish rule extended from 1498 to 1757. The English became longtime rulers until the granting of political self-government in 1956. Since then, Trinidad and Tobago has undergone constitutional changes through independence in 1962 to the Republican status it has now held since 1982.

Table 8.1

Population and Land Distribution, Number and Percentage and Size of Households by Administrative Regions, 1980, 1990

Region	Acreage	Population 1980	Population 1990	Households 1990	Distribution 1990 (%)	Average Household Size 1990
Port-of-Spain	2,368	58,427	50,878	12,654	4.60	3.37
San Fernando	1,600	34,154	30,092	6,871	2.50	3.85
Arima	2,986	24,645	29,695	6,165	2.24	4.30
Point-Fortin	6,272	16,710	20,025	4,986	1.82	3.73
St. George	227,241	384,624	445,620	100,376	36.52	3.93
Nariva/Mayaro	225,277	31,167	36,781	7,760	2.82	4.33
St. Andrew/ St. David	231,486	50,937	62,944	13,857	5.04	4.25
Caroni	136,951	141,319	177,189	38,546	14.03	4.38
Victoria	201,011	187,009	210,833	45,762	16.65	4.32
St. Patrick	160,640	107,202	120,129	26,471	9.63	4.25
Tobago	40,743	39,524	50,282	11,298	4.15	3.95
Trinidad and Tobago	1,235,750	1,075,718	1,234,388	274,846	100.00	4.05

With respect to its economic resource base, Trinidad and Tobago has remained almost wholly dependent upon its primary production of petroleum, natural gas, and related products, which provided extensive funds to support accelerated housing construction for only a brief time. The "bonanza" was relatively short-lived, and the collapse of oil prices on the international market in 1985 ushered in austerity and restructuring imperatives. From this time on, the state's preoccupation with meeting external debt repayments has adversely affected plans for social and welfare investments, especially towards housing. The harsh economic times have been marked by high unemployment rates (rising to over 20 percent), by appreciable reductions in family incomes, and by losses of jobs for many who formerly had been favorably placed with respect to access to housing. A considerable proportion of citizenry has been returned to increased dependency upon the state at a time when it is struggling with meeting the needs of the poor, and addressing an accumulated housing deficit that is at near-crisis proportions. The following sections critically document the successive phases of state policy making, the successes and failures that led to the present situation; scarcely one of promise, but with a plethora of lessons to be heeded.

Housing in the Early Period of Colonialism

History books do not normally reserve a place for housing issues in the lives of people whose history they so meticulously detail. Confirmation of this is evident in the index of a very detailed historical publication covering the period from 1498 to 1900, which makes no mention of housing in relation to the plantation slaves from Africa nor the East Indian indentured laborers or Chinese who were the former's replacements in the plantation labor force (Carmichael 1948). Yet, the barrack-styled units (fig. 8.1) and densely packed "creole" and "ajoupa" types (see Klass 1961 and Hudson chapter 2 of this volume for more detailed descriptions of these styles) characterized vernacular housing provisions which were essential to the maintenance and survival in the sugar industry of these early times (fig. 8.2). In contrast, high-ranking officials belonging to the government administration and to the plantocracy of estate owners and overseers housed themselves in replicas of "great houses" derived from colonial architectural styles of the mother countries. Here, a brief interpretation of colonial housing conditions can be elicited from accounts of the social and economic conditions and the history of Trinidad and Tobago's plantation economies. The Spanish Cedular of 1789 formulated by Trinidad's Governor Chacon made stipulations to the effect that owners were required to provide adequate accommodation for their slave workers so as to protect them from the weather and that they should permit no more than two persons to a room. The laws relating to immigration in 1899 further stipulated that employers of immigrant labor should provide suitable dwellings, and should keep these in sufficient repair, well roofed and water-tight. There were also specifications with respect to the dimensions of single and family dwellings. But these stipulations could hardly be interpreted as a state policy intended to meet housing needs. Rather, they were intended to maintain the health of members of the labor force who were of immense value to the plantation economy.

Fig. 8.1. Barracks housing, Chancery Lane, Port of Spain.

Fig. 8.2. Trinidadian "Creole" vernacular housing.

The Evolution of Early Housing Forms before 1956

The conditions under which estate workers were housed were almost wholly determined by the requirements of the plantation economy, which consisted of large sugar estates and other similar agricultural holdings given to the growing of staple crops: coffee and cacao, for example. Barrack-type units were the first to emerge, some of which can still be seen today, even in the capital city of Port of Spain (fig. 8.1). These were deliberately designed to serve the system of agricultural estate production, which required a clustering of housing accommodation to provide close proximity to the workplace and to exercise control over the work force residing therein. The succeeding phase of indentureship occasioned further modification of plantation and rural housing styles, commensurate with the ethnic composition of the laboring populations of East Indian and Chinese extraction. Ajoupa-type' units were thus added to the low-income population housing stock, which was predominantly rural in location (see Hudson chapter 2).

In the years which followed emancipation and indentureship, those who fled the plantation established widely scattered village settlements, with shelter provisions acquired at the most modest means. But, according to Woodville Marshall's (1971) account on the ascent of a Caribbean peasantry, many workers still remained tied to the plantation, if not to their original place of enslavement. Only knowing plantation work, many sold their labor in return for permanent residential accommodation on the plantation. Accounting for the rise and fall of the peasantry, Marshall contends that many of the workers eventually broke loose from this arrangement due to insecurity of tenure, low wages, and high rents. Of those who established themselves as reconstituted peasants, many only possessed a "house-spot" and a "garden," being merely able to acquire the smallest of land holdings.

The population of Trinidad and Tobago was under one hundred thousand in 1861, a year that strategically marked three decades since the end of mercantilist activity and the transportation of enslaved and indentured workers to work on sugar estates and to live in the most rudimentary of housing conditions. Another three decades later, as revealed by the census data of 1891, 74 percent of the gainfully occupied population were still relatively unskilled: they were classified as agricultural and general laborers, as well as engaged in low-ranking, personal-service occupations. There was hardly much of a change in their overall housing conditions, therefore, even with the exodus of workers from the estates and plantations. The plantocracy retained responsibility for the provision of housing their workers, which they accomplished in their time-honored manner: meagerly.

There is little evidence, too, of a state housing policy which sought to address other citizens' needs at this time, since there was not even a recognition of the existence of an aspiring peasantry. As Marshall (1971) puts it: "Neither the Colonial Office nor the local legislature exerted themselves, at first, to assist peasant development. Government's attitude was modified only when discontent and restlessness among peasants and labourers combined with prolonged depression in the sugar industry during the 1890s and again in the 1930s, became widespread" (2). Instead, several commissions were appointed to enquire into the causes of discontent and disturbances which arose among the laboring population. These included the Royal West Indian Commission in 1897, the Sugar Commission of 1929, and the Moyne Commission of 1939.

The social conditions and ensuing events which led up to these enquiries merit recounting. According to the 1931 census, the population constituted 448,000 persons, made up of agricultural workers and their dependents, and the condition of the working class was described as "a social and economic study of poverty" (Central Bureau of Statistics 1949). The accuracy of this assessment is endorsed by events in the lives of the ordinary people, who participated in riots, and the workers, who participated in strikes: both were protesting against the sugar and oil industries. The emergence and participation of trade unions culminated in the memorable strikes of the 1937 era. Increasingly desperate living conditions, escalating rents, and the general unavailability of work, therefore, fueled discontent. Disturbances spread from estate to estate.

These critical years, then, were dubbed a period of "Working Class Revolt." They marked the emergence of trade unionism with an agenda dedicated to fighting for better wages and working conditions for working-class people. The efforts extended beyond the sugar workers. It is reported that "the rise of a new and vigorous oil industry caused the kind of industrial development which led to the demand for a better quality of labour requiring higher wages and better working and housing conditions" (Ramdin 1982: 89). The reference to housing is significant, since at this time any improvement in the shelter situation of the population rested heavily with prospects for meeting the related needs for meaningful and secure employment and better wages.

This indeed was among the terms of reference of a Colonial Advisory Committee set up in the wake of the 1937 riots and mandated to "study the most effective means of bettering health, wages and hours of work, housing and working conditions and the enforcement of minimum wage legislation," this being one of five major areas of focus. Still, as reported (Ramdin 1982: 147), despite the implementations of both the Forster and Moyne Commissions of 1937 and 1939 (and the passing of the Slum Clearance and Housing Ordinance No. 41), there was scarcely any improvement in the industrial and social conditions of the workers. They were receiving poor wages below the rising cost of living, and many were underemployed. In reference to housing and sanitation, the situation was described as "deplorable and indefensible and compounded by illiteracy" (Ramdin 1982: 6).

Neither extensive land distribution nor the adoption of an agrarian policy followed, so much so that yet another enquiry into the conditions of the population had to be instituted (Simey 1948). Repeating previous commissions' findings, Lord T. S. Simey's 1946–48 appraisal of living conditions in his frequently referenced *Social Welfare Planning in the West Indies* bore testimony to the fact that the bulk of the population had been left to fend for itself. "Philanthropic sentiments" did not translate into actions, however.

For all of the years following and beyond the 1940s, the low-income population was destined to remain too poor to independently afford decent shelter of its own. Between 1901 and 1946, no significant transformation in the occupational profile of the largely unskilled work force was evident, there being little indication that a significant proportion of the population had sufficient means to provide themselves with housing beyond the modest levels of earlier plantation days. According to the census of 1946, the population of gainfully occupied workers was still largely unskilled, constituting 48 percent, and made up of agricultural laborers and persons engaged in low-ranking occupations; in particular, urban personal services. The proportion of skilled workers scarcely increased at all: from 16.9 percent in 1891 to 17.6 percent in 1946.

The population of 544,624 in 1946 was distributed in 135,384 households, a significant number, 22,837 (16.5 per cent), being one-person households. There were 57,986 dwelling houses, 5,740 divided dwellings, 8,589 barrack-type dwellings, and 5,988 rooms in yards. Small families of five persons and less made up 48.6 percent of the total and large families of six and more members, 49.9 percent. According to the 1946 census data, 37.5 percent of the dwellings were one-roomed and 43.8 percent had two or three rooms. The average family and household size was 4.02, whilst the ratio of persons per room averaged 1.77.

A surrogate indicator of the physical quality of the housing at this time is construction materials. In this regard, a relatively high proportion (32.8 percent) of units were constructed of "tapia," a low-cost, nondurable material constantly in need of replacement and/or repair. Some 49.6 percent of the houses were constructed of wood, a more durable material, yet certainly not "modern" and socially accepted as a suitable building material for this urbanizing society. These then were the general characteristics of the housing situation which the newly independent state inherited in the post-colonial decades. With this as the benchmark, the state might genuinely claim some credit for improving the overall quality of housing in Trinidad and Tobago, both in terms of numbers provided and in terms of improvements of the physical quality of life and environmental conditions for some, if not all, of its citizens.

State Involvement in Housing
Provision Begins: 1956-1972

When the first national government of Trinidad and Tobago, the Peoples National Movement (PNM), won its mandate to administer the affairs of state in 1956, there were distinct policy issues to be faced, not the least of which were those concerned with housing. From this time on, there has been no dearth of rhetoric on the part of the state, claiming housing provision to citizens in need as a priority. Housing policy statements have been clearly documented and enunciated in as many forums as opportunities presented themselves, with government officials or technocrats elaborating upon elements of the policy framework(s) within which housing programs are to be mounted. This was the contextual platform for the state's position on housing: distinguished, in part, in terms of a post-colonial legacy and as a rhetorical stance at the threshold of self-government. The housing situation was, to put it mildly, grim: a consequence of accumulated neglect over so many years of colonial administration.

State provision of housing effectively began in the post-colonial years, so that, between 1956 and 1960, only a modest yield of 348 units was realized. It was the problems of the overcrowding of the capital city of Port of Spain and the uncontrolled settlement of its immediate precincts at Malick and Morvant, and of the southern town of San Fernando and its encroaching environs of Pleasantville, that brought early responses from the state to the critical housing situations in those rapidly urbanizing areas. These areas had been the recipient of urban-bound streams of migrants from almost every rural area throughout the country (Government of Trinidad and Tobago n.d.), as well as from neighboring West Indian islands.

At the institutional level, a Sugar Industry Welfare Fund was established, an aided self-help educational program mounted, and a National Housing Census conducted in 1957. During 1957–62, well over 36,000 applications for housing were received. In response, the state only managed to provide 5,900 units; most were rental apartments at locations in East Port of Spain and eastern San Fernando. So intense was the demand, especially from low-income households, that a National Housing Authority (NHA) was established in 1962, with responsibilities and functions of a much wider scope than its predecessor, the Planning and Housing Commission. This institution had the responsibility for executing state housing policies and did so at first through the allocation and maintenance of rental units and the supervision of housing loans and mortgages.

The first explicit housing policy was documented in the second Five Year Development Plan of 1964–69. The state undertook responsibility for directly providing housing in the form of apartment units (flats), to be administered by the National Housing Authority. NHA was mandated to service the housing needs of the low-income sector in particular, but it was also authorized to implement financial schemes to assist lower middle-income prospective homeowners. Then, the Trinidad and Tobago Mortgage Finance Company was established in 1965, with an operating capital of TT$4.8 million, and tax concessions were given to private developers as incentives to participate in these housing provision plans. The latter, however, restricted their interest to meeting middle-income households' needs. These policy-backed incentives and the state's own efforts resulted in some 10,869 units being built between 1957 and 1968. The state, however, all-too-quickly became the sole provider of housing for low-income groups in society.

Another dimension of the state's involvement in the housing sector was with respect to urban redevelopment and especially the clearance of urban slums, which had become visible "eye-sores" to those in authority. An Urban Redevelopment Corporation (URC) was established in 1971 in response to what appeared to be unceasing in-migration to an already overcrowded capital city, Port of Spain. In this regard, the "City Proper" (as the census depicted it) had reached a peak population of 93,954 persons in 1960, so that this perceived pressure on city resources and infrastructure "rationalized" state action. The problems (real or imagined is not at issue) posed by this uncontrolled pattern of settlement have been highlighted in studies by Simpson (1974), Clarke (1974), Hewitt (1975, 1977) and Conway (1981).

URC undertook a comprehensive sociodemographic study of the East Port of Spain area during 1971–72 (see fig. 8.3), intending to redevelop the area, while at the same time addressing the issue of small-island immigration, which was felt to be causing such peripheral overcrowding (see Conway 1981 for a dissenting view). Redevelopment action was also to entail the removal of persons from squatter areas around the city, temporarily relocating them into decanting centers until more permanent arrangements could be made for their resettlement. Little came of these efforts, in large part because the nation's economic health at the time was scarcely favorable: bluntly, state revenues were depleted. When the cost of carrying out the redevelopment programs was realized, the state lacked the revenue, the political will, or both to carry out any major redevelopment in the Laventille area, beyond some apartment building and squatter-relocation efforts. Success Village, a planned site for redevelopment in the Laventille hills of East Port of Spain, was commandeered by those able to afford such modest housing. Once again, the poor were left to their own devices.

Substantial Housing Provision in the Period 1973-1985

By 1975, the state coffers had made significant economic recovery through the

Fig. 8.3. John John (East Dry River), Laventille Hills, East Port of Spain.

receipt of unprecedented high revenues derived from the sale of oil and natural gas on the international market, beginning in 1974. The next seven years came to be known as the "oil boom years." In part prompted by this economic windfall, the state was to become much more involved in the provision of housing units than it had ever planned to be. With prosperity, heightened activity in the construction sector ensued. However, the problem of low-income housing provision was not about to be solved, nor was any of the burden shared by private developers and financiers. Low-income housing was to remain a problem that nobody else wanted. The state therefore redefined its housing policy as follows: a) to become involved in land development; b) to construct multiple-occupancy accommodation units; c) to provide soft loans to prospective homeowners to aid in the purchasing of units; d) to encourage the mass production of houses.

Was it that then Prime Minister Dr. Eric Williams (1971) was being disingenuous when he pronounced that "[t]he Government was bound to adopt policies and plan its own action which, when undertaken, can lead in some co-ordinated fashion, to a solution which does not cut across the grain of the government industrial, social and economic policies and its priority of providing for the low income groups"? As if to prove Eric Williams right, there were contradictions arising from the pursuit of all these ambitious housing objectives all at once. What followed was the establishment of a rather extensive and complex state machinery which became involved in various aspects of housing delivery. The private sector was known for its reluctance to serve the interest of low-income groups, but they were promptly coopted by the state into the web of activities designed to provide housing. Substantial funds were channeled through approved financial institutions, but by the time all the qualifying prerequisites for accessing these funds were processed, only those better-off persons with incomes sufficient to afford the mortgages offered stood to benefit. It was then left to the state once more to take on the responsibility of providing for the poor. Although during this period an intense program of housing construction was undertaken, the numbers fell far short of satisfying the needs of those most in want. Similar shortfalls in production performance occurred in the French Caribbean, as detailed in chapter 11 by Condon and Ogden. Estimates suggest that only 25 percent of the housing units built during this "boom" period went to low-income persons (tables 8.2 and 8.3). What were some of the reasons for this sad state of affairs?

Table 8.2

Balance Sheet Indicating Housing Demand and Supply for Trinidad and Tobago, 1980–1990

Demand		Supply	
1.1 Total households 1980 Units in good condition 10–20 yrs. old—58% existing	235,100 136,360	1.1 Public sector provision Ongoing: 1981–85 Projected:1985–90	 5,000
1.2 Units in poor condition (over 20 yrs. old)	98,740	2.0 Private sector provision	
1.3 Overcrowding— households sharing	23,620	Individuals Developers Additions/Repairs	 1,653
2.1 Total deficit up to 1980	122,360	Total	10,110
2.2 Increments to households 1980–90—4,200 per annum	40,200		
Add replacement from 20 yr. old units in 1980 19,700	59,900		
2.3 Total demand to 1990	182,260		
Total Annual Demand	18,230	Average Total Annual Supply	10,100

Table 8.3

New Dwellings and Additions to Housing Stock, 1961–1990

Year	Number of Units
Pre-1961	72,115
1961–69	4,609
1970–77	6,713
1978	8,438
1979	9,669
1980	7,761
1980–87	10,845
1988	7,067
1989	6,435
1990	4,506

Eckstein (1981) describes the escalation in housing costs that took place during 1974–77 as "unbelievable" and contends that the prevailing oil price–induced bonanza was largely responsible. At the onset, there was a shortage of funds available to financial institutions as well as limited investment opportunities. Consequently, there was too much inflexibility in government legislation as it related to the composition of investment portfolios. In effect, the oil revenues quickly built to a glut of domestic financial capital, and, with too few outlets for investment, conditions were ripe for an untrammeled diversion of huge sums into housing-sector transactions. There ensued a lot of speculation on all fronts of the housing and real estate markets. Every item's price spiraled upwards—housing, land, wage rates for construction workers, the price of building materials, and the fees charged by professionals in the construction industry (Eckstein 1981). A plot of land which fetched TT$4,200 in 1974 became valued at TT$35,000 a year or so later. A house which could be bought for TT$15,000 in 1973 was selling for TT$117,000 and a TT$40,000 house for TT$280,000. All these price changes occurred in five years or less. This was the inflationary scenario at the time. Furthermore, there was a strong bias towards mortgaging loans and agreements for building, which disadvantaged lower-income people even further. Rapidly rising costs and the imposed terms and conditions of long-term borrowing in the private market, therefore, provided further legitimacy to the state's wholesale involvement in the provision of low-cost housing.

Ellis (1983) estimated the value of varying elements of construction cost which prevailed during this oil boom period, as well as appraised the shift from conventional methods to the system method of prefabricated and high-density housing construction. Extensive increases in all of the component elements of labor, material, and transport pushed home-building costs from TT$29.47 per square foot in

1975 to TT$118.00 in 1982 for a typical, low-income house. The rate of price increase averaged between 1.5 percent and 2 percent per month (Ellis 1983).

For the record, the state became more involved in the actual construction of low-income housing during this period than it had ever been before. There were no fewer than four public agencies entrusted with carrying out state housing policies. The National Housing Authority was charged with the responsibility of maintaining existing housing estates, seeing to the needs of low-income earners, providing emergency shelter to the temporarily dislocated and persons made homeless, and overseeing the development of construction sites and the administration of lending programs. A National Insurance Property Development Company was also established to administer and monitor large housing projects, and a Housing Task Force became involved in the design and delivery of several housing projects. In addition, the state established financial institutions to undertake the disbursing of loans to prospective homeowners, although this latter facility more commonly served middle-income buyers.

In order to meet the number of units targeted to be built in the specified time, large-scale residential projects were designed and prefabricated construction systems employed. Ellis (1983) held the view that this shift to the system method of building provided understandable trade-offs, since the faster completion rate offset high production costs. Others criticized the state's redirection and argued that the prevailing labor situation was one of a large, unemployed work force ready and waiting to be absorbed into conventional building ventures. As if in negation of his opinion, Ellis's calculations had shown that it was less costly to build single housing units than the high-density flats and apartments that the state undertook to promote. Eventually, other fiscal disadvantages surfaced, but not before several thousands of these type of units were produced (table 8.3).

As a result of this extensive involvement, the state alone provided some 8,200 units at residential estates which now bear the names Malabar, La Horquetta, Maloney, Bonair, and Valencia in the north of the country and Embarcadere in the south: all located where "building-space" was available for parceling such large areas. These were, by design, high-density housing projects constructed by prefabricated systems methods. They served to relocate thousands of persons, many of whom had grown used to town and city life and were very much dependent upon urban/metropolitan services such as health, education, recreation, and the full range of means to earn a livelihood. Here in these distant state-created "dormitory communities," as they came to be called, many of these estate residents continued to commute to the cities (Port of Spain and San Fernando) on a daily basis to access the services and jobs they were attached to, such as schools, employment, and other types of retailing services. The problems of long commutes and the daily living stresses which arose are worthy of study, but are beyond the scope of this chapter.

Political Change, State Policy, and Program Shifts, 1986-1991

Trinidad and Tobago's State policies for housing provision abruptly changed with the defeat of the Peoples National Movement (PNM) government after thirty years of rule, in 1986. The National Alliance For Reconstruction (NAR) defeated the PNM and brought radical changes of policy with respect to housing provision for the needy. The policy measures NAR enunciated were as follows: a) to undertake responsibility for providing various forms of relief to the housing situation of the population; b) to promote initiatives in housing technology, in particular, and to use indigenous types of materials and methods in housing construction; c) to provide support for self-help efforts; d) to establish a facility within the housing sector which would have the capability of producing trained professionals and technicians with skills in construction technology; e) to promote the development of communities in newly developed housing estates; and f) to develop mechanisms for proper evaluation of housing programs.

These objectives were to be achieved through a variety of measures: the provision of high-density housing; the institution of land banking and development; the involvement of the private sector; the resettlement of communities; and squatter regularization and rent control. A National Settlement Programme was subsequently instituted with an organizational structure consisting of a Project Execution Unit and a specialist consultant in housing programs. The program was supported by special loans from the Inter-American Development Bank for Reconstruction (IADB).

The philosophy underlying the settlement approach was derived from the concept of the *"Sou Sou,"* a Trinidadian Creole expression describing the practice of achieving things in an incremental fashion, "bit by bit," as it translates literally. The term "Sou Sou Land" had been adopted earlier, in 1983, as the project name for the activity of a private, nongovernmental organization whose objective was to provide land for the landless who wished to make a start in acquiring their own homes. One advocate described the Sou Sou Land approach as the birth of a home-grown initiative that had the potential for laying a basis for a genuine Caribbean approach to providing civilized environments for people (Laughlin 1988). One of its underlying principles was that, even amidst a situation of economic hardship, shelter could be provided for those in need at terms and prices that would be affordable.

Not too long after the launching of this new initiative, the NAR minister of finance, Selby Wilson, commenced his address to a housing conference, with a statement to the effect that his government was dedicated to finding new and creative ways of achieving the goals and satisfying the needs of lower-income groups for housing within the constraints of limited resources. He assured the gathering that his government was committed to the view that there should be an appropriate partnership in which government and all the social and economic groups fully participated in the development process, since the state was fully cognizant of its responsibility to ensure that all social groups were entitled to the basic amenities of life. The policy of the state would be extended further, the minister assured his audience, to enable the creation of an environment that was conducive to facilitating the flow of resources to the housing construction sector. Specifically, financial incentives and appropriate infrastructure would be provided to encourage private-sector activity in housing construction and to direct such activity through policies and programs which would make housing more accessible to the poor and thereby help the improvement and enhancement of the housing stock.

The enunciation of such a progressive housing policy seemed inopportune, since it was being expressed at a time when stringent economic stabilization and adjustment measures were beginning to dominate state decision making. In the same year, 1987, the NAR government of Trinidad and Tobago adopted structural adjustment measures under direction from the World Bank, which carried conditionalities principally designed to curb public-sector spending, even in relation to social sector programs. Housing became affected, along with education and health: all suffered reductions. The details of these economic measures are too extensive to be presented here, but the conditionalities were such that, even when the state was provider, the affordability of housing was severely compromised.

Undaunted, the NAR's principal housing strategy was the adoption of the *Settlement Programme* approach as a vehicle for providing shelter for low-income persons in need. The Settlement Programme initiated in 1987 marked a dramatic shift in the state's usual approach to addressing the nation's housing problems. No longer was there to be direct involvement by the state in constructing and distributing finished housing units. Rather, the state perceived itself as an "enabler" and "facilitator," providing affordable land as well as attractive financing arrangements to enable prospective homeowners to acquire their own homes. The regularization of squatters was to be another aspect of the strategy towards housing provision. Renovating depressed urban areas was another part of the strategy, and the incremental development of decentralized settlements yet another.

The state, therefore, rationalized the adoption of the settlement emphasis as a synthetic approach, encompassing issues of population distribution, housing and land development, and the provision of social services. It was felt that resolution of these settlement issues could be better achieved within a framework in which social and economic planning are pursued together. Settlements could be planned and organized at the national, regional, and local levels. The state sought to justify this focus, arguing that such a settlement approach was the more appropriate means of addressing the housing problem within a wider context, where other social and economic needs are being determined and planned.

The philosophy behind this new synthetic approach was outlined in an address given by the acting minister of housing at a housing seminar in 1988. In his speech the following principles were espoused. The needs of lower-income groups were particularly urgent ones, estimated to be 80 percent of the total unmet amount. Housing and homeownership constituted a stabilizing force in the society. Land distribution policy is essential to the shelter/settlement solution. Measures employed to solve the settlement/shelter problem could also stimulate economic activity, and the private sector must also be an active partner in housing provision for the poor and needy (Sanderson 1988).

The Settlement Programme outlined by the NAR was clearly guided by these interpretations and perceptions of the housing and settlement needs of the poor. Lands were to be developed and distributed to qualified applicants. Existing squatter communities were to be provided with rights to the parcels of land which they occupied, and badly needed infrastructure would be provided or the available infrastructure upgraded in a manner which would enhance the present landscape. The provision of basic amenities, such as piped water, drainage, electricity, and sewer disposal, would be part of the package also.

Despite these good-intentioned pronouncements by the state, duly qualified with an admittance of its reduced financial circumstances, the promised delivering of low-income housing seemed to be at odds with reality. Fiscally, the country was on the verge of economic bankruptcy and under IMF/World Bank stringency terms. The number of housing units estimated to be needed was between eight and ten thousand every year, through to the year 2000, if any impression on the accumulated deficit which had accrued over the many years of inactivity within the housing sector were to be made (table 8.2). The state may have been quite aware of what the needs were, but clearly lacked the financial resources to adequately address the problem.

The performance of the Trinidadian State therefore has to be assessed against the limiting economic circumstances which prevailed. The options which were chosen were directed towards providing prepared housing sites with the services required to build viable communities. Self-help initiatives were encouraged, and the provision of starter homes on a limited scale constituted the main thrust of housing policy. Notwithstanding the stringencies accompanying any state action, the issue of lowering standards sparked off intense debate among planners and construction professionals, who felt that building codes, health and sanitary requirements, proper drainage, and other essential infrastructural facilities ought to be met. These issues remained a major bone of contention. On the one hand, the realities of the economic situation suggested that the rigid standards normally applied to building construction could be eased somewhat in order to keep costs within affordable limits. On the other hand, the state could not be party to the violation of established building codes.

By the end of the NAR government's term of office, few of the policy objectives had been achieved or were even underway. Out of the checklist consisting of creating viable settlements, providing land for the landless, creating job opportunities, revitalizing villages, creating small farming communities, and cultivating self-reliance, self-help, and self-sufficiency among the many groups, most were far from having been realized. And, since the five-year term seemed rather short to realistically expect so comprehensive an outcome, reasonable speculation was aired about whether such laudable objectives were ever achievable in the first place.

Housing Policy and Program Continuities(?)—1991 to the Present

There is always the danger that, with a change in regime, ongoing policies and programs are discontinued prematurely or, perhaps worse, completely reversed. Such a situation becomes even more critical where economic resources are in short supply and where new political priorities must be established because of the reversal of political mandates. Trinidad and Tobago appeared ripe for discord in housing policy, and yet another change in direction, as was done when the NAR came into power. But for the fact that certain special circumstances instrumental to the preservation of continuity prevailed, events could have proven to be more disruptive for the future of housing provision. In the same way that the NAR government in its 1986–91 term inherited the unfinished business of incomplete housing projects left behind by its predecessor, the PNM, returning to office in 1991, was obligated to continue the outgoing government's Settlement Programme. Continuity had to be maintained, since to a large extent the program was conceived and funded by means of an external IADB loan, and such external pressures very much dictated domestic agendas in Trinidad and Tobago during this period of restructuring.

Thus, in 1992, the newly appointed PNM minister of housing made a public pronouncement to the effect that the government's housing strategy was embodied in a Settlement Programme which seeks to facilitate the provision of shelter to the population, particularly to low-income groups. The program involved the establishment of two subprograms, namely, a Sites and Services component and a Squatter Regularization program, with costs born by the state and by assistance from the Inter-American Development Bank. The Sites and Services subprogram was concerned with the provision of housing infrastructure, including all-weather roads, sewers, water, and electricity. Five thousand residential building lots were targeted to be made available to prospective purchasers at a minimum cost of TT$15,000 each. Buyers were to be provided with mortgaging facilities in sums ranging from TT$20,000 to TT$70,000. As part of the assistance package, standardized designs and technical assistance were to be made available.

These schemes were devised, in a sense, to address some of the failings of previous state housing programs whereby residential communities were built without essential social facilities such as schools, community centers, and recreational facilities. In this latest scheme, community centers were to be integrated into each housing development plan. The Trinidadian (PNM) government viewed its responsibility, first, as enabling different groups in need of housing to avail themselves of a range of options and services provided within a comprehensive housing policy framework. The elements of this framework were indeed comprehensive and may well be seen as an inventory of the shortcomings which had beset previous housing policies. The issues seemed well identified, however, but the problem remained whether these noble intentions could be achieved. The state was to continue its role as enabler, and policies and programs were intended, above all, to encourage self-help initiative, provide building lots and physical infrastructure, develop sites and services, as well as control population distribution. They were also intended to exert some control over the financial markets and provide incentives to stimulate the home-building industry.

The money needed to finance the housing program had previously been negotiated with the IADB and was to constitute a US$66.1 million loan to be drawn down in tranches every four years. The first was disbursed in 1990 and up to 80 percent was targeted to be spent on the major beneficiaries of the National Settlement Programme, specifically low-income groups. The objective was to underwrite government's effort to improve living standards among low-income households and to establish self-sustaining communities. The cost of developing serviced lots would amount to US$47.6 million and squatter regularization was to be pursued at a cost of TT$27.2 million.

The yield from this investment was expected to benefit 5,000 households who themselves had to provide up to TT$20,000 to purchase lots measuring approximately 4,500 square feet. To support this comprehensive approach towards housing programming and delivery, the state's administrative machinery had to be strengthened, and new organizational structures put in place. First, the capability of the National Housing Authority had to be enhanced through technical arrangements. Next, a Project Execution Unit was established and staffed with appropriate professional and technical personnel. Other component parts of the program included technical assistance in the provision of financial management, technical planning, and operational procedures; technical reviews of past policies with respect to shelter and land development; the establishment of housing data bases, especially with respect to applicants for housing assistance over the years, existing tenants of NHA-owned housing units, and beneficiaries of NHA housing loans; the undertaking of studies intended to provide data and information to assist in improving housing policies; and enabling the private sector to participate as a partner in providing affordable homes for the population. A Housing Information System, which was to provide specific types of data required for directing programs in housing and settlement, was also planned.

All of the above programs were new aspects of housing administration never before incorporated into state machinery in Trinidad and Tobago. They were organizational innovations that appeared to promise major benefits from this IADB loan agreement. But the added cost proved phenomenal. The administrative and organizational machinery to support these policies and run the specific housing programs required financial support equal to or even greater than that for the five thousand beneficiary households themselves. The squatter regularization programs also proved to be a costly exercise, requiring cumbersome and time-consuming investigative and legal procedures. The lands occupied by squatters had to be surveyed and the boundaries of each occupant's plot determined before titles could be granted. These procedures proved to be costly and occasioned much delay and time overruns.

With the new PNM government settled into its term of office, and the stringency of loan conditionalities becoming less onerous in the 1990s, there are gradual shifts in policy directions, including some redirection to those pursued in the past. Perceiving that the worst of economic hard times were over, or nearing their end, the state has begun to make policy adjustments. In particular, there appears to be an emerging return to direct involvement in the provision of housing to ensure that those who could least afford shelter should not be deprived of this basic amenity. The Squatter Regularization programs have been given the go-ahead, and are proceeding with their mandate, and the Sites and Services program has been somewhat modified from its original rudimentary form. In addition to land provision, prospective low-income earners now receive a range of services, including housing plans in optional designs, low-interest soft loans, and a waiver of associated legal fees. There is to be a return to direct state involvement in construction, as it has sought to pool resources with private-sector interests in the building of housing units. There is a belief that the provision of housing requires that the problem be confronted by nothing short of such a collective effort.

Conclusion: Have State Housing Policies Worked?

Trinidad and Tobago's colonial history bequeathed a legacy of housing need that has plagued the country throughout its thirty-some years of political independence. The housing situation in Trinidad has been highlighted in this eventful account of the state policy's twists and turns, with regime effects instrumental in both the changes of policy and in performance standards. The polarization of society that was a legacy of colonial times still prevails in contemporary relations, and housing reflects this polarization, as much today as it did in colonial times. Societal changes that have brought material gains to a substantial number of Trinidadians during the post-colonial years have brought progressive changes to the country's housing stock. Many among the emergent middle class have had their housing needs met very satisfactorily. On the other hand, the state's demonstrations of responsibility to the poor have invariably been late; the state has reacted only when low-income housing needs have become acute and have manifested themselves in extreme ways, such as by widespread squatting.

In Trinidad, as in other Caribbean emerging countries, state housing policies do not stand alone and cannot be divorced from other critical welfare aspects which relate to issues such as the development of human resources, the provision of employment opportunities, the promotion of good health, and the channeling of energies into healthy social activities, including recreation. The state, either in partnership with, or as mediator of private-sector activities—both domestic and international—has overseen considerable progress in the development of infrastructure, of amenities, and of social-welfare support institutions. Perhaps housing was doomed to be a neglected sector when there were other urgent deficiencies to be addressed in the cause of "development" and "modernization."

The early periods of direct state involvement in housing provision might have been lacking in performance, but they tackled a daunting backlog. The private sector showed some capability, when opportunities presented themselves, but it too had diverse portfolios to address. This has been effectively demonstrated by the extensive involvement of the private sector in the provision of housing which matched the activity of the state during the 1974–83 period of economic prosperity. On the other hand, the performance of the state, and the continual mismatch between its rhetorical stances and actual performance, is less laudable (Conway 1984).

The OPEC-generated "boom-and-bust" years promised much, then punished many. The country's ensuing economic crisis, followed by IMF and World Bank (neoliberal) restructuring imperatives, scarcely gave housing a place in the policy-making arena. Housing price declines, many bankruptcies, housing repossessions, and widespread mortgage defaulting brought the not-so-poor into the debate. Now it was not only the poor who were in need, but middle-class homeowners also.

This enlarging of the "housing problem" presents the state with a political conundrum it will have difficulty resolving. The state has joined forces with the private sector to bring about what has been, so far, very much an elusive feat. Regime effects have been minimized by the continuities mandated under the IADB loan. This suggests that a way forward might be fashioned through such external directives of a progressive nature. However, the most recent PNM policy packages represent yet another experimental phase in the housing experience which has now become part and parcel of the state's approach to housing provision in Trinidad and Tobago.

In the meantime, self-help housing initiatives, plus an avoidance of legal means to acquire shelter, are still the only autonomous responses available to the majority of the poor in need of this basic good. Squatter regularization has proved to be a slow and cumbersome process, though a progressive move, so very late in coming. The twist and turns in policy directions and the cyclical ebb and flow of the country's economic standing have contributed to a perpetuation of unmet housing needs in Trinidad and Tobago. The way forward appears still to be more experimental than purposeful, still tentative rather than committed. Housing remains an *undervalued right, denied to the most needy,* a need more readily identified in political speeches and as a voting draw than as a priority activity that the Trinidadian State is committed to fulfilling.

References

Carmichael, G. (1948) *The History of the West Indian Island of Trinidad and Tobago.* London: Alvin Redman.

Central Bureau of Statistics. (1949) *The West Indian Census 1946.* Jamaica: Trinidad and Tobago Central Bureau of Statistics.

Clarke, C. (1974) "Urbanization in the Caribbean." *Geography* 59: 223–32.

Conway, D. (1981) "Fact or Opinion on Uncontrolled Settlements in Trinidad." *Exstics* 286: 37–43.

———. (1984) *Trinidad's Mismatched Expectations: Planning and Development Review.* University Field Staff Report. Hanover, N.H.: No. 26.

Eckstein, J. (1981) *Inflation in Land and Housing in Trinidad and Tobago.* CSO Research Papers No 17. Central Statistical Office, Trinidad.

Ellis, F. (1983) *Housing Construction Cost: A Review.* Caribbean Conference on Housing, Port of Spain, Trinidad.

Government of Trinidad and Tobago. (n.d.) *National Development Plan 1964–1968.* Port of Spain, Trinidad.

———. (n.d.) *Macro Economic Development Framework 1986–1995.* Port of Spain: Ministry of Finance.

Hewitt, L. (1975) "A Demographic Analysis of Urbanization in Trinidad and Tobago." Unpublished M.Sc. diss. University of the West Indies, St. Augustine.

———. (1977) *Some Dimensions of the Housing Problem in Trinidad and Tobago.* CSO Research Papers No. 13. Central Statistical Office, Trinidad.

Klass, M. (1961) *East Indians in Trinidad: A Study of Cultural Persistence.* New York and London: Columbia University Press.

Laughlin, I. (1988) *The Sou Sou Land Story a Non Governmental, Non Profit Land Reform Initiative in Trinidad and Tobago.* Trinidad: HEM Printers.

Marshall, W. T. (1971) "Notes on Peasant Development in the West Indies since 1838." In T. Monroe and R. Lewis, eds., *Readings in Government and Politics in the West Indies,* 34. Mona, Jamaica: Department of Government, University of the West Indies.

Potter, R. B., and O'Flaherty, P. (1995) "An Analysis of Housing Conditions in Trinidad and Tobago." *Social and Economic Studies* 44, 165–83.

Ramdin, R. (1982) *From Chattel Slave to Wage Earner: A History of Trade Unionism in Trinidad and Tobago.* London: Martin Brian and O'Keete.

Sanderson, Minister (acting NAR minister of housing). (1988) Address to a Conference on Housing, Port of Spain, Trinidad.

Simey, T. S. (1948) *Social Welfare Planning in the West Indies.* London: Colonial Office.

Simpson, J. (1974) *Internal Migration in Trinidad and Tobago*. Mona, Kingston, Jamaica: Institute of Social Economic Research, The University of the West Indies.

Williams, E. (1971) "Slavery in the Caribbean." In T. Monroe and R. Lewis, eds., *Readings in Government and Politics in the West Indies*, 19. Mona, Jamaica: Department of Government, University of the West Indies.

Chapter 9

Self-Help Housing Strategies in Cuba: An Alternative to Conventional Wisdom?

Kosta Mathéy

Until 1959, Cuba's political and social conditions resembled those of other Caribbean islands. Cuba was ruled by an oligarchy with a dictator as president. Mining and plantation agriculture were the major economic activities and were controlled by foreign companies. But what suddenly changed the setting from one day to another was the victory of Fidel Castro's rebel army. A revolutionary government took power and soon opted for a socialist plan. Thus, housing, like other social services, was to be provided in line with a national economic plan and distributed according to need instead of according to an individual's ability to pay. Many expected the revolution to offer a blueprint for a better, egalitarian society.

This chapter reviews the record of Cuban housing provision to recent times, when the "Special Period" brought about by the collapse of the Soviet Union and its support for the Castro regime, and the subsequent tightening of the economic embargo by the United States Congress and the Clinton administration, virtually brought the process to an abrupt halt. After a brief discussion of the pre-revolution context, the chapter details the revolutionary regime's alternative housing strategies, their ideological bases, legal frameworks, and performance record, with particular attention being paid to the different forms of *microbrigades*. Presented as an "alternative," *socialist* self-help approach to meeting Cuba's housing needs, the conceptual bases underlying the revolutionary model are given some coverage. Hence, I next deal with the problems of commodification, of double exploitation, and issues of pacification, affordability, replicability, and technical deficiencies, among other comparative hypotheses (Bamberger 1982; Burgess 1977; Harms 1976; Ludwig and Cheema 1987; Ramirez and Burgess 1988; Peattie 1987). In this second part of the account, an assessment of possible differences in the self-help approach in Cuba, compared to practices elsewhere in the region, is attempted. A final section deals with the Special Period, precipitated in 1990, and continuing to the present.

Cuba's record and demonstrably different mechanisms for assuring shelter provision pose an alternative "vision," yet they scarcely present a viable model for others to embrace. The mobilization of people into microbrigades, the deregulation of renting and housing exchanges, and other such *socialist* mechanisms can scarcely be envisaged as part of any other Caribbean country's policies, where U.S. hegemony, advocacy of neoliberalism, and the power of the global capitalist system dominate domestic (national) self-determination. Despite this pragmatic "reality," Cuba's housing programs are a worthy yardstick to evaluate other programs that similarly dependent Caribbean countries have practiced—Duany's Puerto Rico, for example, or Condon and Ogden's French Caribbean *Départements D'outre mer*. This chapter presents this alternative vision.

Pre-Revolutionary Housing Provision

Before the arrival of the Spaniards, most ordinary dwellings were self-built. The traditional hut, today locally known as *bohío* (also *choza, bajareque, barbacoa,* or *caney*), was constructed of organic materials only—particularly of *yagua* (the very durable shaft leaves of the royal palm), of *guano* (palm leaves), and of *tabla* (wooden trunks) (fig. 9.1). Its plan could be circular, elliptical, or rectangular, although the latter form became dominant. The Spaniards added interior walls to the formerly undivided interior and introduced solid walls of earth or stone for more prestigious residences which were built by their own craftspeople (Pérez de la Riva 1952; Weiss 1972). The *bohío* was used in towns and villages alike, until colonial authorities tried to ban this type of structure from the towns due to fear of fires. In the urban setting the courtyard type house became common until the more compact bungalow type, with a veranda (*portal*) towards the street, found its way from North America. In rural areas, the *bohío* can still be found today. In the capital, la Habana, where most nonsugar-based industrial development occurred, overcrowded rented tenements appeared from the beginning of the century, complemented by informal, self-built slums in the 1950s. According to Hamberg (1990: 37), about half of the total housing stock was considered substandard at the time of the revolution and squatter settlements were relatively scarce at 5–7 percent of the housing stock. A larger number of squatter settlements also appeared in Santiago de Cuba, the country's secondary town, both before and after the revolution.

Fig. 9.1. A Cuban bohío.

Revolutionary Housing Strategies and Performance

Following the revolution, Cuban housing policies consisted of measures affecting both the physical construction of dwellings and of legal reforms. Of these, the latter seemed to be more important than the former, particularly during the initial period following 1959. It granted full security of tenure, made speculation and private letting almost impossible, cut rents by half, and abolished them for slum dwellings altogether. Later on, through the 1984 Housing Act (amended in 1989, see *Gazeta Oficial del la República de Cuba* 1984, 1989a), most tenants in state-provided housing were made homeowners, which shifted the responsibility of management, repair, and maintenance to the users (except for the external and common parts of apartment blocks), but established a uniform type of tenure throughout the country. In any analysis of the various programs for physical housing development, a distinction seems useful between state-provided and self-built programs, with the addition of a third, mixed alternative: the microbrigades, a remarkably innovative scheme original to Cuba.

State-Built Housing

State-built housing, the conventional socialist supply model, accounts for about one-third of the new houses built in Cuba after the revolution. The majority were constructed by the Ministry of Construction (MICONS), the Sugar Ministry (MINAZ), and the Ministry of Agriculture (MINAGRI). Most of the construction followed repetitive standard plans (*proyectos tipicos*), a strategy introduced in the first years of the revolution when there was a shortage of architects and engineers. To speed up the pace of construction, prefabricated building systems were promoted, with a uniform number of floors, large and repetitious concrete panels, and the parallel orientation of long, linear buildings to facilitate the use of a hoist. This type of mass housing has been increasingly criticized—including by Fidel Castro himself—for its monotonous appearance and for its cultural incompatibility with living traditions, particularly in smaller towns and rural areas (Ortega et al. 1987: 37; Segre 1984: 357). Only after 1990, due to the effects of the economic crisis and the shortage of building materials, have individually designed low-rise developments using more traditional materials become common, as in the rural "Plan Turquino" program (González 1994).

Self-Help Housing Practices

Although the majority of dwellings constructed after the revolution were (often illegally) self-built, such practice was not supported through state programs for most of the time—apparently as a result of being considered incompatible with socialist principles. Indeed, one of the first proponents of self-help housing policies, Smiles, considered it a prevention strategy against socialism (Briggs 1958: 14). Real socialism in Eastern Europe usually opted for a policy of industrialized mass housing which was to be provided by the state and would take advantage of rent pooling and the economies of scale. Apart from Engels's (1975) general criticism, private housing, including self-help, was specifically associated with landlordism, where the generation of profits (exploitation) is the only incentive. Nevertheless, those self-help housing practices in Cuba which eventually received government assistance fell into three groups: 1) early self-build settlement projects; 2) the so-called "*construcción por esfuerzo propio*"—representing the majority of all constructed houses (fig. 9.2); and 3) cooperatives.

In the early days of the revolution, a few conventional self-build settlements were permitted, under the Self-Help and Mutual Aid Program, to rehouse underprivileged residents from urban slum areas in Havana (Hamberg 1986: 593). Altogether, some 3,400 units of this type were built in the years 1960–61. The program was discontinued because, among other reasons, a continuation of the same social segregation which the residents had suffered before was feared in the new settlements. Some of the existing informal settlements, however, were considered to be fit for improvement and received the infrastructure they formerly lacked, such as water, electricity, sewage, streets, and social amenities (Coyula 1985: 39). Although a brief experiment, the program was effective in eradicating approximately forty squatter settlements. In an indirect manner, this also represented state support of self-help housing processes—similar to the more recent upgrading schemes in other developing countries.

In 1964, the issue of self-help housing was taken up again at an official level in the First National Housing Conference, when this option was specifically recommended for rural areas to replace the supposedly primitive *bohíos* with durable houses built to modern standards (Ortega et al. 1987: 17). However, the notion did not meet with much enthusiasm on the part of the Ministry of Construction (MICONS) and the Ministry of Agriculture (MINAG). The most visible outcome remained an architectural competition for house types suitable for self-building (Anonymous 1965). A similar competition was repeated in 1983.

The reform of the constitution in 1976 established local governments (*poder popular*) that possessed a certain degree of autonomy. Faced with an evident housing shortage at their doorstep, many provincial towns used their powers to support individual self-build efforts by the citizens through the allocation of building sites and construction materials—even if this was not backed by official government policy until 1984. In that year, at the national architects' conference, self-help became a priority political issue in Cuba for the first time. The debates at

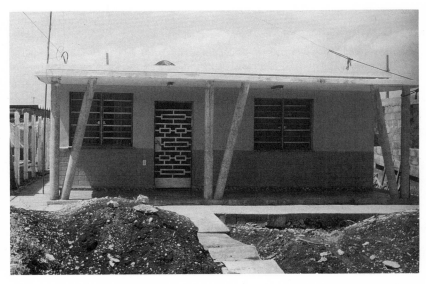

Fig. 9.2. Typical house built by "esfuerzo propio" (individual self-help).

that conference were influenced by the results of the 1981 housing census. This had revealed that, between 1976 and 1980, only 164,000 dwellings had been officially created either directly through the state sector or through the microbrigades, although the net increase of the housing stock accounted for a total of 246,000 units (Hamberg 1986: 603). The striking difference between these figures represented "informal" constructions, most of them built by their occupants in self-help efforts. The 1981 census also indicated that some 50 percent of the self-built units had serious structural problems (Anonymous 1989b: 21)—a result of the lack of professional expertise and limited access to standard building materials. The building materials industry was, on the whole, a state monopoly, and the production plans had never accounted for this demand for private house building. Acknowledging this surprising discovery and considering the debates at the architects' conference, the 1984 housing law included particular provisions to support self-help housing— namely credit, technical assistance, and official outlets for standard quality building materials.

In the following years, completely new neighborhoods were laid out and sites allocated to families who wanted to build, especially on the periphery of medium-sized towns. Standard construction plans could be purchased from municipal or provincial architects' offices, but individual designs were also prepared by these offices for a slightly larger fee. The necessary building materials were released in stages according to the calculated quantities from the official outlets, where also the necessary tools and machinery, like concrete mixers and the like, were borrowed (although not always available). Professional artisans were often hired for jobs which required special skills, for example, electrical installations, casting a concrete slab, or welding iron gates. Credits of up to 5,000 pesos were available— and sufficient at state prices—to pay for materials and assistance, except for the owner's own labor input. Repayment of the loans could be stretched over as long as 20 years, depending on the individual family's income. In 1989, some 130,000 self-built houses were under construction (Anonymous 1989b: 9), considerably more than in the state-provided sector.

Certain limitations of individual house-building practices, such as a lack of expertise, unproportionally high technical assistance requirements, and the need for many helping hands for specific building tasks (like casting a concrete floor) can be overcome through collective forms of self-help, namely, cooperatives. Agricultural cooperatives had already existed for a considerable time and were encouraged to engage in housing construction, too. In their case, house building remained a marginal activity among several other cooperative tasks and was financed directly with credits from the National Bank (which also supervises the building process) in addition to the cooperative's own funds and the farmers' private savings (Anonymous 1989b: 35).

In the urban context, the 1984 housing law also promulgated regular housing cooperatives. The idea was that several individual self-builders would form a team, build their own houses together, and thus benefit by sharing skills and technical support. The construction of multifamily blocks was particularly encouraged in order to save land and infrastructure. After completion of construction, the cooperative would dissolve and the members become individual owners, like any other self-help builders.

Despite the favorable provisions laid down by law, very few housing cooperatives actually formed. However, from 1986 onwards, all political support was directed towards the newly emerging microbrigades (see below), which were considered a superior form of collective self-help. Eventually, in the 1988 amendment to the General Housing Law, the section dealing with housing cooperatives was replaced with new provisions in support of the various forms of microbrigades which had sprung up again in the mid-1980s (López 1987; Mathéy 1989). And up to the Special Period, when natural economic restructuring priorities dominated all else, the microbrigades were the most dynamic element of Cuban housing provision both in terms of new building and in the maintenance and renovation of the existing housing stock. Because they represent a unique feature in Caribbean housing, and indeed elsewhere in the Third World, their particularities will be discussed in greater detail.

The Microbrigade Movement

The microbrigades represent a mixture between self-help and state-provided housing. The idea of the microbrigades was first aired publicly by Fidel Castro in 1970. The workers within an office, factory, or any other place of employment should be given the possibility of building houses for themselves and for their colleagues, he proposed. For this purpose, some of them would be released from their normal work duties and integrated into building brigades (microbrigades), while their colleagues who stayed behind were to guarantee maintenance of the previous level of productivity in the unit—if necessary through extra labor input (plus trabajo). In practice, however, the U.S. trade embargo had interrupted the supply of raw material and spare parts, which was an important factor in decreasing production and overstaffing of many work centers. Thus, the microbrigades presented the possibility of making productive use of an otherwise underutilized labor force. The microbrigadistas (members of a microbrigade) continued to receive their regular salary from their employer, and therefore their income might even exceed the level normally obtainable by unskilled workers within the building industry. All the dwellings constructed by a microbrigade would then be distributed amongst the workers of the base work unit—whether brigadistas or not—according to the individuals' housing needs and work merits of the respective applicants.

Within a few months after Castro's 1970 speech, the first microbrigades started on an experimental basis. The model was found to be feasible and efficacious, and more and more microbrigades were formed. By the year 1978, more than 1,100 teams, incorporating a total of some 30,000 brigadistas had been formed and had completed 82,000 dwellings (Ortega et al. 1987: 22 and 36; Segre 1984: 356). The movement was strongest in the capital Havana, since here the house building activity of the state sector—the conventional channel for the production of mass housing—was intentionally kept to a minimum in order to let the historically underserviced provinces catch up (fig. 9.3). Complete satellite cities around the capital were built by the microbrigades. Typical examples include Alta Habana, Reparto Electrico, San Augustin, Cotorro, and Alamar. The latter was designed to house some 150,000 people (Ortega 1987: 23) and became the most famous of all.

Fig. 9.3. Microbrigade in Old Havana.

At that time almost all the houses built by the microbrigades were four- or five-floor walk-up flats following standard designs (like the type E-14) and building systems (e.g., SP-72, "Gran Panel IV," "IMS"; for details see Ortega et al. 1987: 22, 36, and 37). To reduce urban monotony, the facades were gaily painted, or green areas were cultivated between the blocks. However, a contributing factor to the maintenance of the high social status of these settlements was that, unlike architecturally similar public housing developments in socialist Europe, the inhabitants were not social problem cases, but honorable workers selected for these dwellings due to their outstanding work and social histories.

Despite the recognized achievements of the microbrigades, the movement almost came to a standstill by the late 1970s. There was more than one single reason for this, but it was evident that the ongoing institutionalization and restructuring of the national economy played a major role. More particularly, it was argued that the predominantly artisan building technology used by the microbrigades was not very efficient, and that both the quality of the product and the productivity of the process could be raised by relying more on industrialized systems—which in turn would require a skilled labor force and not the laymen of the microbrigades. Another criticism concerned the selective distribution principles of the microbrigade houses, excluding some of those with the greatest housing needs, namely, people without employment (including old-age pensioners, single mothers, and the like) and certain key professions with staff shortages (education, health). Also, the employers (work centers) themselves became increasingly reluctant to release their workers to join a microbrigade once the earlier mentioned production problems, which had frequently caused overstaffing, had been largely overcome. Last but not least, a new economic and management system, which had been introduced in the second half of the 1970s, required the self-financing of these enterprises and called for a more economical and product-oriented use of the employed labor force.

With respect to housing production it was planned that the gap which was left behind by the dissolved microbrigades would be filled by additional—and more efficient—*state brigades*. These would also incorporate some previous microbrigadistas who preferred to remain in the building trade instead of returning to their original workplace (but were now paid directly by the Ministry of Construction). However, for various reasons, the expected increase in the output of houses built directly by the state did not materialize. It seemed that the possible productivity gains through industrialization had been overestimated—an experience also shared by Eastern European countries. In addition to this structural limitation, the newly formed state brigades were not primarily used for housing construction, but diverted to nonresidential projects with higher political priority.

At the same time as the housing output of the state sector dropped (which includes microbrigades for statistical purposes), housing demand increased, in large part because the generation born during the 1960s baby boom reached marrying age in the 1980s. Between 1958 and 1988, the country's population had increased by 58 percent (Anonymous 1989b: 9). While the housing deficit generated considerable dissatisfaction and popular pressure, the politicians recognized the need to attribute a much higher priority to housing issues than in the past. The 1984 housing law was an expression of that development, but it also signaled that it was unrealistic to expect the state sector alone to supply all the dwellings needed within the coming years. The mid-1980s policy change—surprising to many—can also be interpreted as an early manifestation of a wider political reorientation, which had become known as the "rectificación de los errores" (the correction of past mistakes).

As part of the rectification process, many political decisions of the 1970s were revised, and the phasing out of the microbrigades was one of the measures undertaken. In another speech in June 1986, Fidel Castro himself proposed a revitalization of the microbrigades. He said that it would be absurd to let the microbrigade movement die, considering its past merits, and he added that the microbrigades would be particularly useful for those factories or other productive units which suffered temporary work stoppages for one reason or another. After referring to the old criticism of selective distribution of microbrigade flats, Castro noted that it was decided that the new Micros (microbrigades) should not just build housing for the benefit of their own worker community, but should cater to general needs as well (Granma, 9 June 1986).

Less than four months after this 1986 speech, some 75 new microbrigades with 2,400 workers had been formed in Havana, and most of them had started to work on site by the end of the year. By November 1988, the number of microbrigadistas had risen to almost 38,000 (in 10,000 brigades), the largest participation since the 1970s. Some 3,000 dwellings were finished in less than two years, and another 25,000 were under construction in 1989. In addition, the new micros also constructed social infrastructure and services.

Although the old microbrigade concept of the 1970s was rejuvenated, it was not duplicated point by point. In Havana, which once again became the principal arena of the program, the explicit goal was to start "a radical transformation of the capital," a statement hinting at the new urban and architectural emphasis to be followed. Similarly, as in Europe, the euphoria for large-scale housing development on the urban periphery had passed. The need for urban repair and conservation, particularly of historic neighborhoods, had been recognized and resulted in various reconstruction and infill projects. It became obvious that industrialized building systems, the domain of the Cuban Ministry of Construction, were neither a sensible nor economical solution for these tasks. The microbrigades, on the other hand, had an obvious advantage in doing such a labor-intensive job with their typical artisanal approach. Of course, urban renovation is only one of several areas where microbrigades became active. In the less densely populated peripheral areas of the city, they continued to build standard-design blocks of flats, and occasionally they finished off high-rise buildings after the basic structure had been erected by MICON's own construction teams.

Microbrigade projects in existing neighborhoods required a close coordination with the local administration and implied a social responsibility towards the resident population. Therefore, the new microbrigades were separated from the Ministry of Construction and obtained their own independent institutional organization corresponding to the geographic structure of local government units, the *Poder Popular*. Many microbrigade zones even opened their own design offices, as in Habana Vieja, or employed individual architects working or living in the neighborhood. The decentralized form of organization also permitted a more flexible architectural approach, the use of local materials and the recycling of salvaged building components, closer links with the neighborhood, and, last but not least, a pooling of technical assistance, supervision, education, and catering services among several microbrigades.

The biggest difference concerning new microbrigades compared to the previous practice was their explicit social responsibility. Only 60 percent of all the dwellings produced by them went to the brigadistas and their colleagues in the unit's workplace. The remainder were offered to the *Poder Popular* for distribution among those members of the community who needed a house, but were not connected with any microbrigade (for example, their workplace may have too few employees, or the applicants may be unemployed, old, or disabled). In addition to housing, the microbrigades simultaneously provided urgently needed buildings for community facilities—such as *circulos infantiles* (child care centers), schools, polyclinics, surgeries, and homes, offices, and hospitals for neighborhood doctors and nurses. To handle even bigger projects, like the zoo, the botanical garden, the aquarium, the eighteen pavilions belonging to the scientific-technical exhibition EXPOCUBA, or the buildings to accommodate the 1991 Pan-American Games, several microbrigades cooperated with regular state building enterprises. The listing suggests that—at least in Havana—microbrigade activity concentrated on those kind of projects which were most visible to the public eye (excluding, for example, sewers, industries, or traffic construction); an indication of the supplemental, political, and educational role of the new micros.

Each microbrigade consists of not fewer than thirty-three workers, an arbitrary, historic number which had been established at the outset of the movement and which has not been changed since. In the evenings and at weekends, relatives and colleagues often join and help. Assistance is also offered by the brigadistas' work center. For example, any trucks or machinery not in use over the weekends may be borrowed by the micros, and certain products and services provided by the centers are not billed. Also the microbrigades themselves economize by reconditioning broken machines or trucks already abandoned by other firms. The extended weekly working time in a microbrigade of sixty hours, compared to forty-four in a regular job, together with a better work morale (that is, less absentee-ism), is reported to result in higher productivity levels compared to the regular state building brigades of the Ministry of Construction.

Due to the fast growth of the microbrigade movement in 1987, coupled with the increased number of building permits issued for individual self-help housing, the demand for building materials very soon exceeded available supply and represented the greatest obstacle to an expansion of the movement at that time. Thirty-eight new building materials factories were set up, ten of which were exclusively operated by microbrigades.

The Social Microbrigades

A more recent variation of the microbrigade concept is the "social microbrigade," which had been introduced in late 1987, taking up the experience of a local initiative in Las Güásimas (1983–87), a neighborhood (barrio) in the province of La Habana. In this model the workers were not recruited from the same work center, as in the 1970s microbrigades, but all lived in the same neighborhood—the one in which the microbrigade operated. The main objective of this type of microbrigade was the repair or renovation of the existing housing stock and urban infrastructure (fig. 9.4). New constructions remain an exception and are generally limited to informal settlements, or "barrios insalubres," where many poor dwellings need to be replaced by new structures.

Because these social microbrigades are not linked to an existing work center, many unemployed people from within the neighborhood can be incorporated, particularly young adults. Also housewives and the elderly can be provided with a paying job. Those without previous professional training have the possibility to participate in training schemes. Apart from the paid members working full-time, the social microbrigades also incorporate voluntary workers, who are either neighbors joining the unit during their free time or individuals given paid leave from their regular work center. Because of the specific local conditions, the size of the brigade is not fixed and can vary considerably. This and similar decisions are left to delegados (elected councilors) of the circumscripción (election district or ward), who set up the brigade.

It is important to note that the social microbrigades have several functions. Apart from addressing the housing problem and maintaining the urban fabric, they also provided jobs for the increasing number of unemployed youths. A guaranteed income, improved housing opportunities, and the social control of the neighborhood were incentives to offset the inconveniences of hard physical labor and long working hours in the microbrigades. As an additional advantage it has also been pointed out that the residents may take greater care of the houses they

Fig. 9.4. Social microbrigade in an informal settlement at the periphery of Havana.

live in, and that they were better equipped to carry out future maintenance jobs by themselves once they have participated in renovating or rebuilding a house.

Limitations in Practice

Although the new microbrigades achieved impressive results within a relatively short period after their implementation, they were not without problems. As mentioned above, the building materials industry was by no means prepared for such a rapid increase in demand, and the shortages in materials delayed the completion of most microbrigade projects. There were not enough talented architects to provide tailored designs for all projects, nor experienced engineers and foremen to guarantee a smooth work organization on site, all of which negatively affected progress and workmanship. Particularly in the social microbrigades, the resulting frustrations and delays caused considerable variability among the brigadistas' performances and production rates. For instance, in the Van-Van project, in Santiago de Cuba, only 50 percent of authorized posts could be filled in 1988. These difficulties were, however, not an inherent feature of the concept but rather attributable to the premature start of too many microbrigades at the same time with too little preparation.

The crumbling of the COMECON block, the end of cheap oil imports from the Soviet Union, and the ensuing economic crisis that these events precipitated, brought almost all microbrigade building activities to a standstill in the early 1990s. Cement production and transportation systems suffered severe cutbacks during this Special Period, made even more crisis-ridden by the tightened economic embargo. The building industry had tried to adapt to this new situation through the introduction of alternative building technologies, including stabilized soil blocks and micro-concrete roofing tiles (Bancrofft 1994; Kruckenberg and Vollmann 1994; Mathéy 1994b). There has been some success in this transition to the use of alternative technologies. For example, in 1993, among the 25,000 housing units completed nationwide, 15,700 were of the so-called low-energy type. And some 2,700 of these can be attributed to the social microbrigades. The reality of the Special Period, however, is a widespread scaling back of housing enterprises, while the country and the Castro regime have had to focus on providing the immediate necessities of life, addressing the day-to-day hardships of acquiring food, clothing, medicine, keeping people gainfully employed, and maintaining the people's support of the new economic restructuring programs, drastic though they may be. I discuss the limited and highly uncertain future the Special Period offers for housing initiatives in the final section of this chapter.

A Different Type of Self-Help?

As mentioned in the introduction, many limitations of self-help housing practices worldwide have been associated with the conditions of the capitalist economy. A review of the main arguments and their comparison with the Cuban experience will highlight some important differences in the outcome of the strategy in both settings. The comparison draws on recently published empirical research analyzing different forms of self-help housing in Cuba (Mathéy 1993a).

One of the issues recently discussed in this context is the process of *commodification*. It has been said that typical self-help housing projects promote the introduction of market relationships and thus contribute to the expansion and stabilization of the capitalist economy. Typical instances where this can happen are the expedition of land titles in squatter legalization procedures, the obligation to use industrialized building materials for their compatibility with the building regulations, the expansion of bank loans to low-income people, or the spreading of the DIY market. Even if such instances of commodification may appear favorable to the individuals concerned given their particular circumstances, they need not be indispensable for the improvement of housing conditions. In the Cuban case some processes linked to self-help housing can be interpreted as an indicator of "commodification," although they lack a clear linkage to a capitalist's interest; for example, land (or land-use rights, to be accurate) is sold to self-builders, but the prices are very modest and speculation is avoided by limiting ownership to one single plot per family. Industrial building materials are generally used, but they are distributed through the state at subsidized rates—and every effort is made to avoid excessive consumption. Also bank loans are granted for house building, but they are almost interest-free. Most of the tools used for construction are borrowed from individuals or belong to an institution—there is no commercial DIY market anyway.

The accusation of *double-exploitation* is one of the oldest arguments raised in connection with self-help housing policies. It has been argued that the low wages paid in the formal sector exclude the cost of adequate housing, and therefore the workers have to extend their working days through self-building activities—usually in the evenings and at weekends. Further in Cuba both individual and collective self-help builders work a considerable number of extra hours to obtain or improve shelter. In the case of the microbrigades unpaid "extra labor" (*plus trabajo*) is a formal part of the concept, and officially implies working sixty hours per week instead of the regular forty-four. Individual house builders work similar hours, if their income earning job is accounted for in the calculation. In practice, however, the brigadistas work even longer—up to eighty-four hours per week. However, some doubts can be raised whether double-exploitation is the correct term for what we observe. First, it is important to remember that the Cuban revolution relies heavily on popular mobilization, and considers nonmaterialistic, voluntary labor a key element in social development. Secondly, my own and others' (Hoffmann 1994) participant observation in microbrigades (but also in other forms of voluntary labor, like tomato picking at weekends) suggests that labor intensity in both regular and voluntary jobs varies considerably and does not necessarily correspond with our concept of exploitation or with typical conditions of waged employment in a capitalist economy. One underlying factor may be that it is very difficult to get sacked from a job in Cuba—and if it should happen, the consequences are not dramatic. The other is a more informal attitude towards the job in general and in all forms of self-help building. This is underlined by the incorporation of volunteers from the neighborhood or from the same work center, and the work atmosphere allows for communication and distraction. When working long hours the workers do similar things to those they would do otherwise: talking to neighbors and colleagues, even shopping is done in between; the reality can be interpreted in a utopian way as an integration of the productive and the reproductive spheres of life. This does not mean that work is not done. If the conditions require it, a job is completed in triple shifts, operating day and night. An idealistic attitude becomes apparent in the considerable number of workers who join a microbrigade without even needing or wanting better accommodation. Hoffmann (1994) reports from a microbrigade in Bayamo in which less than half of the brigadistas needed a flat. My guess for Havana is 10 to 20 percent of the workers do not require new housing.

The main reason, however, why self-help housing policies have been advocated all over the world is an assumed *reduction in housing costs* for low-income households. This will be achieved through not accounting for the owners' labor cost, the use of local building materials, and more flexible (lower) standards. In the Cuban case this hypothesis cannot be confirmed, either in respect to the absolute construction costs, nor for the current housing costs of the residents. In the case of microbrigades, first, most of the self-help input is waged, and, secondly, the savings in the rents are marginal (less than 5 percent of income). In individually self-built houses the costs were higher than normal, basically due to higher standards. Cost savings are definitely not a motivation to engage in self-help housing.

Affordability may also be enhanced by improving the job opportunities for the participants (that is, through training schemes). Unfortunately, the demand for qualified construction workers is not unlimited, thus this option cannot work for all. Furthermore, commercial builders in capitalist developing countries have commonly failed to link training schemes with their house-building projects for low-income people, since profit margins are small anyway. In Cuba, however, the microbrigades regularly offer such training, and a certain proportion of the participants remain in the building trade thereafter. Ironically, the higher-income perspectives do not lead to better housing opportunities in this setting.

Social integration also has aspects other than higher income. Particularly in the theoretical discussion lead by John Turner (1976) it was suggested that for the poor home building can be a first step towards integration into society and offers a chance for upward social mobility. However, within a class society, social upward movement can, by definition, only be an option for a very few—otherwise different classes are bound to disappear altogether. Socialist societies, on the contrary, attempt to overcome the segmentation into classes and all other kinds of discrimination, including by race and sex. Self-help projects can, by incorporating everybody into the labor process, emphasize equal opportunities and serve to unify different sections of society. For example, the Cuban microbrigade system overrules the customary division between white-collar and blue-collar workers, since even staff from ministries form brigades where they work under the guidance of ordinary building workers. Therefore, the microbrigades can be considered an anticlass advancement. Also gender discrimination and sexual division of labor is reduced, though to a lesser extent, through explicitly incorporating women in the construction labor force. For example, within the conventional microbrigades, women represented 22 percent of the total labor force in 1988, being the highest ratio by international standards (ILO 1984). The social microbrigades go even further and incorporate, in many cases, more than 50 percent women (fig. 9.5). Aside from the numerically impressive result, sexual equality in respect to the *quality* of the job seems still further away. Women brigadistas often specialize in interior finishing jobs (tiles, painting) or operating the lift, occupations that require care but not much physical strength (although several of the women seemed much stronger than their male counterparts). They are always, of course, expected to run the canteen. In conclusion, we may suggest that self-help practices in Cuba help to overcome fragmentation into social classes and, within limits, lessen gender inequalities. Furthermore, the greater involvement of women in the construction sector is not counterbalanced by enhanced responsibilities among the men in the distribution of household chores—a limitation of the generally positive observation.

Another controversial issue in connection with self-help housing policies is *political mobilization and pacification.* In the capitalist world, the introduction of self-help housing programs was often part of a political strategy to pacify social unrest, as was the case with the U.S.-financed Alliance for Progress in Latin America, right after the Cuban revolution. Empirical research in many countries confirms that organized political resistance and apparent unity in the low-income communities often disintegrate in the course of assisted self-help housing projects due to internal conflict, the stress arising from house building, which demands several thousand working hours plus organizational duties, and as a result of administrative control through planning authorities and funding agencies (Rodríguez 1972; Schmidt-Relenberg, Karner, and Kohler 1980). On the other hand, progressive planners and academics recurrently assert that self-help programs can also politically mobilize the residents and prepare the path towards grassroots democracy (Fadda 1987; Glaeßner, 1984; Nelson 1979). Also in Cuba, the mobilizing

Fig. 9.5. Women participate in the construction labor force.

aspect has been considered an important part of the microbrigade concept, particularly with reference to the thinking of Che Guevara, who called for nonmaterial initiatives in the interest of the revolution. Empirical data, however, do not confirm a linkage between collective self-help building activities and political mobilization. Indeed, a reverse relationship was observed (up to 17 percent below the average—see Mathéy 1993a: 107). But, after all, in Cuba there are other channels—the mass organizations—specifically aiming at political mobilization. However, massive mobilization does happen through microbrigades in a different way: that is, through *work* mobilization. Hoffmann (1994), for example, cites the case in which a microbrigade was able to mobilize a voluntary labor force of up to five times its own size on a weekend.

A major political problem of self-help housing lies in the *anti-social character* of self-help per se, or, in other words, the law of the jungle. Some people even suggest that self-help is a synonym for capitalism: those people equipped with particular capabilities or with more financial resources will benefit from self-help more than others, but the old, the sick, and the poor are bound to lose out. This observation is generally true for all individual forms of self-help, and in a competitive (capitalist) environment it also applies to collective forms like normal housing cooperatives (because only those who will not draw on the resources of the group without contributing their equal share will be allowed to join). Socialism cannot fundamentally alter the anti-social aspect of individual self-help initiatives, but through its local and mass organizations—which are a typical feature in most socialist states—it has the necessary infrastructure to organize self-help activities on a collective basis without excluding the weak from its harvest. This is demonstrated by the Cuban microbrigades, which assign only 60 percent (50 percent before 1989) of houses produced to the brigade itself. The remaining dwellings are put aside to satisfy "general need" and are distributed among the local neighborhood—the allocation is made through an elected local committee according to the criteria set by the community.

In the European or North American context, with its relative affluence, more attention can be paid to the qualitative aspects of everyday life. In those regions, self-help housing activity has been praised for its *nonalienating work* character, and as a source of personal satisfaction through self-expression. However, as Harms (1976) noted a decade ago, such a connotation seems rather absurd in the typical Third World setting, where to obtain shelter the poor have no other alternative than to build their own houses. In the Cuban case no official claim was ever made that self-building projects were meant to enable self-expression or the like, though a few individual cases may be found where such a suggestion might be justified. More remarkable, however, are the evolving opportunities of job rotation, which may also contribute to job satisfaction. As mentioned before, the Cuban microbrigade system allows laborers and employees to leave their regular jobs for a limited period—typically one or two years—and to integrate themselves into a microbrigade where they engage in construction. During this period, they maintain their previous salaries and may return to the original workplace. Although there can be no doubt that the prime motivation for joining a brigade is to improve housing conditions rather than the desire to engage in heavy physical work, it must be remembered that some brigadistas join although they are not searching for accommodation. This observation suggests that for some participation in a brigade can provide personal fulfillment and social pride.

Another recurrent argument in the self-help debate is concerned with the *architectural and technical qualities* of a dwelling. John Turner and others argue that because the motivation for building is the creation of use values instead of exchange values, more care is dedicated to quality. Of course, the appearance of neither regular Third World squatter settlements nor formal self-builders' programs easily confirms this hypothesis—but then, the commodity nature of housing can never be excluded in such settings (Burgess 1977; Drakakis-Smith 1981; Pasteur 1979). In Cuba, property speculation is very difficult; therefore, the production of use value can be assumed to be dominant in construction. Even design-imposed living patterns could be made more "rational," involving, for example, more shared facilities (laundries, child care, shared flats, communal kitchens, dining rooms, and shops). In practice, however, only a reduction of building failures was reported from state assistance in self-help housing initiatives (Hamberg 1986: 608), whereas, with few exceptions, the architectural outcome was not better than in nonassisted or state-produced housing.

The last concern about all self-help housing programs in the Developing World is their limited *affordability and replicability.* In capitalist countries, projects of this kind tend to be isolated ventures with no significant quantitative impact in relation to overall need. Land speculation, overheads, administration, and the like raise the cost far beyond the target group's ability to pay, and the high subsidies impede replicability. A different experience is demonstrated in the Cuban case. It shows that when greater political priority is attributed to shelter, assisted self-help housing can have an important impact in solving the housing problem—as in the two periods of massive microbrigade mobilization: between 1971 and 1979 more than 80,000 dwellings were built by the microbrigades, and provided shelter for about 20 percent of the city populations in Havana and Santiago de Cuba. The more recent movement, which started in 1986, incorporated almost 40,000 workers, a greater number than at any time in the past. To this number the impact of the social microbrigades must be added, as well as the assisted self-builders in *construcción por esfuerzo propio*—the latter sector alone had 130,000 units under construction before the present crisis started (Anonymous 1989b: 9).

In conclusion the comparison suggests that self-help housing can offer a realistic solution to the housing problem in Cuba, and such self-help housing produces quantitatively and qualitatively superior results compared to both spontaneous self-building and assisted self-help programs in other Latin American countries. The Cuban experience differs with respect to several of the typical limitations of self-help by reducing commodification and by improving affordability, replicability, social integration, and technical quality. However, no evident difference is apparent regarding construction costs, political mobilization, the quality of architecture, or provision of collective amenities. Other topics, including double exploitation, personal satisfaction, income generation through training opportunities, and social integration, allow ambiguous interpretations, which are dependent on political or philosophical values.

Current Housing Problems and Future Options

The promising vitalization of self-help housing activities in Cuba through state assistance has been harshly interrupted by the crisis arising from the breakup of the COMECON economic community. Particularly serious is the scarcity of crude oil, which has caused a sharp drop in the production and transport of cement and almost all other building materials. Not only have the state-built housing schemes been discontinued, but also the material assistance to the microbrigades and to individual self-builders has been heavily cut. Local communities are being encouraged to engage in decentralized activities instead and to rely as much as possible on their own resources—not only in the field of housing. To facilitate such an approach, far-reaching organizational and administrative reforms have been started.

Among these, the newly created *Concejos Populares,* which represent the smallest unit of government and which operate at the *barrio* level are particularly relevant. Their delegates are personally known to the neighbors and are able to assess local needs and resources best. If necessary, the Concejos Populares can install a so-called *Taller de Transformacion Integral de Barrio* in their neighborhood, which provides the technical expertise and logistical base for further development of the barrio, including social, cultural, economic, and physical upgrading initiatives (Leinauer et al. 1994). In Havana, networking between various *talleres* is facilitated through the *Grupo por el Desarrollo Integral de la Capital,* an independent advisory office staffed with high-ranking professionals, which can also assist in establishing direct links with international aid donors, particularly of the NGO type. Thus, decentralization is now touching the grassroots level—and may open new perspectives in self-help housing processes too. Several new initiatives have already sprung up, such as the local production of building materials in neighborhood-run building yards, but it is too early to identify a general pattern (Mathéy 1994a).

Conclusion

The evidence from Cuba confirms that the established debate on self-help housing policies, based as it was on experiences in capitalist countries alone, is incomplete. For example, the effect of commodification through self-help housing programs appears to be insignificant in Cuba when compared with capitalist countries. Political *mobilization* through self-help programs alone was found to be difficult to achieve in both systems. The contrary effect of *pacification,* a typical result in the capitalist context, does not appear to operate, either. Also, in Cuba, assisted self-help housing does not seem yet to produce better use values than other forms of house building, except for a reduction in building failures. But for the quantitative aspect, both forms of self-help housing in Cuba, the microbrigades and the *construcción for esfuerzo propio,* have produced most impressive results and are a significant contribution towards solving the housing problem—at least until the beginning of the current period of crisis. At this moment, the radical and promising steps towards decentralization seem to open new avenues to self-help housing processes and, if applied to a wider context, possibly to overcome the present problems of socialist development as well.

Particularly at a time when the socialist project has been abandoned in Eastern Europe, it is noteworthy that in Cuba the socialist context and the operation of microbrigades have demonstrated new possibilities in the realm of self-help housing. Moreover, some elements of the Cuban experience, particularly that of the *social microbrigades,* incorporate a number of progressive elements which could be assimilated in other economies too (Mathéy 1993b). The wholesale adoption of the socialist model is not advocated, nor is it a realistic "demonstration-model" for other Caribbean dependencies, however.

Reforms during the Special Period continue apace, as the Castro regime struggles to ride out the crisis. It is still too early to judge what kind of mixed-economy model will evolve and what aspects of the socialist project will be incorporated into the new restructured programs, whether in housing provision, or any other social service sector. The embargo is continuing the crisis, the Castro regime has its focus on survival, and housing provision is scarcely at the head of the agenda, if indeed it ever was (Hamberg 1986).

Whether the self-help approach Cubans used will be a frame of reference for future housing policy in other Caribbean countries cannot be ascertained today. Socialist ideology is so at odds with the tenets of the capitalist, neoliberal agenda that, unless the approach is cast in different mold, the lessons might never come to light. Inclusion in this comparative collection might, however, be a fruitful introductory step: this is its intention.

References

Anonymous. (1965) "Concurso para viviendas por medios propios." 1964. *Arquitectura Cuba* 333 (1965): 29.

———. (1989b) "Cuba Politica Habitacional y su Financiamiento." Paper presented by the Cuban delegation at the VI réunion del comité technico de ALIDE (Asociación Latinoamericano de Instituciones Financieras de Desarrollo) in La Habana, Cuba, 17–20.

Bamberger, M. (1982) *Evaluation of Sites-and-Services Projects, The Evidence of San Salvador.* Washington, D.C.: World Bank.

Bancrofft, R. (1994) "Die Entwickung von neuen Baustoffen und die Wiederentdeckung traditioneller Konstruktionsmethoden in Cuba." In K. Mathéy, Hrsg., *Phänomen Cuba: Alternative Wege in Architektur, Stadtentwicklung und Ökologie,* 195–204. Karlsruhe: Lehrstuhl für Städtebau und Entwerfen.

Briggs, A. (1958) "Self-Help—A Centenary Introduction." In S. Smiles, *Self-Help* (orig. 1858), 7–13.

Burgess, R. (1977) "Self-Help Housing: A New Imperialist Strategy? A Critique of the Turner School." *Antipode* 2 (9): 50–60.

———. (1987) "Petty Commodity Housing or Dweller Control. A Critique of John Turner's View on Housing Policy." *World Development* 6: 1105–34.

Coyula, M. (1985) "Vivienda, renovación urbana y poder popular: Algunas consideraciones sobre La Habana." *Arquitectura y Urbanismo* 2: 12–17. English version: "Housing, Urban Renovation and Popular Power." *Trialog* (Darmstadt, West Germany) 6 (1985): 35–40.

Drakakis-Smith, D. (1981) *Urbanization, Housing, and the Development Process.* New York: St. Martin's Press.

Engels, F. (1975) *The Housing Question.* Moscow: Progress Publishers.

Fadda, G. (1987) "Urban Social Movements in Caracas: Their Connection with Urban Policies. A Case Study: 'El Barrio la Moran.'" *Trialog* (Darmstadt, West Germany) (13/14): 12–17.

Gazeta Oficial de la República de Cuba. (1984) "Ley General de la Vivienda." 22 Dec., La Habana, 101–22.

———. (1989a) "Ley General de la Vivienda." 3: 5–32.

Glaeßner, G. J. (1984) *Vertrauen auf die eigene Kraft: Selbsthilfe-projekte und Ko-operativen in der Dritten Welt.* Berlin.

González, D. (1994) "Der Plan Turquino. Ein Programm zur Verbesserung der Wohn- und Lebensbedingungen in den Bergregionen Cubas." In K. Mathéy, Hrsg., *Phänomen Cuba: Alternative Wege in Architektur, Stadtentwicklung und Ökologie.* Karlsruhe: Lehrstuhl für Städtebau und Entwerfen.

Hamberg, J. (1986) "The Dynamics of Cuban Housing Policy." In R. Bratt, C. Hartman, and A. Meyerson, eds., *Critical Perspectives on Housing,* 586–624. Philadelphia: Temple University Press. Reprinted as *Under Construction: Housing Policy in Revolutionary Cuba.* New York: Center for Cuban Studies, 1986.

———. (1990) "Cuba." In K. Mathéy, ed., *Housing Policies in the Socialist Third World,* 35–70. London: Mansell.

Harms, H. (1976) "The Limitations of Self-Help." *Architectural Design* 46: 230–31.

Hoffmann, D. (1994) "Die Microbrigade der Kämpfer. Beobachtungen zu Wohnungsbau und Stadtteilsanierung in Bayamo." In K. Mathéy, Hrsg., *Phänomen Cuba: Alternative Wege in Architektur, Stadtentwicklung und Ökologie,* 149–60. Karlsruhe: Lehrstuhl für Städtebau und Entwerfen.

ILO. (1984) *ILO Year Book of Labour Statistics.* Geneva: International Labour Organization.

Kruckenberg, A., and H. Vollmann. (1994) "Chichi Padron—Planen und Bauen in der 'Periodo especial: Erfahrungen aus Santa Clara.'" In K. Mathéy, Hrsg., *Phänomen Cuba: Alternative Wege in Architektur, Stadtentwicklung und Ökologie*, 205–18. Karlsruhe: Lehrstuhl für Städtebau und Entwerfen.

Leinauer, I., B. Hunkenschroer, K. Wolff, S. Heerde, and M. Stilo. (1994) "Cayo Hueso, ein Barrio in La Habana." In K. Mathéy, Hrsg., *Phänomen Cuba: Alternative Wege in Architektur, Stadtentwicklung und Ökologie*, 99–122. Karlsruhe: Lehrstuhl für Städtebau und Entwerfen.

López, S. (1987) "Las Microbrigadas: Una Manifestacion revolucionaria de la Participacion Popular en el Campo de las Construcciones." Paper presented at the Conferencia Internacional sobre la Vivienda y el Urbanismo, La Habana, Palacio de las Convenciones, Feb.

Ludwig, R., and S. Cheema. (1987) "Evaluating the Impact of Policies and Projects: Experience in Urban Shelter and Basic Urban Services." *Regional Development Dialogue* (Nagoya, Japan; Pergamon) 8 (4): 190–229.

Mathéy, K. (1989) "Microbrigadas in Cuba: A Collective Form of Self-Help Housing." *Netherlands Journal of Housing and Environmental Research* 4 (1).

———. (1992) "Self-Help Housing Policies and Practices in Cuba." In K. Mathéy, Hrsg., *Beyond Self-Help Housing*, 181–216. London and New York: Mansell. S.

———. (1993a) *Kann Selbsthilfe-Wohnungsbau sozial sein? Erfahrungen aus Cuba und anderen Ländern Lateinamerikas*. Hamburg and Münster: LIT.

———. (1993b) "Wildes Siedeln? Die Dritte Welt kommt nach Europa—mögliche Konsequenzen für die Wohnungsversorgung." In J. Brech, Hrsg., *Neue Wege der Planungskultur. Orientierungen in der Zeit des Umbruchs*. Frankfurt/Darmstadt: Wohnbund/Verlag für wissenschaftliche Publikationen.

———. (1994a) "Methoden Partizipativer Erneuerungsstrategien: das Beispiel Pogolotti." In K. Mathéy, Hrsg., *Phänomen Cuba: Alternative Wege in Architektur, Stadtentwicklung und Ökologie*, 83. Karlsruhe: Lehrstuhl für Städtebau und Entwerfen.

———. (1994b) "Periodo Especial. Wie Cuba die ökonomische Krise ökologisch zu meistern versucht." In K. Mathéy, Hrsg., *Phänomen Cuba: Alternative Wege in Architektur, Stadtentwicklung und Ökologie*, 189–94. Karlsruhe: Lehrstuhl für Städtebau und Entwerfen.

Nelson, J. M. (1979) *Access to Power, Politics and the Urban Poor in Developing Nations*. Princeton: Princeton University Press.

Ortega Morales, Gonzáles, Alfonso Lourdes, Angela Rojas Avalos, Gilberto Hernández Garmendía, and Obdulio Coca Rodríguez. (1987) *Nuevas Tendencias en la Politica habitacional y la produccion de viviendas en Cuba. Panorama de su Desarrollo (Band 27)*. Hamburg: Arbeitsbereich Städtebau, Objektbezogene Stadtplanung im Forschungsschwerpunkt 6. Technical University, Hamburg-Harburg. 87 pages plus Annex.

Pasteur, D. (1979) *The Management of Squatter Upgrading: A Case Study of Organization, Procedures and Participation*. Farnborough, Kent: Saxon House.

Peattie, L. (1987) "Affordability." *Habitat International* 11 (4) (1987): 69–76.

Pérez de la Riva, F. (1952) "La habitación rural en Cuba." *Revista de Arquelogía y Etnología* (La Habana) Enero-Diciembre.

Ramirez, R., and R. Burgess. (1988) "Affordability and No Cost Recovery! Conceptual and Political Issues around World Bank Housing Strategies." *Trialog* 18 (Darmstadt, West Germany): 9–12.

Rodríguez, A. (1972) "De Invasores a Invadidos." *Revista Latino-americano de Estudios Urbanos Regionaes* 4 (2): 101–42.

Schmidt-Relenberg, N., H. Karner, and V. Kohler. (1980) *Selbstorganisation der Armen*. Frankfurt: Vervuert.

Segre, Roberto. (1984) "Architecture in the Revolution." In C. R. Hatch, ed. *The Scope of Social Architecture*, 348–60. New York: Van Nostrand.

Turner, John F. C. (1976) *Housing by People. Towards Autonomy in Building Environments*. London: Marion Boyars.

Weiss, J. E. (1972) (2d ed., 1979) *La Arquitectura Colonial Cubana,* vol. 1 and 2, Siglos XVI/XVII, La Habana.

Wolff, K., I. Leinauer, B. Hunkenschroer, and St. Heerde. (1993) *Ein steiniger Weg. Stadterneuerung in La Habana/Cuba—der Barrio Cayo Hueso.* Projektbericht No. 26. Institut für Stadt-und Regionalplanung der TU. Berlin: Technische Universitat.

Chapter 10

From the *Bohío* to the *Caserío:* Urban Housing Conditions in Puerto Rico

Jorge Duany

Like other aspects of Caribbean Creole culture, Puerto Rican housing reflects the intense mixture among Amerindian, European, African, and other elements. Key strands of a Caribbean style in architecture were brought to the island by different people and blended together (Slesin et al. 1985).

However, contemporary houses have replaced many traditional elements in Puerto Rico. Wood is no longer the most important building material, being replaced by a combination of cement, brick, and steel. Dwellings have incorporated structures that were formerly separated from the main frame, such as kitchens and bathrooms. Modern building technologies have displaced traditional crafts. Suburban developments have supplanted many of the rural settlement types of earlier eras, and the architectural styles of European and American metropoles dominate over vernacular forms. Thus, contemporary housing reflects the historical and cultural transformations of this Caribbean society during the twentieth century. It could scarcely be otherwise: houses present a mirror image of a society at a particular point in time (Jopling 1988).

This chapter surveys the historical and contemporary situation of housing in Puerto Rico. Because urban centers currently have the largest number of housing units on the island, the focus will be on the main cities, especially the San Juan metropolitan area. Special attention is paid to urban lower-class households, which must cope with inadequate housing conditions, particularly in public housing projects, working-class neighborhoods, and squatter settlements. The chapter also centers on Santurce, the core of San Juan, as an example of constant state intervention in housing provision for the urban poor. Indeed, Santurce's experience encapsulates many of the housing problems of the island and the Caribbean region.

To begin, the historical evolution of housing conditions in Puerto Rico is traced since the colonial era under Spain and later the United States, when most of the population lived in rural huts called *bohíos*. Second, the counterpoint between self-help housing, *arrabales,* and government-sponsored housing, *caseríos,* is reviewed. Third, a working-class neighborhood, Barrio Gandul, is examined in detail to illustrate present housing conditions in Santurce. Fourth, efforts by the Puerto Rican government to deal with inadequate housing conditions are evaluated, particularly the massive relocation of urban squatters to public housing projects. Finally, appropriate planning strategies aimed at improving housing conditions in Puerto Rico's urban centers such as Santurce are identified. In essence, it is argued that the state has consistently undermined self-help initiatives by poor households in Puerto Rico, and, as a result, urban housing conditions have deteriorated despite active government intervention over the past four decades.

Historical Background:
The *Jíbaro* and the *Bohío*

Like most Caribbean countries, Puerto Rico was predominantly rural until well into the twentieth century. For most of its history, the vast majority of the population lived in the countryside, scattered in small farms and isolated towns. Until the nineteenth century, most Puerto Ricans were either subsistence farmers (*jíbaros*) or sharecroppers (*agregados*) who lived in small *bohíos* (figs. 10.1, 10.2, and 10.3). Towards the end of the seventeenth century, Puerto Rico had only two major urban centers: San Juan on the northeast coast and San Germán in the southwest. Both were small in size and simple in style, except for their military and religious buildings (Jopling 1988). Much of the island's central mountainous region remained uninhabited until the second half of the nineteenth century. City life in Puerto Rico, the Dominican Republic, and Cuba did not challenge the prevailing, isolated rural housing practices until the end of the century (Rigau 1992).

The island's physical features largely determined the geographic distribution of the population during the first three centuries of Spanish colonization. The coastal plains were much more amenable to settlement than the rugged interior. Until the eighteenth century, most of the Puerto Rican population was concentrated on the north coast, while the mountainous region attracted few settlers. The most important economic activities—cattle raising and commercial agriculture—were

Fig. 10.1. A typical bohío in the Puerto Rican countryside, made with dry branches and thatch, the most common dwelling of highland peasants, or jíbaros.

Fig. 10.2. A rural bohío made with yaguas, with one room for a family of eight.

Fig. 10.3. A self-built casita, *a peasant house with wooden walls and zinc roof.*

carried out in the northern lowlands. During the nineteenth century, the western highlands developed in response to the growth of coffee agriculture. By 1899, population density was higher in the western and northern regions of the island than in the southern and eastern regions (Picó 1975).

During the nineteenth century, Puerto Rico was transformed from a neglected military outpost into a booming agricultural colony. Sugar in the lowlands and coffee in the highlands became the leading export crops. The settlement patterns of sugar plantations and coffee *haciendas* differed considerably. *Haciendas* consisted of isolated peasant households surrounded by a few acres of cultivated land. In contrast, plantations were characterized by nucleated villages of wage laborers. Meanwhile, small holder areas, growing tobacco and minor crops, harbored rural settlements intermediate between the clustered plantation villages and the scattered *hacienda* communities (Quintero Rivera 1981, 1987). These differing environments shaped the class solidarities and world views of agricultural workers in Puerto Rico. Not surprisingly, the coastal lowlands and inner highlands developed distinct subcultures that persisted well into the present century.

In Puerto Rico as in other Caribbean countries, the ethnic groups that populated the island left a deep imprint on Creole architecture (Jopling 1988; see also Duany 1985). However, local conditions invariably shaped immigrant tastes and styles. *Bohíos* built with indigenous materials such as wood, cane, palm trees, *yagua,* and thatch housed lower-class peasants of various ethnic origins. Because of their low cost, simple design, and adaptability to the tropical climate, *bohíos* became the most common vernacular house in Puerto Rico (see figs. 10.1 and 10.2). As late as 1878, about one-third of the island's houses were *bohíos* (Sepúlveda Rivera 1989). In nineteenth-century Santurce, most buildings were *bohíos,* where the majority of the free black population lived scattered away from the main road (Sepúlveda and Carbonell 1988). Urban *bohíos* represented modifications of rural housing types popular in Puerto Rico since pre-Columbian times.

During the early Spanish period, upper-class urban houses were vernacular versions of stone and adobe houses found in Spain, particularly Andalusia. In San Juan, Spanish houses were often built with local materials and designs adapted to the tropical climate (Sepúlveda Rivera 1989). Housing types differed considerably according to social class. Wealthy Spaniards and Creoles occupied spacious stone houses with ample windows and doors allowing for ventilation. Lower-class residences, mostly inhabited by mulattoes and blacks, were similar to the *bohíos* of the countryside (Castro 1992).

By the end of the eighteenth century, San Juan had developed a Spanish pattern of residential differentiation. At the center of the city, near the plaza, stood the best residences with stone or brick walls and wooden roofs, whereas thatched *bohíos* with dirt floors dominated the outskirts of the city. This form of social stratification derived from colonial regulations, which distributed space according to social status outward from the town's center to the periphery. The farther one lived from the urban nucleus, the lower one's standing in the class hierarchy (Sepúlveda Rivera 1989).

In the plantations, African slaves were usually housed separately from their masters. Slave quarters, or *barracones,* reflected European rather than African architectural styles. Barrack-type houses also came to dominate Puerta de Tierra, a black working-class community outside San Juan. Here wealthy landlords built large wooden structures, which they then subdivided, renting the small units to poor tenants. Puerta de Tierra thus contained a large concentration of overcrowded *casas de vecindad,* as these multiple dwelling tenements came to be known (Sepúlveda Rivera 1989). On the northeastern coast of the island, near Loíza, the descendants of free blacks and African slaves built houses that resembled the African-inspired dwellings found elsewhere in the Caribbean. However, the major African contribution to Puerto Rican housing was the technical expertise of black carpenters and other artisans who helped build *hacienda* and town houses for the upper classes (Jopling 1988).

Nineteenth-century immigrants to Puerto Rico came from Corsica, Mallorca, Spain, the Canary Islands, and Latin American and Caribbean countries such as Venezuela, Santo Domingo, and Haiti. As a result, local architecture incorporated new ethnic elements, especially in the coffee-growing regions of the western and central parts of the island, where most immigrants settled. In towns such as Ponce and Yauco, Catalan and Corsican merchants recreated their own housing styles (Rigau 1992). In San Juan, a neoclassical style prevailed as a symbol of the Spanish colonial establishment (Castro 1992; Vivoni Farage 1992).

During the nineteenth century, Puerto Rico's population became increasingly urban. By 1878, about 21 percent of the population was classified as urban. San Juan was the most densely populated city, with an average of twenty persons per dwelling. The city eventually expanded beyond its walled limits, beginning with Puerta de Tierra (Sepúlveda Rivera 1989). At the same time, residential interaction between different social groups increased within the city. In 1846, a typical San Juan neighborhood housed members of the elite as well as the popular sectors, such as seamstresses and bakers. As Negrón Portillo and Mayo Santana (1992) note: "San Juan had some streets where merchants, affluent property owners and professionals (Puerto Ricans, Spaniards, and South Americans) apparently concentrated. But there was a larger number of streets with a more varied composition, with neighbors of different social sectors, occupations, and skin color" (71; my translation). Landlords often subdivided large housing structures into smaller rental units, occupied by lower-class tenants, including slaves, many of them black or mulatto. Female-headed households were common, especially among blacks. Slave men as well as women often engaged in domestic service; others practiced skilled trades.

Population growth and economic development during the nineteenth century led to the proliferation of new towns and the expansion of old ones. Nonetheless, "many towns were but small villages with a few thatched *bohíos* around the Church, which only came to life on Sundays and some holidays" (Sepúlveda Rivera 1989: 103; my translation). Toward the end of the Spanish colonial period, urban centers such as Mayagüez and Ponce expanded quickly. Although San Juan's population increased steadily, the city lost its traditional dominance over the island's export trade. Mayagüez, Guayama, and Ponce became important commercial ports in their own right. The rise of a Creole urban bourgeoisie consolidated Puerto Rican cities as seats of economic and political power in the Spanish colony (Rigau 1992).

A Creole style emerged among the urban middle classes and rural upper classes. Elite houses incorporated European elements, such as hip roofs and open balconies, selected for their appropriateness to the Puerto Rican environment. Private residential designs developed a new architectural language for a thriving urban bourgeoisie (Rigau 1992). But even the *jíbaros'* humble dwellings adapted Taíno and African components to local conditions. According to Jopling (1988), Puerto Ricans created a distinctive social and spatial order based on various architectural styles, building techniques, and symbolic repertoires.

Changes under United States Rule

The American occupation of the island in 1898 and its subsequent colonial administration transformed the agrarian structure to suit the demands of huge sugar corporations, or *centrales*. These enterprises tended to concentrate landownership into a few large estates, especially in the coastal lowlands, thus reversing an earlier trend towards the dispersion of rural property. At the same time, coffee declined as the island's chief export. In less than ten years, the metropolitan administration converted the seigneurial *hacienda* economy into a modern-day plantation system. By 1930 the agrarian transformation was complete: Puerto Rico became a typical Caribbean sugar island, characterized by *latifundios,* extreme concentration of capital and labor, the predominance of capitalist relations of production, and a monocultural export economy producing for a single foreign market and importing most of its basic goods from the metropolis (Scarano 1993).

The development of monocultural agriculture between 1900 and 1930 was accompanied by massive migration from the mountains to the coasts. As sugar plantations expanded their control over land and labor, highland workers moved to the lowlands near the *centrales* in search of jobs. Unable to eke out an existence from the soil, landless peasants and *hacienda* workers also migrated to the towns and cities, which were fast becoming the dynamic centers of the economy. The three largest port cities—San Juan, Ponce, and Mayagüez—absorbed much of the island's population growth under American rule. Urban labor markets became saturated with unskilled workers from the countryside.

The United States occupation of Puerto Rico also transformed housing conditions on the island. Metropolitan styles initially influenced the design of public buildings and upper-class residences, but the lower classes soon incorporated American motifs into their houses. Even poor country dwellings adopted American styles such as Art Deco and materials such as metal roofing. By 1920, the Spanish Revival was a popular architectural idiom in Puerto Rico as well as in the United States. Local architects designed both institutional and residential buildings with romantic images of Spain in mind (Rigau 1992). Common people adorned their houses with wide arches, brick tiles, and whitewashed walls reminiscent of Spanish times. After 1940, suburban residential developments adopted an international style of architecture following the United States model. *Urbanizaciones* such as Puerto Nuevo and Levittown became endless rows of identical, box-type, cement-block, single-family dwellings.

Rural working-class houses still differed considerably from those in Puerto Rico's urban areas (Pérez Velasco 1984). One-room *bohíos* were the most common housing type among agricultural laborers during the first two decades of U.S. domination. On sugar plantations, workers were crowded into barrack-type quarters with wooden walls and zinc roofs. Squatting in isolated and dispersed farmsteads was the leading form of rural occupation in the inner highlands. The rugged mountain topography discouraged the creation of agricultural villages among subsistence farmers. As late as 1950, three-fourths of upper Loíza's population lived in remote *bohíos* (Augelli 1955). Housing conditions in the inner highlands had not changed much since the days of Spanish colonization.

In the towns and cities, workers often built their own houses, although many rented rooms in *casas de vecindad,* especially in Old San Juan, Puerta de Tierra, and Santurce. The practice of leasing small plots of land continued in urban centers. Large-scale migration from rural to urban areas created more housing problems in the already overcrowded and inadequate structures of working-class neighborhoods. Living conditions deteriorated for many workers between 1898 and 1920.

The Great Depression of 1930 shook the foundations of the plantation system. Puerto Rico's sugar industry never recovered from that international crisis of the capitalist market, and has undergone progressive deterioration ever since. During the 1930s and 1940s, more rural dwellers migrated to the cities, especially to San Juan's growing squatter settlements (see figs. 10.4 and 10.5, for examples). Former peons, sharecroppers, small farmers, and rural wage laborers were forced to flee the countryside due to the decline in demand for agricultural labor. A sustained movement of people took place from the coffee-growing regions of the interior to the coastal cities, especially to the peripheries of major urban centers. The crisis of the agricultural sector nourished Puerto Rico's urban proletariat.

Fig. 10.4. Small huts built with zinc, yaguas, and cardboard, ripe for infectious diseases, ca. 1940.

Fig. 10.5. El Mangle, a shantytown built over public marshlands in the south of Santurce during the 1930s, later removed as part of the urban renewal program.

Economic crisis also stimulated political change on the island. In 1940, the Popular Democratic Party led by Luis Muñoz Marín came to power, campaigning against large sugar interests. "Bread, land, and freedom" became the rallying cry for the *populares*, who adopted the traditional *pava* hat of the *jíbaros* as their symbol. In 1947, the PPD-controlled government launched "Operation Bootstrap" to modernize the economy and improve living standards. This program came to be known as "industrialization by invitation," because it relied on massive investments for industrial development from capitalists in the United States, lured by tax exemption laws and the availability of cheap labor. By reorganizing the land tenure system and promoting the proletarianization of human resources, Operation Bootstrap imposed the death sentence on an already moribund plantation economy. The government's development strategy also encouraged further migration from rural to urban areas, where most factories were located, and to the United States. In 1952, the Popular Democratic Party negotiated for the establishment of the *Estado Libre Asociado,* or Commonwealth status, for Puerto Rico, thus attaining a greater degree of local autonomy from the U.S. federal government. Under Commonwealth status, industrialization proceeded rapidly and urbanization hastened its pace.

During the 1950s, new settlement types appeared in Puerto Rico (Augelli 1955). *Arrabales,* lower-class urban agglomerations resulting largely from rural migration, such as El Fanguito in Santurce, quickly replaced *haciendas,* isolated farms, and towns, the traditional modes of settlement on the island since Spanish times. After World War II, hamlets, little towns, and suburbs proliferated. The American suburban division was the most recent type to develop on the island, mainly as a result of the increasing use of the automobile as the dominant means of private transportation. Living in an *urbanización* became the hallmark of upward social mobility in postwar Puerto Rico.

The emerging pattern of urbanization of the greater San Juan conurbation has been extraordinary suburban growth, first in Santurce, then in Río Piedras and Hato Rey, and finally in the adjacent municipalities of Bayamón, Guaynabo, and Carolina (see Duany 1987). After World War II, San Juan experienced a boom in housing construction, both privately and publicly financed. The city expanded largely through the division of rural properties into small plots of land sold to urban dwellers. With time, the Spanish colonial pattern of residential differentiation, where the rich lived near the city center and the poor on the fringes, was inverted. Since 1960, upper-status groups have moved to the peripheries of the cities, while the lower-status remain closer to the city center (Schwirian and Rico-Velasco 1971: 88–89). Modern San Juan looks more and more like a typical American city in its physical and sociological features: the upper-class flight to the suburbs, the marginalization of old downtown areas, the concentration of capital resources and services in a financial district, and the residential segregation of rich and poor. The result has been a growing polarization of the San Juan metropolitan area, with the urban poor concentrated in the central districts of Old San Juan, Santurce, and Hato Rey; the middle classes in the outlying areas of Río Piedras, Carolina, and Bayamón; and the most affluent groups seeking ever more remote locations in Guaynabo and Cupey to isolate themselves from the poor.

Two main models of ecological organization—the Spanish and the American—coexist in the San Juan metropolitan area. Although Old San Juan and Río Piedras were laid out according to the Spanish gridiron plan, Santurce was not. Thus Santurce became a hodgepodge of diverse neighborhoods with no central business district, inadequate plazas, and few community centers. According to Caplow and Wallace (1964), San Juan was an unnucleated city, an amorphous structure lacking a main core of economic activity. This unnucleated pattern has serious socioeconomic disadvantages, such as the dispersion of functions and people, and the ineffectiveness of the public transportation system. Nonetheless, San Juan has avoided many of the problems of American cities, such as severe racial and ethnic segregation. Still, San Juan has been unable to provide adequate shelter for its poor population. Since the 1920s, squatter settlements have mushroomed throughout the city.

Arrabales: The Growth of Self-Help Housing, 1920-1950

Arrabales are squatter settlements usually located on public lands with little commercial value such as the shores of mangroves and swamps. The largest *arrabales* were located on low ground on the sides of the Martín Peña Channel and the San José Lagoon in Santurce and Hato Rey. Although many *arrabales* are now centrally located, they remain physically and socially isolated from other urban communities.

San Juan's shantytowns were crowded with former rural dwellers, many of whom could not find stable employment and were forced to participate in the informal economy and/or rely on public welfare. Job opportunities for shantytown residents were largely confined to blue-collar and service occupations, such as irregular construction work and domestic service (Safa 1974). *Arrabales* originally had poor access to public services, such as piped water, electricity, and security. Because of inadequate living conditions and because they were built on contiguous plots of land, *arrabales* became fertile ground for tuberculosis, syphilis, and other contagious diseases.

The shantytowns of San Juan were built by the cooperative efforts of individuals and their families. Many houses were placed on piles to ensure air circulation and protect them from the tidal waters. Wooden floors were supported by posts. Families filled the mangroves and built small channels to drain the water around their homes. An unskilled worker usually initiated the construction process with a few simple tools, gathering makeshift materials from various sources, such as cardboard, wood, and cans. Relatives and neighbors commonly helped to finish and improve the house. To this extent, many self-built houses in San Juan were initially the product of unalienated labor with an essentially use-value for the families that occupied them (see Conway 1982). *Arrabal* shacks were urbanized versions of *bohíos,* wooden or cement box-type structures painted with vivid colors, evoking the memory of an agricultural past (Jopling 1988). However, shantytown houses varied considerably in style and condition according to their occupants' social status (Caplow and Wallace 1964).

In Puerto Rico, shantytown development has undergone four distinct phases: 1) the establishment of working-class communities on private lands, from the beginning of the twentieth century until the end of the 1920s; 2) the settlement of public lands by squatters, from the 1920s through the 1950s; 3) the government control of shantytown expansion, along with consolidation of existing settlements, from the 1950s until the late 1960s; and 4) the confrontation of new squatters by the state since the late 1960s (Stevens 1985; Cotto 1993). In the 1990s, new squatter communities faced increased government hostility, continuing the state–civil society conflicts (Cotto 1994).

The first *arrabales* emerged in the 1920s when rural workers were displaced from their agricultural lands. The most infamous of these settlements was El Fanguito, near the Caño Martín Peña (Maldonado 1947). Like other *arrabales,* El Fanguito was built clandestinely on the swamplands of Santurce. Small huts were made from discarded boxes, barrels, cans, and other materials like *yagua,* tin, and galvanized iron (see fig. 10.4). El Fanguito residents developed serious health problems as a consequence of overcrowding, poverty, and insanitary conditions. Lack of social control was associated with crime, juvenile delinquency, prostitution, and alcoholism.

Across the San Juan Bay, in Cataño, lower-class rural migrants also built shacks on marginal lands during the 1940s. Former peasants became urban unskilled workers, mostly in manufacture, construction, and services (Ramírez 1977). Economic conditions were marked by poverty, unemployment, underemployment, and low educational levels. Despite inadequate physical conditions, residents considered the shantytown a good place in which to live. At least they retained some autonomy from the government and a sense of community solidarity.

Shantytowns emerged on the periphery of the San Juan metropolitan area just as the government removed existing slums in Old San Juan. The first public housing project was built in Puerta de Tierra in the 1930s. By the end of the twenties, shantytowns were sufficiently large to attract public attention, especially in Santurce and Hato Rey. During the 1930s and 1940s, most residential growth took place in the form of unplanned settlements. Indeed, the squatter settlement population grew more quickly than the rest of the urban areas. By 1950, about half of Santurce's population lived in *arrabales* (Stevens 1985). The so-called "Slum Belt" extended for several miles on the northern side of the Martín Peña Channel and around the San José Lagoon.

Although the local government opposed the expansion and consolidation of squatter settlements, occupants were not evicted without compensation if they had built complete houses. Thus, rural migrants quickly built makeshift shacks to prevent their immediate eviction, first in accessible sites and later over swamps and open water. For many lower-class migrants, unauthorized occupation of public lands was the only alternative to renting high-priced private dwellings. Shantytowns represented the major form of residence of the urban poor and the first place of settlement for most newly arrived rural migrants in San Juan from the 1940s to the 1960s (Safa 1974). By the end of the decade, many squatters were second-generation urban dwellers, excluded from the formal labor and housing markets of the city. As Cotto (1993: 122) notes, poor people were forced to "rescue" private or public property to provide their own shelter. Land invasions were common well into the 1970s but decreased in frequency after 1975 with the consolidation of several legal measures to control and penalize the squatters (Cotto 1994).

Safa (1974) explains the emergence of San Juan's shantytowns as a response to the expansion of the urban industrial proletariat. In turn, the city's growing population reflected its increasing importance as the chief port of trade as well as the political and administrative center of the island under United States rule. Some shantytowns provided stable settings where rural migrants could gradually adapt to the city. In the 1960s, Safa (1974) described one shantytown as "a very cohesive community" (61). Mutual aid and solidarity among neighbors was a common coping strategy, reinforced by kinship, ritual kinship, and friendship ties. Lack of economic competition among shantytown families minimized class conflicts and racial differences.

Physical conditions in the *arrabales* tended to improve over time. Originally, squatters had no access to public services such as police and fire protection. Most houses had piped water but lacked toilets, bathtubs, and showers and rarely had electricity (Hollingshead and Roger 1963). During the 1950s and 1960s, public services were installed in many squatter settlements. Residents rebuilt and renovated many houses. Mangroves were filled and rescued from the water. The physical quality of life in the *arrabales* improved both as a result of private initiative and public rehabilitation (Stevens 1985). Some of these self-built housing developments managed to become full-fledged urban communities, such as La Perla in Old San Juan. However, many Puerto Rican shantytowns did not last long enough to upgrade into working-class neighborhoods as in other Latin American countries, because they were removed by the government's urban renewal program.

Enter the State: Relocating the Poor in *Caseríos*, 1950–1968

In the 1950s, the Commonwealth government defined *arrabales* as deteriorated neighborhoods in need of state intervention. As in other Latin American countries, local planners typically viewed shantytowns as "social cancers" and eyesores to be eradicated.[1] Moral outrage was mixed with economic considerations. As Stevens (1985) notes, "[I]t is practically cheaper to eliminate an entire *arrabal* and build low-cost housing units, than to rehabilitate one" (189; my translation). The state initially discouraged repairing shantytown houses to prevent their proliferation. But land invasions continued unabated during the 1940s. Squatters organized themselves to improve the physical conditions of their communities and press for government services (Cotto 1990). Squatters obtained many government concessions during Felisa Rincón de Gautier's *(Doña Fela)* incumbency as mayor of San Juan in the 1950s and 1960s.

Regardless of the squatters' efforts, government authorities decided to eliminate the largest shantytowns, such as El Fanguito and Barrio Hoare in Santurce. As part of this urban renewal program, the state expropriated large tracts of land to construct new roads, parks, clinics, and other public works, as well as for private development (Cotto 1990). By 1962, most of El Fanguito had been cleared and its families had been relocated in public housing projects, working-class neighborhoods, and *urbanizaciones* (Safa 1974). Most of El Fanguito's two thousand families were relocated to the San José housing project in Río Piedras (Sepúlveda and Carbonell 1988). More recently, in 1986, Barrio Tokío in Hato Rey was removed to make way for the government's much touted land-water transportation scheme, popularly known as *Agua-Guagua*.

Since the 1950s, therefore, state policy has been oriented toward eliminating shantytowns, building public housing projects, and relocating shantytown dwellers in the projects. Major government efforts to improve the living conditions of squatter settlements began during the 1950s with the construction of Barrio Obrero as the first publicly planned working-class neighborhood in Santurce (Sepúlveda and Carbonell 1988). Later efforts included paving streets and installing running water and electricity in existing settlements, but mostly they focused on building new public housing facilities, or *caseríos*. With massive amounts of U.S. federal funds, the Commonwealth government was thus able to provide low-cost housing for *arrabal* families.

In 1957, the Commonwealth government created the Urban Renewal and Housing Corporation (CRUV) to coordinate the elimination and rehabilitation of shantytowns, as well as the construction of public housing projects. By 1966, CRUV had built 33,500 public housing units and relocated 26,000 shantytown families (Alvarado 1967). CRUV sponsored the construction of both single and multiple dwellings, condominiums for moderate-income families, and apartment buildings for senior citizens. Furthermore, CRUV provided low-interest mortgage loans to foster homeownership, good citizenship, and family stability (Government Development Bank 1969). However, CRUV's main activity was the construction of public housing projects throughout the island, especially in the San Juan metropolitan area. By 1993, Puerto Rico had 332 *caseríos* with an estimated 225,000 residents (*San Juan Star* 1993a).

Caseríos consist of several tenement structures of various heights, typically three or four stories. *Caseríos* are usually large and compact settlements, such as Lloréns Torres in Santurce with 2,000 housing units and Nemesio Canales in Río Piedras with 1,150 units (*San Juan Star* 1992). In contrast to shantytowns, *caseríos* were built on dry land, made with concrete, and subdivided into one-family apartments, with plumbing, electricity, and sanitary facilities (see figs. 10.6 and 10.7). The buildings were architecturally sound and the apartments were larger than shantytown homes. Although the government built much public housing during the 1950s and 1960s, *arrabales* grew almost as fast as *caseríos* because of the continuing inflow of rural migrants to the city (Hollingshead and Rogler 1963).

In the beginning, most shantytown dwellers accepted the state's urban renewal program, but many later protested their relocation to public housing projects. According to the former head of the planning board, Rafael Picó (1952), opposition to shantytown clearance came mainly from unscrupulous speculators who rented

Fig. 10.6. El Falansterio, one of the first public housing projects in Puerto Rico, built in Puerta de Tierra on the outskirts of Old San Juan during the 1930s.

Fig. 10.7. One of the first low-cost housing developments in San Juan, urbanización Eleanor Roosevelt, during the 1940s.

illegal structures without owning the land. On the other hand, Picó argued, the Commonwealth government built modern *caseríos* and sided with "the suffering and exploited tenants of the *arrabal*." The government perceived squatter settlements as overcrowded and unhealthy centers of infection, promiscuity, and delinquency (see also Alvarado 1967). Public housing projects were proposed as an alternative, with better physical facilities, more recreational space, and lower rents than shantytowns. By the middle of the 1950s, the growth of *arrabales* had slowed down. Some residents were able to move out and buy a house in modern-style *urbanizaciones*. However, the most important force retarding the growth of *arrabales* was the government's effort to relocate shantytown dwellers to public housing projects.

The public perception of shantytowns as social problems led the state to an extensive urban renewal program designed to improve the living conditions of the urban poor in Puerto Rico (González Díaz and Vargas Acevedo 1988). The construction of large-scale housing projects such as Lloréns Torres and San José helped to restructure the city according to social class divisions. Thus, public housing projects were built for the poor; some *urbanizaciones* catered to the lower-middle class, such as Roosevelt and Reparto Metropolitano; some were oriented toward the upper-middle class, like University Gardens and Hyde Park; and still others, like Miramar and Condado, were reserved for the elite.

Urban renewal policies produced unintended results. As former shantytown residents moved to public housing projects, their family organization changed. Although the projects represented an effort to improve the poor's living conditions, they undermined traditional values and practices. Relocation disrupted the large kin networks and contiguous residential patterns of shantytown dwellers. United States federal housing policies made it difficult to reconstruct the residents' coping strategies, such as mutual assistance and frequent interaction among relatives and friends. Moreover, relocation created new problems for public housing residents, such as an imposed distance on formerly stable households and extended families. In short, public housing projects represented "a radical change in ecology and community organization for the *arrabaleños*" (Bryce-Laporte 1968: 535).

Whereas most shantytown dwellers liked their homes, most public housing residents disliked theirs (Hollingshead and Rogler 1963). Public housing residents questioned government restrictions, such as prohibiting relatives, boarders, and livestock in their apartments. *Caserío* dwellers also resented the uprooting of their families and communities as a result of resettlement. Lower-class norms constantly clashed with government regulations. Furthermore, *caserío* dwellers preferred a home of their own—but not in the *caserío*. According to Caplow and Wallace (1964: 229), most Puerto Ricans preferred a single-family house on its own landscaped plot of ground, however small, rather than row houses or low-rise apartments. Some would rather live in a *bohío* than in a *caserío*.

Public housing residents complained about increasing vandalism, theft, and drug addiction among the young. Men especially disliked public housing because it eroded their traditional male authority as economic providers and homeowners. Conversely, project regulations favored the maintenance of single female-headed households among the urban poor. Kinship and friendship ties disintegrated, and patterns of cooperation and trust weakened as a result of such housing dislocations. Public housing projects were characterized by a loss of social control, particularly among teenagers. In short, relocation increased the dependence of the poor on the government and reduced working-class consciousness and solidarity (Safa 1974).

Thus, the social impact of urban renewal practices on poor communities has been largely negative in Puerto Rico. The massive destruction of housing units, stores, and other familiar structures altered the residents' lifestyle. Planners rarely took into account the need to recreate a neighborhood's social institutions, such as churches, schools, and stores in the projects. Many people resisted the move to public housing because they preferred to have their own home, no matter how humble. Government expropriation of shantytowns created a sense of impotence and insecurity among displaced residents. Families and friends were dispersed throughout the metropolitan area and in strange surroundings. Tenants of the *caserios* lacked a sense of privacy and power over their own lives. Public housing projects tended to deteriorate over time, as opposed to shantytowns, which tended to improve (Ramírez 1977).

Recent Developments, 1968-1993

In 1968, the residents of shantytowns and public housing projects voted en masse to help elect a new government in Puerto Rico. Political participation by the urban poor represented a protest against the Popular Democratic Party, in power since 1940. Most of the urban poor were opposed to the elimination of shantytowns and the construction of more housing projects. Many hoped that the new administration would rehabilitate their communities without forcing them to move (Ramírez 1977). Instead, the New Progressive Party basically continued the housing policies of the previous administration, taking a hard line against squatter settlements.

By the end of the 1960s, relations between squatters and the state had become increasingly antagonistic. One commentator interprets land invasions (or "rescues") as an urban popular struggle against the state (Cotto 1993). The *rescate* movement engaged in nontraditional forms of popular mobilization and negotiation, such as mass rallies, pickets, vigils, and caravans. Squatters formed regional organizations and obtained the support of some government corporations, as well as religious, civic, and political groups. The state apparatus sometimes reacted with the use of violence, evicting squatters by force. However, government agencies also established new social-welfare programs, such as land distribution and construction projects. Thus, the destabilizing potential of land invasions met with the expansion of public services designed to uphold the moral and legal authority of the state (Cotto 1993). In the end, the *rescate* movement was coopted, dismantled, or incorporated into conventional political organizations.

The 1980 invasion of Villa Sin Miedo escalated conflicts between the state and popular sectors. Several families took over an abandoned farm, La Dolores, in Canóvanas, and built wooden and zinc shacks similar to the shantytowns of the 1950s. Most squatters were unemployed, could not afford to pay rent, or had been unable to secure public housing. The community was well organized and connected with political, religious, and labor leaders. The squatters eventually brought water and electricity into the area. By 1982, over 250 families were living in Villa Sin Miedo (*El Nuevo Día* 1982a).

By then, the government had decided to evict the squatters. Although some families relocated voluntarily, most stayed and defied an eviction order. In May 1982, more than 300 police officers stormed the area and forced the squatters to leave. Houses were burned or torn down immediately. Residents fought the police by burning tires, throwing stones and Molotov cocktails, and shooting police officers. When the confrontation ended, a policeman had been killed and two were injured, along with three residents. Most of the squatters were set free and relocated in a nearby community. The government, then controlled by the New Progressive Party, blamed the episode on a politically motivated movement against the state (*El Mundo* 1982; *El Nuevo Día* 1982b).

Perhaps more important, *caseríos* had become undesirable places to live in. Few people wanted to move to public housing projects because of increasing social problems and government restrictions. For instance, U.S. federal legislation required that public housing residents pay a proportion of the income earned by all household members (*Diálogo* 1993a). Thus, *caserío* dwellers did not report many employed residents in their household in order to reduce their monthly rent. Household members were often hidden from public authorities even though they resided temporarily or permanently in the *caserío*. Moreover, public policy destabilized households and fostered the separation of married couples. In sum, the government bureaucracy penetrated even deeper into the private lives of *caserío* dwellers.

In 1992, the Commonwealth government transferred the administration of housing projects to private corporations. This decision was based on the deplorable physical and social conditions of the *caseríos*, which had become synonymous with uncollected trash, illegal drugs, crime, unemployment, school dropouts, delinquency, and welfare dependence (*Diálogo* 1993a). Since then, private corporations have repaired many *caserío* buildings, initiated beautification projects, and managed federal funds more efficiently than the local government. Still, public housing residents perceive the need for better services, such as public transportation, recreational parks, health clinics, and day care centers (*Diálogo* 1993b).

Public opinion as well as the state have stigmatized *caseríos* as the main causes of the island's alarming crime rate. Vigilance over the *caseríos* has increased both in frequency and intensity, with more police officers assigned to these areas and spectacular raids against suspected drug smugglers. Between 4 June and 10 September 1993, the local police and National Guard took over twenty public housing projects as part of a tough-minded government campaign against crime (*San Juan Star* 1993a). The island's public housing projects have thus come under a veritable state of siege. Popular images of *caseríos* have come a long way from the days when the government proposed them as solutions to the problems of the urban poor. Nowadays, *caseríos* are more likely to be seen as part of the problem. The "social cancer" has spread from squatter settlements to public housing projects.

In the late 1980s and 1990s, several sectors of the Puerto Rican urban population have organized their communities to defend themselves against crime. These efforts tend to develop among the middle and upper classes, which attempt to control access to their neighborhoods, based on the premise that criminals come "from outside." "Building walls thus appears as the short-term 'solution' to the security problem in the country and not as the unequivocal expression of the fragility of the social order in Puerto Rico" (Román 1993: 57; my translation). Each month, more and more *urbanizaciones* are closed off to vehicular traffic in a desperate attempt to ward off criminals. Some middle-income communities also attempt to renovate their physical environment, by installing better street lights, painting schools, repairing basketball courts, or maintaining local parks. These private initiatives reflect the state's inability to provide such services efficiently. The situation is even worse in lower-class communities like Barrio Gandul.

Inside Barrio Gandul:
A Working-Class Neighborhood

Barriadas are lower-class neighborhoods in the inner city, such as Barrio Obrero, Tras Talleres, and Barrio Gandul in Santurce. These neighborhoods are usually located near a central business district such as Santurce's Stop 15, where many residents can find employment, do their shopping, and find cheap transportation. Many houses were once adequate structures that have since been subdivided and converted into overcrowded tenements (Safa 1974). In some ways, *barriadas* are the Puerto Rican equivalent to American ghettoes, characterized by low standards of living, inadequate housing structures, overcrowding, disease, delinquency, and drug addiction. However, Puerto Rican slums differ from their mainland counterparts in that their residents do not belong to an exclusive ethnic or racial minority, but rather to a single social class: the urban proletariat. Some *barriadas* in Santurce and Río Piedras have recently received a large influx of foreign immigrants, especially from the Dominican Republic. Nonetheless, Dominican residents are not a majority in any of Santurce's neighborhoods, not even in Barrio Gandul, one of the largest Dominican communities in Puerto Rico.

Elsewhere I have traced the historical development of Barrio Gandul since the beginning of the twentieth century (Duany, Hernández Angueira, and Rey 1995). What follows is a synopsis of that essay. Like other parts of Santurce, Barrio Gandul became a working-class community between 1900 and 1930. During this period, Barrio Gandul was still part of San Juan's suburban periphery. Similar to other areas close to the Martín Peña Channel, the land was marshy and covered with mangroves, with little real estate value. Low rents, central location, ease of transportation, and job availability accordingly attracted poor immigrants to the *barriada*. These same factors continued to attract Dominicans in the 1980s.

In its early years, Barrio Gandul was defined by its easy access to the trolley and the railroad station on Stop 15. Thus, many of the train's mechanics and operators settled with their families in Barrio Gandul and nearby Tras Talleres. In 1915, a causeway and drawbridge extended the highway from Santurce to the outlying city of Bayamón across the San Juan Bay. Stop 15 was the only connection between Santurce and Bayamón until Stop 18 was extended and linked with the bridge to Bayamón in the 1950s. Thus, Barrio Gandul lost its character as a way station between San Juan and the rest of the island. Although the neighborhood was increasingly in the center of the metropolitan area, it became marginal to the city's development, which moved towards the suburbs.

Many residents recall the origins of Barrio Gandul. The name of the neighborhood derives from the large number of *gandul* plants (pidgeon peas) that once grew there. The original inhabitants of Barrio Gandul worked the land of a wealthy landowner, don Vicente Balbás Peña, whose heirs still own much of the property. Poor families typically built their houses on leased plots of land, as in rural areas. Many residents were rural migrants, especially from the island's central highlands, who moved to Santurce in the 1930s and 1940s. Only one out of four residents of the blocks under study had been born in Santurce. Many had come from rural municipalities such as Morovis, Camuy, Vega Alta, and Fajardo.

Old residents remember the dirt roads and wooden shacks that dominated the landscape at the turn of the century. "Gandul was then an area of swamps and mangroves, surrounded by ditches to drain the water from the swamps," said a woman who arrived in 1918 (Cruz Rodríguez et al. 1990: 9; my translation). Another neighbor remarked that Ernesto Cerra Street resembled an open-air market full of vegetables and fruits. Some residents missed the old days when Barrio Gandul was safer and more lively. "The community was poor but it was fantastic," according to a woman who grew up in the neighborhood. "We used to live here with pride, tranquillity, and happiness." Many residents liked the area because it was accessible and close to bus stops, movie theaters, pharmacies, and schools, among other places.

Barrio Gandul has recently become an undesirable place to live in. "Stop 15 has gained a bad reputation as a center of infection for AIDS," lamented a young resident. "I've lost my affection for the neighborhood," said a property owner. Drug addiction, alcoholism, prostitution, and homelessness are now common in the area. Heightened concerns over a rising crime rate have also tarnished the neighborhood's reputation. Local residents and the general public perceive Barrio Gandul as a crime-ridden area, although participant observation and police statistics suggest that this *barriada* is much safer than other parts of Santurce. In any case, the neighborhood has been stigmatized as a site of social problems.

Barrio Gandul contains various types of dwellings. The most common type along the main thoroughfares is a multiple-story building with small apartments and rooms for rent. Many structures have two floors, often occupied by a small business on the first floor and a residence on the second floor. The area's cross streets contain mostly single-story houses, usually with a small apartment or converted unit in the backyard. Most structures are built with cement, but some have wooden and tin roofs. Many plots of land have more than one structure as a result of an irregular settlement pattern established since the *barriada*'s inception. In the late 1980s, about 55 percent of the housing units were considered in good condition, whereas 45 percent had deteriorated or were inadequate (Estudios Técnicos 1989).

Barrio Gandul shows other signs of urban blight. In 1990, 15 percent of the housing units were vacant. The cost of housing was relatively low because rents are controlled by law. Most housing units are rented for less than two hundred dollars a month (DACO 1988). Among the residents, 7 percent had moved to the neighborhood between April and June of 1990. Thus, the neighborhood has high vacancy and residential mobility rates.

The racial composition of Barrio Gandul is not known precisely because the census of Puerto Rico does not collect data on race. However, our study suggests that about 55 percent of the residents were black or mulatto, and about 45 percent white. With regard to ethnic composition, Barrio Gandul has one of the highest proportions of foreign immigrants in Santurce. We found that about a third of the residents were of Dominican origin. Apart from the Dominican Republic, foreign immigrants came from St. Kitts, Anguilla, Dominica, Cuba, and Colombia. A few Puerto Ricans were born in the United States.

The socioeconomic characteristics of Barrio Gandul are predominantly those of a working-class population. In 1980, one-third of the area's families lived under the poverty level and about 17 percent of the residents were unemployed. Most employed persons were service and blue-collar workers with less than a high school education (U.S. Department of Commerce 1984). According to our study, most households in Barrio Gandul operated on the margins of the formal economy. Residents typically pooled resources, based on temporary, occasional, and seasonal labor as well as off-the-books employment and public assistance. The primary source of income for most residents was not regular employment, but a combination of casual, welfare, and other sources including retirement and disability pensions. In sum, Barrio Gandul's residents tend to have low socioeconomic status and a precarious attachment to the formal labor force.

The neighborhood also has a complicated land tenure system. A recent study of one of the blocks determined that half the residents rented their units and the other half owned them (DACO 1988). Furthermore, many homeowners leased plots of land from the Balbás Peña Estate and many tenants sublet rooms to other residents. Thus, the neighborhood has a four-tiered tenure system, from boarders and tenants to lessees and landowners. Residents of Barrio Gandul share the dilemma of not owning the land with other Santurce neighborhoods, such as Barrio Figueroa and Alto del Cabro. Lack of legal access to the urban land market has also been found in other Third World Cities (Conway 1985).

To date, most efforts to rehabilitate Barrio Gandul have proven unsuccessful. The neighborhood faces serious obstacles to organizing and developing a sense of community. It is deeply split between Puerto Rican and Dominican residents, between landowners and lessees, and between merchants and residents. Community institutions, such as schools and churches, do not adequately represent local interests and needs. As a result, Barrio Gandul has been unable to develop community projects to address its many social problems: poverty, unemployment, drugs, and alcoholism. In many ways, the neighborhood is typical of lower-class communities in Santurce, the San Juan metropolitan area, and other urban centers in Puerto Rico. At the same time, Barrio Gandul differs from other *barriadas* because of its high concentration of foreign immigrants, particularly from the Dominican Republic. The latter feature has only furthered the neighborhood's marginalization, because many Dominicans are undocumented and lack access to state protection.

State Policies and Self-Help Alternatives

Since 1947, the Puerto Rican government has pursued an active role in urban planning within the framework of its leading development strategy, Operation Bootstrap. The government's main approach has been to contain the growth of shantytowns in the inner city, build massive public housing projects, and foster the development of *urbanizaciones* around the periphery of San Juan and other cities. Consequently, public housing projects have replaced shantytowns as the most common settlement type for the urban poor, and suburban developments for the middle class have sprawled throughout and beyond metropolitan areas. In the process, the State has largely ignored self-help housing initiatives by the urban poor. Furthermore, public housing structures have displaced vernacular forms of habitation and traditional household arrangements. As in other Caribbean islands, public policymakers have paid little attention to folk architectural traditions and have focused on the preservation of Spanish colonial houses and monuments.

In the 1990s, Puerto Rican society is faced with the mixed results of past state interventions in urban housing: some positive, much disappointingly negative. Physical conditions have undoubtedly improved for the majority of the Puerto Rican population. Few people now live in wooden and thatched *bohíos* as they did in the past. In Santurce, modern roads, parks, and buildings have supplanted the most squalid shantytowns. Public housing projects have provided adequate shelter as well as basic services such as plumbing and electricity. Dilapidated and overcrowded tenements in the inner cities have been removed or renovated. Government rent controls have ensured a minimum housing stock for low-income tenants in major urban areas.[2] U.S. federal mortgage loans have enabled middle-income residents to become homeowners in suburban private developments. Owners now occupy nearly two-thirds of all housing units in Puerto Rico (U.S. Department of Commerce 1991).

Over the past few decades, the housing situation has improved substantially, especially in urban centers. The proportion of inadequate housing decreased from 80 percent in 1940 to 32 percent in 1965 (Alvarado 1967), although it remained around 30 percent in 1981. By 1990, only 11 percent of all housing units in Puerto Rico were considered inadequate, deteriorated, or dilapidated. Three out of four units had concrete walls and roofs. Only 5 percent lacked complete plumbing facilities. Most urban units had access to running water, bathroom facilities, and showers (U.S. Department of Commerce 1993, 1991; Centro de Datos Censales 1993).

Still, urban housing conditions are far from adequate. The local planning board projected that 26,714 new units would have to be built by 1980 to satisfy the needs of San Juan's population (Junta de Planificación 1978). In 1990, 54,320 housing units on the island were judged as substandard (U.S. Department of Commerce 1993). Moreover, social conditions for the urban poor continue to deteriorate. In the inner cities, many housing structures have been abandoned or left in disrepair. Public housing projects have become a focus of popular discontent, both from residents and outsiders who view the *caseríos* as the culprits of the island's criminal activities. The quality of life in the *caseríos* has tended to decrease over time. For lower-class people, the option of owning a house has become more remote and dependence on the government has deepened. Middle- and upper-class neighborhoods have segregated themselves from surrounding communities in an effort to fend off crime. A deeply polarized society has led the state to take increasingly repressive measures against the urban poor.

Since the 1950s, state policies in Puerto Rico have favored suburbanization to the neglect of the old urban centers. The city's core was abandoned to the vagaries of the market, with the consequent loss of population and deterioration of infrastructure. Zoning laws increased the separation between home and workplace as central areas were reserved for commercial use and peripheral ones for residential use. The specialization of land uses created severe traffic congestions in urban centers, compounded by growing reliance on the private automobile. City life became increasingly unmanageable for people who sought better housing and working conditions in the suburbs (Pumarada 1992).

During the 1980s, the Commonwealth government re-evaluated some of its policies towards urban centers. Law 148 for the rehabilitation of Santurce provides a case in point (Estado Libre Asociado de Puerto Rico 1988). The law's objectives included retaining and increasing the area's population; promoting the physical, economic, and social rehabilitation of lower-class neighborhoods; and occupying and renovating vacant structures. To implement its goals, the Puerto Rican Legislature commissioned planning and zoning studies favoring high-density and multiple-function structures in the urban core. New zoning regulations, adopted in 1992, were also aimed at strengthening and protecting the use of public spaces in Santurce. Finally, the regulations attempted to control the consolidation of urban plots of land to curb the expansion of multiple-story dwellings in residential neighborhoods.

In 1989, the president of Puerto Rico's Senate formed an ad hoc Committee for the Rehabilitation of Santurce to assess these proposals. The committee identified several major problems. First, planners failed to incorporate various sectors of the population in the proposals' design and implementation. For example, most Dominican immigrants and other groups of residents were not consulted on their needs and preferences. Second, the new regulations favored "re-peopling" the area, rather than retaining the existing population. As a result, the rehabilitation of Santurce is expected to entail greater gentrification and the replacement of poor neighborhoods by middle- and upper-class residents. Third, the local demand for goods and services was not surveyed. Thus, the integration between businesses and neighborhoods cannot be adequately promoted and financed. Finally, the new guidelines overlooked the rich vernacular architecture of Santurce's poor neighborhoods, focusing instead on its historic monuments and public buildings. Now as before, state intervention underestimated self-help housing initiatives.

Looking towards the Future

The Puerto Rican government should explore other planning alternatives to provide adequate housing for the urban poor. First, policies encouraging agglomeration into large metropolitan areas should be reassessed. To date, the extreme concentration of the island's population in San Juan and its surrounding munici-palities has created more problems than it has solved. Pollution, congestion, and crime besiege this burgeoning urban center. Moreover, the flight of upper-income groups beyond the borders of the city has depleted the tax base and thereby con-tributed to decrease the quality of public services in inner-city areas. Government planning should attempt to control the further growth of greater San Juan by de-centralizing economic activities in Puerto Rico. One move in this direction has been the promotion of new industrial parks outside the San Juan metropolitan area, in places such as Barceloneta and Humacao.

Second, the Commonwealth government should support self-help initiatives by poor households. Most state interventions in urban areas have replaced self-built houses with public housing projects. In the end, this policy has proven in-effective, as the current crisis with the *caserío* program suggests. Instead, govern-ment resources should be geared toward rehabilitating lower-class neighborhoods, as has recently been attempted in Alto del Cabro and Cantera. Urban housing policies should make use of existing resources within the community, such as artisanal construction labor and building expertise. Housing types should reflect the residents' needs and aspirations, rather than metropolitan models imposed by government planners. A viable, if partial, solution to the housing problems of the urban poor is to direct state resources to encourage the gradual improvement of shantytowns and working-class neighborhoods rather than invest in more public housing projects.[3]

Third, the state must recognize that self-help efforts by the urban poor are not sufficient to meet their needs for shelter. Policymakers must also intervene in the laws and regulations governing the distribution of urban space, as they did in Santurce after 1988. Among other measures, planners should continue to control housing rents, maintain mixed uses of space, provide a wide range of public ser-vices, promote community economic development, and attract diverse sectors of the population back to the city centers. Moreover, the state might well remove some of the structural constraints to the development of affordable housing. For example, privately owned estates can be expropriated and the land sold at low prices to the occupants of self-built structures, as has happened in Barrio Gandul. Financial incentives can help subsidize the physical improvement of lower-class neighborhoods rather than promote their wholesale removal and replacement by middle-class developments as a housing solution. Nothing less than a full-scale restructuring of current housing policies will significantly alter the living condi-tions of the urban poor in Puerto Rico today.

At this juncture, the state must re-evaluate its traditional stance vis-à-vis urban centers in Puerto Rico. The Commonwealth model of industrialization, urbaniza-tion, and migration has largely been discredited. New development strategies are in order. The privatization of public housing projects will not by itself solve the housing problems of the urban poor. Decentralization of the urban economy, on-site rehabilitation of lower-class neighborhoods, and community economic development are currently being explored. Policy measures should be geared toward increasing the population of the inner cities, stemming the uncontrolled growth of suburban settlements, improving the living conditions of public housing residents, and fostering the mixed uses of urban spaces. Private urban renewal efforts (such as "gentrification") should not displace lower-class households from their neighborhoods. Instead, government resources should support the gradual improvement of self-built houses and the development of full-scale urban communities. Finally, vernacular architectural styles should be preserved where possible as adaptive responses to local conditions.

Over the past four decades, urban housing conditions have ameliorated in Puerto Rico. Still, the island continues to have dilapidated and overcrowded inner-city neighborhoods like Barrio Gandul. Urban squatting remains a viable alternative for some lower-class households, although it is now not as widespread as in the 1930s and 1940s. A lopsided housing market favors the construction of more upper- and middle-class residences in suburban areas. Affordable housing for the poor, even the working poor, is becoming increasingly scarce. Government efforts to serve as a direct provider and manager of lower-class housing have collapsed. Such developments point to the need to rethink the way the government, private enterprise, and local communities can collaborate to develop long-term solutions to the housing problems of the urban poor. No new comprehensive model of urban renewal has yet emerged; perhaps the publication of this volume will stimulate further discussion on this pressing issue. In the meantime, Puerto Rico, like other Caribbean societies, enters the twenty-first century without effectively meeting its collective demand for shelter.

Notes

The illustrations for this chapter were obtained from Ana María Biascoechea, "El problema de la vivienda de la clase pobre en Puerto Rico y los proyectos del gobierno para mejorar dicha situación," (B.A. thesis, Colegio Universitario del Sagrado Corazón, 1944). Reproduced with permission of the author and the Biblioteca Madre María T. Guevara, Universidad del Sagrado Corazón. Many thanks to my brother, Raúl Duany, for help with the reproduction of the photographs.

1. As Santiago-Valles (1991) argues, the image of a "society under siege" was one of the key elements of the official discourse on Puerto Rico during the 1940s. The island's urban landscape, particularly the squatter settlements of San Juan, became the setting for this ideological representation. Conway (1985) notes that many urban planners in the Third World shared a negative view of self-help housing during the 1950s and 1960s.

2. In 1046, the local legislature approved the Reasonable Rent Law, covering about 200,000 housing units, mostly in the urban centers of San Juan, Ponce, and Mayagüez. The law currently controls about 60 per cent of Santurce's 20,000 rental units (*San Juan Star* 1993b).

3. For an overview of changing perspectives towards self-help housing in Third World cities, see Conway (1985).

References

Alvarado, C. M. (1967) "Los programas sobre la habitación urbana del Estado Libre Asociado de Puerto Rico." *Bienestar Público* 22 (87): 17–33.

Augelli, J. P. (1955) "Rural Settlement Types of Interior Puerto Rico: Sample Studies from the Upper Loíza Basin." In C. F. Jones and R. Picó, eds., *Symposium on the Geography of Puerto Rico,* 325–68. Río Piedras: University of Puerto Rico Press.

Bryce-Laporte, R. S. (1968) "Family Adaptation of Relocated Slum Dwellers in Puerto Rico." *Journal of Developing Areas* 2: 533–40.

Caplow, T., S. Sheldon, and S. E. Wallace. (1964) *The Urban Ambience: A Study of San Juan, Puerto Rico.* Totowa, N.J.: Bedminster Press.

Castañeda, I., N. Domenech Abreu, and O. Figueroa Navedo. (1987) "Una identificación de necesidades y recursos en las personas deambulantes de Santurce." Master's thesis, University of Puerto Rico.

Castro, M. de los Angeles. (1992) "La arquitectura del viejo San Juan: Mudanza de valores y persistencia de un estilo." In M. Méndez Guerrero, ed., *San Juan de Puerto Rico,* 25–35. Madrid: Ediciones de Cultura Hispánica.

Centro de Datos Censales, Universidad de Puerto Rico. (1985) *Perfil demográfico de la población de Puerto Rico: 1980.* Escuela Graduada de Salud Pública, Programa Graduado de Demografía, Universidad de Puerto Rico, Recinto de Ciencias Médicas.

———. (1993) "Perfil demográfico de la población de Puerto Rico, 1990." *Noticenso: Boletín del Centro de Datos Censales* 7 (1).

Conway, D. (1982) "Self-Help Housing, the Commodity Nature of Housing, and Amelioration of the Housing Deficit: Continuing the Turner-Burgess Debate." *Antipode* 14 (2): 40–46.

———. (1985) "Changing Perspectives on Squatter Settlements, Intraurban Mobility, and Constraints on Housing Choice of the Third World Urban Poor." *Urban Geography* 8 (2): 170–92.

Cotto, L. (1990) "La ocupación de tierras como lucha social: Los rescates de terreno en Puerto Rico: 1968–1976." *Revista de Ciencias Sociales* 29 (3–4), 409–30.

———. (1993) "The *Rescate* Movement: An Alternative Way of Doing Politics." In E. Meléndez and E. Meléndez, eds., *Colonial Dilemma: Critical Perspectives on Contemporary Puerto Rico,* 119–29. Boston: South End Press.

———. (1994) "Globalización, luchas urbanas y afirmación cultural en Puerto Rico, 1992." Paper presented at the XIX Annual Conference of the Caribbean Studies Association, Merida, Mexico, 24–28 May.

Cruz Rodríguez, A. I., N. García Trinidad, V. E. Díaz Vázquez, and N. I. Ortiz Navarro. (1990) "Perfil sub-barrio Gandul: Santurce, Puerto Rico." Unpublished paper, Graduate School of Social Work, University of Puerto Rico.

DACO (Departamento de Asuntos del Consumidor) Puerto Rico. (1988) "Estudio sobre la ley de alquileres razonables en Puerto Rico." Unpublished data.

Diálogo (San Juan). (1993a) "¿Por dónde vamos? A un año de la privatización de los residenciales públicos." Sept. issue: 10.

———. (1993b) "Un llamado a valorar la opinión de los residentes." Sept. issue: 14.

Duany, J. (1985) "Ethnicity in the Spanish Caribbean: Notes on the Consolidation of Creole Identity in Cuba and Puerto Rico, 1762–1868." In S. D. Glazier, ed., *Caribbean Ethnicity Revisited,* 15–39. New York: Gordon and Breach Science Publishers.

———. (1987) "*Buscando ambiente:* Estratificación social y minorías étnicas en San Juan, Puerto Rico." *Revista de Ciencias Sociales* 26 (1–4): 103–38.

Duany, J., L. Hernández Angueira, and C. A. Rey. (1995) *El Barrio Gandul: Economía subterránea y migración indocumentada en Puerto Rico.* Caracas: Nueva Sociedad.

El Mundo. (1982) "Consumado el desahucio." 19 May, 1, 17A.

El Nuevo Día. (1982a) "Crece la comunidad de Villa Sin Miedo." 30 Mar., 11.

―――. (1982b) "Lágrimas por un hombre del pueblo." 20 May, 4.

Estado Libre Asociado de Puerto Rico, Cámara de Representantes. (1988) Ley Número 148. Rehabilitación y desarrollo de Santurce. 4a. Sesión Ordinaria, 10a. Asamblea, 4 de agosto.

Estudios Técnicos. (1989) "Inventario de estructuras para el sector central de Santurce." Unpublished data. Prepared for the Puerto Rico Planning Board.

González Díaz, E., and N. Vargas Acevedo. (1988) "Ciudad, población y vida cotidiana: La cuestión urbana en el Puerto Rico 'moderno.'" *Revista de Ciencias Sociales* 27 (1–2): 1–16.

Government Development Bank, Puerto Rico. (1969) *A Special Report on Puerto Rico Urban Renewal and Housing Corporation*. San Juan: Government Development Bank of Puerto Rico.

Hollingshead, A. B., and L. H. Rogler. (1963) "Attitudes Towards Slums and Public Housing Conditions in Puerto Rico." In L. J. Duhl, ed., *The Urban Condition*, 229–45. New York: Basic Books.

Jopling, C. F. (1988) *Puerto Rican Houses in Sociohistorical Perspective*. Knoxville: University of Tennessee Press.

Junta de Planificación de Puerto Rico. (1978) *Situación de la vivienda en Puerto Rico: 1977–80*, vol. 2. Santurce: Junta de Planificación de Puerto Rico.

Maldonado, C. D. (1947) "Arrabales en la zona de San Juan." B.A. thesis, College of the Sacred Heart, Santurce.

Negrón Portillo, M., and Mayo R. Santana. (1992) *La esclavitud urbana en San Juan*. Río Piedras: Centro de Investigaciones Sociales, Universidad de Puerto Rico/Huracán.

Pérez Velasco, E. J. (1984) "La condición obrera en Puerto Rico (1898–1920)." *Plural* 3 (1–2): 157–70.

Picó, R. (1952) "La eliminación de arrabales y los programas de vivienda." *El Mundo*, 12 Dec.

―――. (1975) *Nueva geografía de Puerto Rico: Física, económica y social*. Río Piedras: Editorial Universitaria.

Pumarada, R. (1992) "Leon Krier y la recuperación de la ciudad." In L. Krier, *Completar Santurce: Estudio preliminar para el plan maestro de un barrio*, 11–18. San Juan: Oficina de Asuntos Urbanos, Oficina del Gobernador.

Quintero Rivera, A. G. (1981) *Conflictos de clase y política en Puerto Rico*, 3d edition. Río Piedras: Centro de Estudios de la Realidad Puertorriqueña/Huracán.

―――. (1987) "The Rural-Urban Dichotomy in the Formation of Puerto Rico's Cultural Identity." *New West Indian Guide* 61 (3–4): 127–44.

Ramírez, R. L. (1977) *El arrabal y la política*. Río Piedras: Editorial Universitaria.

Rigau, J. (1992) *Puerto Rico 1900: Turn-of-the Century Architecture in the Hispanic Caribbean, 1890–1930*. New York: Rizzoli.

Román, M. (1993) *Estado y criminalidad en Puerto Rico*. San Juan: Publicaciones Puertorriqueñas.

Safa, H. I. (1974) *The Urban Poor of Puerto Rico: A Study in Development and Inequality*. New York: Holt, Rinehart, and Winston.

San Juan Star. (1982) "Uncertain Future Clouds Life in Project." 8 Nov., 10–11.

―――. (1993a) "Police, NG Swarm into Hato Rey Project." 8 Sept., 7.

―――. (1993b) "Updating Rent Control Law Could Further Stifle Affordable Housing." 11 Sept., 23, 24.

Santiago-Valles, K. A. (1991) "Social Structure and Contested Subjectification in Puerto Rico, 1940–1985." Paper presented at the XVI International Congress of the Latin American Studies Association, Crystal City, Virginia, 4–6 Apr.

Scarano, F. (1993) *Puerto Rico: Cinco siglos de historia*. San Juan: McGraw-Hill.

Schwirian, K. P., and Rico-Velasco, J. (1971) "The Residential Distribution of Status Groups in Puerto Rico's Metropolitan Areas." *Demography* 8 (1): 81–90.

Sepúlveda, A., and Carbonell, J. (1988) *Cangrejos—Santurce: Historia ilustrada de su desarrollo urbano (1519–1950)*. San Juan: Centro de Investigaciones CARIMAR/Oficina Estatal de Preservación Histórica.

Sepúlveda Rivera, A. (1989) *San Juan: Historia ilustrada de su desarrollo urbano, 1508–1898*. San Juan: Centro de Investigaciones CARIMAR.

Slesin, S., S. Cliff, and J. Berthelot. (1985) *Caribbean Style*. New York: Clarkson N. Potter.

Stevens, R. W. (1985) "Los arrabales de San Juan: Una perspectiva histórica." *Revista de Ciencias Sociales* 24 (1–2): 155–200.

U.S. Department of Commerce, Bureau of the Census. (1984) *1980 Census of Population and Housing: Census Tracts. San Juan, Puerto Rico*. Washington D.C.: U.S. Government Printing Office.

————. (1991) *1990 Census of Population and Housing: Summary Population and Housing Characteristics. Puerto Rico*. Washington, D.C.: U.S. Government Printing Office.

————. (1993) "Puerto Rico to Receive Economic, Social, and Housing 'Portrait' Drawn from 1990 Census Long Form." Press Release. Public Information Office, U.S. Department of Commerce, 29 Jan.

Vivoni Farage, E. (1992) "El Capitolio de Puerto Rico, 1907–1929: Origen y transformación de un ideal." In C. Rafucci, S. A. Curbelo, and F. Picó, eds., *Senado de Puerto Rico, 1917–1992: Ensayos de historia institucional*, 51–102. San Juan: Senado de Puerto Rico.

Chapter 11

Housing and the State in the French Caribbean

Stephanie A. Condon
and Philip E. Ogden

> The housing sector, in the same way as health, is one of those aspects of
> national "solidarity" for which state intervention is of prime importance,
> especially in allowing many households access to a dwelling in relation to
> their financial means.
>
> (Antilla 1994: 27)

This quotation from a recent survey of housing policies in the French Caribbean
islands of Guadeloupe and Martinique hints at a number of themes which this
chapter seeks to develop. Housing conditions have improved rapidly since 1945,
and especially over the last twenty years. By 1990, for example, a quarter of the
dwellings were less than eight years old, and traditional shack housing ("*cases*")
had declined from around one in three dwellings in 1982 to one in eight in
Martinique and from one in two to one in five in Guadeloupe. The role of the
French state has been crucial in determining the rate and nature of the modernization of the housing stock.

Three principal aspects underpin the later empirical information on which this
chapter is based: first, the nature and significance of the islands' status as *départements d'outre mer*; second, the way in which the housing policies of metropolitan France have evolved and been adapted to the specific needs of the Carib-

bean; and, third, the pressures which the changing demography and economy of the islands have placed on housing provision. For these principal reasons, the case of the French islands is distinctive in the wider Caribbean environment, as a reading of this essay in comparison with the others in this volume will readily demonstrate. This chapter seeks to outline the distinctive background in a little more detail, to trace some of the principal housing pressures during the first two decades after *départementalisation,* to sketch current housing conditions and, finally, to develop some ideas about the specific role of the French state over the last twenty years. The sources on which the chapter relies include the successive population censuses up to the most recent in 1990, contemporary studies, and a number of reports by, and interviews with, those principally concerned with the development of housing policy.

The designation of the islands as *départements d'outre mer* in 1946 lies at the heart of any understanding of socioeconomic change over the following half century. As documented elsewhere (for example, Murch 1971), the decision to integrate the islands administratively and politically into metropolitan France meant that they became increasingly distinctive in the wider Caribbean context, that much policy was developed and determined according to the imperatives of the central French state (Domenach and Picouet 1992; Condon and Ogden 1991a, 1991b), but that specific initiatives were taken, again from the métropole, to respond to the particular Caribbean context. For example, for De Gaulle and successive French governments, the overseas departments were something of a showcase for a French version of postcolonialism; and, further, the maintenance of the status itself depended on a political peace created both by local social investment and by a deliberate policy of encouraging emigration to the métropole (Condon and Ogden 1991a: 509). For the islands themselves, as Gastmann and MacDonald (1989: 251) have indicated, a further consequence has been the growth of an increasingly urban consumerism dominated by metropolitan French and Western values. The development of policy has been in the context of the overseas departments and territories (DOM-TOM) as a whole (that is, principally, Guadeloupe, Martinique, Réunion, Guiana), and the point of comparison is increasingly with *départements* of metropolitan France. There is hardly any mention in the French literature of comparisons with the rest of the Caribbean, which gives the scope of the present volume added interest.

Housing policies in the Caribbean owe as much to the politics of metropolitan France as they do to local conditions. As we have documented elsewhere, for the Afro-Caribbean population who had migrated to the métropole (Condon and Ogden 1993), public housing in various forms became central from the 1960s onwards when urbanization and a legacy of generally very poor housing conditions emphasized the role of HLM *(Habitations à loyer modéré)* and other state-assisted housing. In the Caribbean, three elements were of importance in the way central housing policy was adapted: first, and by far the most important, direct state funding came through the budgets of the *Ministère de l'Equipment* with, second, some of the more general policy parameters being set by the ministry for the overseas departments and territories (DOM-TOM); and, finally, the detailed application of some aspects of housing policies was determined by the elected departmental and local councils. A later section of this chapter documents in detail the specific schemes created for the Caribbean context. Whilst the consequent improvements in housing conditions cannot be doubted, there have been a number of implicit and explicit cultural conflicts in the way housing policy, defined essentially in Paris, has been applied. One such eloquent testimony to the fate of a bidonville in Fort-de-France is provided by Patrick Chamoiseau's (1992) recent novel, *Texaco*.

The demography of the islands has evolved rapidly and, together with general changes in population distribution, urbanization, and changing economic structures, has had a major impact on the political importance attached to housing provision. Rapid population growth became a principal feature of both Guadeloupe and Martinique during the 1950s and 1960s; the population of the islands increased by one-third between the censuses of 1954 and 1967. This prompted the government to encourage emigration to the métropole and also to embark upon a more integrated policy of social development in the islands themselves. Emigration and fertility control produced a considerable slackening of population growth from 3.1 percent per annum in 1954–61 to 0.1 percent per annum in 1974–82. This was, however, reversed during the 1980s, as emigration faltered in response to changing economic conditions in metropolitan France, and a certain degree of return migration occurred (Condon and Ogden 1996). Urban growth continued apace through most of the postwar period, with the principal towns of Fort-de-France (in Martinique) and Pointe-à-Pitre (in Guadeloupe) attracting an increasing number of rural-urban migrants (Jolivet 1985: 109). This reflected, in turn, the collapse of agricultural production and a sharply increased concentration of employment in the tertiary sector, not least in the public services (Narfez 1976: 116). The status of overseas departments has certainly brought a sharp rise in standards of living for certain categories of the population, whilst they have stagnated or worsened, in relative terms, for others (Dagas and Meyer 1993). As we show below, whilst housing conditions for many have improved dramatically, "islands of deprivation" persist for some. The influence of the state on the wider demographic environment is also evident. The French islands have amongst the highest levels of life-expectancy and lowest levels of infant mortality in the Caribbean (Guengant 1993) and are on a par with those in the métropole, with infant mortality at 6.2 per thousand in Martinique, for example, by 1992. Other factors are also likely to lead to renewed population growth: while fertility was down to 2.1 children per woman by 1992, the young age structure produced a crude birth rate of 16.9 per thousand and crude death rate of 5.8, such that population growth will continue to provide an urgent background against which housing policies will have to be set. For example, assuming roughly current demographic trends, the population of Martinique is likely to grow from 371,000 in 1992 to 431,000 by 2010 (INSEE 1993a: 33). Of particular significance for housing policy is household change. While average household size declined sharply during the 1970s and 1980s, the number of households increased dramatically. In Guadeloupe, for example, households increased from a little under 77,000 in 1974 to over 112,000 by 1990, and in Martinique a medium projection of demographic trends suggests an additional 32,000 households will need to be housed between 1990 and 2000 (Conseil Général 1993: 18), in addition to the urgent need for improvement in current housing conditions.

Housing policies were implemented, then, against a background of rapid sociodemographic change. Before discussing the nature of housing stock improvement and the impact of policy on housing conditions throughout French Caribbean society, we will turn first to one of the principal generators of social change and one directly affecting both conditions and policy in housing, that is, migration to the towns.

Traditional Housing and the Rural Exodus

But what saved me was the knowledge that the town was there. The town, with its bright new opportunities, selling promises of a life without sugar cane or békés (white plantation owners). The town, where one's toes would no longer be mud-coloured. The town, which fascinated each and every one of us.

P. Chamoiseau (1992: 43–44)

Slavery and colonization clearly have made an impact on the built environment in Caribbean societies. What is less clear is the extent to which African traditions have influenced housing types (Leiris 1955: 48). The *case* is typically a wooden construction composed of a single room, built in a manner to enable future extension if necessary. A variety of building materials is used, wood panels protecting an inner shell of wattle, daub, or other vegetable matter, perhaps replaced later by zinc sheeting on the wind-facing walls. Kitchen duties, washing, and other household activities are performed outside the *case,* the cooking facilities being protected by a sheltering roof usually made of corrugated iron.

Under colonization, slaves could take no initiative in the building of their dwellings, neither in location, materials, nor design. Slave huts were often large, occupied by groups centered around the master's large home. With the abolition of slavery and the gradual constitution of small property during the nineteenth century, the *cases* and their inhabitants dispersed throughout the islands (Menauge 1977; Baptistide 1982). The essential characteristics of the slave hut persisted, but in a smaller form (roughly three meters by six meters), inhabited by a single household and surrounded by a garden (perhaps shared) for the cultivation of ground provisions or raising poultry (Mintz 1984; Chivallon 1993: 17). Other plots at some distance from the *case* were sometimes owned. This is a form of housing "adapted to self-sufficient societies, in harmony with the environment in which the inhabitant finds his or her building materials and most foodstuffs" (Berthelot and Gaumé 1984: 80). There are slight architectural differences between the Martiniquan and the Guadeloupean *case,* the former being placed on a stone ledge, the latter, either on four large stones (Grande-Terre) or on short stilts (Basse-Terre). An important feature of the *case* is that it is a mobile structure, a legacy of colonization when slave huts were moved to different fields according to plantation requirements (Coit 1988: 13). The true *case* has remained mobile to this day, indicating the closeness of the relationship of people with their homes rather than with the land. Coit (1988: 16) also argues that the heritage of slavery has meant a lack of tradition in skilled building craftsmen and thus only elementary building skills have been passed from one generation to the next (cf. Leiris 1955: 79).

Mobility rapidly became a way of life for many people after emancipation. Women would travel on foot to the nearest town to sell a tray of vegetables, people would go to church on Sunday, men unable to support their families solely from the produce of their garden plot would travel to work elsewhere, often farther afield than the neighboring factory or distillery, thus avoiding renewed dependency on the plantation system (Revert 1949: 293). Many of these mobile workers would build a temporary shelter—an *ajoupa*—near their place of work, returning to their homes on their days off. However, sugar factories, fearing labor shortages, offered housing with garden plots to workers often free of charge, housing that Revert (1949: 294) described in the 1940s as being among the poorest.

The transport revolution transformed mobility on the islands in the 1930s. People began to travel into town by *taxis pays,* trucks converted into buses. Gradually, those who had become accustomed to going regularly into town to work, to sell their wares, or for other reasons, began to look for permanent settlement there, and the rural *case* became a temporary residence linked to the garden plot (Revert 1949: 297). The movement steadily accelerated during the 1940s, then took off in the 1950s. Following the model set by the mulatto bourgeoisie from the mid-nineteenth century, people left the countryside. Rather than being the response to opportunities offered by an expanding economy, since this was nonexistent (Lasserre 1961: 627), migrants were seeking social advancement, plus the advantages of a new consumer society and services introduced through *départementalization* (Letchimy 1985: 126; Jolivet 1985; Zobel 1974).

The towns of Fort-de-France (Martinique) and Pointe-à-Pitre (Guadeloupe) had already emerged as major urban complexes by the end of the eighteenth century. In the nineteenth century, they gradually overtook in importance the older port cities of St. Pierre and Basse-Terre (Gastman and MacDonald 1989: 239–40). At the same time, the smaller townships, linked to the plantation system under colonization, expanded with the creation of central sugar-processing factories in the mid-nineteenth century, and later, upon *départementalisation,* they were attributed service functions (Bertile 1984: 33). With the sugar crisis and the unemployment that ensued, the rural exodus then directed itself to the main towns from the latter part of the nineteenth-century (Gastman and MacDonald 1989: 243; Jolivet 1985). Subsequently, Fort-de-France received many former inhabitants of St. Pierre after the eruptions of the volcano Mont Pelée (1902 and 1929), and Pointe-à-Pitre's public works schemes following the 1928 hurricane attracted numerous workers to the town (Revert 1949: 292; Lasserre 1961: 604–5). Yet, migration to the main towns rose most sharply from the late 1940s. The towns were totally unprepared for this massive arrival, and available rented housing or decent land upon which to set down one's *case* were rapidly taken up. It was then that the problem of shantytowns really began to dominate the problems of urban housing, as will be discussed more fully subsequently. The town of Fort-de-France saw its population grow from 60,648 inhabitants to 96,943 between the 1954 and 1967 censuses. Between the same dates, the growth of the two main Guadeloupean towns was less spectacular, Basse-Terre growing from 11,837 to 15,833 and Pointe-à-Pitre from 26,160 to 29,160. However, as during previous decades, the growth of the latter was constrained by the city limits and spilled over into neighboring Abymes, which, during the same period, more than doubled in size, from 18,425 inhabitants in 1954 to 39,947 in 1967.

Urban concentration since has continued unabated. By 1990, over 90 percent of the population in both islands lived in urban areas, and the population of Fort-de-France had increased to 133,920 and Pointe-à-Pitre/Abymes to 124,422. For some groups, lifestyles changed radically as the whole of French Caribbean society was transformed. Overall, living standards have improved enormously since the 1950s, but, at the same time, the island societies have become more complex. Intermediate groups have formed as an extension to the mulatto middle class born in the nineteenth century, the most notable being that of the public-sector employees, who enjoy a stable income and various other advantages (Leiris 1955; Giraud 1979). This group stands in stark contrast to a good third of the active population, striving to make a living from seasonal employment and odd jobs interspersed with periods of full or semi-unemployment (Domenach and Guengant 1981; Blérald 1986). Since *départementalisation,* the islands' economic structures have changed from a largely agricultural to a service base, for the rural exodus signified a move from rural to urban employment for an increasing number of people. Thus, in 1961, around 48 percent of the islands' active population was employed in the primary sector, and by 1974 the proportion had fallen to 22 percent in Guadeloupe and to 18 percent in Martinique. At the same time, the proportion of the active population working in the tertiary sector rose from around 30 percent to 55 percent in Guadeloupe and to 63 percent in Martinique (Dépt. de la Martinique 1965, Table A; Dépt. de la Guadeloupe 1965, Table 2).[1] Another aspect of change profoundly affecting lifestyle was the fall in birth rate, and thus a reduction in family size, which occurred first in the towns. For example, in Martinique in 1967, fertility was 25 percent lower in Fort-de-France than elsewhere in the island (Léridon 1970: 106). Demographers attributed the fertility decline in the islands to a combination of the movement to towns and modernization (Charbit and Léridon 1980).

Such lifestyle changes were accompanied for some by access to modern homes. Yet, the majority of the new households were still obliged to build their own *case* or, for those having moved their *case* to the town, gradually convert the *case* into a more permanent, sound dwelling. As soon as it became financially feasible for the household to do so, the owner of the *case* would replace the wooden walls, beginning with those facing the oncoming winds, with bricks or concrete if they were affordable (fig. 11.1). Next, the floor would be replaced by cement. If there was space around the *case,* additional rooms might be added on to the initial structure. As a general rule, the corrugated iron roof and the wooden or cardboard room separations were retained. This conversion of the *case* could take several years, depending on the income changes of the household, and was carried out by both inhabitants of the poorer, country areas and of the outskirts of towns. As

Fig. 11.1. Traditional self-built housing in an urban setting with building materials piled up awaiting use, Morne-à-L'eau, Guadeloupe.

Menauge (1977: 1) concluded, this conversion was not only a necessity, but an ideal for the poorest sections of the community, which had neither access to modern homeownership nor to the rental sector. For, despite sizable building programs in the 1960s and 1970s, in both the private and public housing sectors, a considerable portion of the islands' populations was left with no choice but to build their own homes.

The Evolution of Housing Conditions

In a number of respects, the last two decades have proved revolutionary for the islands in terms of the type of housing provided and the level of domestic comfort. Poor conditions were widespread until the mid-1970s, but thereafter an extensive program of new building and improvements brought at least basic provision to the majority of the population. Nevertheless, poor conditions do persist in certain geographical areas and for certain socioeconomic groups and reflect the degree of social polarity which the particular sort of economic development encouraged by *départementalisation* has created.

The accompanying tables are eloquent testimony to the pace and extent of change. Table 11.1 indicates the extraordinary level of housing activity since 1982, in response to population and household growth, to private initiative, and to concerted state action to improve housing provision. Thus, by 1990, almost one-third of all dwellings in both islands had been built since the previous census in 1982, and only one-half dated from before 1975. Table 11.2 indicates that this was accompanied both by a decline in the average number of persons per dwelling and an increase in the average number of rooms per dwelling, the latter increasing from around 2.5 in 1961 to 3.7 in 1990.

There were two particularly important aspects to this process, which had a major effect both on the landscape and on the general level of housing provision. First was the decline in the number of *cases*,[2] especially in Martinique. By 1990,

Table 11.1

Age of Housing Stock in Guadeloupe and Martinique

Date	Percentage			
	All Dwellings		**Principal Dwellings**[a]	
	Guadeloupe	**Martinique**	**Guadeloupe**	**Martinique**
Before 1975	48	54	49	54
1975-1982	21	18	21	19
After 1982	31	28	30	27

SOURCE: INSEE (1993a, 1993b: 45).
NOTE: [a]Excluding second homes and empty dwellings.

Table 11.2

Evolution of Number of Persons per Household and Number of Rooms per Dwelling, Guadeloupe and Martinique, 1961-1990

Date	Ave. No. of Persons per Household		Ave. No. of Rooms per Dwelling	
	Guadeloupe	Martinique	Guadeloupe	Martinique
1961	4.1	4.2	2.5	2.7
1967	4.2	4.4	3.0	3.0
1974	4.2	4.2	3.4	2.8
1982	3.7	3.8	3.5	3.4
1990	3.4	3.3	3.7	3.7

SOURCES:INSEE (1993a, 1993b: 47).

there were still around 40,000 in the two islands (table 11.3), but they accounted for only 18 percent of the housing stock, compared to 63 percent in Guadeloupe and 53 percent in Martinique in 1974 (Cazenave 1991: 24). Second, there is the growth of blocks of flats, largely in the public sector. By 1990, over 40,000 dwellings were in this category (table 11.3), concentrated particularly in the principal urban areas, representing an increase from 5 percent in 1974 to 18 percent by 1990. Thus, in Fort-de-France 32 percent and in Pointe-à-Pitre 79 percent of all dwellings were in this category. The vast majority were rented rather than owned. In general, in the two islands, about one-third of all homes were rented, 46 percent owned both house and land, 16 percent owned the house but not the land, and about 6 percent were housed by their employers.

Housing tenure is nevertheless an inadequate indicator of housing standards, for the owner-occupier group includes households at both ends of the socioeconomic scale. Whilst employers, the self-employed, professionals, and waged farm workers gained increasing homeownership during the 1960s and 1970s, it was also the least well-off section of society that tended to be homeowners, for a number of reasons. Thus, apart from the fact that collective housing units were too expensive for such households, traditional housing suited their lifestyles, and they were able to build and modify their own homes using cheap materials. The other groups—white-collar workers in both the private and public sectors, middle and top executives, and waged fishermen—were attracted by the relative comfort of rented housing. Thus, as Menauge (1977) points out, insofar as departmental status of the islands encouraged home renting, the consequence was improved housing conditions and, indirectly, raised social status of the occupants of such housing. Moreover, the status of certain households, notably those enjoying two public-service salaries, rose rapidly during the 1970s and formed a "public-sector middle class" with increasing access to second homes. Often, these were former permanent homes of the households concerned, but a growing number of new second homes were being built from the late 1960s.

The improvement in housing conditions has been dramatic since the mid-1970s. Table 11.4 demonstrates, for example, that as late as the census of 1974 only around one-third of houses had inside running water, only a half had elec-

Table 11.3

Main housing types and levels of comfort in Guadeloupe (G) and Martinique (M), 1990

Housing Type		Number	Percent of total	Percentage of households:		
				with inside WC and bath	with fridge	with TV
Habitation de fortune	G	5566	4.95	9	34	28
	M	3561	3.34	14	35	36
Case traditionnelle	G	21,850	19.43	46	75	63
(traditional shacks)	M	8,844	8.30	33	62	61
Maison traditionnelle	G	13,286	11.81	55	80	65
(traditional house)	M	9,376	8.80	57	78	75
Maison en dur	G	50,941	45.29	85	91	81
(solid construction)	M	65,274	61.27	88	92	89
Immeuble collectif	G	20,855	18.52	93	95	74
(flats)	M	19,481	18.29	96	95	85
Total	G	112,478	100	71	85	79
	M	106,536	100	79	87	82

SOURCES: Cazenave (1991: 25); Zabaleta (1991: 29), from 1990 census data (INSEE, 1991: 16).

tricity, and considerably fewer had inside lavatories and bathrooms. This certainly represented some progress on 1954, when the census revealed that only 19.5 percent of dwellings in Martinique and 14 percent in Guadeloupe had electricity, and 16.5 percent and 6.8 percent had running water. By 1990, these basic amenities had become the norm for the majority of households, and refrigerators, telephones, and televisions had become very widespread. Table 11.5 demonstrates that by 1990 the basic goods did not vary enormously by socioprofessional groups: only washing machines and freezers had failed to make a major impact amongst the less well-off. Zabaleta (1991: 27) has calculated that if we take provision of fridge, freezer, washing machine, and television, we can see two extremes: 27 percent of all households in Guadeloupe and 24 percent in Martinique have all four; 11 percent in Guadeloupe and 9 percent in Martinique have none of the four. Within this general picture of rapid improvement, particularly compared to the low base of the 1960s and early 1970s, there is nevertheless a need for caution. The very improvement in conditions for the majority draws attention to the remaining poor conditions for a large number, concentrated both socially and geographically. From the outset, investment in housing and infrastructure has been concentrated in the main towns. In the rural areas, water and electricity supplies long remained patchy. Thus, table 11.3 shows that, in 1970, some 29 percent of households in Martinique lacked the combination of inside lavatory and bathroom. In 1980, 35 percent of the households of Guadeloupe and 15 percent of those of Martinique were without a water supply and some villages still had no sewage-disposal system. This was, inevitably, strongly linked to housing type: traditional housing was still very underequipped. Cazenave (1991: 23–24) notes that this "precarious" housing came to renewed public attention at the time of Hurricane Hugo in 1989 in Guadeloupe, when the ten thousand houses destroyed were particularly concentrated amongst the poorest. Much of the worst housing is also the oldest, but there is a continuing problem of recent uncontrolled speculation and housing construction "au sauvage," houses built on vacant land, without planning permission, and, therefore, without basic infrastructure (Cazenave 1991: 25–26).

Composite definitions of housing deprivation vary. Map 11.1 shows the geography of one measure of deprivation in 1990. This is defined as dwellings without both electricity and water; those with water but no electricity; those with electricity and no water; and those with electricity and water but the latter outside the dwelling (fig. 11.2). This includes a total of 14,809 (13.9 percent) for Martinique and 22,491 (20 percent) for Guadeloupe. The number of people living in such

Table 11.4

Evolution of Housing Conditions in Guadeloupe (G) and Martinique (M)

| | | Percentage of houses | | | | |
		1961	1967	1974	1982	1990
Water supply in home	G	7	47	32	68	83
	M	18	34	40	78	90
Electricity	G	25	40	55	77	89
	M	23	32	45	72	90
Inside WC	G	10	22	47	55	78
	M	12	25	36	63	89
Shower or bath	G	—	—	38	62	74
	M	—	—	29	52	83
Mains drainage	G	—	—	—	25	36
	M	—	—	—	23	38

SOURCES: INSEE (1993a, 1993b: 47).

Table 11.5
Household Equipment by Selected Socioprofessional Groups, Guadeloupe (G) and Martinique (M), 1990

		Agriculture	Managers / Professionals Professionals	Professions	Employees	Workers	All
Fridge	G	77	99	97	90	79	83
	M	80	99	97	92	83	87
Freezer	G	35	61	53	39	28	35
	M	33	59	50	33	25	31
Telephone	G	76	90	84	74	60	71
	M	81	94	91	85	77	83
Air Conditioning	G	4	44	26	11	5	11
	M	2	22	10	3	2	5
Washing-machines	G	52	89	83	66	48	58
	M	43	86	78	57	43	52
Television	G	75	91	90	86	75	79
	M	78	88	90	86	80	82
Car	G	50	93	87	86	75	79
	M	60	93	87	54	52	53

SOURCES: INSEE (1993a, 1993b: 67).

conditions was 66,458 (17 percent) in Guadeloupe and 42,312 (11.9 percent) in Martinique. A more subtle definition of *précarité* by researchers at the National Statistical Institute (INSEE) takes into account the type of housing construction and includes all the *habitations de fortune* (temporary shacks); those traditional *cases* which lacked either water or electricity or WC or inside bathrooms and those traditional houses without both water and electricity (Dagas 1992: 27). This gives totals for Guadeloupe of 18,000 (16 percent of the total) and for Martinique of 10,000 (9.4 percent) (see Conseil Général 1993; Zabaleta and Nema 1992: 30). It is also worth noting that Dagas (1993: 41) in a later article draws the definition of *précarité* rather wider and the number of such dwellings rises to 36,786 (32.7 percent) in Guadeloupe and 18,702 (17.6 percent) in Martinique. This brings into the definition not only the traditional shacks but also a large number of dwellings of solid construction that lack one or more of the basic elements of comfort of inside running water, electricity, WC, or bathroom. Similarly, Cazenave (1991: 23–24) calculated that some 32,000 dwellings in Guadeloupe and 22,000 in Martinique lacked the combination of water, electricity, inside lavatories, and bath or showers in 1990. Whichever measure is used, there has certainly been a great improvement. Using the Dagas (1992) definitions above, for example, the decline has been from 55.2 percent in Guadeloupe and 38.7 percent in Martinique since 1982, though the number of people living in poor conditions is still very substantial.

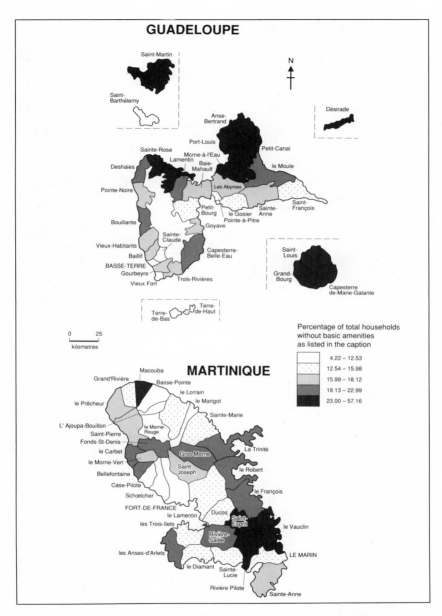

GUADELOUPE

Saint-Martin

Saint-Barthélemy

N

Anse-Bertrand

Désirade

Port-Louis

Petit-Canal

Sainte-Rose

Morne-à-l'Eau

Lamentin

Baie-Mahault

le Moule

Deshaies

Les Abymes

Pointe-Noire

Petit-Bourg

le Gosier

Sainte-Anne

Saint-François

Bouillante

Pointe-à-Pitre

Goyave

Sainte-Claude

Vieux-Habitants

Capesterre-Belle-Eau

Saint-Louis

Baillif

BASSE-TERRE

Grand-Bourg

Gourbeyre

Vieux Fort

Trois-Rivières

Capesterre-de-Marie-Galante

Terre-de-Bas

Terre-de-Haut

0   25

kilometres

Percentage of total households
without basic amenities
as listed in the caption

	4.22 – 12.53
	12.54 – 15.98
	15.99 – 18.12
	18.13 – 22.99
	23.00 – 57.16

MARTINIQUE

Macouba

Grand'Rivière

Basse-Pointe

le Lorrain

le Prêcheur

le Marigot

Sainte-Marie

L' Ajoupa-Bouillon

le Morne-Rouge

Saint-Pierre

Fonds-St-Denis

le Carbet

Gros Morne

La Trinité

le Morne-Vert

Saint-Joseph

Bellefontaine

le Robert

Case-Pilote

Schœlcher

le François

FORT-DE-FRANCE

le Lamentin

Ducos

Saint-Esprit

les Trois-Ilets

le Vauclin

Rivière-Salée

les Anses-d'Arlets

LE MARIN

le Diamant

Sainte-Lucie

Rivière Pilote

Sainte-Anne

Map 11.1. Basic housing deprivation in Guadeloupe and Martinique, 1990 (includes all those dwellings without electricity and water, those with water and no electricity, those with electricity and no water, and those with electricity and water but the latter outside the dwelling). Adapted from INSEE (1991: Table Log 1.1 Res).

Fig. 11.2. Traditional housing with limited conversion and television aerial, Vieux Bourg, Grande-Terre, Guadeloupe.

In both departments, as map 11.1 shows, the worst housing is located in pockets of poverty, both in the countryside and in the main towns. Thus, levels of deprivation are particularly marked in the small fishing and farming communities of eastern and southern Martinique, in northern Guadeloupe, and in the outlying island dependencies of Désirade, Marie Galante, and St. Martin. Yet, these pockets of poverty also exist at the heart of the cities, sometimes in tightly knit communities, sometimes lying starkly adjacent to much better-off housing. There is obviously a general relationship between these poor housing conditions, unemployment, and low incomes. But both Dagas (1992) and Zabaleta and Nema (1992) point out further subtle contrasts between rural and urban. In rural areas, the most disadvantaged households are frequently the old or large families; in urban areas, they tend to be found amongst the young and single-parent families. Indeed, the report by the Conseil Général (1993: 14) demonstrated that one-person households, those with no employed persons, and the elderly were particularly overrepresented in the poorest housing. These dwellings were also the smallest (67 percent had only one or two rooms compared with 12 percent in Martinique as a whole), and they had the highest proportion of owners of the house but not the land on which it stood.

The question of poor housing conditions in the two principal cities of Fort-de-

France and Pointe-à-Pitre remains critical. Areas such as Texaco in Fort-de-France or La Batelière in the suburb of Schoelcher may have improved markedly, and areas such as Volga Plage or Canal Alaric are well on the way, but a dozen or so areas of deprivation remain in the capital. In Pointe-à-Pitre, the Boissard quarter is now infamous: some 1,319 of its 2,472 dwellings fall within the definition of deprivation by Dagas (1992) given above. Three-quarters of the housing consists of old *cases,* 40 percent have neither running water nor lavatories, and unemployment stands at 40 percent. Yet, only 14 percent have no electricity and levels of provision in the basics of refrigerators and televisions approach the departmental average (Dagas 1992: 28). Overall, there is still much work for urban planners to do. But Zabaleta and Nema (1992: 31) remind us how far the French islands have progressed, certainly in comparison with many other Caribbean states, as elucidated in this volume. Of the 1,713 small-area census divisions used in 1990, 500 had no dwellings which qualified under the definition of deprivation used, and only 34 had more than 40 percent of the housing stock in this category. Yet, this very dispersal of a certain proportion of the poor housing stock represents a particular challenge for policymakers.

Housing Policies and the Upgrading of Housing Stock: Modern Homes for All?

> For concrete was the town par excellence, the definitive signal that one was making one's way in life.
>
> Chamoiseau (1992: 391)

The housing conditions for a large part of the French Caribbean population have thus been transformed. Much of this transformation would not have been possible without the intervention of the state in terms of planning and funding. The main housing problems facing the island departments four decades ago were those facing the rest of France.

First, there was a general need for house building throughout the country because of the high number of young households forced to cohabit with parents through lack of available dwellings, and this shortage was greatest in the towns, where the population growth was highest. Second, thousands of existing dwellings were in urgent need of modernization or reconstruction. In many rural areas and on some urban fringes, considerable numbers of homes lacked water supply, toilet facilities, and electricity, or perhaps enjoyed only one of these basic amenities. As late as 1961, 46 percent of the population of mainland France had no access to sewage disposal systems and 14 percent had no drinking water supply (CGP 1965: 41) and still in 1968, 55 percent of dwellings lacked at least one basic amenity (CGP 1971: 53). On the outskirts of the major cities, notably Paris, Lyons, and Marseilles, shantytowns—known as the *bidonvilles* and most usually housing foreign migrants—sprang up in areas devoid of infrastructure (Castles and Kosack 1973; Hervo and Charras 1971). In the shantytowns of Pointe-à-Pitre and Fort-de-France, settlements were characterized by the vernacular housing type, dwellings either having been transported from the rural areas or built on the occupant's arrival in town. Yet, the shantytowns were to be far from temporary in the French Caribbean, as house-building programs never managed to catch up with the backlog of housing need.

During the period of postwar national reconstruction, emphasis in France generally was laid upon the industrial and service sectors and relatively little investment was made in the housing sphere. The severity of the housing crisis soon became so apparent that, at the beginning of the 1950s, the state took a series of measures in order to finance construction and renovation (Duclaud-Williams 1978). Yet, the accumulation of shortages in most types of housing since the 1920s meant that the effects of new housing policies remained fairly limited for many years to come. Throughout the 1950s and 1960s, the national plan's stated aims of between 400,000 and 500,000 new homes to be built in mainland France, of which over half were to be in the social sector (CGP 1957, 1961, 1966; Topalov 1987). The overseas departments have always been treated separately from the mainland in terms of funding, allocation of building finance and planning being decided by departmental committees. Targets would be set, as in mainland France, and applications made to the relevant ministries (housing, social services, and others) for supplementary grant aid.

There have been several differences between mainland France and the Caribbean departments in the treatment of housing provision. First, in the Caribbean, most housing finance during the last forty years has been public in origin, enabling the construction of low-cost individual and collective housing (De Panisse 1985: 136). Second, for two decades, most social housing construction in France was financed by the *aide à la pierre,* a global construction aid by the state, consisting of grants to house builders in order to reduce rent levels. The 1977 Housing Finance Act then personalized state housing aid and replaced the *aide à la pierre* with *aide à la personne,* a system of personalized housing benefits, aid to prospective homeowners on low incomes, and agreements between social housing construction companies and the social services for the building of good quality, low-rent flats (Toubon and Tanter 1991). Yet, this reform was not extended to the overseas departments, and so *aide à la pierre* has remained predominant in the islands. Third, finance originating in compulsory payroll deductions, crucial in facilitating the access of thousands of salaried workers and their families to social housing in mainland France since 1954 (Condon and Ogden 1993; Condon 1995), has been of negligible importance in the Caribbean, given the lack of large employers. Finally, in the Caribbean, considerations of housing quality, adaptation of housing to local conditions, and creation of local solutions to housing the poor have often preceded similar initiatives in mainland France (De Panisse 1985).

A recurrent complaint in five-year-plan reports drawn up by the Caribbean departmental housing committees since the early 1960s relates to the slowness of progress. Even after investment began to be directed to housing, away from the modernization of ports and road systems, achievements continued to fall far short of targets (Baptistide 1982; Comby 1971). For example, in 1977, Menauge estimated that four thousand dwellings per year would have to be built over the next ten years in order to meet needs in Martinique, but given the low level of construction in the mid-1970s (two thousand dwellings per annum), he remained pessimistic (1977: 2). Likewise, in Guadeloupe, from 1971 to 1975, only one-third of the total dwellings built were social housing units, so the fact that roughly four thousand households built *cases* during this period was a further reminder that social housing programs remained insufficient (Baptistide 1982). Baptistide criticized the whole system of social housing in the departments, the *aide à la pierre,* housing allocation, and rent levels, insofar as it benefited a mere 15–20 percent of the population, 60 percent of the poorest population being left to find its own housing solution.

Thus, the challenge to the state since the 1950s has been that of the shanty-towns and urban slums. Lasserre describes how these were already a feature of the landscape of Point-à-Pitre in the mid-nineteenth century, as migrants set down their *cases* on undrained, mosquito-ridden swampland between narrow strips of raised land serving as paths. Further, Lasserre explains how the local council, faced with regular rebuilding of various parts of the town after fires, earthquakes, and hurricanes, did not have the financial means to drain and rebuild the whole area (Lasserre, 1961: 601–4). Migrants were also victims of rich town dwellers, who bought up areas of unserviced land, then rented plots at exorbitant rates to *case* owners (Pamphile 1985), a practice surviving into the 1950s as Lasserre observed in Guadeloupe. Throughout the postcolonial period, little was done to improve housing for the masses. Although works were begun in the 1930s, notably on the area to be known as the Assainissement (Pointe-à-Pitre), achievements by the 1950s were minimal. Massive urbanization was not accompanied by any town planning, and squatting on unoccupied state-owned land, over which local authorities had no control, continued and increased.[3] Eventually, after visits from various ministerial delegations, the state set up town planning offices in the main centers, and grandiose schemes were drawn up, to be financed by the special investment body for the overseas departments (FIDOM). Yet, in the mid-1970s, over half the housing stock in the islands was still declared to be in need of renovation (or, in some cases, destruction) (Bertile 1984: 120).

The task facing the new departmental authorities was enormous. In the main towns, upon which the state's assimilation policies were focused, poor quality housing struck a vivid contrast with the image of prosperity and progress that, as part of the French nation, the towns were intended to reflect. At the 1954 census, 43 percent of dwellings were in very poor condition (Lasserre 1961: 627; INSEE

1956: 102–7), and only one-third of dwellings in Pointe-à-Pitre had electricity, and 15 percent a water supply (44 percent and 29 percent respectively in Fort-de-France). As Revert (1949) pointed out, "in its most simple form, the rural case is not squalid. This is because of its rustic surroundings, the salubrity of the ground upon which it is built, and its garden. Quite the opposite are the intolerable urban slums, built from bits of old plank or wooden crates, with roofs improvised out of easily-rusting metal from petrol barrels" (31). The inhabitants of undrained areas attempted to keep their *cases* dry by raising them on large stones and using planks to cross the open drainage channels. As a midwife in Guadeloupe in the early 1960s recalls: "I went to attend to a birth in a house in Pointe-à-Pitre and as I went inside the house, Plop! I went through the floor. It was made of wood from crates of course, and my foot sunk into this viscous, green water, and I had to deliver the baby with my legs covered in that stuff!" (Interview in Pointe-à-Pitre, Nov. 1993). Urban *case* occupants had to fight a constant battle on two fronts: first, against insanitary conditions and regular flooding of their homes, and, second, against departmental planners determined to remove the shantytowns and to prevent their further spread. For the state, such settlements were incompatible with the strictly planned urbanization of the islands, as well as being seen as a health and fire risk. The fate of these settlements and of their inhabitants much depended upon the personality and policies of the town mayor (local council leader).

In Fort-de-France, the role of the mayor, Aimé Césaire, was all important in the fate of shantytowns such as La Trenelle, Volga-Plage, and Texaco. From the late 1950s, Césaire placed emphasis on the housing of the most needy. In order not to contravene state law, Césaire took advantage of loopholes, delimiting areas of publicly owned land upon which people were allowed to build "light-weight, temporary buildings," whilst awaiting rehousing (Paquette 1969a: 175–76). Only the departmental (state) authorities had the power to give out building permits. Moreover, the local authorities received no state aid for housing at the time. Thus, in the absence of any alternative solution to housing the newcomers, the Fort-de-France local authority closed its eyes to the process underway.[4] Conversion of the wooden *cases* proceeded within the outside walls of the *case*, beyond the watchful eyes of the departmental authorities, and, when completed, the permanent, solid structure emerged as a butterfly from its chrysalis. Furthermore, when a *case* was declared by the local authority to be fit for habitation, the occupant could obtain an improvement loan from the social services.

The *Texaco* shantytown, born in the 1960s, was located on the storage area of the petrol company. Two decades later, there were still 205 *cases* in various stages of conversion, of which only one-quarter were sound, and there was still no infrastructure in the district except for drinking water (Letchimy 1985: 127–28). In the meantime, there had been various slum clearance projects in other parts of the town (infrastructure, social service intervention, clearance, and rehousing).

For areas like Texaco, Letchimy (1985) has stressed that, although housing is poor and unemployment high, they constitute cohesive communities in which people develop new coping strategies reflected in types of *case* construction, the informal economy, and forms of sociability. Thus, it is necessary to adapt solutions accordingly; for example, reconstruction and rehousing should take place in the same neighborhoods.

In the case of Pointe-à-Pitre, the increasing degradation of housing conditions in the Quartier de l'Assainissement during the 1950s and into the 1960s was due to the density of housing within the narrow confines of the town boundary. Efforts by the council to extend the 1840 town boundary limits had been to no avail. Thus, Pointe-à-Pitre's urban growth spilled over into neighboring Abymes. In Abymes, conditions were much less dramatic. Spontaneous settlements, and later the Delacroix *cité de transit,* enjoyed much more space, and people could continue to keep poultry or pigs and grow fruit and vegetables around their homes.

In 1960, 5,863 *cases* were enumerated in the Quartier de l'Assainissement, with only 84 square meters of land per *case*. The city plan recommended that housing plots should be at least 200 square meters after renovation (Paquette 1969b: 129). Paquette quotes the mayor, Henri Bangou, as saying in 1964 that he saw the urban development of Pointe-à-Pitre in terms of the complete removal of the *cases* from the town. By 1969, 3,500 *cases* had been removed from the Assainissement (60 percent of the surface area), but only 900 replacement dwellings had been completed, and 800 were under construction. People were encouraged to take their *cases* elsewhere (moving costs being paid by the council), but most tried to stay as near the town center as possible. Later, on seeing that the Laurisque *cité de transit*—officially temporary housing in which people from the Assainissement had been rehoused—was becoming a permanent feature and that no immediate solution seemed possible, Bangou admitted that a gradual conversion of a proportion of the houses would have its advantages for both the inhabitants and the town.[5] The council then provided washing and toilet facilities and, later, a school. As it turned out, the Laurisque *cité* became so much a part of the town that its inhabitants were forgotten. A survey in the area in 1980 revealed that many inhabitants had lived in this area, just a couple of kilometers from "Bangou's modern city," for over fifteen years, enduring very poor housing conditions and much social hardship (Boquet 1985).

Despite the low construction rate and the persistence of shantytowns, great transformations were taking place due to state intervention. Built according to national standards and on the French model for very low-cost housing, collective housing was introduced into the islands and became the mainstay of urban housing programs. In the 1940s, individual four- or five-story blocks had been built by private speculators, but collective social housing construction began the 1950s with the creation of the SIDOM, state-aided private housing companies and housing cooperatives. The intention was that the SIDOM should house the poorest households. Yet, the large state housing projects, such as the Ensemble Floréal in Fort-de-France and the Quartier de l'Assainissement in Pointe-à-Pitre, proved to be inaccessible to these very households (fig. 11.3). The estates tended to house people leaving older housing in the town centers, people with stable incomes, rather than those having left the countryside, and those without stable employment (Paquette 1969a: 186). From the outset, the main towns had wanted to create their own public housing companies, but, funding being refused, they were powerless to do so. When, in the early 1970s, such companies (OPHLM) were created, instead of housing poorer households, as generally do their counterparts in mainland France, they housed middle-income households in comfortable flats (De Panisse 1985: 140). Moreover, during this decade, the SIDOM, in addition to no longer making a profit, ran into financial difficulties due to the inability of some households to keep up with their rent payments, to the relatively high cost of maintenance and management, and to rising building costs. Clearly, new solutions had to be sought.

Experimental schemes had begun in the 1950s. For example, in 1954, five hundred single-family houses, each with a garden plot, were built in the Raizet district of Pointe-à-Pitre. However, despite strong demand, most could not afford

Fig. 11.3. Area of social housing, Quartier de l'Assainissemenet, Point-à-Pitre, Guadeloupe.

them, and this was why the emphasis came to be placed on collective housing in the 1950s and 1960s, in addition to the fact that town-center land values were high. The problem of housing provision had been recognized, and the planning offices had begun to look at adapted solutions by the late 1960s. It was thus that the "site and service" experiment was initiated in a number of towns. In Guadeloupe, the aim was to equip between nine hundred and one thousand plots per year, but the complexity of the financing mechanism and the general lack of enthusiasm meant that less than half the target was achieved. An evaluation of the experiment revealed that the occupants considered that the sites were poorly designed and that the occupants were inadequately informed (Direction Départementale de la Guadeloupe 1974). Yet, from this original experiment, others were born. In 1977, the LTS ("Truly social" housing) was created to enable the poorest households to become homeowners. It consisted of a virtually completed house, financed entirely by state grants, the occupant then being responsible for completion in his or her own time. Since then, various reworked versions of the LTS, sometimes including cover of the cost to the occupant by the social services, have been launched to enable low-income homeownership, whilst other schemes have been drawn up to provide low-cost rented housing (Henry 1993; Arrès-Lapoque 1992). Much of this has been speeded up by the creation in 1978 of an innovative financing mechanism, the LBU (*Ligne Budgétaire Unique*), a specific funding system bringing together the various existing mechanisms for housing in the overseas departments. Yet, while this constitutes a simplified mechanism, its creation has coincided with the progressive withdrawal of the state from housing finance nationally (CGP 1980: 90; Lacaze 1989). An event such as the extensive housing destruction in Guadeloupe left by Hurricane Hugo was necessary to prove that the beginning of state withdrawal had been premature and inappropriate with respect to the Caribbean departments and combination of state and European funding since has been injected into housing schemes for the poor (Tardivon 1992).

Whilst some critics argue in favor of aligning housing benefits totally on the national system (Bertile 1984), others warn against encouraging a dependency syndrome (Baptistide 1982). It must be remembered that the alignment of other benefits—in particular, family allowance, pensions, unemployment benefit—took place very gradually over the three decades subsequent to *départementalization* (Constant 1987). They remained at a lower rate than those paid to residents of mainland France, the percentage difference in some cases being paid to social action funds (for example, to fund school canteens). The most recent major social benefit, the RMI,[6] provided to an increasing number of households in the islands, is paid at a 20 percent lower rate than in mainland France. The problem remains that many households are excluded from the limited housing benefits extended to the overseas departments. Bertile (1984: 234–36) has explained how, by not taking into account local conditions, single, young households and pre-retirees are excluded from family housing benefits. Other types of household are also excluded owing to various criteria pertaining either to household income, number of persons in the household, domestic hygiene, or to the number of days worked in a year (a minimum of ninety days is specified, which in a context of high unemployment, is particularly ill-adapted). Similarly, many very poor families have been excluded from recent social housing schemes. New legislative measures have been sought since 1990 to remedy the incompatibility of the housing benefit system with local conditions (Direction Départementale de l'Equipment de la Martinique 1991), but for the present little has changed.

Due to the massive rural exodus and the concentration of population growth in the towns, over the years, housing in the French Caribbean has increasingly become an urban problem. Today, around 90 percent of the islands' populations live in urban areas (Cazenave 1991). From the outset, construction and improvement of housing was funded first in the main towns, and conditions in the rural areas long remained generally poor. At the same time, rural emigration led to a worsening of urban housing conditions, since the towns were struggling to get the upper hand on slum clearance. The hard core of very poor housing has been reduced, as the level of overall housing stock has been raised. Slum clearance programs and housing renovation funding have continued, sometimes coinciding with urban social intervention programs, such as the national *Développement Social des Quartiers* (DSQ) programs, in areas of particular social hardship. Much has been done to improve housing for the most deprived households through various innovative schemes, but these have only reached a minority of households and planners continue to look for new alternatives (La Lettre de l'IDEF 1993; Tardivon 1992). In a recent interview, the Martiniquan town planner Serge Letchimy presented his main concerns for the future. In his opinion, it is necessary to double the rate of construction, and so double the LBU funding to multiply low-cost house-building schemes and to provide more efficient information about the various options open to households (Antilla 1994: 24–25). Yet, as in Guadeloupe (Tardivon 1992: 27; Henry 1993), a number of local economic, social, and legal obstacles still prevent construction and renovation needs being met, but, above all, housing policy and finance remains a central state decision in which local authority desires play a minor role (Ministère des DOM-TOM 1991: 113).

Final Comments

This chapter has suggested that the remarkable changes in housing provision in the French Caribbean since the War, and more especially over the last three decades, must be seen in the context of the status of the islands as *départements d'outre-mer* and of the general evolution of the housing policies of the French state. While as shown by the other chapters in this volume there are similarities between the French islands and other parts of the Caribbean—for example, in housing types and the importance of rapid urbanization—their political status has drawn Martinique and Guadeloupe firmly into the orbit of metropolitan France.

Improvement in housing conditions has been particularly rapid, and most households now have basic amenities. Nevertheless, two important questions dominate current housing policy. First, the existing housing stock is still in need of much further improvement, with some limited but acute areas of real deprivation remaining. Waiting lists for public housing are long. Second, a number of factors mean that pressure on housing provision will grow rather than diminish: the number of new young households is rising sharply; the rate of emigration has declined; there is a growing trend towards return from metropolitan France; and some immigration from neighboring islands. Current housing policy encompasses a wide variety of schemes for both the public and the private sector, but lacks a clear and coherent overall plan of land use, finance, and political control. In view of past experience, increased funding of plots of land fully equipped with drains, water and electricity supplies should be made available, on which households can build their own homes or occupy low-cost housing which they can improve gradually; home improvement grants should be more abundant; and further housing for rent or purchase in village or small town centers should be built.

Notes

1. With respect to the latter statistic, the difference between the islands can be explained by the centralization of many regional administrative head offices in Martinique, encouraging further concentration of services in the island.
2. The housing categories discussed here are those defined by INSEE for the 1990 census. There are five types: *habitations de fortune* (temporary shacks); *cases traditonnelles* (traditional shacks); *maisons traditionnelles* (traditional houses); *maisons en dur* (houses of solid construction, i.e., brick and concrete rather than wood); *immeuble collectif* (flats). The classification is applied on the ground by the census enumerators, following guidelines issued by INSEE.
3. Often on state-owned land commonly known as the "50 pas géométriques." A legacy of the Ancien Régime, comprising stretches of land extending roughly eighty-one meters inland from the natural coastal waterline.
4. The battle between the shantytown inhabitants and the departmental authorities and the role of Césaire in allowing the settlement to remain is vividly described in Chamoiseau (1992: 366–90).
5. Another important point is that, under the French political system, the larger the town's population, the greater its council's share of the state budget and its tax income. Thus, it was in Pointe-à-Pitre's interest to retain its large population. Since building space was lacking, the solutions found were the building of blocks of flats and the reclamation of the mangroves on the northwestern limits of the town. By 1969, 17.5 hectares of land had been reclaimed and 1,800 *cases* were relocated there.
6. *Revenu Minimum d'Insertion*, a form of supplementary benefit introduced by the Socialists in 1988, bringing the household's income up to a predefined threshold level.

References

Antilla. (1994) "Habitat and immobilier." *Antilla* 17 (special issue): 3–34.

Arrès-Lapoque, P. (1992) "La politique de logement dans l'outre-mer Français." *Les Cahiers de l'Habitat* 16: 6–11

Baptistide, J. C. (1982) "Le logement." *Atlas des Départements Français d'Outre-Mer: 3) La Guadeloupe*. Planche 15. Talence, Centre d'Etudes de Géographie Tropicale du CNRS.

Berthelot, J., and M. Gaumé. (1982) *L'habitat populaire aux Antilles*. Point-à-Pitre: Editions Perspectives Créoles.

Bertile, W. (1984) *Le logement dans les Départements d'Outre-Mer*. Rapport au Premier Ministre de la Députe de la Réunion.

Blérald, A. P. (1986) *Histoire économique de la Guadeloupe et de la Martinique du 17ème siècle à nos jours*. Paris: Karthala.

Boquet, M. (1985) "La rénovation urbaine à Pointe-à-Pitre." *Les Dossiers de l'Outre-Mer* (78/79): 80–84.

Castles, S., and G. Kosack. (1973) *Immigrant Workers and Class Structure in Western Europe*. London: Oxford University Press for the Institute of Race Relations.

Cazenave, J. (1991) "Les insuffisants progrès de l'habitat." *Antiane Eco* 14: 23–26.

CGP (Commissariat Général du Plan). (1957) *Troisième plan de modernisation et d'équipement. Rapport de la Commission de l'Equipement Sanitaire et Social*. Paris: CGP.

———. (1961) *Quatrième plan de l'équipement et de la productivité (1962– 1965)*. Paris: CGP.

———. (1965) *Cinquième plan. Rapport des Commissions*. Paris: Imprimerie des Journaux Officiels.

———. (1966) *Cinquième plan 1966–1970: Commission de l'Habitation. Rapport Général et rapports spéciaux annexes*. Paris: Editions du Moniteur des Travaux Publics.

———. (1971) *Sixième plan de développement économique et social 1971–1975. Rapport général. Les objectifs généraux et les actions prioritaires*. Paris: La Documentation Française.

———. (1976a) *Septième plan de développement économique et social 1976–1980. Rapport général*. Paris: La Documentation Française.

———. (1976b) *Préparation du septième plan. Rapport des Commissions*. Rapport de la Commission des Départements d'Outre-Mer; Rapport du Comité Habitat. Paris: La Documentation Française.

———. (1980) *Préparation du huitième plan. Rapports des Commissions*. Rapport du Comité des Départements et Territoires d'Outre-Mer; Rapport de la Commission Habitat et Cadre de Vie (annexes). Paris: La Documentation Française.

———. (1983a) *Préparation du neuvième plan. 1984–88. Rapport du groupe de travail Financement du logement*. Paris: La Documentation Française.

———. (1983b) *Préparation du neuvième plan. Annexes au rapport de la Commission Nationale de Planification. Tome 5: Développement décentralisé et équilibre du territoire: Intergroupe DOM-TOM*. Paris: La Documentation Française.

Chamoiseau, P. (1992) *Texaco*. Paris: Gallimard.

Charbit, Y., and H. Léridon. (1980) *Transition démographique et modernisation en Guadeloupe et en Martinique*. INED Travaux et Documents Cahier No. 89, Paris, Presses Universitaires de France.

Chivallon, C. (1993) "Les paysans Martiniquais ou l'histoire d'un territoire et d'une indentité contestés." *Géographie et Culture* 7: 3–26.

Coit, K. (1988) *Housing and Development in the Lesser Antilles*. Paris: UNESCO.

Comby, J. (1971) "Le problème du logement dans la société et l'économie Martiniquaise." *Cahiers du CERAG* 23: 1–158.

Condon, S. A. (1993) *L'accès au logement: filières et blocages. Le cas des Antillais en France*. Rapport au Plan Construction et Architecture, Ministère de l'Equipement, Paris.

———. (1995) L'accès au logement: filières et blocages. Le cas des antillais en France. Collection 'Recherches.' Plan Construction et architecture, 55, Paris.

Condon, S. A., and Ogden, P. E. (1991a) "Emigration from the French Caribbean: The Origins of an Organised Migration." *International Journal of Urban and Regional Research* 15 (4): 505–23.

———. (1991b) "Afro-Caribbean Migrants in France: Employment, State Policy and the Migration Process." *Transactions, Institute of British Geographers* New Series 16 (4): 440–57.

———. (1993) "The State, Housing Policy and Afro-Caribbean Migration to France." *Ethnic and Racial Studies* 16 (2): 256–97.

———. (1996) "Questions of Emigration, Circulation and Return: Mobility Between the French Caribbean and France in the 1980s and 1990s." *International Journal of Population Geography* 2 (1): 35–51.

Conseil Général de la Martinique. (1993) *Tendances générales du développement de la Martinique. Poids et occupation de l'habitat précaire.* Conseil général de la Martinique and Direction départementale de l'équipement de la Martinique. Report.

Constant, F. (1987) "La politique Française de l'immigration antillaise de 1946 à 1987." *Revue Europeénne des Migrations Internationales* 3 (3): 9–30.

Dagas, S. (1992) "Guadeloupe: le logement défavorisé en poches." *Antiane Eco* 17: 27–29.

Dagas, S., et P. Meyer. (1993) "Guadeloupe et Martinique: de fortes inégalités de revenu." *Antiane Eco* 20: 34–35.

De Panisse, H. (1985) "La naissance et le dèveloppment de l'habitat social dans les DOM." *Les Dossiers da l'Outre-Mer* (78–79): 135–41.

Département de la Guadeloupe. (1965) *Cinquième plan. Rapport de la Commission locale du plan.* Unpublished report.

Département de la Martinique. (1965) *Cinquième plan 1966–1970.* Unpublished report.

Direction Départementale de l'Equipement de la Martinique. (1991) *Etude sur les besoins en logement à la Martinique. Rapport final de synthèse.* CODRA (Bagneux) et CEPCOM (Fort-de-France). Unpublished report.

Direction Départementale de la Guadeloupe. (1974) *Les structures d'accueil: pour ou contre?* Ministère de l'Equipement/DDG.

Domenach, H., and J.-P. Guengant. (1981) "Chômage et sous-emploi dans les DOM." *Economie et Statistique* 137: 3–21.

Domenach, H., and M. Picouet et al. (1992) *La dimension migratoire des Antilles.* Paris: Economica.

Duclaud-Williams, R. H. (1978) *The Politics of Housing in Britain and France.* London: Heinemann.

Gastmann, A. L., and S. MacDonald. (1989) "The French West Indies." In R. B. Potter, ed. *Urbanisation, Planning and Development in the Caribbean,* 237–51. London: Mansell.

Giraud, M. (1979) *Races et classes à la Martinique.* Paris: Editions Anthropos.

Guengant, J.-P. (1993) "Caraïbe: des enfants pour l'émigration." *Antiane Eco* 20: 12–18.

Henry, H. (1993) "Logement social: la percée du LES." *Antiane Eco* 20: 36–38.

Hervo, M., and M. A. Charras. (1971) *Bidonvilles.* Paris: F Maspéro.

INSEE. (1956) *Résultats statistiques du recensement général de la population des départements d'outre-mer (1.07.54) Antilles Françaises: Martinique et Guadeloupe.* Paris: INSEE.

———. (1991) *Recensement général de la population. Logements. Population. Emploi. Guadeloupe and Martinique.* Paris: INSEE.

———. (1993a) *Ter 93. Martinique. Tableaux Economiques Régionaux.* Martinique: Service Régional de l'INSEE.

———. (1993b) *Ter 93. Guadeloupe. Tableaux Economiques Régionaux.* Guadeloupe: Service Régional de l'INSEE.

Jolivet, M. J. (1985) "Migrations et histoire dans la Caraïbe française." *Cahiers de l'ORSTOM* 21: 93–113.

La Lettre de l'IDEF. (1993) "Ville, habitat, logement." *La Lettre de l'IDEF* 80. Numéro spécial: Réalités familiales, sanitaires et sociales dans les DOM, 50–54.

Lacaze, J. P. (1989) *Les Français et leur logement. Eléments de socio-économie de l'habitat.* Paris: Presses de l'Ecole Nationale des Ponts et Chaussées.

Lasserre, G. (1961) *La Guadeloupe. Les îles et leurs problèmes,* vol. 2. Bordeaux: Université de Bordeaux.

Leiris, M. (1955) *Contactes de civilisations en Martinique et en Guadeloupe.* Paris: UNESCO/Gallimard.

Léridon, H., et al. (1970) *Fécondité et famille en Martinique.* INED Travaux et Documents, Cahier No. 56. Paris, Presses Universitaires de France.

Letchimy, S. (1985) "La restructuration et la réhabilitation du quartier Texaco à Fort-de-France." *Les Dossiers de l'Outre-Mer* (78/79): 126–34.

Menauge, J. (1977) "Le logement." *Atlas des Départements Français d'Outre-Mer: 2 La Martinique.* Planche 16. Talence, Centre d'Etudes de Géographie Tropicale du CNRS.

Ministère des DOM-TOM/Ministére de l'Equipement. (1991) *Etats généraux de l'habitat des Départements d'Outre-Mer. Paris 1991. Les actes de la rencontre.* Paris.

Mintz, S. W. (1984) *Caribbean Transformations.* Baltimore and London: Johns Hopkins University Press.

Murch, A. (1971) *Black Frenchmen: The Political Integration of the French Antilles.* Cambridge, Mass.: Schenkman.

Narfez, R. (1976) "De l'ambiguïté de la départementalisation sociale en Guadeloupe et Martinique." *Cahiers de l'Anthropologie* 4: 115–18.

Pamphile, J. (1985) "Quelques aspects de la construction spontanée (Fort-de-France, Martinique)." *Les Dossiers de l'Outre-mer* (78/79): 74–79.

Paquette, R. (1969a) "Une cité planifiée et une cité spontanée (Fort-de-France, Martinique)." *Cahiers de Géographie du Québec* 28: 169–86.

———. (1969b) "Divergences de politique en matière d'habitation populaire dans les villes antillaises: une ville française et une ville anglaise." *La Revue de Géographie de Montréal* 23 (2): 123–36.

Revert, E. (1949) *La Martinique. Etude géographique.* Paris: Nouvelles Editions Latines.

Tardivon, P. (1992) "La reconstruction: le LES object de controverse." *Les Cahiers de l'Habitat* 16: 25–29.

Topalov, C. (1987) *Le logement en France. Histoire d'une marchandise impossible.* Paris: Presses de la Foundation Nationale de Sciences Politiques.

Toubon, J. C., and A. Tanter. (1991) "Les grands ensembles et évolution de l'intervention publique." *Hommes et Migrations* 1147: 6–18.

Zabaleta, E. (1991) "Le foyer à l'heure du modernisme." *Antiane Eco* 14: 27–29.

Zabaleta, E., and M. Nema. (1992) "Martinique: les oubliés de l'habitat." *Antiane Eco* 17: 30–32.

Zobel, J. (1974) *Rue cases nègres.* Paris: Presénce Africaine.

Chapter 12

Caribbean Housing Futures: Building Communities for Sustainability

Dennis Conway
and Robert B. Potter

Meeting the shelter needs of the poor in the twentieth century has proved difficult in many Caribbean countries. First and foremost, the postcolonial experiences of countries differ, as do the casual ensembles involved, the role of the state, the rigidities of existing land tenure systems, and the self-help autonomous responses of the rural and urban poor. The chapters in this volume have provided evidence of the woeful state of housing provision throughout the Caribbean. Colonial legacies of neglect in this arena provided such accumulated deficits that state action was always inevitably insufficient in scope. Inadequate and inappropriate planning models further hampered state effectiveness. Vernacular and appropriate styles of housing have been disparaged in favor of more costly, imported technologies, and this despite the time-honored persistence of the latter. On the other hand, self-help housing initiatives, whether state-assisted or not, have scarcely compensated for state and private-sector neglect of the accommodation needs of the poor in most Caribbean societies. Furthermore, the uncontrolled and, in some cases, unrestricted patterns of low-density residential subdivision have led to constraints in the supply of land for housing. Additionally, clear distortions in the housing and land markets characterize Caribbean nations.

Taken together, the contrasting examples evidenced in this book suggest there has been a fundamental lack of understanding among the region's decision makers—whether state agencies, consulting academies, or public-private partnerships—of the interrelated nature of the housing, planning, and urbanization processes in the Caribbean. State and public responses to housing provision have been driven by inappropriate objectives and have relied on "modern" transferred models of housing and building codes, which have proved to be poorly suited to the local environment. The autonomous responses of the poor have been little understood by the state; their needs, by and large, have been met by their own "sweat equity." Several of the contributors to this volume chart disappointing histories of lost opportunities and identify sequences of problems that ineluctably have contributed to extremely poor records of housing provision.

Comparative Insights

Beyond the general critiques of state inaction during the postcolonial period, the general denigration of folk, vernacular housing styles, and, by default, the poor's reliance on self-help autonomous initiatives, what specific conclusions might we draw from the differing cases our contributors have documented? Are there other subregional generalizations or comparative perspectives that emerge from these recent historical records of Caribbean societies' housing and settlement patterns? While elaborating on each chapter's main points in the first section of this chapter, some generalizations, albeit despondent and somewhat critical in tone, do materialize. Following on its heels, however, in the next section we draw upon the more positive accomplishments, or inadvertent happenings, from which we develop our "vision" of how the future of Caribbean housing might better be ensured.

In his chapter on "Homes and Heritage," Hudson reminds us that there is a deep heritage of vernacular housing throughout the Caribbean, and that popular styles were every bit as creative and distinctive as the "great houses" and the transported Europeanized versions that were the venerated forms of the plantation cityscapes and town houses of these colonial dependencies. The modern era, however, has seen the wholesale replacement of both popular and elite "antiquated" styles with a new set of transported styles, technologically modern in appearance and metropolitan in design and construction. "Concrete" is viewed as a sign of status and of social value, and this theme resonates through several of the contributions, for example, the discussions of the French West Indies, Puerto Rico, and Cuba's Havana.

Next, Watson and Potter's focus on chattel housing in Barbados serves to remind us of the overwhelming importance of land tenure relations and the significance for the Caribbean poor that secure access to land affords. On the other hand, insecurity has had major implications for the *physical* quality of housing in Barbados, with "tenantries" fostering traditions of incremental housing construction as well as the mobility of structures. Although the Barbados State prevaricated in its approaches to providing better security of tenure to rural and urban areas alike, changes in the 1980s have occurred which promise a better future. There was a move to privatization in the 1980s, which favored middle- and upper-class residential development and housing provision, but legal accommodations to better house the poor were also secured for the post-1980 period. When compared to other post-1980s experiences, there are signs of progress in Barbados's housing situation.

Potter's own chapter on "Housing and the State in the Eastern Caribbean" again stresses the variety in the *physical* qualities of housing that the poor experience. Small island vernacular housing is characterized by its identity as separate dwelling units, the incremental enlarging of units to accommodate growing families, and, significantly, *the common practice of sharing among extended family groups*; a trend Gilbert (1993) noted is growing in importance in Latin America. Gilbert (1993) linked such "sharing" practices with the shrinking of self-help housing opportunities and the increasing dependence of Latin America's urban poor on rental arrangements. In the Caribbean, however, other informal and noncommodity arrangements among family and kin exist, like "tenant-at-will" agreements (Conway 1981, 1982). Potter also provides a normative model, using "articulation theory" to personify the role and behavior of the state in these peripheral capitalist societies in its priority setting of housing initiatives for the poor. It is all too clear from this conceptual standpoint that the poor in the eastern Caribbean have generally been left to fend for themselves in the scramble for shelter. They invariably have been kept marginalized in their housing ventures, both geographically and socially, regardless of the island in question. One interesting and generalizable insight that emerges concerns the structural prompting of state action in the housing arena. Not inconsequentially, *direct* state intervention seems to occur only in response to environmental disasters, or during crisis periods of political regimes, or when one triggers the other. Then, housing rehabilitation, disaster-mitigation, state redistribution of international disaster relief funds come to be applied to housing renovation, and the poor's lot is addressed; that is, until the crisis is passed or the hurricane damage is repaired.

The next two chapters, by Eyre and Klak, are complementary accounts of the changing situation in Jamaica. Eyre, drawing upon decades of scholarship focusing on the expansion and diversification of self-help settlement in the island, both in Montego Bay as well as Kingston, reminds us of the variety of self-help housing forms that have arisen in Jamaica. As Potter, Watson, and Hudson have also observed in their eastern Caribbean contexts, a long tradition of self-help housing building exists in Jamaica, in both rural and urban areas. Since the 1950s, the shantytown dwellers have been assured by the state that they can "control their own lives," that they can invade abandoned or unused land. Now, the same political patricians are reversing their rhetorical stances, telling the poor that it is unlawful, anti-social, even criminal to invade and self-help. The immediacy of the crisis is only too apparent, though the solution is scarcely obvious.

As Eyre intimates, the Jamaican State, regardless of the regime, has a long tradition of avoiding its responsibilities to directly undertake housing programs. Klak's chapter details the performances of two of the state's largest public-private partnership programs and finds common cause with Eyre's conclusions. Stressing regime effects and the different institutional arrangements underway in Jamaica, Klak's analysis and theoretical treatment is thorough and convincing. The poor are by and large excluded from state agency initiatives, and major programs such as Jamaica's National Housing Trust (NHT) and the Caribbean Housing Finance Corporation (CHFC), as well as the Government's Ministry of Construction (Housing), or MOC(H), serve the middle classes, while denying the poor the access to credit and to land and housing loans they so desperately need. Furthermore, the social interests of the politically and economically more powerful continue to be served in the latest period of neoliberal restructuring in Jamaica. Klak's opinion is that the state's roles need to be dramatically reviewed if shelter provision is going to be taken seriously, because the conditions of underdevelopment and of external dependency that dominated Jamaica's colonial and postcolonial experiences remain an ongoing constraint to the development of a progressive housing policy for the island. We concur.

The next two chapters also document the problems of state-directed policies, but deal with the other two largest Commonwealth Caribbean counties, Guyana and Trinidad and Tobago. Peake's chapter focuses on Guyana and charts the fate of housing provision accompanying the destructive decline of fortunes of that South American country under the Burnham regime. One distinctive feature noted in Guyana's Cooperative Socialist experiment with state-directed housing provision was reliance on governmental rental housing for the poorest classes. This failed to meet housing demand in its entirety, but it did provide shelter for the party faithful, such was the patronage system the PNC developed. However, since the mid-1990s, the state has withdrawn from such direct involvement in housing provision, and squatting has been on the increase as a consequence. Peake finds solace in the progress being made in the 1990s, with the passing of Forbes Burnham and the replacement of his inept People's National Congress administration by the People's Progressive Party. Indeed, she expresses optimism that a "revival" is underway, while reminding us that the housing situation in Guyana is still in a state of crisis, and that unmet need is as great as ever.

Peake's observations on what the future holds for Guyana are upbeat, however. Clearly, in Guyana, as elsewhere in the Caribbean, an upturn of economic fortunes is likely to signal an upturn in overall welfare, and more employment opportunities are going to be translated into shelter improvements among other investments. The nadir may be past in Guyana's case, the worst over. The Guyanese people have always demonstrated resourcefulness, and Peake's thoughtful conclusion of a more optimistic future for the poor in terms of their housing provision reflects this persuasion. Structural adjustment has dictated a greater reliance on private market forces, and the public sector's role is now as an "enabler" of housing provision initiatives, rather than as a direct provider. Guyana's housing stock is in a deplorable state, but Peake sees the state's transition towards policies to facilitate self-help, site and infrastructure upgrading, and to undertake programs of squatter regularization, as promising avenues. Trinidad also appears to be on a similar track.

Hewitt's chapter, which documents the twists and turns of state policies in Trinidad, does not promise such a dramatic revival, however. The "boom and bust" nature of the Trinidad experience in the period between 1973 and 1985 was more dramatic in its cyclical intensity. Trinidad and Tobago shared a common legacy of colonial neglect by the British along with Jamaica and Guyana, through to each country's political independence in the early 1960s. Each newly independent, fledgling government made distinctive attempts to chart a different postcolonial path. Forbes Burnham's Guyana experimented with Cooperative Socialism, Michael Manley's Jamaica tried Democratic Socialism, and Eric Williams in Trinidad attempted a middle way with his State Capitalism model (Ambursley and Cohen 1983). The Trinidad State promised much and rarely followed through on its promises. State provision of housing for the burgeoning low-income classes failed to deliver the numbers needed. On the other hand, the urban poor who flocked into the low-income suburban peripheries of Port of Spain and San Fernando gained access to land for their housing through rental and tenantry arrangements. So, in the first two decades of the country's rapid urbanization experience, self-help housing initiatives proved to be of some sufficiency. Only when restrictions in land availability became more pronounced during and after the 1973 "boom" period did squatting intensify and become a common practice among Trinidad's poor and needy.

Hewitt's identification of the rapid growth of middle-class demands for residential space points to another encumbrance the poor face in their struggle for shelter. In Trinidad, as elsewhere in the region where upward social mobility has been experienced by a sizable proportion of the people, the consumption of residential space by the middle class imposes great stress on the system. This is especially the case in Caribbean countries where the needed and expected supportive infrastructure is concentrated around the capital cities, or in the coastal zones of the smaller islands. Trinidad and Barbados housing provision patterns reflect this pattern (see Potter's chapter), and in both cases the middle-class consumption of living space, not to mention the political power of the middle classes, disadvantage the poor in their search for appropriate accommodation. Duany also documents a similar tale in the growth and spread of Greater San Juan in Puerto Rico, in chapter 10 of this collection. Then, when scarcity prevails, and the state has to choose which constituency to satisfy, it is the poor who find themselves marginalized. The poor's housing needs play second fiddle to those of the middle class, their superiors in this contest for political patronage. So it goes in Trinidad.

The remaining three chapters address state provision and autonomous self-help housing responses in other cultural realms of the Caribbean, beyond the British Commonwealth cases. Widely differing experiences of "hegemonic-dependency" mark the three: from Cuba's relations with the Soviet Union and the Eastern Bloc, to Puerto Rico's neocolonial association with the United States, and to metropolitan France's *départements d'outre mer* of Martinique, Guadeloupe, the dependencies, and the French Antilles.

Mathéy's chapter, dealing with the provision of housing in Havana, challenges us to consider this experience and evaluate it as a radical alternative. Does Cuba represent a "different type of self-help approach," a viable socialist alternative? The *microbrigade* certainly emerges as a progressive community force, and self-help housing in Havana is, by and large, a consequence of microbrigade activities. Here, Cuba's experience differs from that of any other Caribbean people. Then there is Mathéy's articulate review of the conceptual bases for self-help under a socialist regime that firmly illuminates the differences between the Cuban socialist models of state housing provision and other state models in the region. Mathéy deals with several contentious and debatable issues: property commodification questions, double-exploitation concerns, social integration, political mobilization and pacification issues, and the dangers inherent in the anticommunal characteristics of self-help under capitalism—individualism, landlordism, and sweat-equity investments. Under socialism, building communally is viewed as nonalienated work, and Cuban *microbrigade* activities demonstrate this progressive aspect of Havana's experience. On the other hand, the crisis brought on by the withdrawal of Soviet support, the hardships of the recent "Special Period," and the national priorities of the Castro regime, which relegate housing provision to relative insignificance, all point to a hiatus in state policymaking, and to the need for drastic revisions in the way the country is managed and planned. Under a mixed economic model, can housing provision be left to the initiatives of *microbrigades,* and to self-help, autonomous, communal activities? It is too early to judge, and Mathéy leaves us with Cuba's experience as a model, not to be followed so much as to be examined for its positive attributes and creative aspects. We see at least one element as progressive: namely, "building community."

Duany's thorough documentation of the transitions Puerto Rico's housing stock has undergone, from *bohíos,* to *arrabales,* to modern *caserios,* places shelter provision as an integral part of the island's modernization experience. The social value of housing remains center stage in his elaboration of the transformations underway in Greater San Juan, the island's primate city, especially during the period from 1920 to 1950. It was during this era that the mushrooming of *barriadas* and *arrabales* occurred. And the state's responses were predictable: "eradication" was an early strategy, replaced by benign neglect and avoidance later. Duany's in-depth inspection of the transition of one such *barriada,* Barrio Gandul, highlights the social fabric of the livelihoods of its residents, and the class-related transitions of status the neighborhood has undergone.

Puerto Rico's housing experience does mirror that of other Caribbean countries, even though the Commonwealth's ties with the United States also serve to set it apart, in terms of the dramatic social upheavals that accompanied "Operation Bootstrap," and the island-dependency's modernization experience. "Concrete" styles reflect status, whilst vernacular styles are denigrated as "old-fashioned." U.S. metropolitan values are so reinforced by the circulatory lives many Puerto Ricans lead that the people's consumption patterns are driven as much by the mainland as they are by the island. Housing is viewed in similar bimodal terms, and the poor struggle here, as they do on the mainland.

Duany's evaluation of future planning directions is more forbidding than optimistic. He advocates dramatic changes in the state's approach to housing provision: to move away from the role as provider of flawed, or failing, *caserios* and to move towards the roles of "enabler" and "facilitator" of self-help initiatives by communities themselves. In Duany's model of the future, there are parallels with Peake's suggestions for Guyana, and there are lessons the Jamaican State might well heed. In this exposé of Puerto Rico's "progress," there are salutary cautions that other Caribbean governments should note as well. Later, in the chapter we build further on the conclusions derived from the richness of these island-specific investigations, and the comparative insights that they provide.

The final case study by Condon and Ogden extends the comparative frame to include the francophone Caribbean. More specifically, the housing situations in the French *départements d'outre mer,* Martinique and Guadeloupe, are examined. The role of the French State, the direct and dominant involvement of metropolitan *and* insular institutions, makes this case distinctive. Here, decisions in Paris, as well as Fort-de-France and Point-à-Pierre set housing agendas in these *départements.* And the major transformations experienced in the modernization of these islands' housing stocks, especially during the last two decades, suggest that such "dependency" relations have their positive aspects (see also McElroy 1995).

Very rapid urbanization and extremely high growth rates of the populations of the French islands' capital cities inevitably forced the incoming rural poor to adopt self-help strategies to build their *cases* (homes). Like San Juan, the ensuing growth of *bidonvilles* in underdeveloped or marginal areas of the cities alarmed the state apparatuses. State-provision of accommodation—in this case, the large-scale building of blocks of rental flats—was intended to lessen the pressure. In large part, it succeeded, at least in the capital cities. Moreover, the growing demands for residential space by middle-class households was also met by public-sector action and delivery. Yet, while there has been progress and improved housing under central state guidance, the problems that the *bidonvilles* created, and the problems that created them (unemployment, marginal employment regimes, as well as construction industry incapacity), continue to this day in these French *départements*. The upgrading programs have been far from successful. Some eradication programs displaced *bidonvilles*, only to have others spring up elsewhere, and the rate of unit replacement needed to house the poor must be doubled if it is to make a dent in the overall accumulated deficit. The particular bimodal responsibility the French State operates poses its own problems and is distinctly different from other contexts. On the other hand, the provision of housing and finance according to central state dictates markedly reduces the authority and responsibility of the local state. While the French West Indies is yet another comparative example from which lessons can be derived, to reach a more equitable housing situation, the particular model of administration employed is not one we can promote or suggest is worth emulating. We intend, rather, to distill the major essences of messages derived from this contribution, and the others, to draw out the positive signals that the authors have alluded to.

And there are positive signs that can be derived from some of the contemporary Caribbean experiences elaborated in this volume, which could have transferability and regional relevance for urban planning and a future where accommodation for all might be attainable, in a sustainable manner. Mathéy's chapter detailing Cuban experience suggests that an alternative is possible. Condon and Ogden's investigation of the state's role in housing provision in Martinique and Guadeloupe intimates that a more committed state apparatus might ameliorate the situation. Hewitt's identification of a progressive role played by the Inter-American Development Bank in Trinidad suggests that international, external agencies can play their part in directing a more progressive future of shelter provision. Concerns for a stronger commitment to appropriate housing styles, as expressed in the contributions of Hudson and Watson and Potter, suggest another possible avenue. The state *can* be an enabler and facilitator of self-help initiatives of the poor, and the flawed and failed policies of the past need not signal avoidance of, or withdrawal from, the sector.

Looking to the Future

Rather than dwelling further on the shortcomings of past state policies or on the problems the poor have faced in their scramble for adequate shelter, together with the disappointing records, the flawed models, the despondent situations many, if not all, Caribbean societies face, we prefer to conclude this comparative investigation looking towards the future. Yes, we frame our deliberation within the current crisis the Caribbean faces, because the shortcomings of present policies and plans have been only too forcibly documented in the preceding chapters. However, we attempt to reconcile the contemporary state of affairs with a future agenda that is *necessary* for a sustainable future. It is not beyond our remit to promote actively the idea that housing must be seen as an inalienable *human right*. The future should offer hope and promise for a better and more meaningful life for Caribbean people, where appropriate shelter, and a "home as haven," can be expected as a *basic right* for all members of the regional community (Leckie 1989). Looking to the future demands that we undertake a radical rethinking of priorities and this, of necessity, demands radical changes from existing common practice.

HABITAT's visions (see Conway 1985; UNCHS 1983) and UNEP's Agenda 21 for "Promoting Sustainable Human Settlement Development" (see UNEP 1992) are lofty ideals that appear beyond the financial capacities of most restructuring Caribbean countries.[1] What then are the insights we can bring to this discourse? Shelter should be a basic human right, as Leckie's (1989) legal arguments propose. Self-help, autonomous responses by the people are not to be viewed solely as desperate measures by the marginalized and underprivileged. They must also be interpreted as empowering efforts. Lest the state be thought to be exonerated by the advocacy of self-help strategies, we, in fact, see the need for more state activism, more state responsibility, more state accountability if a sustainable future is to be promoted. Prevailing rigidities and inequities in land markets and the resultant legacies of distorted land and housing markets are not so easily redressed (Conway 1985; Palmer and Patton 1988). Prevailing patterns of unfettered residential sprawl in the form of middle-class, subdivision-led land conversions threaten any sustainable future for island economies where the landscape resource base is an integral aspect of the tourism bundle (Hudson 1986). As an ever-more avid consumer of urban residential space, the middle class now joins the elite classes in the future power struggle for adequate shelter. The state's activism and progressive intervention to assure equity in shelter provision has never been more needed than today (see also Hardoy and Satterthwaite 1989).

Several emerging themes appear as part of our vision for promoting sustainable human settlement development in the Caribbean: 1) building community; 2) popular participation and local empowerment; 3) progressive, state-enabling solutions; 4) appropriate (vernacular) housing styles; 5) environmental sustainability; and 6) economic wealth with environmental health. Accordingly, each of these themes is addressed in the account which follows.

"Building Community": Turner's Vision

With the wisdom that he has always brought to the issue, John Turner reproaches one and all with a firm reminder that "building community" would be his preferred description for the project that academic writers have labeled "self-help housing." Turner sees this more holistic vision as capturing the essentials he attempted to provide in his 1972 co-authored book, *Freedom to Build*; namely, an emphasis on people's cooperative activities in building and consolidating local, communal-environmental relationships, rather than focusing on housing as a product, a proto-commodity, a commodity, a fixed-capital investment, or an architectural style. In this connection, it is useful to reiterate John Turner's latest contribution to the discourse, which is to be found in one of our contributor's latest anthologies, Kosta Mathéy's *Beyond Self-Help Housing* (1992). Turner (1992) offers the following proposition, that we also take up here in our collection:

> Social justice, peaceful and sustainable development depend on primary resource economy; this depends, in turn, on the proper matching of human relations and organizations in essential and complementary tasks: necessary local activities, those which must match the infinite variety of personal and local needs and priorities, must be predominantly self-managed (whether self-built or not). Enabling institutions and supporting infrastructures, on the other hand, require governmental command or competitive commercial structures according to the natures, relationships, scales and context of the tasks. As the capacity to make the most economic and creative use of resources is in local hands, the overall task is to discover ways and means by which state powers and market forces can enable and support personal creativity and local initiative—a search for symbiosis but a competition for hegemony. (xi)

Popular Participation and "Place" Empowerment

In rejecting the modern era of architecture and planning, postmodernism involves a return to vernacular, traditional, premodern, small-scale forms. Thus, Turner's ideas have their representation in the postmodernist discourse on "imagined communities" (Anderson 1983) and "place reconstruction" (Harvey 1992), along with Heideggerian (Heidegger 1966, 1971; Relph 1976), and Marxian traditions on the power of capitalist (materialist) social relations over the immediate experiential world. Harvey, invoking the framework of the "Lefebvrian matrix" (as detailed in his *The Condition of Postmodernity,* Harvey 1989; see also Lefebvre 1991), reminds us that "place is becoming more important to the degree that the authenticity of *dwelling* (our emphasis) is being undermined by political economic processes of spatial transformation and place construction" (Harvey 1992: 12).

Linking the authenticity of dwelling with community power, Harvey (1992) argues convincingly that local communities will be the spatial locales where resistances that focus on alternative constructions of place will inevitably come about in response to peoples' search for authentic senses of community and authentic relations with nature as their urban-societal context is structured and restructured by the increasing penetration of global forces of money, technological rationality, along with commodification and capital accumulation. Harvey (1992) goes on to stress that such authentic communities (read Turnerian self-built communities) may arise as autonomous creations of seemingly powerless and marginalized people—that is the poor—but they survive "by an accommodation to the power of money, to commodification and capital accumulation, and to modern technologies" (19). These are scarcely the idealized, radical communities of social resistance, politically motivated social movements dreamed of by intellectuals seeking grassroots power bases (Castells 1978). More important, they are likely to emerge as highly differentiated "built communities," capable of inserting and reinserting themselves into changing space relations, responding in flexible ways to an ever-changing future shaped in part by global-to-local relations, and in part by state intermediation with its resultant accompaniment of local communal resistances, which are not solely expressions of exclusionary local behavior on the part of the powerful, wealthy, and privileged, but include *all* communal resistances seeking "place-representation" (Harvey 1992).

Leeds (see Sanjek 1994), with reference to his empirical research among the favelas of Brazil, has also argued in favor of the flexibility that the social organization of "localities" can provide, where the localities are more than merely residential communities. Rather, they are territorially-based flexible entities, which can respond effectively to the extraordinary exigencies of life arising from the imposition of external controls by supralocal organizations and state institutional directives, primarily the use of people's informal and personalized relationships facilitated by proximity within the locality. Whether the conceptual label is "place-representation," "localities," or "spontaneous shelter," the generalizable theme among all these notions is that communal-territorial responsibilities are best manifest in people's empowerment and participation in the decisions that affect their daily lives and those of their families and loved ones, including the provision of shelter and a home as haven.

A Progressive State

Hardoy and Satterthwaite (1989) have also advocated the need for the state to reassess approaches to low-income housing provision. They have added their voices to Turner and other progressives, suggesting that the path forward must be the adoption of a "popular approach" to housing policy formulation. Thereby, solutions to problems of urban finance, housing, land access, the siting and standards of urban infrastructure, environmental quality, and essential amenities must be formulated locally, by local people, on the basis of local experience, local custom, knowledge and information. Reviewing the evidence of thirty years of squatter settlement growth and development in the cities of the Third World, Hardoy and Satterthwaite, far from suggesting a diminished role for the state, advocate a radical change in state praxis: "more activist, more developmental, more decentralized, more representative and more supportive of citizens' efforts" (Hardoy and Satterthwaite 1989: 304). The same authors have mobilized much the same argument with respect to enhancing environmental conditions in Third World cities, noting the need for good city governance (Hardoy, Mitlin, and Satterthwaite 1992).

Today's neoliberal agenda appears decidedly inappropriate in this context. Letting market forces prevail might serve as an "economic wisdom" for international trade, though this is not the place to debate such a contentious assertion. But it scarcely makes sense in terms of the impacts of such regularization of land and housing markets in the Caribbean on housing provision for the poor. On the contrary, the woeful records of housing provision in so many Caribbean countries—where the state has either demonstrated a general lack of political will or has deemed housing provision for the poor among its lowest priorities, thereby letting the market forces decide—suggests that the state must take a progressive stance on managing both land and housing supply for the people. Now, more than ever, the Caribbean state has a responsibility to intervene and ensure the poor have access to land and housing, either via squatter regularization (for example, in Trinidad and Tobago) or other forms of legislative provisions of security of housing tenure sensitive to each particular Caribbean country's contexts (for instance, Barbados's tenantries). Elsewhere (Conway 1985; Potter 1993a), we have enlarged on the necessity for state-enabling initiatives to intervene on behalf of the poor to ensure adequate land supply and housing security for their needs.

Despite its disappointing record in the past, the state can intervene positively, given the necessary political will. There is still too wide a gap between promises and fulfillment, as several of the contributions to this volume have documented, but it is to be hoped that the messages contained in this volume will prompt some progress. Matching state rhetoric with practice may not be such an impossibility after all. Over thirty years of experience of urbanization, of state and self-help practices, bounded by the structural limitations posed by the changing global contexts, might suggest that the future needs to be rethought. Certainly, a fundamental reordering of ideas as to what constitutes Caribbean "development" and state-directed objectives towards achieving a sustainable future for the region's people should have shelter provision as one dimension of such a future agenda. It seems clear that appropriate vernacular forms should be part of any future solution.

Appropriate Vernacular
Housing Styles

Not only might the vernacular house be construed as an indigenous form of resistance to colonial domination (Lewis 1983), but it presents policymakers and needy people alike with an appropriate and cost-effective, popular dwelling style that has the requisite flexibility and adaptability to serve as an appropriate regional model, culturally sensitive as well as practical (Potter 1993a). Maintenance, upkeep, adaptability to upgrading, repairing, and investing sweat-equity in one's home, is valued, if there is due recognition given to the sociocultural integrity of the distinctive architectural forms of the region's vernacular housing types. We are not arguing that the vernacular house should be seen as an endpoint, rather the reverse, with it being employed as the starting point in housing upgrading and consolidation processes.

If society continues to treat the modern form as the status symbol of class position, while disparaging the vernacular, then to the Caribbean poor the sociocultural "use-values" of the self-built home as shelter, as affordable accommodation, as private space, as a "haven" will always be thought of as transitory, if not demeaning, and, therefore, worth escaping. They will aspire to acquire the more costly, modern, modular design, never mind that it embroils them in markets where their negotiating position is marginal and fraught with risk. Further to their disadvantage, these markets remain dominated by land and housing developers more responsive to middle- and upper-class residential tastes in the consumption of space than to the modest needs of the poor, however desperate the shelter shortage. There is therefore an imperative need for Caribbean societies to better value their vernacular housing heritages, for the state to progressively and idealistically embrace policies and programs which value such housing styles, provide means for access to land where appropriate housing can be located and tenure assured, and for the Caribbean people themselves to begin to recognize the richness in diversity of their cultural landscapes, with built environments given equal attention to those scenic landscapes that they, and their tourist visitors, have taken for granted as their tropical heritage. The increasingly extensive use of vernacular house types, in the form of tourist-related structures, in hotels and commercial shopping centers bears witness to a further postmodern twist to this current situation (Potter and Dann 1994; Dann and Potter 1994).

Housing the Poor, Uncontrolled Urbanization, and Urban Environmental Concerns

Building communities, whether state-promoted, state-aided, or state-enabled, cannot be accomplished without the people's unalienated commitment to their social responsibilities: their sense of belonging to a community, of concern for each and everyone's welfare and communal "basic rights," and of self-worth that derives from feelings of equality, identity, and humanitarian existence, and of future security for all. The sustainability of contemporary urban environments in the Caribbean, as elsewhere in the developing "South" is not a given—far from it (Potter

1993b). The uncontrolled urbanization that has been, and still is, the common experience poses a challenge for future environmental conditions.

Not before time, a concern for environmental conditions among the residential communities of the urban poor has become an issue of global relevance (Hardoy, Mitlin, and Satterthwaite 1992). Concern first manifested itself in megacities like Mexico City, Sao Paulo, and Rio de Janeiro, where environmental pollution threatened people's "living and breathing," where deplorable environmental living conditions and the lack of sewerage treatment created health hazards for the communities' children, and where making a living from working the city's refuse heaps also posed health threats to children. The environmental problems facing residents in the burgeoning squatter settlements were not limited to these extreme situations, however. Smaller rapidly urbanizing cities in Latin America had their own examples of marginalized barrios (Hardoy, Mitlin, and Satterthwaite 1992). Environmental conditions in the uncontrolled peripheral settlements, in *colonias miserias* and shantytowns of the largest cities of Caribbean countries—the region's most rapidly urbanizing, primate cities such as San Juan, Puerto Rico, Kingston, Jamaica, Port au Prince, Haiti, even Port of Spain in Trinidad—also appeared similar, if not indicative of the enormity of the Latin American problem (Clarke 1974).

The notion that our global future might revolve around achieving "sustainable cities" has gained currency, largely in reaction to the environmental deterioration of urban living in most advanced capitalist countries, but also because of the more than apparent spatial congruence of mass poverty and environmental degradation in the low-income urban communities of Asia (Douglass 1992). Furthermore, Douglass and Zoghlin (1994) provide a useful schema for understanding how environmental management in such low-income communities might be accomplished, a schema that starts with the household and constitutes four interlocking themes. The first positions environmental management as an integral part of day-to-day, household-level, economic-cum-welfare strategies. These strategies involve family-level and individual-level decisions about the disbursement of household resource allocations among income-producing, habitat-managing, and socio-network-sustaining activities. A third theme is that the capacity for households to engage collectively in improving environmental resource management is contingent upon the particular sets of political, economic, and cultural circumstances they face. These include, for instance, the state and its interventions; the structure of the economy and labor systems; and certain social and cultural institutions that foster reciprocal and redistributive relations in communities (for example, *coup-de-main* in St. Lucia). The fourth theme complements the three previous ones to suggest that certain constellations of factors—including allowance for human agency through leadership, the dedication and commitment of outside as well as internal organizations, and other unexpected sources of empowerment—are more conducive to community-based initiatives than to others (Douglass and Zoghlin

1994). This emphasis on linking community-based environmental management with household decision making suggests there may very well be positive and progressive impacts derived from such local empowerment initiatives in the Caribbean, if a similar state-enabled future can be envisaged and implemented.

Economic Wealth
with Environmental Health

Lest we be accused of futuristic star gazing, or of being too idealistic in seeking environmentally ameliorating solutions at the expense of realistic evaluations of Caribbean development, we need more clarification to substantiate the "soft growth" position we share with others (see Daly 1994). This final point in our argument needs to reiterate that any housing solution cannot be divorced from the equally significant livelihood concerns of the people. Shelter is one basic right among others such as work, health, food, clothing, learning, and maintenance of sociocultural and ethical values (Ekins and Max-Neef 1992). Poverty must be alleviated if a sustainable future is to be envisioned. Expanding economies, raising GNP per capita, increasing capital flows, and designing Caribbean futures on the basis of neoliberal economists' accounting models will not address poor peoples' needs for the basic rights of livelihood (Daly 1994). The uncontrolled patterns of urbanization that have resulted from such myopic policymaking, whether by design or default, are as much a part of impoverishment, poor health, narcotics addiction, patterns of corruption, crime, and human abuses as the resultant residential environments are the hosts of such social excesses of deprivation and destitution. Addressing the shelter needs of the poor alone cannot be achieved successfully without commensurate efforts to alleviate poverty, provide gainful work experiences, provide health care and learning opportunities, and the like. The environmental health of tomorrow's residential communities will be sustainable only if there is "real-life" economic wealth creation of the sort envisaged by Max Max-Neef, Paul Ekins, and Jane Wheelock (see Ekins and Max-Neef 1992).

The themes we have stressed as our vision(s) for promoting sustainable human settlement development in the Caribbean are ones that might well underwrite broader "development" objectives. Building community, popular participation and local empowerment. progressive, state-enabling solutions, environmental sustainability, and economic wealth with environmental health, together with appropriate (vernacular) housing styles, might, taken together, stand as viable themes for a future model of Caribbean sustainable development. We feel that the comparative examination of Caribbean housing provided by this volume will have achieved its purpose if it galvanizes efforts to redesign and rethink the paths the region might take in order to ensure equitable futures for all its sisters and brothers.

Note

1. One outcome of the UNCED Conference in Rio de Janeiro is the comprehensive declarations of Agenda 21. In chapter 7 ideas for "promoting sustainable human settlement development" are forwarded as guidelines for our common future. Core principles of national human settlement strategies are to improve the social, economic, and environmental quality of human settlements and the living and working environments of all people, in particular the urban and rural poor. Such improvement should be based upon technical cooperation activities, partnerships among the public, private, and community sectors, and participation in the decision-making process from community groups and special interest groups such as women, indigenous people, the elderly, and the disabled. Program areas to be prioritized are: 1) providing adequate shelter for all; 2) improving human settlement management; 3) promoting sustainable land-use planning and management; 4) promoting the integrated provision of environmental infrastructure: water, sanitation, drainage, hazardous, and solid-waste management; 5) promoting sustainable energy and transport systems in human settlements; 6) promoting human settlement planning and management in disaster-prone areas; 7) promoting sustainable construction industry activities; and 8) promoting human resource development and capacity building for human settlement development (UNEP 1992).

References

Ambursley, F., and R. Cohen. (1983) *Crisis in the Caribbean*. London: Heinemann.

Anderson, B. (1983) *Imagined Communities: Reflections on the Origin and Spread of Nationalism*. London: Verso.

Castells, M. (1978) *City, Class and Power*. London: Macmillan.

————. (1984) "Space and Society: Managing the New Historical Relationships." In M. P. Smith, ed., *Cities in Transformation: Class, Capital and the State*, 235–60. Beverly Hills: Sage.

Clarke, C. G. (1974) "Urbanization in the Caribbean." *Geography* 59 (3): 223–32.

Conway, D. (1981) "Fact or Opinion on Uncontrolled Peripheral Settlement: Or How Different Conclusions Arise from the Same Data." *Ekistics* 48 (286): 37–43.

————. (1982) "Self-Help Housing, the Commodity Nature of Housing and Amelioration of the Housing Deficit: Continuing the Turner-Burgess Debate." *Antipode* 14 (2): 40–46.

————. (1985) "Changing Perspectives on Squatter Settlements, Intraurban Mobility, and Constraints on Housing Choice of the Third World Urban Poor." *Urban Geography* 6 (2): 170–92.

Dann, G. M. S., and R. B. Potter. (1994) "Tourism and Post-Modernity in a Caribbean Setting." *Cahiers du Tourisme* 185. 43 pp.

Daly, H. (1994) "Sustainable Growth: An Impossibility Theorem." *Carrying Capacity Network: Clearinghouse Bulletin* 4 (4): 1–2, 4, 7.

Douglass, M. (1992) "The Political Economy of Urban Poverty and Environmental Management in Asia: Access, Empowerment and Community-based Alternatives." *Environment and Urbanization* 4 (1): 9–32.

Douglass, M., and M. Zoghlin. (1994) "Sustaining Cities at the Grassroots: Livelihood, Environment and Social Networks in Suan Phlu, Bangkok." *Third World Planning Review* 16 (2): 171–200.

Ekins, P., and M. Max-Neef. (1992) *Real-Life Economics: Understanding Wealth Creation*. London and New York: Routledge.

Gilbert, A. (1993) *In Search of a Home: Rental and Shard Housing in Latin America*. Tucson: University of Arizona Press.

Hardoy, J., and D. Satterthwaite. (1989) *Squatter Citizen*. London: Earthscan.

Hardoy, J. E., D. Mitlin, and D. Satterthwaite. (1992) *Environmental Problems in Third World Cities*. London: Earthscan.

Harvey, D. (1982) *The Limits to Capital*. Oxford: Basil Blackwell.

———. (1989) *The Condition of Postmodernity*. Oxford: Basil Blackwell.

———. (1992) "From Space to Place and Back Again: Reflections on the Condition of Postmodernity." In J. Bird et al., *Mapping Futures: Local Cultures, Global Change*, 3–29. London and New York: Routledge.

Heidegger, M. (1966) *Discourse on Thinking*. New York: Harper and Row.

———. (1971) *Poetry, Language, Thought*. New York: Harper and Row.

Hudson, B. J. (1986) "Landscape as Resource for National Development: A Caribbean View." *Geography* 71 (2): 116–21.

Leckie, S. (1989) "Housing as a Human Right." *Environment and Urbanization* 1 (2): 90–108.

Lefebvre, H. (1991) *The Production of Space*. Oxford: Basil Blackwell.

Lewis, G. K. (1983) *Main Currents in Caribbean Thought: The Historical Evolution of Caribbean Society in its Ideological Aspects, 1492–1900*. Baltimore and London: Johns Hopkins University Press.

Mathéy, K. (1992) *Beyond Self-Help Housing*. London and New York: Mansell.

McElroy, J. (1995) "Bermuda Went the Way of Other Wallet-Wise Territories." *The Christian Science Monitor* 87 (1987), 22 Aug.

Palmer, E. K., and C. V. Patton (1988) "Evolution of Third World Shelter Policies." In C. V. Patton, ed., *Spontaneous Shelter: International Perspectives and Prospects*, 3–24. Philadelphia: Temple University Press.

Potter, R. B. (1993a) "The Neglect of Caribbean Vernacular Architecture." *Bahamas Journal of Science* 1 (1): 46–51.

———. (1993b) "Urbanisation in the Caribbean and Trends of Global Convergence-Divergence." *Geographical Journal* 159: 1–21.

Potter, R. B., and G. Dann. (1994). "Some Observations concerning Postmodernity and Sustainable Developments in the Caribbean." *Caribbean Geography* 5: 92–101.

Relph, E. (1976) *Place and Placelessness*. London: Pion.

Sanjek, R., ed. (1994) *Cities, Classes and the Social Order: Anthony Leeds*. Ithaca and London: Cornell University Press.

Turner, J. F. C. (1992) "Foreword." In K. Mathéy, ed., *Beyond Self-Help Housing*, xi–xiv. London and New York: Mansell.

Turner, J. F. C., and R. Fichter. (1972) *Freedom to Build: Dweller Control of the Housing Process*. New York: Macmillan, 1972.

UNCHS. (1983) *Land for Human Settlements: Recommendations for National and International Action*. Helsinki: United Nations Commission on Human Settlements; HS/C/6/3/Add.1.

UNEP. (1992) *Agenda 21, Chapter 7: Promoting Sustainable Human Settlement Development*. Rio de Janeiro, Brazil: United Nations Conference on Environment and Development.

Appendix

Chapter Abstracts in English, French, and Spanish

Chapter I
CARIBBEAN HOUSING, THE STATE, AND SELF-HELP:
AN OVERVIEW

Dennis Conway and Robert B. Potter

ABSTRACT

The poor's struggle for adequate shelter in the Caribbean has never been easy. Newly independent governments inherited legacies of colonial domination and an accumulated housing deficit. How did these governments fare? How did the people fare? This overview of the present collection of commissioned chapters introduces the themes to be addressed in this volume: the changing roles of the State, of international funding agencies and the Caribbean private housing sectors, in their attempts at low-income housing provision. Also, we concentrate on the ways the poor have sought shelter and accommodation via self-help initiatives: using vernacular styles, autonomous creativity, and State-sponsorship in a few cases. Regionwide coverage is accomplished, of itself a first. Generalizations drawn from these authoritative comparisons between the housing experiences of Cubans, French West Indians, Puerto Ricans, Trinidadians, Jamaicans, Barbadians, Guyanese, and small islanders of the Eastern Caribbean are anticipated.

Chapitre I
LOGEMENT, ETAT ET AUTO-ASSISTANCE
A LA CARAIBE:
UNE VUE D'ENSEMBLE

Dennis Conway et Robert E. Potter

RESUME

La lutte menée par les pauvres pour obtenir un logement convenable dans la région des Caraïbes n'a jamais été facile. Les gouvernements des pays dont l'indépendance est récente ont hérité des résultats d'une domination coloniale et d'un retard accumulé en termes de logements disponibles. Comment ces gouvernements ont-ils géré la situation? Quelle a été la réaction des gens? Cette vue d'ensemble du présent ouvrage réalisé sur commande introduit les sujets traités dans ce volume, à savoir: les changements qui se produisent dans les rôles de l'Etat, des agences de financement internationales et des secteurs privés de l'immobilier dans la Caraïbe lorsqu'ils essaient de fournir des habitations à loyer modéré. Nous portons, en outre, sur les façons dont les pauvres ont cherché à se procurer un abri et un logement par des initiatives personnelles en recourrant à leur créativité personnelle et aux styles populaires locaux, ainsi qu'à l'aide de financement de l'Etat dans quelques cas. Cette étude couvre toute la région et cela constitue en soi une première. Et on s'attend à pouvoir établir des généralisations à partir de ces comparaisons faisant autorité entre les expériences en logement des Cubains, des Antillais français, des Portoricains, des Trinidadiens, des Jamaïquains, des Barbadiens, des Guyanais et des populations des petites îles de la Caraïbe orientale.

Capítulo I
EL ESTADO Y LA INICIATIVA PERSONAL:
UNA PERSPECTIVA SOBRE
LA VIVIENDA EN EL CARIBE

Dennis Conway y Robert B. Potter

RESUMEN

La lucha de los pobres en el Caribe por obtener una vivienda adecuada, jamás ha sido fácil. Los gobiernos recién independizados recibieron legados de la dominación colonial así como un déficit acumulado en lo relativo a la disponibilidad de viviendas. ¿Cómo resolvieron estos gobiernos la situación planteada?, ¿Cuál fue la reacción de sus gentes? Esta perspectiva del presente conjunto de capítulos encargados para este volúmen, presenta los temas a tratarse: el rol cambiante del Estado, de las agencias donatarias internacionales y el sector privado dedicado a proveer vivienda en el Caribe, en sus intentos por porporcionar viviendas a familias de bajos ingresos. El estudio también se concentra en las formas en que los pobres han buscado alojamiento y albergue mediante iniciativas personales: utilizando estilos autóctonos, la creatividad autónoma y el patrocinio del Estado, en unos pocos casos. Este estudio cubre por completo la región y constituye en sí una primicia. Se anticipan generalizaciones a partir de estas comparaciones autorizadas entre las experiencias sobre la vivienda que han tenido los cubanos, los franco antillanos, los puertorriqueños, los habitantes de Trinidad, los jamaiquinos, los de Barbados, los guyaneses y los habitantes de las pequeñas islas del Caribe Oriental.

Chapter 2
HOUSES IN THE CARIBBEAN:
HOMES AND HERITAGE

Brian J. Hudson

ABSTRACT

In their attempts to solve the housing problems of the poor, Caribbean governments, like those elsewhere, commonly make use of modern technology, often importing mass-production methods, design standards and even materials from abroad. The widespread failure of this approach has encouraged governments and international organizations to seek new ways of producing suitable housing economically, often harnessing the labor of the people themselves. Generally ignored, however, are the folk and vernacular traditions of building by which most people have housed themselves for centuries. Largely a syncretic product of transplanted African and European traditions, the "Caribbean popular house" is fast disappearing, yet it represents an appropriate functional response to the physical and cultural environment of the region. Useful lessons may be learned from traditional houses and their methods of construction; and, as an important part of the Caribbean heritage, they are buildings worthy of conservation.

Chapitre 2
LES MAISONS DE LA CARAIBE:
DES FOYERS ET UN PATRIMOINE

Brian J. Hudson

RESUME

En vue de résoudre les problèmes de logement des pauvres, les gouvernements de la Caraïbe, tout comme ceux d'autres régions, emploient souvent des technologies modernes, important de l'étranger, les méthodes de production de masse, les normes architecturales et même des matériaux. L'échec généralisé de cette approche a encouragé les gouvernements et les organisations internationales à rechercher de nouvelles façons de construire des habitations appropriées et économiques et, souvent, à recourir à la main d'oeuvre de la population concernée. Néanmoins, on ignore généralement les traditions populaires et indigènes de construction employées par une grande partie des gens pour se construire leur logement pendant des siècles. La "maison populaire caribéenne" qui est, en grande partie, le produit syncrétique de traditions africaines et européennes transplantées, est en train de disparaître rapidement, alors qu'elle représente une réponse fonctionnelle appropriée au milieu physique et culturel de la région. Des leçons utiles pourraient être tirées des maisons traditionnelles et de leurs méthodes de construction. Ces dernières font partie intégrale du patrimoine caribéen, et par conséquent, devraient être conservées.

Capítulo 2
LA VIVIENDA EN EL CARIBE:
HOGARES Y PATRIMONIO

Brian J. Hudson

RESUMEN

En sus intentos por resolver los problemas de la vivienda para los pobres, los gobiernos del Caribe, así como los de otras partes del mundo, comúnmente utilizan la tecnología moderna, importando, a menudo, métodos de producción masiva, patrones de diseño e incluso materiales del extranjero. El fracaso general de este enfoque, ha alentado a los gobiernos y a las organizaciones internacionales a buscar nuevos métodos de producción económica de viviendas adecuadas, a menudo aprovechando la mano de obra de los propios interesados. Por lo general, se ignoran las tradiciones folclóricas y populares de construcción de viviendas que han sido utilizadas durante siglos por la mayoría de los pueblos. La "casa popular caribeña", en su mayor parte, un producto sincrético de las tradiciones africanas y europeas transplantadas, está desapareciendo rápidamente. Sin embargo, la misma representa una respuesta funcional adecuada al medio físico y cultural de la región. Se puede aprender lecciones muy útiles de las viviendas tradicionales y sus métodos de construcción; y como parte valiosa del patrimonio caribeño, existen edificios que merecen ser conservados.

Chapter 3
HOUSING CONDITIONS, VERNACULAR ARCHITECTURE,
AND STATE POLICY IN BARBADOS

Mark R. Watson and Robert B. Potter

ABSTRACT

The folk architecture tradition of Barbados has been described as being virtually without counterpart anywhere in the world. This essay documents the origins of the traditional movable chattel house in the plantation economy, specifically in relation to the evolution of the plantation tenantries. Subsequently, the spontaneous self-help and incremental upgrading experiences of Barbados are examined in the context of current housing conditions at the national scale. Past, present, and potential future developments in both state and private sector housing policy are then reviewed, with particular attention being paid to key shelter projects, including the upgrading of the plantation tenantries since the passing of legislation in the 1980s, the managerialist influences of the state and private sectors, and what is seen as the continuing importance of financing lower-income households. Throughout, the neglect of the policy potential of the traditional Barbadian house is emphasized in this account.

CHAPITRE 3
CONDITIONS DE LOGEMENT, ARCHITECTURE INDIGENE ET POLITIQUE DE L'ETAT A LA BARBADE

Mark R. Watson et Robert B. Potter

RESUME

La tradition de l'architecture populaire de la Barbade est considérée comme étant unique dans le monde. Ce chapitre apporte des documents sur les origines de la maison en bois démontable traditionnelle dans l'économie de la plantation, notamment par rapport à l'évolution des employés logés sur la plantation. Par ailleurs, l'auto-assistance spontanée ainsi que les expériences d'amélioration croissantes qui ont lieu en Barbade sont étudiées dans le cadre des conditions actuelles de logement au niveau national. Les évolutions passées, présentes et peut-être futures des politiques des secteurs public et privé concernant le logement sont passées en revue. Une attention particulière est en même temps prêtée aux programmes importants pour le logement, dont l'amélioration des maisons des employés agricoles de la plantation depuis la promulgation d'une législation dans les années quatre-vingt, l'influence des sphères dirigeantes des secteurs tant public que privé et, ce que l'on considère comme important, c'est-à-dire, de continuer à financer des habitations à loyer modéré. Cette étude met l'accent sur le manque d'intérêt pour le potentiel d'une politique de la maison traditionnelle en Barbade.

Capítulo 3
LAS CONDICIONES DE LA VIVIENDA, LA ARQUITECTURA POPULAR Y LA POLITICA ESTATAL EN BARBADOS

Mark R. Watson y Robert B. Potter

RESUMEN

La tradición arquitectónica folclórica de Barbados ha sido considerada como sin par en todo el mundo. Este ensayo documenta los orígenes de la casa de madera movible en la economía de plantación, específicamente en relación con la evolución de los agricultores arrendatarios en las haciendas. En consecuencia, la iniciativa personal espontánea y las experiencias de auge cada vez mayor en Barbados, se examinan en el contexto de las condiciones actuales de la vivienda a escala nacional. Se estudian desarrollos pasados, presentes y los posibles desarrollos futuros, tanto en la política sobre la vivienda del sector público como en la del privado, prestando especial atención a los proyectos clave sobre albergue, incluso la evolución de la condición en que se encuentran los arrendamientos agrícolas a partir de la aprobación de la legislación en los años 80, la influencia gerencialede los sectores público y privado y lo que se considera como la importancia siempre vigente de financiar viviendas a familias de ingresos bajos. En todo el relato, se hace hincapié en el rechazo al potencial político de la vivienda tradicional de Barbados.

Chapter 4
HOUSING AND THE STATE IN THE EASTERN CARIBBEAN

Robert B. Potter

ABSTRACT

The small island nations of the Eastern Caribbean, in common with others in the region, possess indigenous self-help housing systems that are based on expandable and moveable wooden housing units. The central argument of this chapter is that such houses, built by the people, for the people, represent a surprisingly neglected architectural, cultural and planning resource. The chapter first assesses housing conditions and quality, and following this, attention turns to state housing policies in the region. The theme is the lack of clear proactive policies in the case of these eastern Caribbean states. With few exceptions, the state has only been seen to intervene directly when the demand for land for commercial purposes has suggested the efficacy of clearing squatters and low-income residents from particular residential areas. Another instance has been where dwellings have been threatened by the likelihood of environmental disasters, such as flooding and storm damage.

Chapitre 4
LOGEMENT ET ETAT DANS LA CARAIBE ORIENTALE

Robert B. Potter

RESUME

Les petits états insulaires de la Caraïbe orientale, tout comme d'autres états de la région, possèdent des systèmes d'auto-assistance pour le logement indigène qui sont basés sur des unités d'habitation en bois qui peuvent être déplacées et agrandies. Ce chapitre porte plus particulièrement sur le fait que de telles maisons qui ont été construites par les gens et pour les gens représentent une ressource de planification, architecturale et culturelle qui, étonnamment, est ignorée. Ce chapitre évalue, d'abord, les conditions et la qualité du logement; ensuite il examine les politiques de l'état en matière de logement en vigueur dans la région. Ce chapitre traite tout particulièrement du manque de politiques dynamiques claires dans le cas de ces états de la Caraïbe orientale. A quelques exceptions près, il semble que l'état ne soit intervenu directement que dans le cas où la demande de terres en vue d'une utilisation commerciale a suggéré une intervention efficace pour chasser les squatters et les habitants économiquement faibles de certains quartiers résidentiels. L'état est également intervenu là où des habitations étaient menacées de la possibilité de catastrophes naturelles, telles que les inondations et les dégâts causés par les tempêtes.

Capítulo 4
LA VIVIENDA Y EL ESTADO EN EL CARIBE ORIENTAL

Robert B. Potter

RESUMEN

Las pequeñas naciones insulares del Caribe oriental poseen en común, con otras de la región, sistemas autóctonos de auto construcción de viviendas, que son unidades habitacionales movibles y expandibles, en madera. El argumento central de este capítulo es que tales viviendas, construidas por el pueblo, para el pueblo, representan un recurso arquitectónico, cultural y de planificación que ha sido sorprendentemente echado a un lado. El capítulo evalúa primero las condiciones y la calidad de la vivienda que se ofrece y a continuación, se concentra en las políticas estatales de vivienda en la región. El tema principal es la falta de políticas pro-activas claras en el caso de estos estados del Caribe oriental. Salvo pocas excepciones, solo se ha visto intervenir directamente al Estado cuando la demanda de terrenos con fines comerciales ha sugerido la eficacia de desalojar a invasores y residentes de bajos ingresos de ciertas áreas residenciales. Otra instancia en que se recurre al desalojo es cuando las viviendas se ven amenazadas por posibles desastres ambientales, tales como inundaciones y tormentas.

Chapter 5
SELF-HELP HOUSING IN JAMAICA

L. Alan Eyre

ABSTRACT

Jamaica has a very long tradition of self-help housing. A majority of rural Jamaicans and a large proportion of urban residents live in dwellings which they have contributed all or most of the construction input by self-help methods. The chapter shows how the whole issue of self-help housing in Jamaica is at a crossroads. Formerly encouraged as a solution to the problems of shelter for the poor, and even championed by socialist politicians, self-help housing is now officially stigmatized as immoral and antisocial. After a hiatus of several decades, confrontation with shantytown dwellers has since 1994 become the order of the day, and the bulldozing of homes has now been put on the national agenda. Five case studies are presented, based on the settlements of Riverton City, Hangman Burial Ground, Whitehall, Flankers, and Holland Bamboo.

Chapitre 5
LOGEMENT AUTO-ASSISTE A LA JAMAIQUE

L. Alan Eyre

RESUME

La Jamaïque a une longue tradition de logements construits par leurs propres habitants. La plupart des Jamaïquains habitant dans les zones rurales, ainsi que très bon nombre des ceux habitant des zones urbaines, vivent dans des habitations, à la construction desquelles ils ont contribué entièrement ou en grande partie à l'aide de méthodes d'auto-assistance. Ce chapitre démontre comment la question de logement auto-assisté se trouve actuellement à un moment critique. Le logement auto-assisté, qui était promu auparavant comme solution aux problèmes de logement pour les pauvres, et même défendu par les hommes politiques socialistes, est, aujourd'hui, officiellement considéré comme immoral et antisocial. Après plusieurs décennies, il y a eu depuis 1994 de nombreuses confrontations avec les habitants des bidonvilles et la destruction de maisons par des bulldozers est à l'ordre du jour national. L'auteur présente cinq études de cas qui portent sur les établissements se trouvant à Riverton City, à Hangman Burial Ground, à Whitehall, à Flankers et à Holland Bamboo.

Capítulo 5
LA CONSTRUCCION DE VIVIENDAS CON RECURSOS PROPIOS EN JAMAICA

L. Alan Eyre

RESUMEN

Jamaica tiene una larga tradición en la construcción de viviendas con recursos propios. Una gran mayoría de los pobladores rurales y una gran proporción de los residentes urbanos, habitan casas que han sido construidas en gran medida o en su totalidad, con métodos de iniciativa personal. El capítulo muestra cómo la cuestión de la contrucción de viviendas con recursos propios en Jamaica se encuentra en una encrucijada. La auto construcción de viviendas, que anteriormente había sido alentada como solución a los problemas de albergue para los pobres, e incluso defendida por los políticos socialistas, se halla actualmente estigmatizada como inmoral y antisocial. Después de una pausa de varias décadas el enfrentamiento con habitantes de las chabolas está, desde 1994, a la orden del día. Igualmente, la remoción de viviendas con aplanadora se incluye ahora en la agenda nacional. Se presentan cinco estudios de caso, basados en los asentamientos de Riverton City, Hangman Burial Ground, Whitehall, Flankers y Holland Bamboo.

Chapter 6
OBSTACLES TO LOW-INCOME HOUSING ASSISTANCE IN THE CAPITALIST PERIPHERY: THE CASE OF JAMAICA

Thomas Klak

ABSTRACT

This chapter reveals a variety of market-related factors which help to explain Jamaica's housing crisis. It focuses on the Jamaican State's role in housing and how it has managed largely to avoid helping what ostensibly is its intended audience, i.e., the most needy and the poor, while it has actually facilitated the private housing market to better meet middle-class housing needs and aspirations. The chapter's aim is to identify the main trends in State policies and practices from the mid-1970s to the present, through regime changes, periods of economic expansion and contraction, to today's neoliberal era. More emphasis is given to the administrations of Manley and Seaga than to the Manley-Patterson government of the 1990s, since the latter's housing priorities and achievements have yet to be fully disclosed. Similarly, most attention is paid to the National Housing Trust, the largest State agency, and the Caribbean Housing Finance Corporation, the second-largest heavily supported by USAID. Long-standing structural adjustment policies influence State housing strategies, but scarcely in positive directions. The poor hold the potential for playing a proactive role in improving their housing conditions. It is up to the State to harness their progressive power, rather than formulate institutional obstacles.

Chapitre 6
OBSTACLES A L'ASSISTANCE POUR LES HABITATIONS A LOYER MODERE A LA PERIPHERIE DU CAPITALISME: LE CAS DE LA JAMAIQUE

Thomas Klak

RESUME

Ce chapitre révèle une variété de facteurs liés au marché qui aident à expliquer la crise du logement à la Jamaïque. Il porte sur le rôle de l'Etat jamaïquain dans le domaine du logement et démontre comment l'état est parvenu, en grande partie, à ne pas fournir une assistance à son public officiellement ciblé, à savoir, les économiquement faibles ainsi que les pauvres, tandis qu'il favorise le marché du logement privé afin d'améliorer les besoins et les aspirations de la classe moyenne en matière de logement. Le présent chapitre a pour objectif d'identifier les principales tendances des politiques et des pratiques gouvernementales, pour la période allant de la mi-décennie des années 70 à nos jours par le biais de changements de gouvernements, de périodes d'expansion et de récession économiques experimentés actuellement jusqu'à l'ère neo-libérale. Une attention est prêtée plus particulièrement aux administrations de Manley et de Seaga qu'aux gouvernements de Manley et de Patterson des années 90, car les priorités et les réalisations de ces derniers relatives au logement n'ont pas encore été complètement révélées. Par ailleurs, un accent particulier a été mis sur le National Housing Trust (Programme national d'aide au logement), la plus grande agence de l'Etat, et la Caribbean Housing Finance Corporation (Société caribéenne de financement immobilier), la deuxième agence la plus grande qui bénéficie en outre d'un concours financier de l'USAID. Des politiques d'ajustement structurel de longue durée influent sur les stratégies de l'Etat en matière de logement, mais rarement de manière positive. Les pauvres ont le pouvoir de jouer un rôle dynamique dans l'amélioration de leurs conditions de logement. L'Etat est responsable de canaliser leur pouvoir progressiste, au lieu de créer des obstacles institutionnels.

Capítulo 6
OBSTACULOS A LA AYUDA PARA LA VIVIENDA A FAMILIAS DE BAJOS INGRESOS EN LA PERIFERIA CAPITALISTA: EL CASO DE JAMAICA

Thomas Klak

RESUMEN

El capítulo revela una variedad de factores relacionados con el mercado que contribuyen a explicar la crisis de la vivienda que experimenta Jamaica. El estudio se concentra en el rol desempeñado por el Estado en asuntos de vivienda y en cómo éste se las ha arreglado, en gran medida, para evitar prestar ayuda a quienes constituyen su público objetivo, vg. los pobres y los más necesitados, al tiempo que ha facilitado el mercado de la vivienda privada para satisfacer mejor las necesidades y aspiraciones de la clase media. El capítulo se propone identificar las principales tendencias en políticas y prácticas estatales, desde la mitad de la década de los 70 hasta el presente, a través de cambio de regímenes, períodos de expansión y de restricción económicas hasta la era neoliberal de hoy. Se ha dado mayor énfasis a las administraciones de Manley y Seaga que al gobierno de Manley-Patterson de los 90, ya que las prioridades y logros de éste último, en lo relativo a la vivienda, están aún por revelarse. De forma similar, se presta gran atención al National Housing Trust (fondo fiduciario para la vivienda), la mayor agencia estatal y a la segunda agencia en tamaño, la Caribbean Housing Finance Corporation, (corporación caribeña de financiación para la vivienda), que recibe un gran apoyo de USAID: Políticas de ajuste estructural que han existido por mucho tiempo, influyen sobre las estrategias del Estado sobre la vivienda, pero, rara vez de una manera positiva. Los pobres tienen la capacidad de desempeñar un papel pro activo para mejorar sus condiciones de vivienda. Al Estado, le queda aprovechar este poder progresista, en vez de formular obstáculos institucionales.

Chapter 7
FROM COOPERATIVE SOCIALISM TO A SOCIAL HOUSING POLICY? DECLINES AND REVIVALS IN HOUSING POLICY IN GUYANA

Linda Peake

ABSTRACT

Overcrowding, insecure shelter, and increasing levels of homelessness are the primary characteristics of the housing situation in Guyana in the early 1990s, and these conditions characterize not only the poor, but the middle classes as well. Two decades after the People's National Congress (PNC) declaration of housing the nation, state-managed housing is in near collapse, and in the cooperative and private sectors, building has been at a virtual standstill. Since before Independence the state has played a major role in the provision of housing for all social groups. Thus, the crisis in housing affects all but the very wealthiest sectors of society. The chapter analyzes the factors that have shaped the development of housing policy in Guyana, commencing with an overview of the urbanization process in general. Attention then turns to the ways in which the PNC shaped housing. The chapter then assesses the current crisis in housing facing the People's Progressive Party (PPP) and the forces most likely to shape future housing provision.

Chapitre 7
DU SOCIALISME COOPERATIF A UNE POLITIQUE SOCIALE DE LOGEMENT? BAISSE ET REPRISE DE LA POLITIQUE DU LOGEMENT AU GUYANA

Linda Peake

RESUME

La surpopulation, les habitations précaires et les niveaux toujours croissants du nombre des sans-abri sont les principales caractéristiques de la situation de logement au Guyana au début des années quatre-vingt-dix, et ces conditions caractérisent non seulement les pauvres, mais aussi la petite-bourgeoisie. Deux décennies après la déclaration du People's National Congress—PNC (Congrès national populaire) en faveur de l'attribution de logement à la nation, le programme de logement géré par l'Etat frôle la ruine, et dans les secteurs coopératif et privé, la construction est actuellement au point mort. Même avant l'indépendance, l'état a toujours joué un rôle important dans la mise de logement à la disposition de tous les groupes sociaux. Par suite, la crise du logement affecte tous les secteurs de la société sauf les plus riches. Le présent chapitre analyse les facteurs qui ont déterminé l'élaboration d'une politique du logement au Guyana. Il donne d'abord une vue d'ensemble du processus d'urbanisation en général et il examine ensuite la façon dont le PNC a influencé le logement. Enfin, il évalue la crise actuelle du logement à laquelle doit faire face le People's Progressive Party—PPP (Parti progressiste populaire) ainsi que les forces qui ont le plus de chances de déterminer la politique future sur le logement.

Capítulo 7
¿DEL SOCIALISMO COOPERATIVO A UNA POLITICA SOCIAL DE LA VIVIENDA? CAIDA Y RESURGIMIENTO DE LA POLITICA DE VIVIENDA EN GUYANA

Linda Peake

RESUMEN

El hacinamiento, el albergue inseguro y el aumento en los niveles de desamparo constituyen las características primarias de la situación de la vivienda en Guyana, a principios de los años 90. Estas condiciones caracterizan no sólo a los pobres, sino también a la clase media. Dos décadas después de que el Congreso Nacional del Pueblo (PNC) declarara construir viviendas para la nación, la gestión de la vivienda estatal se encuentra cercana al colapso y en los sectores cooperativo y privado, la construcción se encuentra virtualmente paralizada. Desde antes de la Independencia, el Estado ha desempeñado un papel importante en la entrega de viviendas a todos los grupos sociales. Por consiguiente, la crisis en la vivienda afecta a todos, menos a los sectores más pudientes de la sociedad. El capítulo analiza los factores que han dado forma al desarrollo de la política de la vivienda en Guyana, comenzando por una perspectiva del proceso de urbanización en general. Luego, el enfoque cambia hacia las maneras cómo el PNC concibió la vivienda. El capítulo evalúa la crisis actual de la vivienda que enfrenta el Partido Progresista del Pueblo (PPP) y las fuerzas que darán forma a la política futura sobre este rubro.

Chapter 8
A CRITICAL REVIEW OF STATE INVOLVEMENT IN HOUSING IN TRINIDAD AND TOBAGO

Linda Hewitt

ABSTRACT

This chapter on State involvement with housing the poor in Trinidad and Tobago critically reviews the evolving situation as the country experiences periods of prosperity and growth, followed by hardship, restructuring, and externally mandated directives. The twists and turns of State policies towards housing the poor and the not-so-poor (especially the middle classes) are scrutinized, and found wanting. Inheriting a legacy of a huge deficit from centuries of colonial neglect, the newly independent State—with the dominating presence of Prime Minister Eric Williams, who was influential in cultivating an impractical, rhetorical style of policy formulation by speech making—by and large, abrogated its responsibility towards housing the urban poor. The poor resorted to self-help strategies, with increasing regularity in the more recent, harsher times under IMF restructuring. The middle classes were also disadvantaged while the regime underwent rationalisation, but their dominance in the urbanizing residential land markets of Greater Port of Spain continued, often at the expense of the poor.

Chapitre 8
UNE CRITIQUE DE LA PARTICIPATION DE L'ETAT AU LOGEMENT A LA TRINITE ET TOBAGO

Linda Hewitt

RESUME

Ce chapitre qui traite de la participation du gouvernement aux efforts de logement des pauvres à la Trinité et Tobago critique la situation en train de développer pendant que le pays connaît des périodes de prospérité et de croissance qui sont suivies de privations, de restructuration et de directives faites de l'extérieur. Les virements et revirements de l'Etat en ce qui concerne le logement des pauvres et des classes moyennes sont examinés de très près et sont considérés inadéquats. Ayant hérité un grand déficit causé par des siècles de désintérêt colonial, l'Etat récemment devenu indépendant, marqué par la présence imposante du premier ministre Eric Williams, qui, a une grande influence en pratiquant un style rhétorique et peu pratique d'élaboration de politiques par les discours, a renoncé à sa responsabilité de fournir un logement pour les pauvres des zones urbaines.

Les pauvres ont donc recouru à des stratégies faisant appel à des initiatives personnelles, et ce d'autant plus pendant les périodes plus récentes et plus difficiles causées par la restructuration inspirée par le FMI. Les classes moyennes se sont également trouvées dans une position désavantageuse lors de la rationalisation du régime. Néanmoins, elles ont gardé leur place dominante sur les marchés immobiliers des zones résidentielles à urbaniser aux alentours de Port of Spain, et ce, souvent, au détriment des pauvres.

Capítulo 8
UN ANALISIS CRITICO DE LA PARTICIPACION DEL ESTADO EN EL RUBRO DE LA VIVIENDA EN TRINIDAD Y TABAGO

Linda Hewitt

RESUMEN

Este capítulo que trata sobre la participación del gobierno en sus esfuerzos por proveer vivienda a los pobres en Trinidad y Tobago, critica la situación que se desarrolla al experimentar el país, períodos de prosperidad y crecimiento, seguidos de privaciones, de reestructuración y de directivas externas. Las idas y venidas de la política estatal en cuanto a la provisión de vivienda a los pobres, y a los no tan pobres—especialmente las clases medias—se ponen bajo escrutinio y son consideradas inadecuadas. Habiendo heredado un gran déficit causado por dos siglos de desinterés colonial, el Estado recientemente independizado, con la presencia dominante del Primer Ministro Eric Williams, quien fue determinante en cultivar un estilo retórico y poco práctico de formular políticas por medio de discursos, ha reconocido su responsabilidad hacia la provisión de viviendas a los pobres de las zonas urbanas. Los pobres han recurrido a estrategias de iniciativa personal, con mayor regularidad en los últimos tiempos que han sido más difíciles a causa de la reestructuración provocada por el FMI. Las clases medias también se hallaron en una posición desventajosa mientras el régimen pasó por la racionalización. De todas formas, estas continuaron dominando en los mercados inmobiliarios de las zonas residenciales a urbanizarse en el gran Port-of-Spain, a menudo a expensas de los pobres.

Chapter 9
SELF-HELP HOUSING STRATEGIES IN CUBA: AN ALTERNATIVE TO CONVENTIONAL WISDOM?

Kosta Mathéy

ABSTRACT

This chapter reviews the record of Cuban housing provision, through to recent times, when the "Special Period" brought about by the collapse of the Soviet

Union, and the subsequent tightening of the economic embargo by the United States administration, virtually brought the process to an abrupt halt. After a brief discussion of pre-Revolutionary times, the revolutionary regime's policies towards housing, their ideological bases, legal frameworks, and the State's performance are examined. In particular, the formation and involvement of *microbrigades* in housing and community development are highlighted as progressive and successful. Then, an assessment of these Cuban self-help strategies as alternatives to other practices in the region is attempted. A final section discusses the problems that the "Special Period" poses for the sustainability of such progressive, *socialist* practices.

Chapitre 9
STRATEGIES DE LOGEMENT AUTO-ASSISTE A CUBA: UNE AUTRE SOLUTION AUX IDEES RECUES?

Kosta Mathéy

RESUME

Ce chapitre passe en revue le record établi par Cuba en matière de construction de logements jusqu'à une époque récente, c'est-à-dire, quand la "Période spéciale" provoquée par la chute de l'Union soviétique ainsi que le strict renforcement de l'embargo économique exercé par le gouvernement des Etats-Unis ont pratiquement provoqué un arrêt brutal. Après une brève discussion de la période pré-révolutionnaire, les politiques du régime révolutionnaire sur le logement sont étudiées ainsi que leur base idéologique, leur cadre juridique et les réalisations de l'Etat. Plus particulièrement, la création des *microbrigades* et leur participation au développement immobilier et communautaire sont soulignées comme étant une initiative progressiste et réussie. Ensuite, une tentative d'évaluation de ces stratégies d'auto-assistance à Cuba comme offrant des alternatives aux pratiques de la région est présentée. La dernière section examine les problèmes que pose la "Période spéciale" pour le maintien de telles pratiques progressistes et *socialistes*.

Capítulo 9
ESTRATATEGIAS PARA LA CONTRUCCION DE VIVIENDAS CON ESFUERZOS PERSONALES EN CUBA: ¿UNA ALTERNATIVA A LAS IDEAS CONVENCIONALES?

Kosta Mathéy

RESUMEN

Este capítulo examina la marca establecida por Cuba en materia de construcción de viviendas a lo largo de los últimos tiempos, cuando el "Período Especial", provocado por el derrumbe de la Unión Soviética y la consecuente aplicación estricta del embargo económico por la administración de los Estados Unidos, hizo que el proceso se interrumpiera abruptamente. Después de una breve discusión sobre los tiempos pre-revolucionarios, se estudian las políticas del régimen revolucionario sobre la vivienda, sus bases ideológicas, los marcos jurídicos y los logros del Estado. En particular, se destaca la formación y participación de las *microbrigadas* en el desarrollo comunitario y de la vivienda como progresista y de resultados positivos. Luego, se intenta una evaluación de estas estrategias de auto construcción en Cuba, como alternativas que se ofrecen a otras prácticas en la región. En la sección final se discute los problemas que plantea el "Período Especial" para el mantenimiento de tales prácticas *socialistas* y progresistas.

Chapter 10
FROM THE *BOHIO* TO THE *CASERIO*: URBAN HOUSING CONDITIONS IN PUERTO RICO

Jorge Duany

ABSTRACT

The historical and contemporary situation of low-income housing in Puerto Rico is surveyed in this chapter. The main focus is on the San Juan metropolitan area, and special attention is paid to urban lower-class households, as they cope with inadequate housing conditions: public housing projects, working-class neighborhoods, and squatter settlements. An in-depth portrayal of *Barrio Gandul,* a working-class neighborhood in Santurce at the core of San Juan, demonstrates the ways the State intervenes in the low-income housing area. Indeed, Santurce's experience encapsulates many of the housing problems of the island. *Caserios,* public housing projects, have become stigmatized as a failure. Nothing short of a major reordering of priorities, and a revitalized sense of purpose and "political will" by the State, will turn the deteriorating situation around for the urban poor in their quest for affordable housing.

Chapitre 10
DU "BOHIO" AU "CASERIO": LE LOGEMENT DANS LES ZONES URBAINES DE PORTO RICO

Jorge Duany

RESUME

La situation historique et contemporaine des habitations à loyer modéré à Porto Rico est examinée dans ce chapitre qui porte sur la zone métropolitaine de San Juan. Une attention plus particulière est prêtée aux classes à faible revenu résidant dans les zones urbaines qui doivent faire face à des conditions inadéquates de logement, telles que des programmes de logements subventionnés par l'Etat, des quartiers ouvriers et des établissements de squatters. Une présentation détaillée du *Barrio Gandul*, quartier de la classe ouvrière situé à Santurce, au coeur de San Juan, démontre la façon dont intervient l'Etat dans les quartiers d'habitations à loyer modéré. En effet, les expériences des habitants de Santurce illustrent bon nombre des problèmes de logement de cette île. L'échec des *Caserios*, habitations subventionnées par l'Etat est généralement admis. Seuls une révision des priorités ainsi qu'une résolution revitalisée et une "volonté politique" de la part de l'Etat, pourront renverser la situation qui se dégrade toujours pour les pauvres des zones urbaines qui sont à la recherche de logement à des prix abordables.

Capítulo 10
DEL *BOHIO* AL *CASERIO*: CONDICIONES DE LA VIVIENDA URBANA EN PUERTO RICO

Jorge Duany

RESUMEN

En este capítulo se estudia la situación histórica y contemporánea de la vivienda de bajos ingresos en Puerto Rico. Se concentra principalmente en el área metropolitana de San Juan, y se presta atención especial a las familias urbanas de más bajos ingresos, al hacer frente a condiciones de vivienda inadecuadas: proyectos de vivienda públicos, barrios de la clase trabajadora, y asentamientos de invasores. Un retrato profundo de Barrio Gandul, un barrio de Santurce, en el corazón de San Juan, donde vive la clase trabajadora, demuestra las maneras en que el Estado interviene en el sector de la vivienda de bajo costo. En realidad, la experiencia de Santurce contiene muchos de los problemas de alojamiento de la isla. Los Caseríos, proyectos de vivienda públicos, se han estigmatizado como un fracaso. Nada menos que un reordenamiento general de prioridades, y un sentido revitalizado de propósito y de "voluntad política" por parte del Estado serán necesarios para que los pobres de la urbe cambien su situación de deterioro en su búsqueda por una vivienda que ellos puedan costear.

Chapter 11
HOUSING AND THE STATE IN THE FRENCH CARIBBEAN

Stephanie A. Condon and Philip E. Ogden

ABSTRACT

Housing conditions in the French Caribbean islands of Martinique and Guadeloupe have improved rapidly since 1945, and especially over the last twenty years. This chapter investigates the nature and evolution of the housing stock and the reasons that underlie its transformation. Three principal aspects underpin the empirical information on which the chapter is based: first, the nature and significance of the islands' status as *departments d'outre mer* and the ways in which this has emphasised the crucial role of the French state; second, the way in which the housing policies of metropolitan France have evolved and been adapted to the specific needs of the Caribbean; and thirdly, the pressures which the changing demography and economy of the islands have placed on housing provision. For these principal reasons, the case of the French islands is distinctive in the wider Caribbean environment.

Chapitre 11
LE LOGEMENT ET L'ETAT AUX ANTILLES FRANCAISES

Stephanie A. Condon et Philip E. Ogden

RESUME

Les conditions de logement dans les îles des Antilles françaises de la Martinique et de la Guadeloupe se sont rapidement améliorées et, plus particulièrement, pendant les vingt dernières années. Ce chapitre examine la nature et l'évolution du parc immobilier ainsi que les raisons ayant conduit à sa transformation. Trois aspects principaux étayent les informations empiriques sur lesquelles ce chapitre est basé: d'abord, la nature et l'importance du statut des îles comme *départements d'outre mer* et les façons dont ce statut a souligné le rôle important de l'état français; la façon dont les politiques sur le logement de la France métropolitaine se sont développées et ont été adaptées aux besoins spécifiques de la Caraïbe; et enfin, les pressions que la démographie et l'économie des îles ont exercées sur la disponibilité des logements. A la lumière de ces raisons principales, le cas des îles françaises se distingue dans la région des Caraïbes.

Capítulo 11
LA VIVIENDA Y EL ESTADO EN LAS ANTILLAS FRANCESAS

Stephanie A. Condon y Philip E. Ogden

RESUMEN

Las condiciones de la vivienda en las islas de Martinica y Guadalupe en las Antillas francesas, han mejorado rápidamente desde 1945, y especialmente en los últimos veinte años. Este capítulo investiga la naturaleza y evolución del rubro de la vivienda y las razones que subyacen en su transformación. Tres aspectos principales sostienen la información empírica sobre la cual se basa el capítulo: primero, la naturaleza y significado del Estado de las islas como *departamentos de ultramar* y en que forma esto ha destacado el papel crítico del estado francés; segundo, la manera en qué las políticas de vivienda de la Francia metropolitana han evolucionado y se han adaptado a las necesidades específicas del Caribe; y tercero, las presiones que los cambios demográficas y económicas de las islas han impuesto sobre la provisión de viviendas. Por estas razones principales, se distinge el caso de las islas francesas en el medio de la región del gran Caribe.

Chapter 12
CARIBBEAN HOUSING FUTURES:
BUILDING COMMUNITIES FOR SUSTAINABILITY

Dennis Conway and Robert B. Potter

ABSTRACT

The chapters in this volume have provided evidence of the woeful state of housing provision throughout the Caribbean. Inappropriate planning models have hampered State effectiveness. Vernacular and appropriate styles of housing have been disparaged in favor of imported technologies, this despite the time-honored persistence of the former. The essays in this comparative collection demonstrate a fundamental lack of understanding among the region's responsible institutions of the interrelated nature of the housing, planning, and urbanization processes in the Caribbean. More specifically, the autonomous "self-help" responses of the poor have been little understood by the State. Several of the contributors to this volume chart disappointing histories of lost opportunities, and sequences of problems that ineluctably contribute to extremely poor records of housing provision. Lessons distilled from the comparisons, however, suggest that a progressive future is possible, given recourse to appropriate, locally sensitive models that incorporate "building community" ideas into their housing programs.

Chapitre 12
L'AVENIR DU LOGEMENT DANS LA CARAIBE:
CONSTRUIRE DES COMMUNAUTES EN VUE DE
LEUR DURABILITE

Dennis Conway et Robert B. Potter

RESUME

Les chapitres de cet ouvrage ont fourni les preuves de l'état de la disponibilité en logements dans la Caraïbe. Des modèles de planification peu appropriés ont entravé l'efficacité de l'Etat. Une architecture populaire adaptée au milieu a été dépréciée en faveur de technologies importées, malgré sa grande longévité. Les essais de ce recueil comparatif prouvent un manque de compréhension fondamental de la part des institutions régionales concernées quant à la nature étroitement liée des processus de logement, de planification et d'urbanisation dans la Caraïbe. Plus spécifiquement, l'Etat n'a pas bien compris les réponses autonomes à partir d'initiatives personnelles des pauvres. Bon nombre de ceux qui ont contribué à ce volume dressent un tableau d'histoires décevantes indiquant des opportunités perdues ainsi que des problèmes qui contribuent inévitablement à des résultats décevants en matière de logements mis à la disposition de la population. Cependant, les leçons qui ont été tirées de ces comparaisons suggèrent qu'un avenir progressiste est possible si des modèles appropriés, sensibles aux besoins des gens et incorporant les idées de "construction communautaire" dans leurs programmes de construction de logements, sont appliqués.

Capítulo 12
FUTURO DE LA VIVIENDA EN EL CARIBE: CONSTRUYENDO COMUNIDADES EN CUANTO A SU SUSTENTABILIDAD

Dennis Conway
y Robert B. Potter

RESUMEN

Los capítulos de este volúmen han dado testimonio del estado lamentable en que se encuentra la disponibilidad de viviendas en todo el Caribe. Modelos de planificación inadecuados han obstaculizado la eficacia del Estado. Se han despreciado estilos arquitectónicos populares en favor de tecnologías importadas, a pesar de la clásica persistencia de los anteriores. Los ensayos de esta colección comparativa demuestran una falta fundamental de comprensión entre las instituciones responsables de la región sobre la naturaleza interrelacionada de los procesos de vivienda, planificación y urbanización en el Caribe. De modo más específico, las respuestas autónomas de las clases menos favorecidas para "construir viviendas con recursos propios" han sido poco comprendidas por el Estado. Varios de los participantes en la realización de este volúmen, documentan historias decepcionantes de oportunidades no aprovechadas y secuencias de problemas que contribuyen, ineludiblemente que se tengan marcas extremadamente bajas de provisión de viviendas. Las lecciones que emanan de estas comparaciones, sin embargo sugieren, que es posible un futuro progresista, dados los recursos para obtener modelos apropiados, de sensibilidad local, que incorporen a sus programas de vivienda ideas sobre la "construcción comunitaria".

Contributors

Stephanie A. Condon

Researcher, Institut National D'Etudes Démographiques, Paris

Dennis Conway

Professor, Department of Geography, Indiana University

Jorge Duany

Associate Professor, Department of Sociology and Anthropology, University of Puerto Rico, Rio Pedras

L. Alan Eyre

Senior Research Fellow, University of the West Indies, Discovery Bay Marine Laboratory

Linda Hewitt

The Registry, St. Augustine Campus of the University of the West Indies, Trinidad and Tobago

Brian J. Hudson

Senior Lecturer, School of Planning, Landscape Architecture and Surveying, Queensland University of Technology

Thomas Klak
Associate Professor of Geography, Miami University, Oxford, Ohio

Kosta Mathéy
Professor Adjunto, Technical University of Havana, and Deputy Professor,
Karlsruhe University

Philip E. Ogden
Professor, Department of Geography, Queen Mary and Westfield College,
University of London

Linda Peake
Associate Professor, Division of Social Science at York University

Robert B. Potter
Professor, Department of Geography, Royal Holloway, University of London

Mark R. Watson
Assistant Housing Consultant, Pieda PLC, formerly Postgraduate Student,
Department of Geography, Royal Holloway,
University of London

Index

165; capitalism, 181; capitalist economy, 177–78, 184; capitalist world, 180, 182, 184; , Castro, Fidel, 164; Castro regime, 177, 184, 248; cement, 183; *choza*, 165; *círculos infantiles*, 174; *circumscripción*, 175; class society, 179; Clinton administration, 164; clothing, 177; collective self-help, 170; COMECON, 176, 183; commercial builders, 179; commodification, 165, 177, 183–84; community, 173–74; community facilities, 174; compact bungalow, 165; competitive (capitalist) environment, 181; *Concejos Populares*, 183; concrete, 169; *construccion por esfuerzo propio*, 167, 182, 184; construction costs, 179; construction materials, 168; construction workers, 179; consumption, 178; cooperatives, 167, 170; Cotorro, 171; courtyard type house, 165; craftspeople, 165; credit, 169; crisis, 184; Cuban revolution, 178, 180; cultural incompatibility, 167; decentralized activities, 183; *delegados*, 175; discrimination, 179; DIY market, 177; double exploitation, 165, 178, 183, 248; dwellings, 169–70; economic crisis, 177; economic embargo, 177; economic restructuring, 170; egalitarian society, 164; elderly, 175; electricity, 168; embargo, 184; engineers, 176; exchange value, 182; experimental basis, 170; EXPOCUBA, scientific-technical exhibition, 174; extra labor input (*plus trabajo*), 170; factories, 173; First National Housing Conference, 168–69; flats, 172, 178; flexible architectural approach, 174; flexible standards, 179; food, 177; foreign companies, 164; formal sector, 178; funding agencies, 180; gender discrimination, 179; gender inequalities, 180; General Housing Law, 1988 amendment, 170; grassroots democracy, 180, 183; green areas, 172; *Grupo por el Desarollo Integral de la Capital guano*, 165; Habana, 165, 171, 173, 175, 178, 182–83, 248; Habana Vieja, 174; high-rise buildings, 174; historic neighborhoods, 173; homeowners, 166; house builders, individual, 178; housewives, 175; housing, 164, 168, 178, 184; Housing

Act, 1984, 166, 169; housing census, 169; housing, commodity nature of, 182; housing construction, 169, 172; housing cooperatives, 169, 181; housing deficit, 173; housing development, large-scale, 173; housing exchanges, 165; housing opportunities, 175; housing provision, 170, 172; housing provision, pre-revolutionary. 165–66; housing shortage, 168; housing stock, 169, 175; housing strategies, revolutionary, 166–70; ideological bases, 164; generation, 183; individualism, 248; industrial development, 165; industrialization, 172; industrialized building systems, 173; industrialized mass housing, 167; infill projects, 173; "informal" constructions, 169; informal settlements, 167, 175; infrastructure, 170, 181; institutionalization, 172; interior finishing jobs, 179; internal conflict, 180; international aid donors, 183; iron gates, 169; job rotation, 181; job satisfaction, 181; La Güasimas, 175; labor force, 170, 172; labor intensity, 178; labor process, 178; land, 170, 177; land speculation, 182; land titles, 177; landlordism, 167, 248; legal reforms, 166; linear buildings, 167; loans, 169; local administration, 174; local communities, 183; local and mass organizations, 181; low-income communities, 180; low-income households, 179; low wages, 178; marginal activity, 167; market relationships, 177; mass housing, 167, 171; massive microbrigade mobilization, 182; medicine, 177; medium-sized towns, 169; microbrigade building activities, 177; microbrigade flats, 173; microbrigade houses, 172; microbrigade zones, 174; *microbrigades*, 164–66, 169–77, 179, 184, 248; *microbrigadistas*, 170, 172–73; micro-concrete roofing tiles, 177; mining, 164; Ministry of Agriculture (MINAGRI), 167–68; Ministry of Construction (MICONS), 167–68, 172–75; mixed-economy model, 184; modern standards, 168; monotonous appearance, 167; multifamily blocks, 170; municipal, 169; National Bank, 169; national economic plan, 164; national

French Caribbean (cont.)
communities, 230; fertility, 219, 223; fires, 233; fishing communities, 230; flats, 236; foreign migrants, 232; Fort-de-France (Martinique), 219, 221–23, 225, 230, 232, 234, 249; France, 232; free market ideology, 116; freezer, 226; French and Western values, 218; French nation, part of, 233; French state, 218; funding, 231; garden, 221; ground provisions, 221; growth rates, 249; Guadeloupe, northern, 230; HLM (*Habitations à loyer modéré*), 218; *habitations de fortune,* 228; health and fire risk, 234; heritage of slavery, 221; homeownership, low-income, 237; household change, 220; households, single, young, 237; housing agendas, 249; housing benefits, 237–38; housing conditions, 225; housing construction "au savage," 227; housing cooperatives, 235–36; housing deprivation, 227; housing destruction, 237; housing finance, 232; Housing Finance Act (1977), 232; housing policies, 238–39; housing provision, 218, 224; housing provision, state's role in, 250; housing renovation funding, 238; housing schemes, 237–38; housing shortages, 232; housing stock, 217, 239; housing tenure, 225; housing types, 239; hurricanes, 222, 233; Hurricane Hugo, 227, 237; immigration, 239; infant mortality, 219; informal economy, 235; infrastructure, 234; innovative financing mechanism, 237; "islands of deprivation," 219; La Batelière, 231; land values, 237; landscape, 224; Laurisque *cité,* 235; Laurisque *cité de transit,* 235; life expectancy, 219; LBU (*Ligne Budgétare Unique*), 237; local social investment, 218; low-cost house-building schemes, 238; low-cost housing, 239; LTS ("Truly social" housing), 237; Lyons, 231; main towns, 227, 230; Marseilles, 231; Martinique, eastern, 230; Martinique, southern, 230; métropole, 218–19; metropolitan France, 239; middle-income households, 236, 249; migrants, 221, 233; migration, 220, 222; *Ministére de l'Equipment,* 219; mobile structure, 221; modernization, 223, 231; Mont Pelée, 222; mulatto, 222; mulatto bourgeoisie, 221; National Statistical Institute (INSEE), 228; new housing policies, 232; overseas departments, 232, 237; owner-occupier group, 225; Paris, 231; payroll deductions, compulsory, 232; pensions, 237; planned urbanization, 234; plantation, 222; Point-à-Pitre (Guadeloupe), 219, 221–22, 225, 231, 233–36, 249; Point-à-Pitre (Guadeloupe) Assainissement, 233; Point-à-Pitre (Guadeloupe) public works schemes, 222; Point-à-Pitre, shantytowns, 232; policymakers, 231; political peace, 218; ports, modernization of, 233; postcolonialism, 218; postwar national construction, 232; poverty, 230; "precarious" housing, 227; pre-retirees, 237; primary sector, 222; public housing, 218, 236; public sector action, 249; public sector employees, 222; "public-sector middle class," 225; Quartier de l'Assainissement (Point-à-Pitre), 235–36; Raizet district (Point-à-Pitre), 236; reconstruction, 231; refrigerators, 226; renovation, 232; rental flats, 249; rental sector, 224; rented housing, 225; rented housing, low-cost, 237; residential space, 249; road systems, 233; running water, 226; rural areas, 227; rural emigration, 238; rural exodus, 222, 238; rural poor, 249; rural-urban migrants, 219; Schoelcher, 231; second homes 225; self-help strategies, 249; semi-unemployment, 222; sewage-disposal system, 227, 231; shantytowns, 222, 231–33, 235; single-parent families, 230; "site and service" experiment, 237; slave huts, 220; slavery, 220; slum clearance projects, 234, 238; social change, 220; social housing schemes, 238; social intervention programs, 238; social polarity, 224; social status, 225; socio-demographic change, 220; solid construction, 228; squatting, 233; St. Martin, 230; St. Pierre, 222; state, 231, 233, 237; state-aided private housing companies (SIDOM), 235; state apparatuses, 249; state-assisted housing, 218; state decision, 238; state intervention, 235; state-owned land, 233; state

Guyana (cont.)
(NGOs),136; out-migration, 122;
overcrowding, 120, 131; parallel market,
131; patronage system, 246; pauperization, 131; People's National Congress
(PNC), 120–28, 246; People's Progressive
Party, 246; petty landlordism, 128;
physical infrastructure, 131; pit latrines,
129; political crisis, 131; political
oppression, 127; private landlords, 126;
private market forces, 247; private sector,
127–28, 134; public education, 131;
public-sector housing, 132; racial
conflicts, 129; range houses, 121; regional
balance, 136; Regional Democratic
Council, 129; rental housing, 124, 126–
28, 246; rents, 132, 134; Revolving Fund,
126; Rose Hall, 122, 135; rural environment, 131; rural population, 126; self-
help housing, 124–27, 132–33, 136, 247;
site upgrading, 247; skilled labor, 126;
slums, upgrading of, 133; social housing
policy, 120–36; socialist objective, 127;
socialist rhetoric, 127; squatting, 129;
squatter settlements, regularization of,
133–34, 247; squatter settlements,
upgrading of, 134; standpipes, 129; state-
directed policies, 247; state land, 134;
state-managed housing, 120; structural
adjustment, 127, 247; Sugar Industry
Labour Welfare Fund (SILWF), 122–23;
sugar plantations, 121; tenants, 128;
tenure, insecurity of, 128; Town and
Country Planning Department, 129; trade
unions, 132, 136; upper-income groups,
127; urban environment, 131; urban
land, 133; urban population, 126; urban
poverty, 133–34; urban productivity, 133;
Urban Rehabilitation Project, 135;
urbanization, 120–22; West Coast
Demerara, 128; Wortmanville, redevelopment of, 123

HABITAT, 251
Haiti, 19; Port-au-Prince, 77, 80; Saint
Domingue, 96
Haitians, 80
hegemonic dependency, 248
hegemonic thinking, 115
"heritage-tourism," 8

higher-income groups, 110
high-interest foreign loans, 111
Hispaniola, 18
"home as haven," 251
homeless, 2
house types: "ajoupa," 26; "creole," 26, 27
housing: administration in Trinidad, 160;
affordable housing, Puerto Rico, 212;
agendas, French DOM, 249; alternative
housing strategies, Cuba, 164; assistance,
109, 112, 115; barrack-styled units,
Trinidad and Tobago, 144, 146, 148;
barrack-type houses, Puerto Rico, 192;
Barbados, 4, 38, 40; benefits, French
DOM, 237–38; Caribbean great houses,
26; chattel housing, Barbados, 8;
collective housing units, French DOM,
225, 235, 237; commodity, housing as,
252; commodity nature of, Cuba, 182;
community sponsored, housing initiatives, 9; conditions, 111, 146, 225;
conference, Trinidad, 155; construction,
152, 155–56, 169, 172, 244; construction
"au savage" French DOM, 227; cooperatives, 125, 169, 181, 235–36; "core
houses," 15, 31, 113; costs, Trinidad,
153; Cuba housing, 4, 164, 168, 178,
184; crisis in Jamaica, 102; deficit in
Cuba, 173; deficit in Jamaica, 113; deficit
in Trinidad, 144; deprivation, French
DOM, 227; destruction, French DOM,
237; disamenity, 56; distortions, 243;
dual housing market, Guyana, 135; elite
houses, Puerto Rico, 193; estates,
Trinidad, 154, 155; exchanges in Cuba,
165; finance, 232; folk, 3, 244; French
West Indies, 4; fund, 108, 112; General
Housing Law, Cuba: 1988 amendment,
170; Guyana, 4; Housing Credit Fund,
Barbados, 44; Housing and Urban
Development Corporation, St. Lucia, 61,
67; Housing Information System,
Trinidad and Tobago, 159; Housing
Rehabilitation Project, St. Lucia, 61;
Housing and Land Development
Corporation, St. Vincent and the
Grenadines, 61; housing disamenity, St.
Vincent and the Grenadines, 59;
indigenous self-help systems, 52; informal
housing system, 72; invasion, Jamaica,

Old San Juan, 195, 200; open-air market, 207; "Operation Bootstrap," 196, 209, 249; overcrowding, 195, 199, 206, 213; *pava,* 196; peons, 195; planning alternatives, 211; plantation economy, 196; plantations, 192; plaza, 192; polarized society, 210; policymakers, 212; political and administrative center, 200; political patronage, 248; pollution, 212; Ponce, 193–94; poor households, 189; Popular Democratic Party, 196, 204; population growth, 193–94; poverty, 199, 208–9; private corporations, 205; private enterprise, 213; private lands, 198; private transportation, 197; privately owned estates, 212; privatization (of public housing projects), 212; prostitution, 199, 208; public buildings, 211; public housing projects, 189, 199, 201, 203–6, 209–10, 212; public lands, 198; public transportation system, 197; Puerta de Tierra, 192–93, 195, 199; Puerto Nuevo, 194; Puerto Rican government, 209, 211; Puerto Rican residents, 209; Puerto Rican slums, 206; Puerto Rico's "progress," 249; Puerto Rico's Senate, 211; recreational parks, 206; rehabilitation, 211; renting, 199; Reparto Metropolitano, 203; repressive measures, 210; *rescate* movement, 204–5; residential mobility rates, 208; retirement, 209; Rincón de Gautier, Felisa, 200; Río Piedras, 197, 201, 207; Roosevelt, 203; running water, 210; rural housing types, 192; rural municipalities, 207; rural to urban migration, 195–96, 199, 201, 207; rural wage laborers, 195; San Germàn, 189; San José Housing Project, 201, 203; San José Lagoon, 198; San Juan, 188–89, 192–95, 197–98, 200, 209, 212, 247–48; San Juan Bay, 199, 207; Santurce, 189, 195, 197–201, 206, 209–11; Santurce's Stop 15, 206–7; segregation, racial and ethnic, 197; self-built housing, 200, 212–13, 248; self-help alternatives, 209–11; self-help efforts, 212; self-help initiatives, 212, 249; senior citizens, 201; shantytowns, 198–201, 203–4, 209–10, 212; sharecroppers, 195; shelter, 213; "Slum Belt," 199; "social cancers," 200, 206; social control, 204; social impact, 204; social institutions, 204; social stratification, 192; socialist alternative, 248; solidarity, 204; South Americans, 193; Spaniards, 192–93; Spanish colonial housing, 210; Spanish colonial pattern, 197; Spanish colonization, 189; Spanish revival, 194; squatter settlements, 189, 194–95, 197–201, 203–6; intervention, *direct,* 245; state policy, 201, 209–11; state provision, 248; stone and adobe houses, 192; sublet, 208; suburbanization, 209, 211, 213; sugar corporations, 194; sugar plantations, 191, 194; symbolic repertoires, 193; Taíno, 193; tax base, 212; tax exemption laws, 196; teenagers, 204; tenants, 208; Tras Talleres, 206–7; unalienated labor, 198; underemployment, 199; unemployment, 199, 205, 208; United States, 194, 196, 208; United States, neocolonial association, 248; University Gardens, 203; urban blight, 208; urban centers, 210; urban communities, 200; urban core, 211; urban dwellers, second generation, 199; urban housing, 189, 210; urban land market, 208; urban lower-class households, 188; urban planning, 209; urban poor, 189, 199, 203–4, 210; urban proletariat, 195, 207; Urban Renewal and Housing Corporation (CRUV), 201; urban renewal program, 200–201, 203–4, 213; urban squatting, 213; *urbanizaciones,* 194, 201, 203, 206, 209; urbanization, 196, 212; US federal funds, 201, 210; US federal housing policies, 203, 205; use-value, 198; vacancy, 208; Vega Alta, 207; vernacular house, 192, 210–11, 213, 249; Villa Sin Miedo, 205; welfare, 208; welfare dependence, 205; working-class neighborhoods, 195, 197; working-class populations, 208; *yagua,* 192; Yauco, 193; zoning laws, 211

"rab" land, 34
Rastafarian, 86
Rastafarian families, 84
Rastafarianism, 84
regime, 103–5
regime effects, 9, 112–14, 116

Trinidad and Tobago (cont.)

Self-Help Housing, the Poor, and the State in the Caribbean was designed and typeset on a Macintosh computer using PageMaker software. The text is set in Berkeley Book, chapter titles are set in Gill Sans Extra Condensed Bold and Gill Sans Ultra Bold. This book was designed by Todd Duren, composed by Angela Stanton, and was printed and bound by Thomson-Shore, Inc. The recycled paper used in this book is designed for an effective life of at least three hundred years.